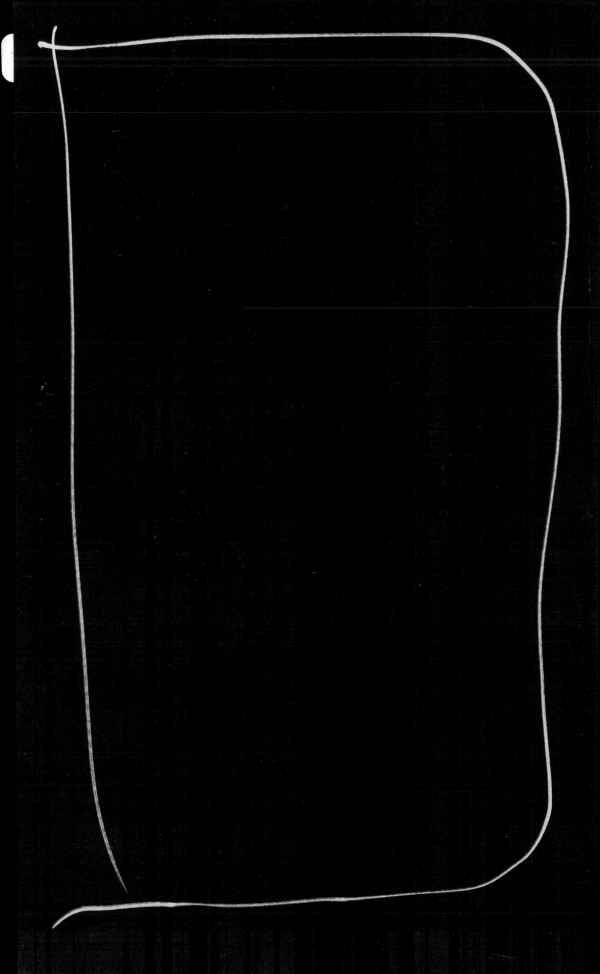

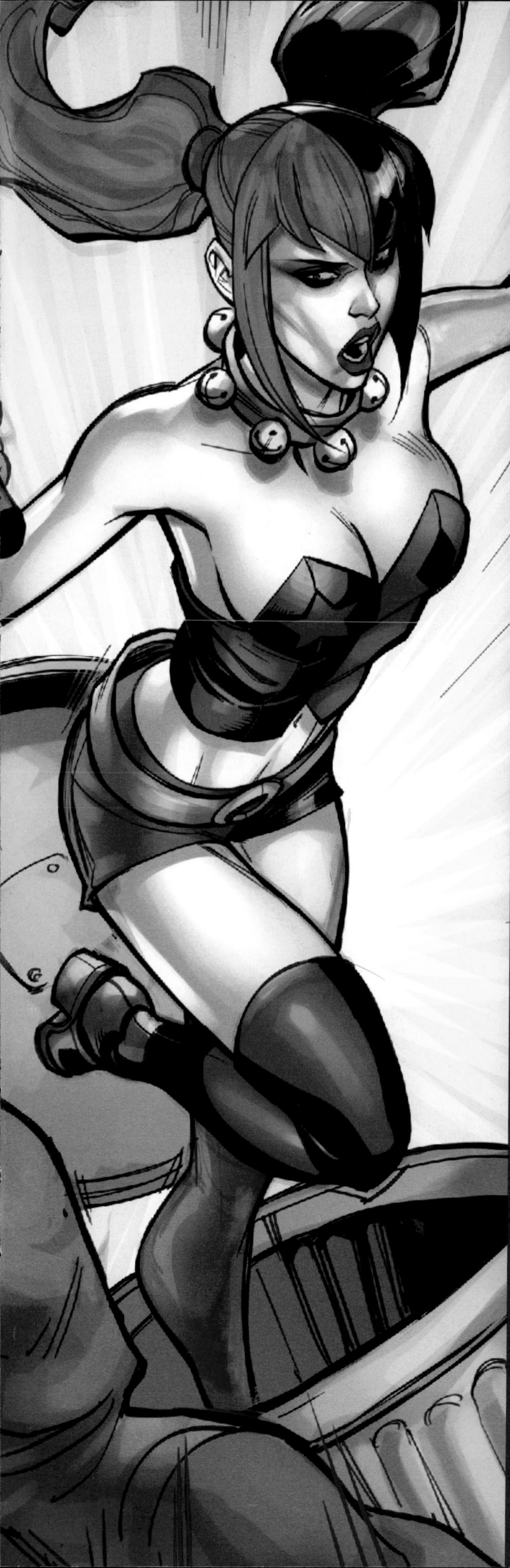

HARLEY QUINN

VOLUME 4

A CALL TO ARMS

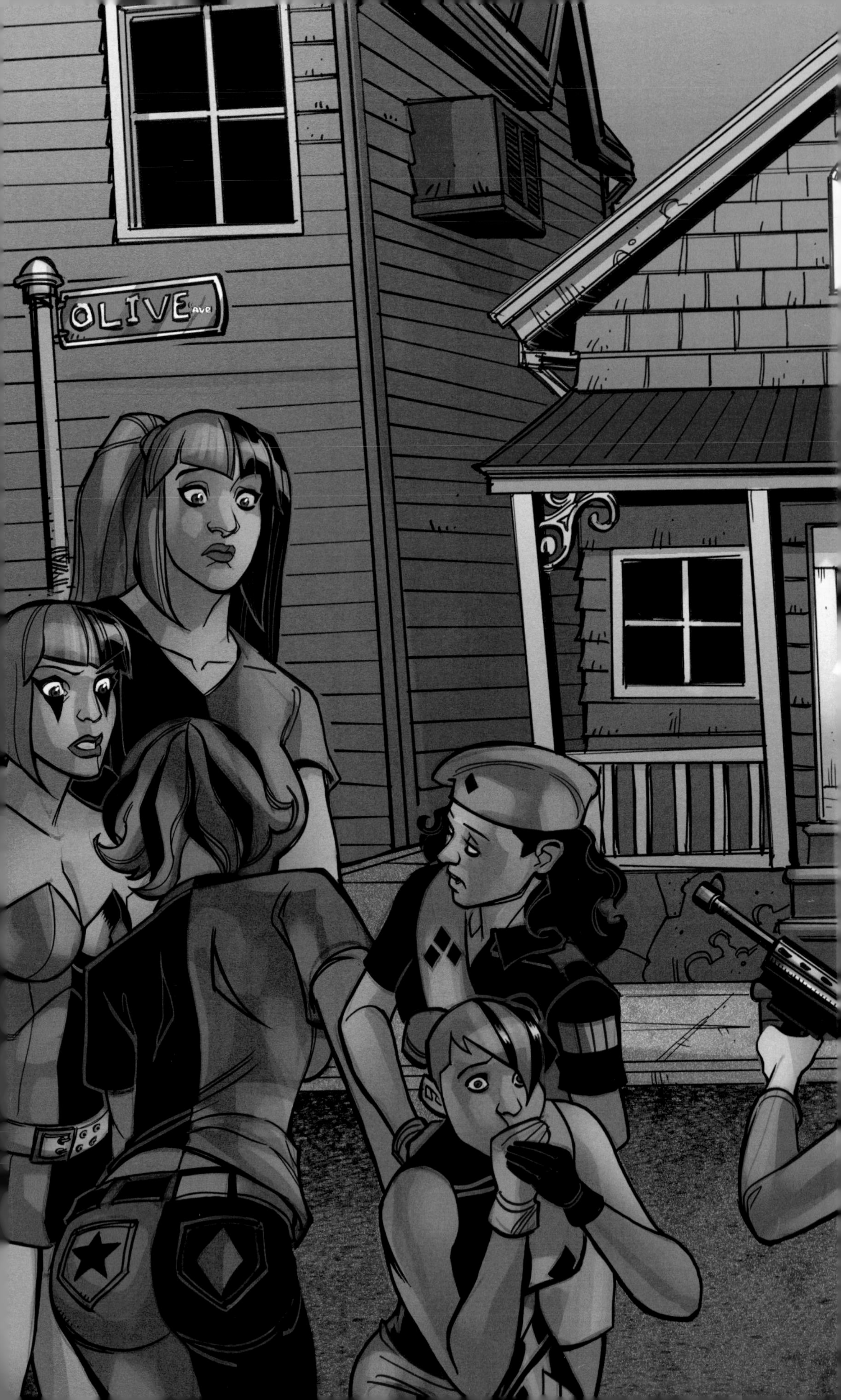
OLIVE AVE

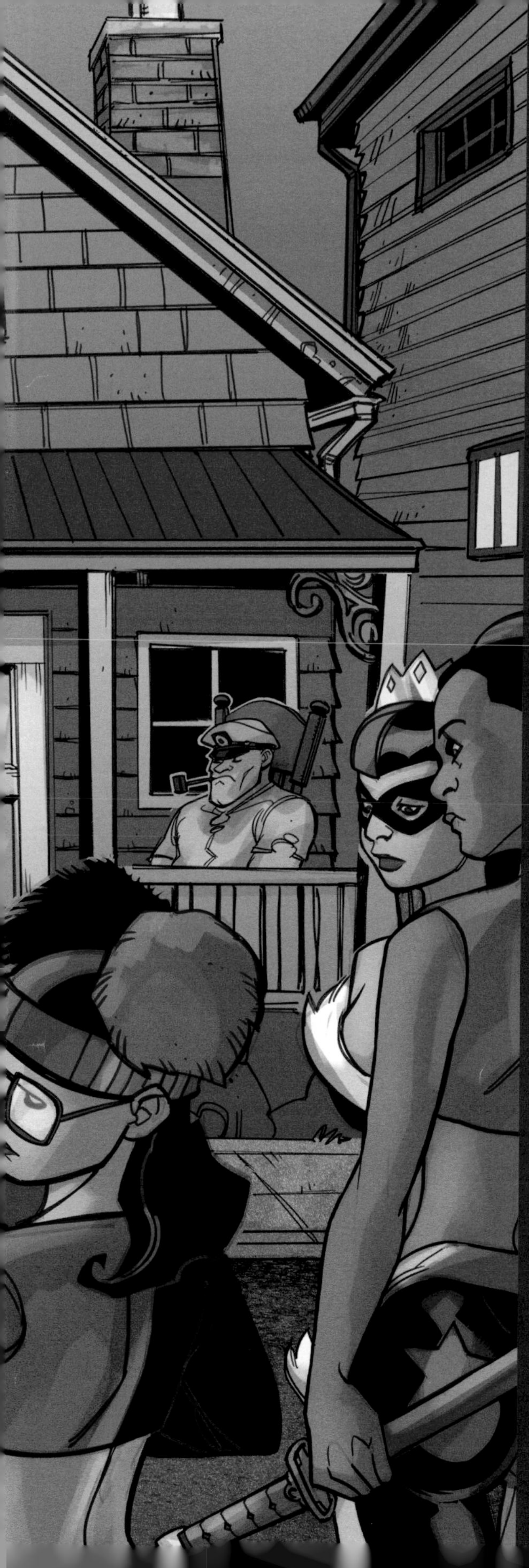

HARLEY QUINN

VOLUME 4
A CALL TO ARMS

WRITTEN BY
AMANDA CONNER
JIMMY PALMIOTTI

ART BY
CHAD HARDIN
JOHN TIMMS
JED DOUGHERTY
BRET BLEVINS
MORITAT
FLAVIANO
PASQUALE QUALANO
MIKE MANLEY

COLOR BY
ALEX SINCLAIR
PAUL MOUNTS
HI-FI

LETTERS BY
JOHN J. HILL
TOM NAPOLITANO
DAVE SHARPE

COLLECTION COVER ART BY
AMANDA CONNER &
ALEX SINCLAIR

HARLEY QUINN CREATED BY
PAUL DINI & BRUCE TIMM

HARLEY QUINN VOLUME 4: A CALL TO ARMS

Published by DC Comics. Compilation and all new material Copyright © 2016 DC Comics. All Rights Reserved.
Originally published in single magazine form in HARLEY QUINN 17-21, HARLEY QUINN ROAD TRIP SPECIAL 1, DC SNEAK PEEK:
HARLEY QUINN #1 Copyright © 2015 DC Comics. All Rights Reserved. All characters, their distinctive likenesses and related elements
featured in this publication are trademarks of DC Comics. The stories, characters and incidents featured in this publication are
entirely fictional. DC Comics does not read or accept unsolicited submissions of ideas, stories or artwork.

DC Comics, 2900 West Alameda Ave., Burbank, CA 91505
Printed by RR Donnelley, Salem, VA, USA. 5/20/16. First Printing.
ISBN: 978-1-4012-6253-2

Library of Congress Cataloging-in-Publication Data is available.

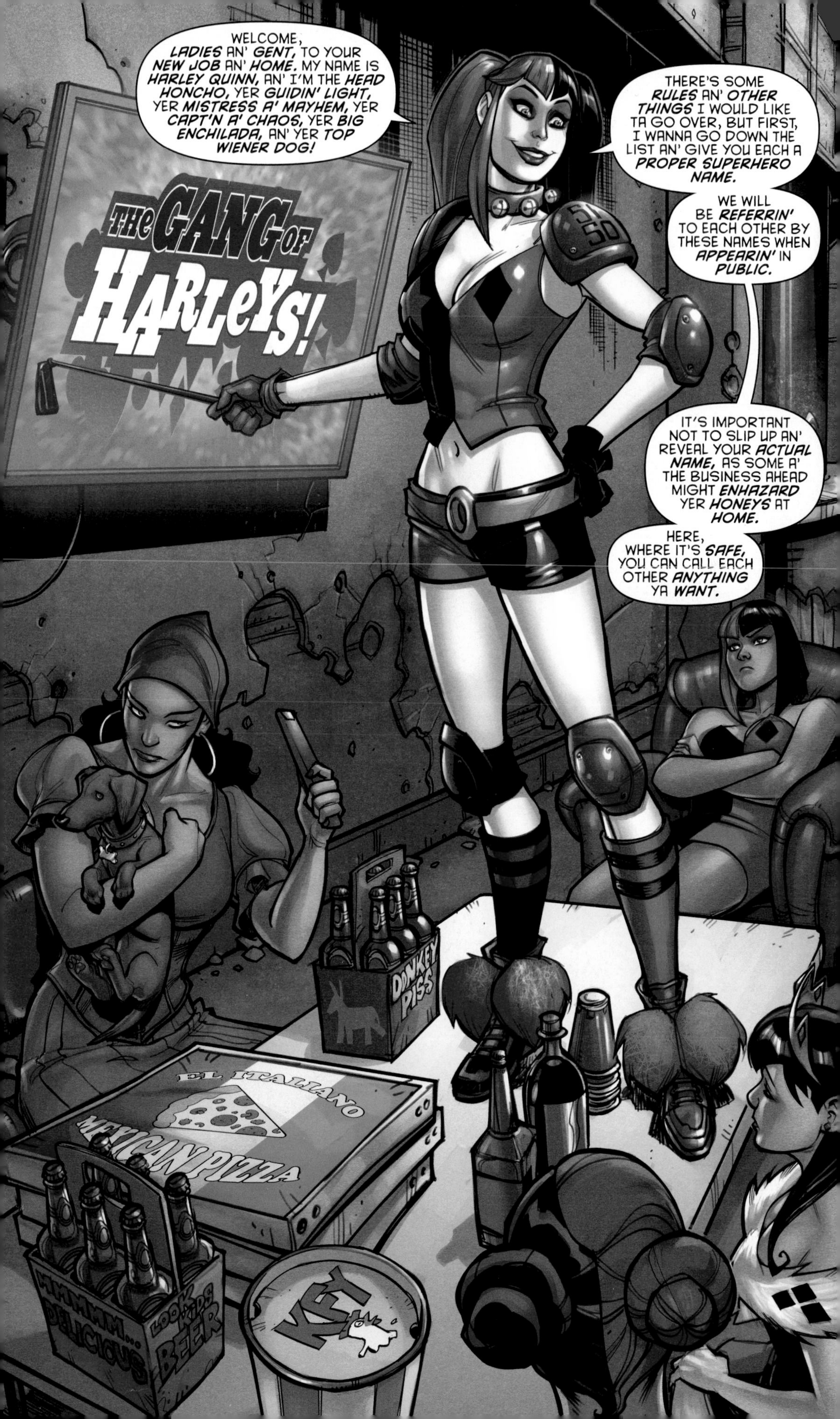
WELCOME, LADIES AN' GENT, TO YOUR NEW JOB AN' HOME. MY NAME IS HARLEY QUINN, AN' I'M THE HEAD HONCHO, YER GUIDIN' LIGHT, YER MISTRESS A' MAYHEM, YER CAPT'N A' CHAOS, YER BIG ENCHILADA, AN' YER TOP WIENER DOG!
THE GANG OF HARLEYS!
THERE'S SOME RULES AN' OTHER THINGS I WOULD LIKE TA GO OVER, BUT FIRST, I WANNA GO DOWN THE LIST AN' GIVE YOU EACH A PROPER SUPERHERO NAME.
WE WILL BE REFERRIN' TO EACH OTHER BY THESE NAMES WHEN APPEARIN' IN PUBLIC.
IT'S IMPORTANT NOT TO SLIP UP AN' REVEAL YOUR ACTUAL NAME, AS SOME A' THE BUSINESS AHEAD MIGHT ENHAZARD YER HONEYS AT HOME.
HERE, WHERE IT'S SAFE, YOU CAN CALL EACH OTHER ANYTHING YA WANT.
DONKEY PISS
EL ITALIANO
MEXICAN PIZZA
MMMMM... DELICIOUS
LOOK KIDS BEER

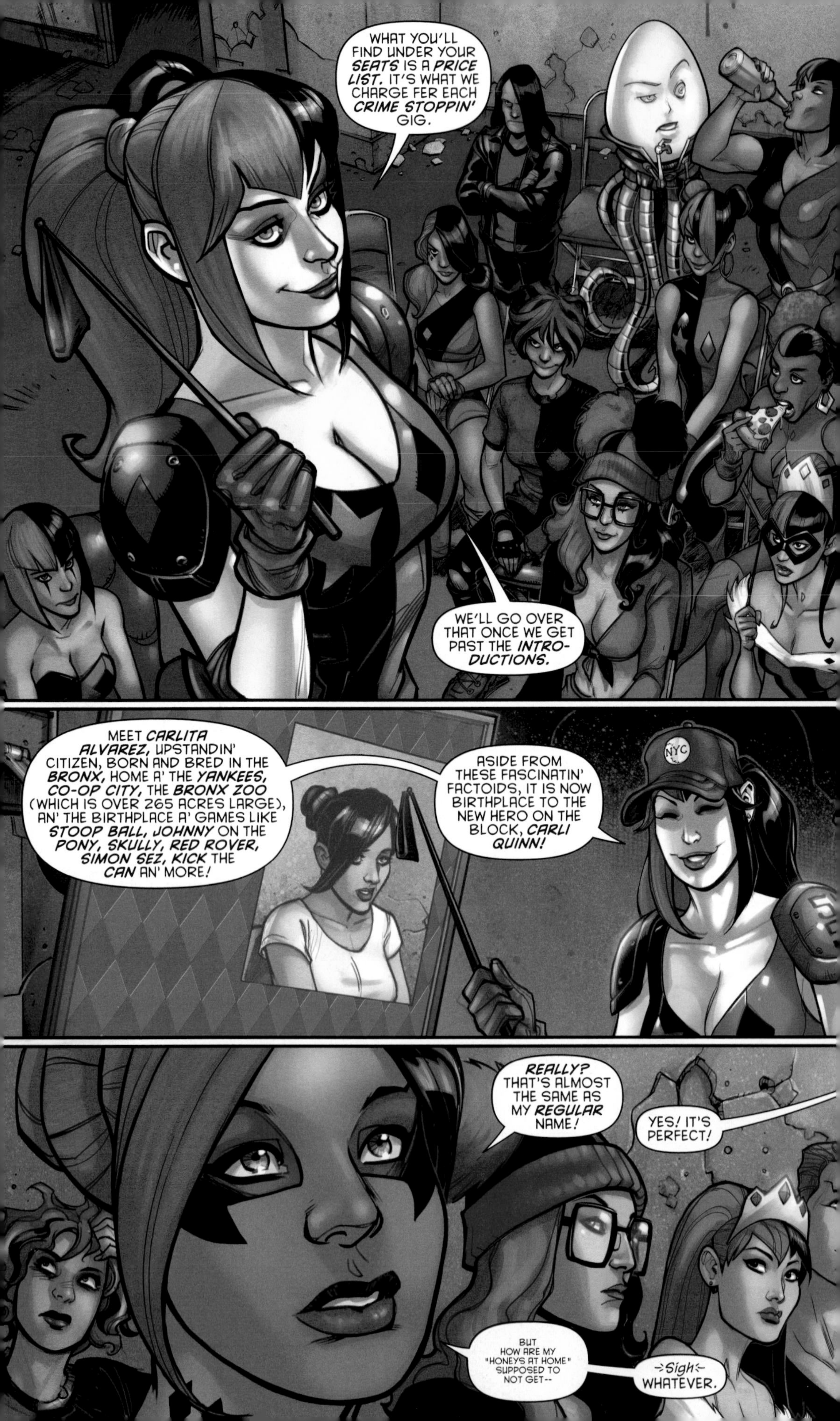
WHAT YOU'LL FIND UNDER YOUR SEATS IS A PRICE LIST. IT'S WHAT WE CHARGE FER EACH CRIME STOPPIN' GIG.
WE'LL GO OVER THAT ONCE WE GET PAST THE INTRO-DUCTIONS.
MEET CARLITA ALVAREZ, UPSTANDIN' CITIZEN, BORN AND BRED IN THE BRONX, HOME A' THE YANKEES, CO-OP CITY, THE BRONX ZOO (WHICH IS OVER 265 ACRES LARGE), AN' THE BIRTHPLACE A' GAMES LIKE STOOP BALL, JOHNNY ON THE PONY, SKULLY, RED ROVER, SIMON SEZ, KICK THE CAN AN' MORE!
ASIDE FROM THESE FASCINATIN' FACTOIDS, IT IS NOW BIRTHPLACE TO THE NEW HERO ON THE BLOCK, CARLI QUINN!
NYC
REALLY? THAT'S ALMOST THE SAME AS MY REGULAR NAME!
YES! IT'S PERFECT!
BUT HOW ARE MY "HONEYS AT HOME" SUPPOSED TO NOT GET--
-Sigh- WHATEVER.

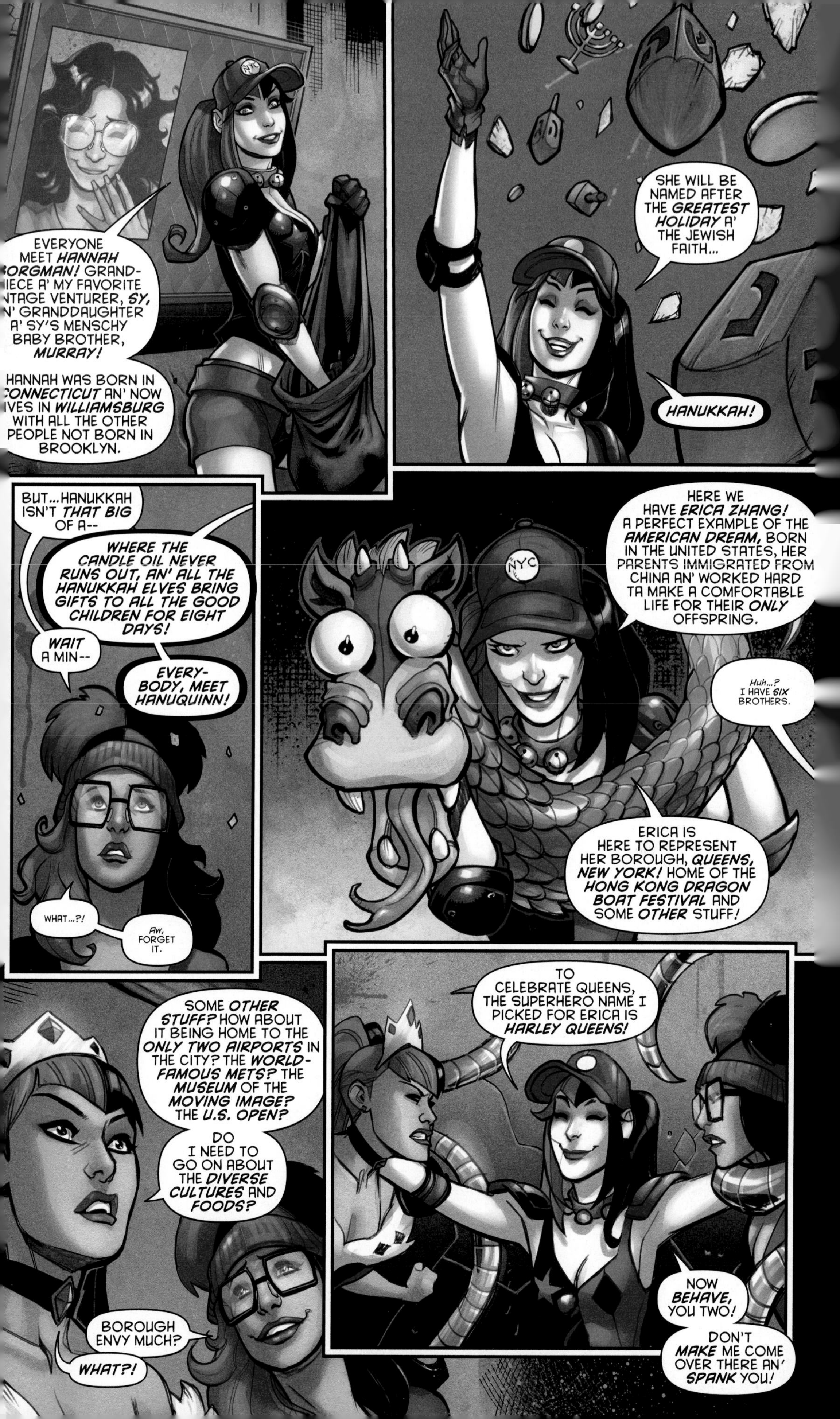
EVERYONE MEET HANNAH BORGMAN! GRAND-NIECE A' MY FAVORITE VINTAGE VENTURER, SY, AN' GRANDDAUGHTER A' SY'S MENSCHY BABY BROTHER, MURRAY!
HANNAH WAS BORN IN CONNECTICUT AN' NOW LIVES IN WILLIAMSBURG WITH ALL THE OTHER PEOPLE NOT BORN IN BROOKLYN.
SHE WILL BE NAMED AFTER THE GREATEST HOLIDAY A' THE JEWISH FAITH...
HANUKKAH!
BUT...HANUKKAH ISN'T THAT BIG OF A--
WHERE THE CANDLE OIL NEVER RUNS OUT, AN' ALL THE HANUKKAH ELVES BRING GIFTS TO ALL THE GOOD CHILDREN FOR EIGHT DAYS!
WAIT A MIN--
EVERY-BODY, MEET HANUQUINN!
WHAT...?!
AW, FORGET IT.
HERE WE HAVE ERICA ZHANG! A PERFECT EXAMPLE OF THE AMERICAN DREAM, BORN IN THE UNITED STATES, HER PARENTS IMMIGRATED FROM CHINA AN' WORKED HARD TA MAKE A COMFORTABLE LIFE FOR THEIR ONLY OFFSPRING.
Huh...? I HAVE SIX BROTHERS.
ERICA IS HERE TO REPRESENT HER BOROUGH, QUEENS, NEW YORK! HOME OF THE HONG KONG DRAGON BOAT FESTIVAL AND SOME OTHER STUFF!
SOME OTHER STUFF? HOW ABOUT IT BEING HOME TO THE ONLY TWO AIRPORTS IN THE CITY? THE WORLD-FAMOUS METS? THE MUSEUM OF THE MOVING IMAGE? THE U.S. OPEN?
DO I NEED TO GO ON ABOUT THE DIVERSE CULTURES AND FOODS?
BOROUGH ENVY MUCH?
WHAT?!
TO CELEBRATE QUEENS, THE SUPERHERO NAME I PICKED FOR ERICA IS HARLEY QUEENS!
NOW BEHAVE, YOU TWO!
DON'T MAKE ME COME OVER THERE AN' SPANK YOU!

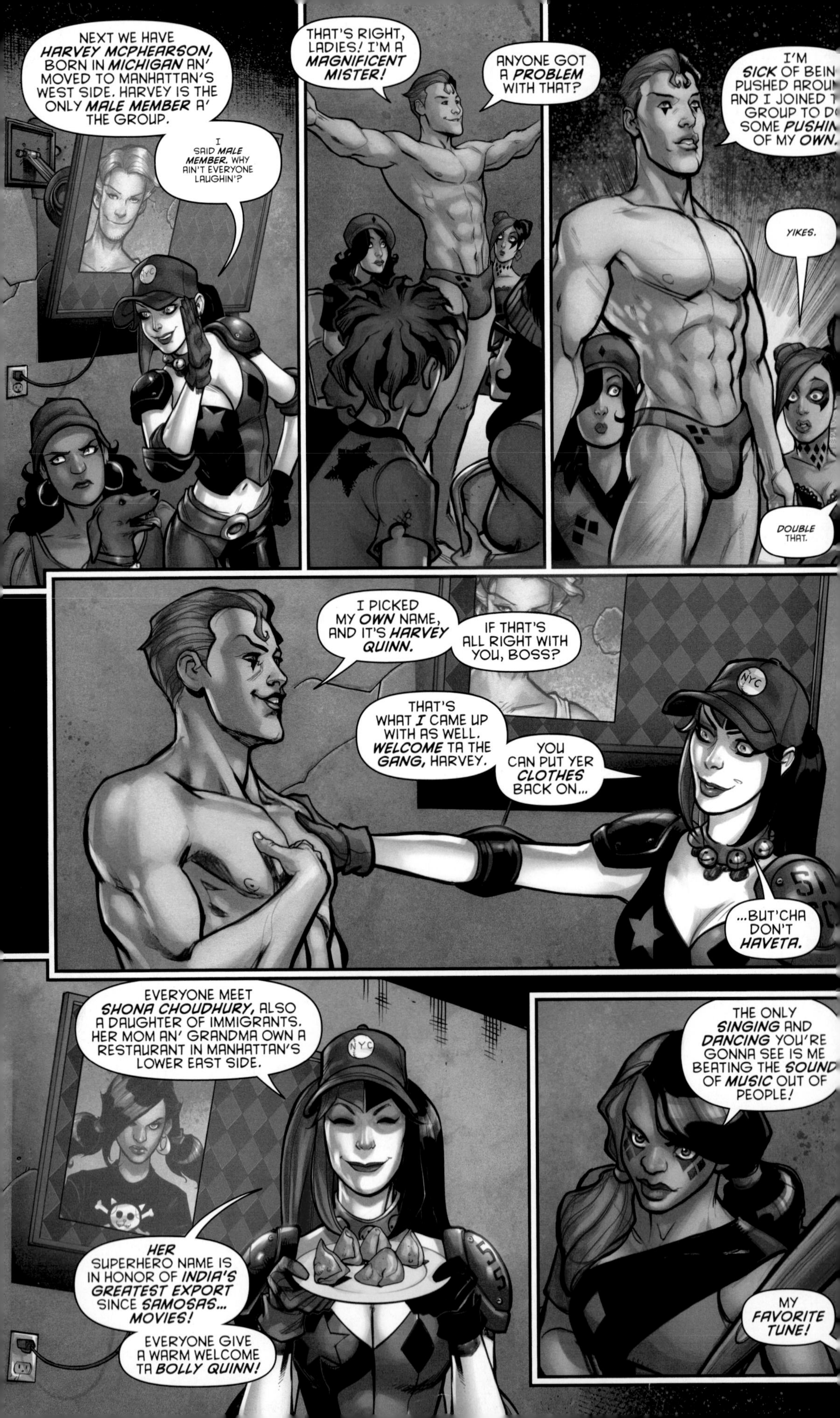
NEXT WE HAVE HARVEY MCPHEARSON, BORN IN MICHIGAN AN' MOVED TO MANHATTAN'S WEST SIDE. HARVEY IS THE ONLY MALE MEMBER A' THE GROUP.
I SAID MALE MEMBER. WHY AIN'T EVERYONE LAUGHIN'?
THAT'S RIGHT, LADIES! I'M A MAGNIFICENT MISTER!
ANYONE GOT A PROBLEM WITH THAT?
I'M SICK OF BEIN PUSHED AROU AND I JOINED T GROUP TO D SOME PUSHIN OF MY OWN.
YIKES.
DOUBLE THAT.
I PICKED MY OWN NAME, AND IT'S HARVEY QUINN.
IF THAT'S ALL RIGHT WITH YOU, BOSS?
THAT'S WHAT I CAME UP WITH AS WELL. WELCOME TA THE GANG, HARVEY.
YOU CAN PUT YER CLOTHES BACK ON...
...BUT'CHA DON'T HAVETA.
EVERYONE MEET SHONA CHOUDHURY, ALSO A DAUGHTER OF IMMIGRANTS. HER MOM AN' GRANDMA OWN A RESTAURANT IN MANHATTAN'S LOWER EAST SIDE.
HER SUPERHERO NAME IS IN HONOR OF INDIA'S GREATEST EXPORT SINCE SAMOSAS... MOVIES!
EVERYONE GIVE A WARM WELCOME TA BOLLY QUINN!
THE ONLY SINGING AND DANCING YOU'RE GONNA SEE IS ME BEATING THE SOUND OF MUSIC OUT OF PEOPLE!
MY FAVORITE TUNE!

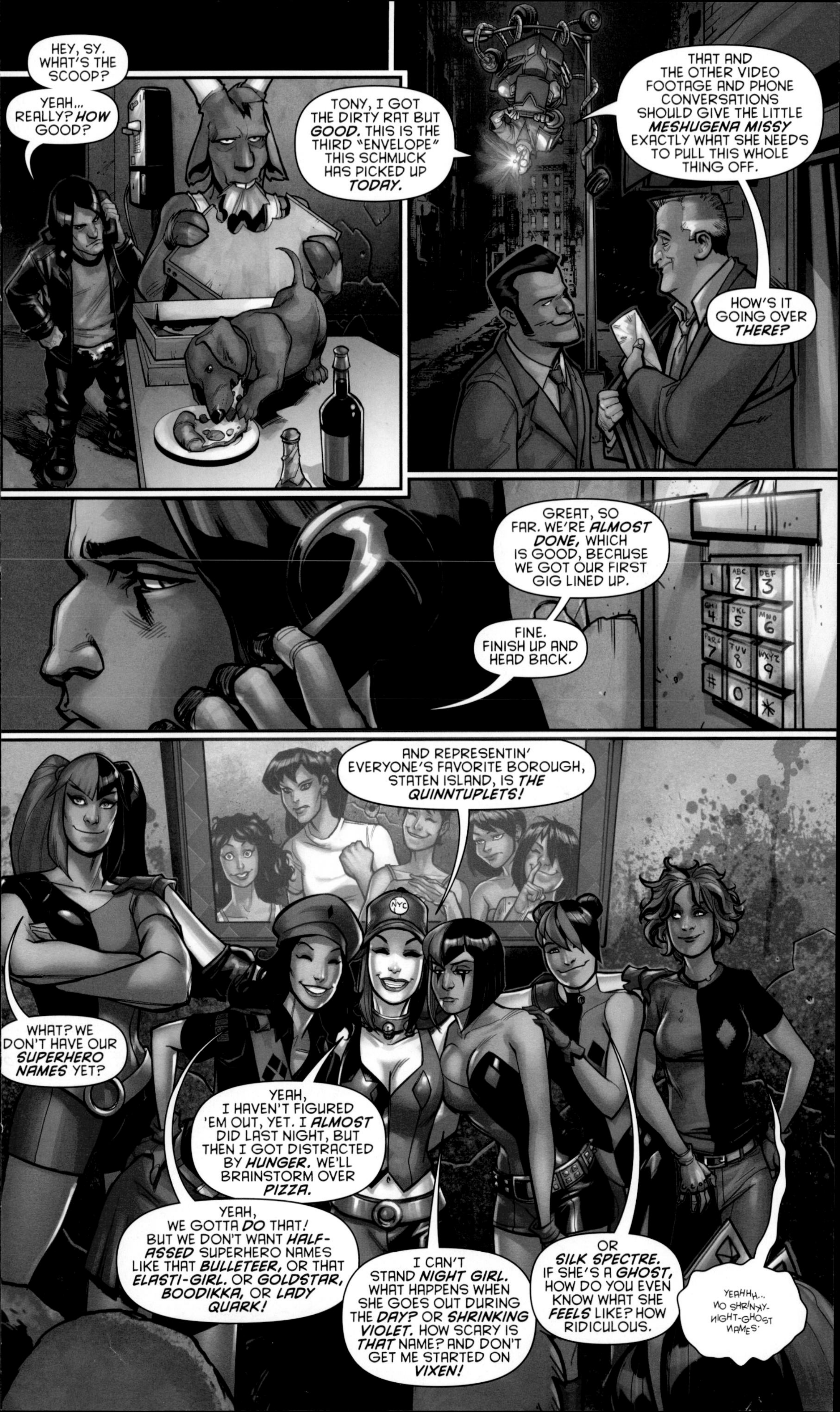

HEY, SY. WHAT'S THE SCOOP?
YEAH... REALLY? **HOW** GOOD?
TONY, I GOT THE DIRTY RAT BUT **GOOD.** THIS IS THE THIRD "ENVELOPE" THIS SCHMUCK HAS PICKED UP **TODAY.**
THAT AND THE OTHER VIDEO FOOTAGE AND PHONE CONVERSATIONS SHOULD GIVE THE LITTLE **MESHUGENA MISSY** EXACTLY WHAT SHE NEEDS TO PULL THIS WHOLE THING OFF.
HOW'S IT GOING OVER **THERE?**
GREAT, SO FAR. WE'RE **ALMOST DONE,** WHICH IS GOOD, BECAUSE WE GOT OUR FIRST GIG LINED UP.
FINE. FINISH UP AND HEAD BACK.
AND REPRESENTIN' EVERYONE'S FAVORITE BOROUGH, STATEN ISLAND, IS **THE QUINNTUPLETS!**
WHAT? WE DON'T HAVE OUR **SUPERHERO NAMES** YET?
YEAH, I HAVEN'T FIGURED 'EM OUT, YET. I **ALMOST** DID LAST NIGHT, BUT THEN I GOT DISTRACTED BY **HUNGER.** WE'LL BRAINSTORM OVER **PIZZA.**
YEAH, WE GOTTA **DO** THAT! BUT WE DON'T WANT **HALF-ASSED** SUPERHERO NAMES LIKE THAT **BULLETEER,** OR THAT **ELASTI-GIRL.** OR **GOLDSTAR, BOODIKKA,** OR **LADY QUARK!**
I CAN'T STAND **NIGHT GIRL.** WHAT HAPPENS WHEN SHE GOES OUT DURING THE **DAY?** OR **SHRINKING VIOLET.** HOW SCARY IS **THAT** NAME? AND DON'T GET ME STARTED ON **VIXEN!**
OR **SILK SPECTRE.** IF SHE'S A **GHOST,** HOW DO YOU EVEN KNOW WHAT SHE **FEELS** LIKE? HOW RIDICULOUS.
YEAHHH... NO SHRINKY-NIGHT-GHOST NAMES.

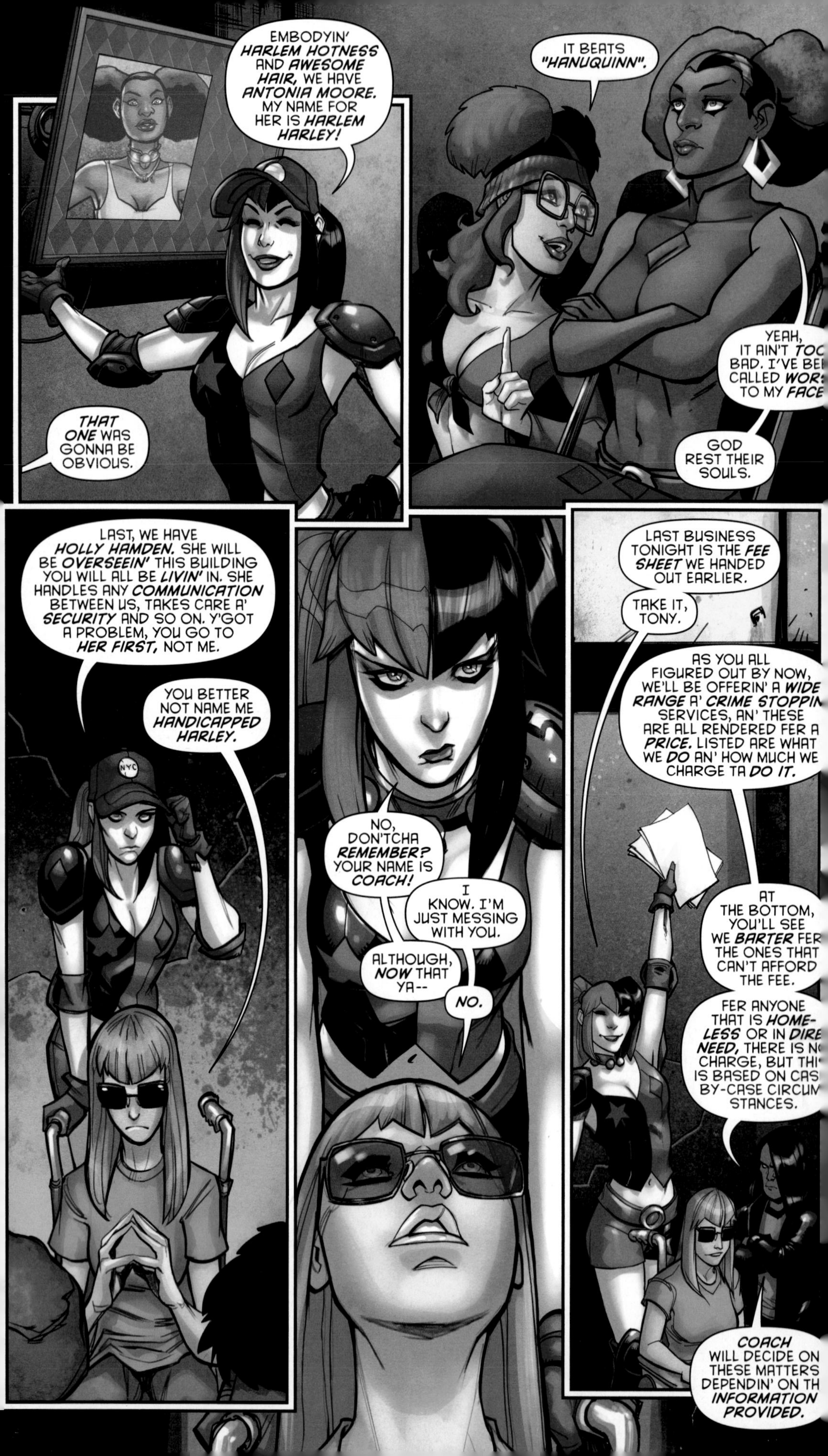
EMBODYIN' HARLEM HOTNESS AND AWESOME HAIR, WE HAVE ANTONIA MOORE. MY NAME FOR HER IS HARLEM HARLEY!
THAT ONE WAS GONNA BE OBVIOUS.
IT BEATS "HANUQUINN".
YEAH, IT AIN'T TO BAD. I'VE BE CALLED WOR TO MY FACE
GOD REST THEIR SOULS.
LAST, WE HAVE HOLLY HAMDEN. SHE WILL BE OVERSEEIN' THIS BUILDING YOU WILL ALL BE LIVIN' IN. SHE HANDLES ANY COMMUNICATION BETWEEN US, TAKES CARE A' SECURITY AND SO ON. Y'GOT A PROBLEM, YOU GO TO HER FIRST, NOT ME.
YOU BETTER NOT NAME ME HANDICAPPED HARLEY.
NO, DON'TCHA REMEMBER? YOUR NAME IS COACH!
I KNOW. I'M JUST MESSING WITH YOU.
ALTHOUGH, NOW THAT YA--
NO.
LAST BUSINESS TONIGHT IS THE FEE SHEET WE HANDED OUT EARLIER.
TAKE IT, TONY.
AS YOU ALL FIGURED OUT BY NOW, WE'LL BE OFFERIN' A WIDE RANGE A' CRIME STOPPIN SERVICES, AN' THESE ARE ALL RENDERED FER A PRICE. LISTED ARE WHAT WE DO AN' HOW MUCH WE CHARGE TA DO IT.
AT THE BOTTOM, YOU'LL SEE WE BARTER FER THE ONES THAT CAN'T AFFORD THE FEE.
FER ANYONE THAT IS HOME-LESS OR IN DIRE NEED, THERE IS N CHARGE, BUT TH IS BASED ON CAS BY-CASE CIRCUM STANCES.
COACH WILL DECIDE ON THESE MATTERS DEPENDIN' ON TH INFORMATION PROVIDED.

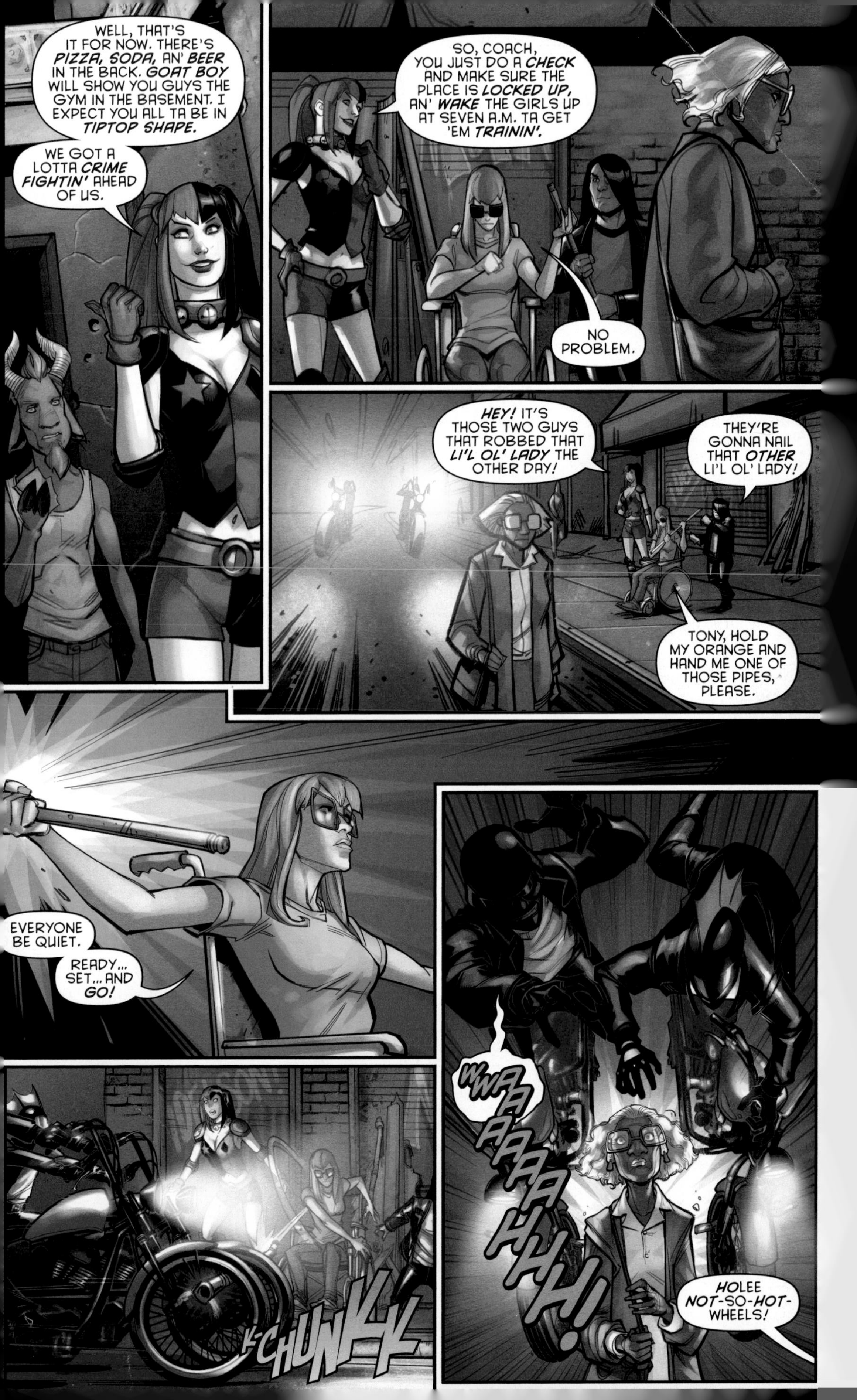

WELL, THAT'S IT FOR NOW. THERE'S PIZZA, SODA, AN' BEER IN THE BACK. GOAT BOY WILL SHOW YOU GUYS THE GYM IN THE BASEMENT. I EXPECT YOU ALL TA BE IN TIPTOP SHAPE.
WE GOT A LOTTA CRIME FIGHTIN' AHEAD OF US.
SO, COACH, YOU JUST DO A CHECK AND MAKE SURE THE PLACE IS LOCKED UP, AN' WAKE THE GIRLS UP AT SEVEN A.M. TA GET 'EM TRAININ'.
NO PROBLEM.
HEY! IT'S THOSE TWO GUYS THAT ROBBED THAT LI'L OL' LADY THE OTHER DAY!
THEY'RE GONNA NAIL THAT OTHER LI'L OL' LADY!
TONY, HOLD MY ORANGE AND HAND ME ONE OF THOSE PIPES, PLEASE.
EVERYONE BE QUIET.
READY... SET... AND GO!
K-CHUNKK
WWAAAAAAAHHH!
HOLEE NOT-SO-HOT-WHEELS!

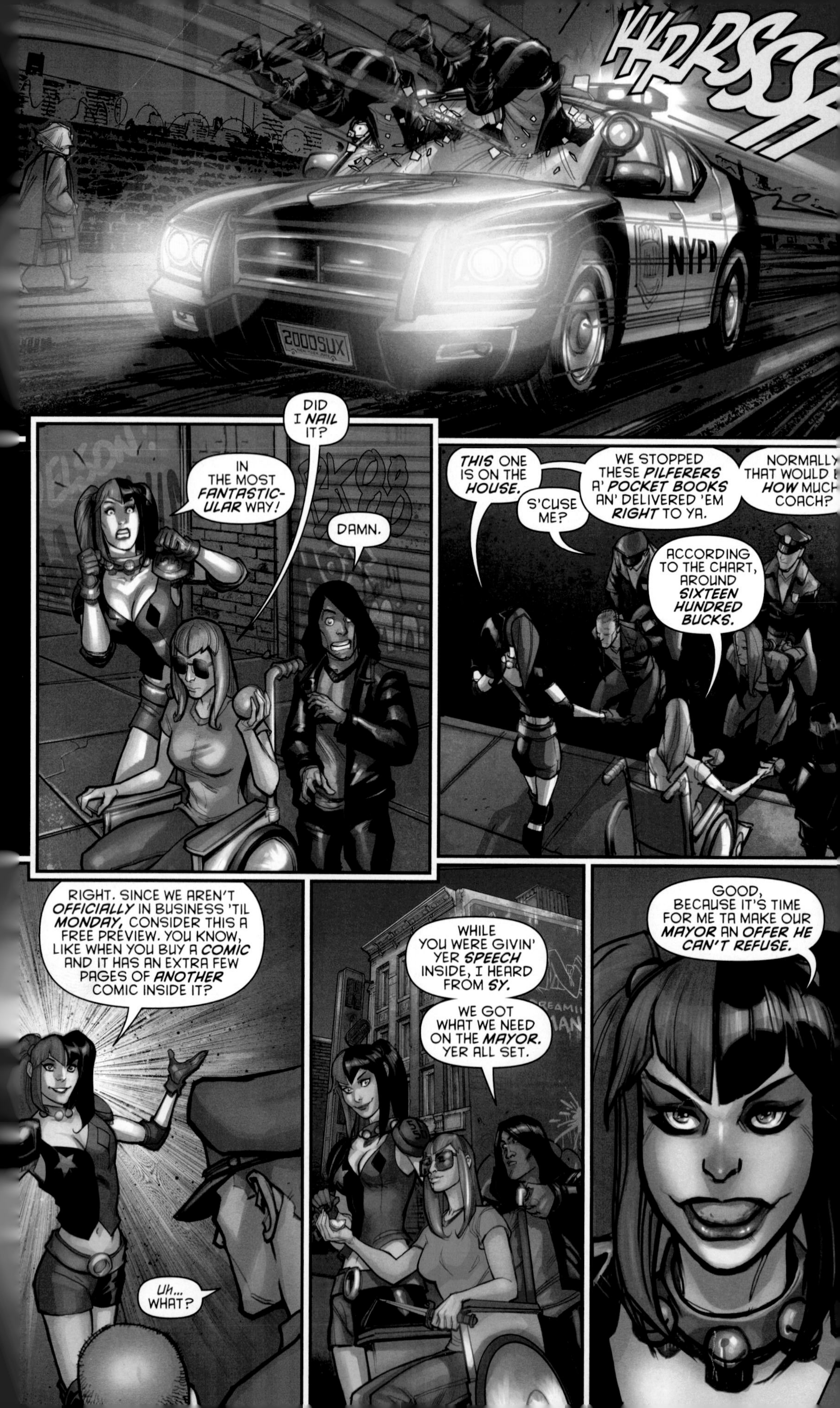

KKRSCSH
2000SUX
NYPD
DID I NAIL IT?
IN THE MOST FANTASTIC-ULAR WAY!
DAMN.
THIS ONE IS ON THE HOUSE.
S'CUSE ME?
WE STOPPED THESE PILFERERS A' POCKET BOOKS AN' DELIVERED 'EM RIGHT TO YA.
NORMALLY THAT WOULD B HOW MUCH COACH?
ACCORDING TO THE CHART, AROUND SIXTEEN HUNDRED BUCKS.
RIGHT. SINCE WE AREN'T OFFICIALLY IN BUSINESS 'TIL MONDAY, CONSIDER THIS A FREE PREVIEW. YOU KNOW, LIKE WHEN YOU BUY A COMIC AND IT HAS AN EXTRA FEW PAGES OF ANOTHER COMIC INSIDE IT?
UH... WHAT?
WHILE YOU WERE GIVIN' YER SPEECH INSIDE, I HEARD FROM SY.
WE GOT WHAT WE NEED ON THE MAYOR. YER ALL SET.
GOOD, BECAUSE IT'S TIME FOR ME TA MAKE OUR MAYOR AN OFFER HE CAN'T REFUSE.

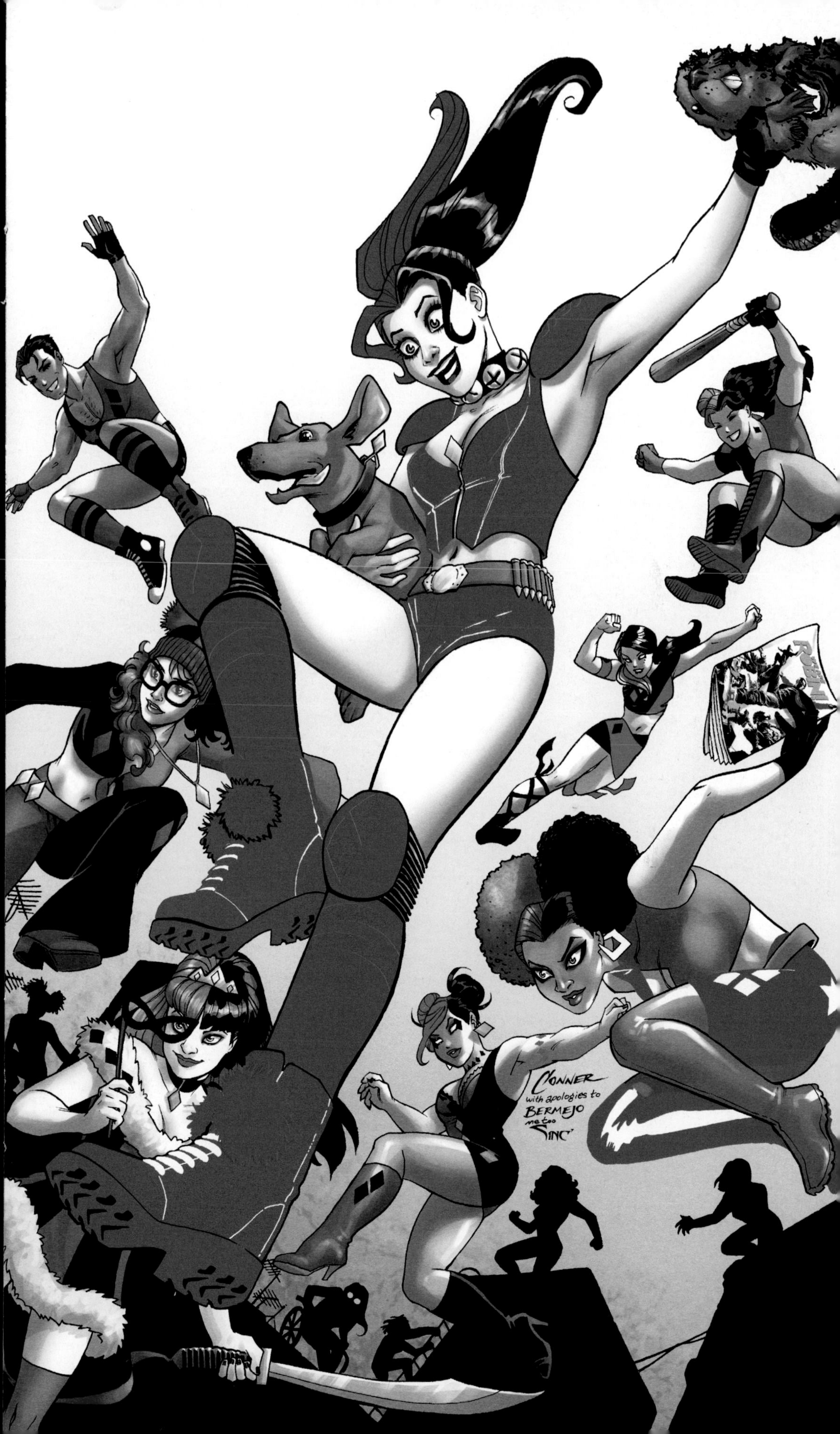
CONNER
with apologies to
BERMEJO
me too
SINC'

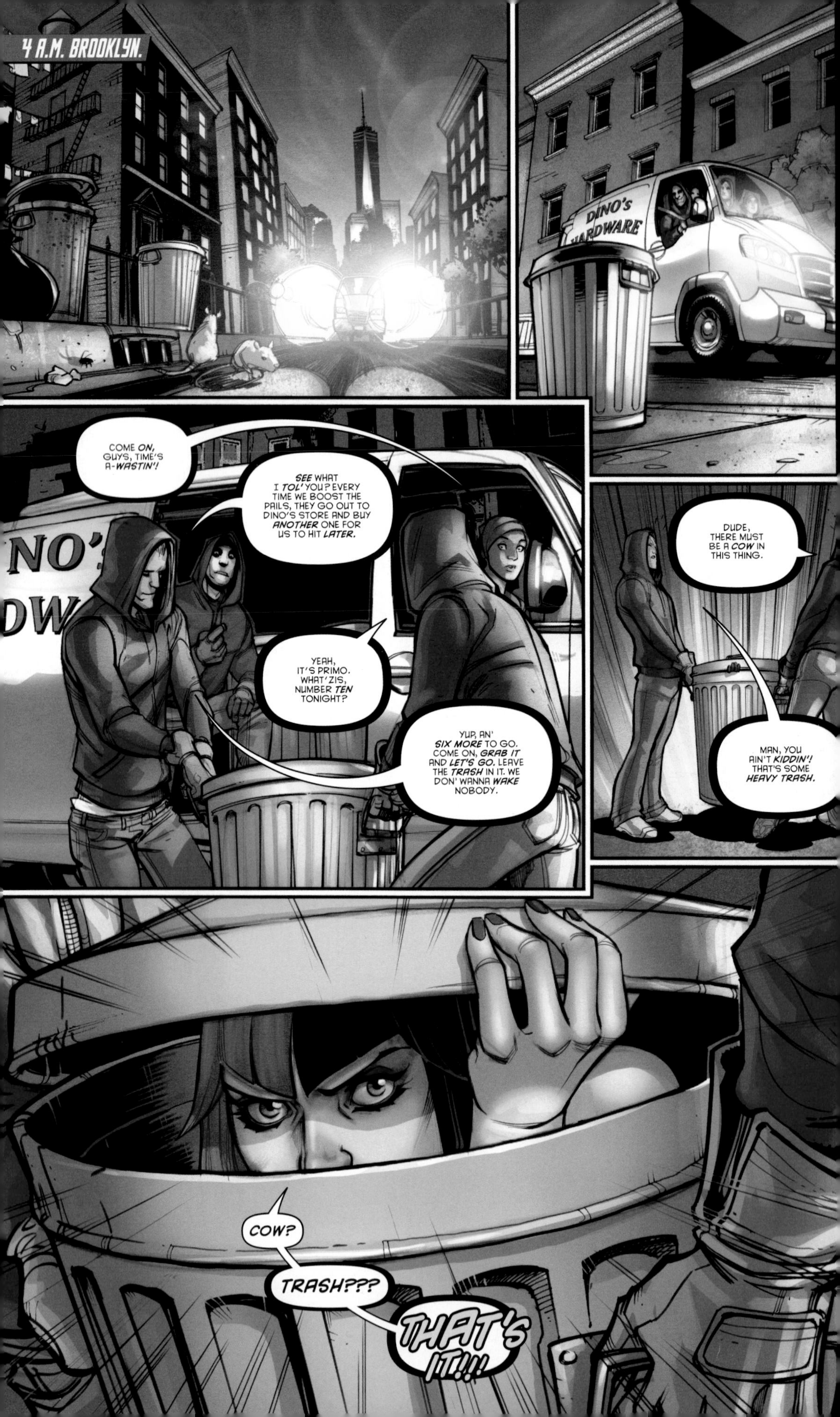
4 A.M. BROOKLYN.
DINO'S HARDWARE
COME ON, GUYS, TIME'S A-WASTIN'!
SEE WHAT I TOL' YOU? EVERY TIME WE BOOST THE PAILS, THEY GO OUT TO DINO'S STORE AND BUY ANOTHER ONE FOR US TO HIT LATER.
YEAH, IT'S PRIMO. WHAT'ZIS, NUMBER TEN TONIGHT?
YUP, AN' SIX MORE TO GO. COME ON, GRAB IT AND LET'S GO. LEAVE THE TRASH IN IT. WE DON' WANNA WAKE NOBODY.
DUDE, THERE MUST BE A COW IN THIS THING.
MAN, YOU AIN'T KIDDIN'! THAT'S SOME HEAVY TRASH.
COW?
TRASH???
THAT'S IT!!!

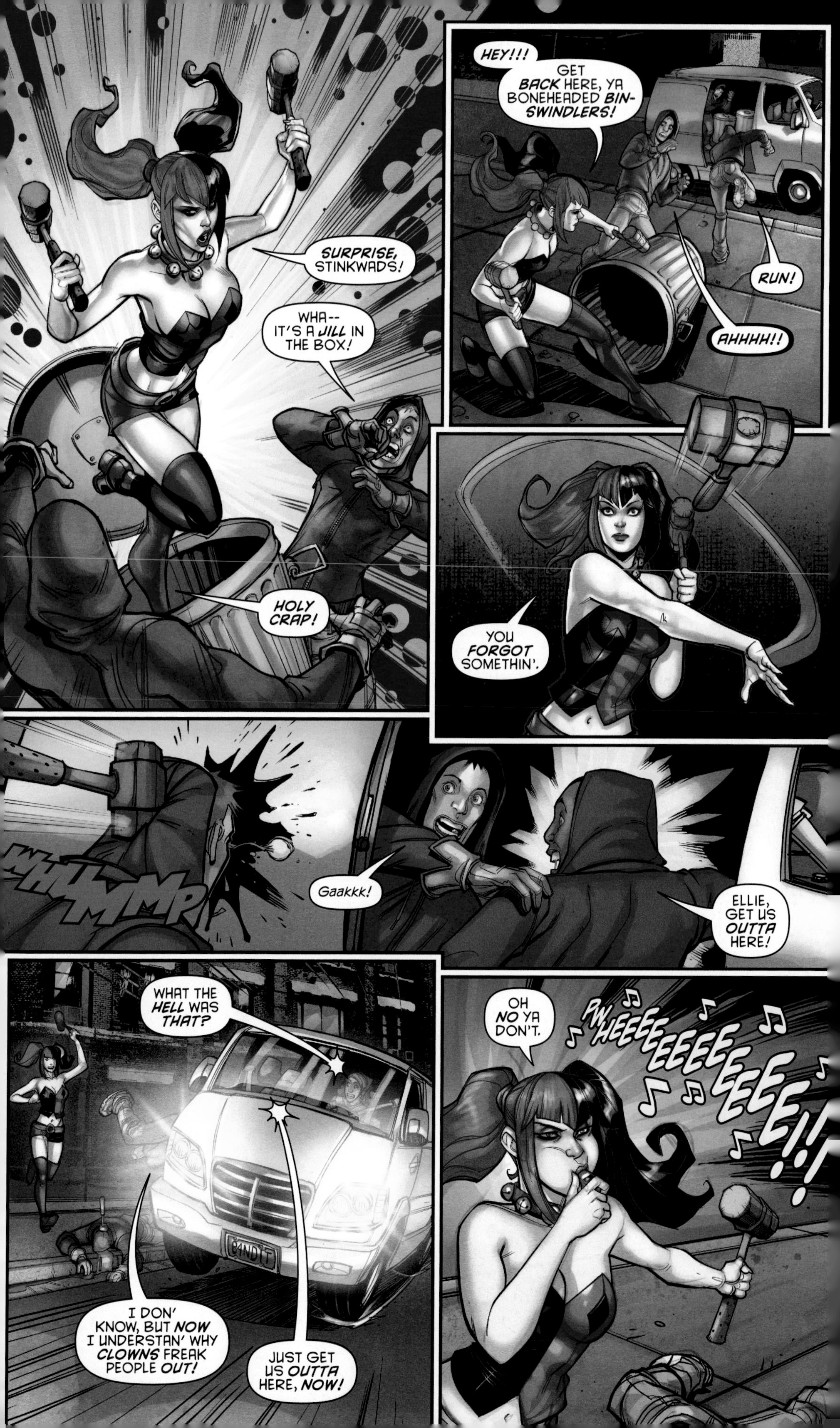
SURPRISE, STINKWADS!
WHA-- IT'S A JILL IN THE BOX!
HOLY CRAP!
HEY!!!
GET BACK HERE, YA BONEHEADED BIN-SWINDLERS!
RUN!
AHHHH!!
YOU FORGOT SOMETHIN'.
WHUMP
Gaakkk!
ELLIE, GET US OUTTA HERE!
WHAT THE HELL WAS THAT?
I DON' KNOW, BUT NOW I UNDERSTAN' WHY CLOWNS FREAK PEOPLE OUT!
JUST GET US OUTTA HERE, NOW!
OH NO YA DON'T.
PWHEEEEEEEEEEE!!!

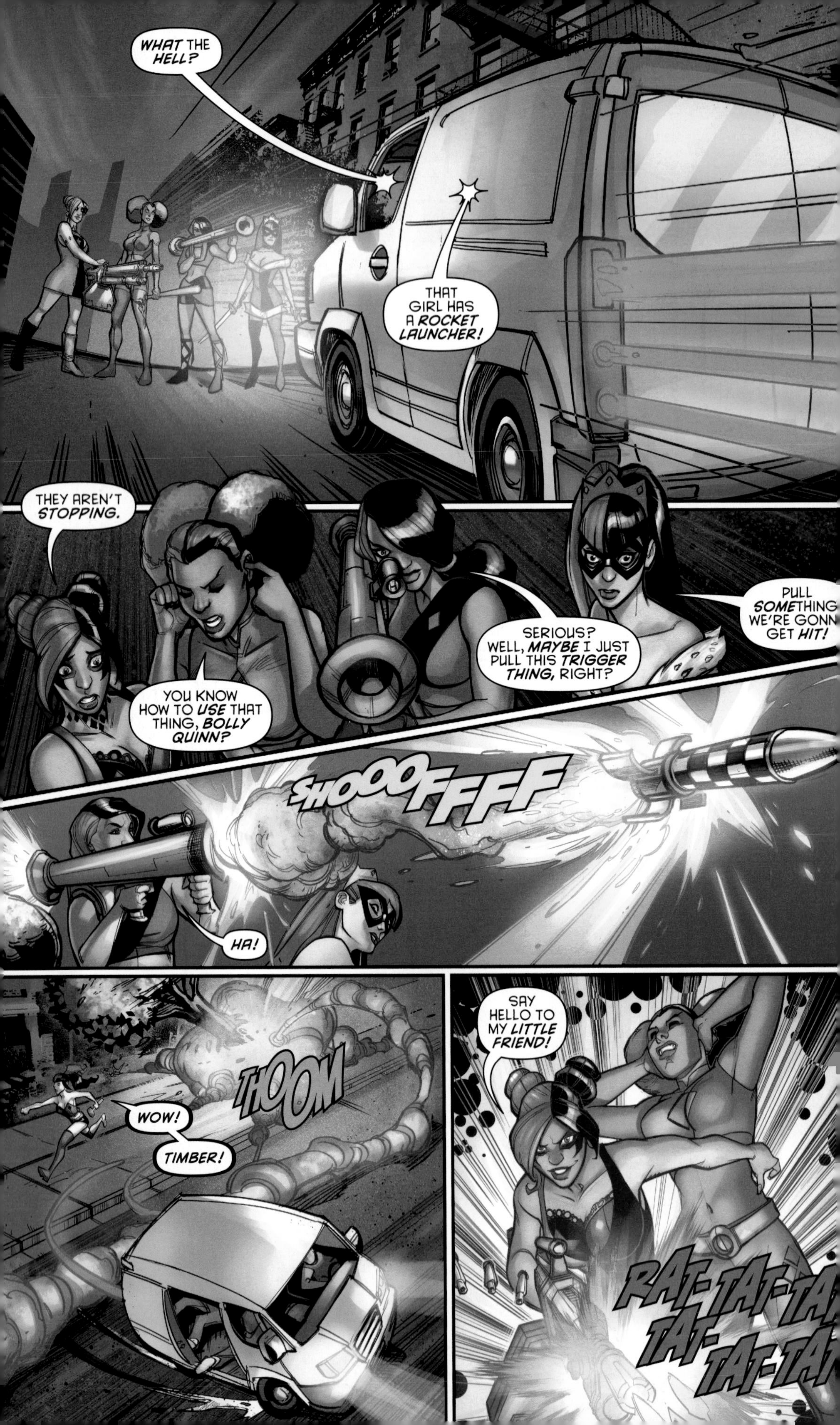
WHAT THE HELL?
THAT GIRL HAS A ROCKET LAUNCHER!
THEY AREN'T STOPPING.
YOU KNOW HOW TO USE THAT THING, BOLLY QUINN?
SERIOUS? WELL, MAYBE I JUST PULL THIS TRIGGER THING, RIGHT?
PULL SOMETHING WE'RE GONN GET HIT!
SHOOOFFFF
HA!
THOOM
WOW!
TIMBER!
SAY HELLO TO MY LITTLE FRIEND!
RAT-TAT-TA TAT-TAT-TA

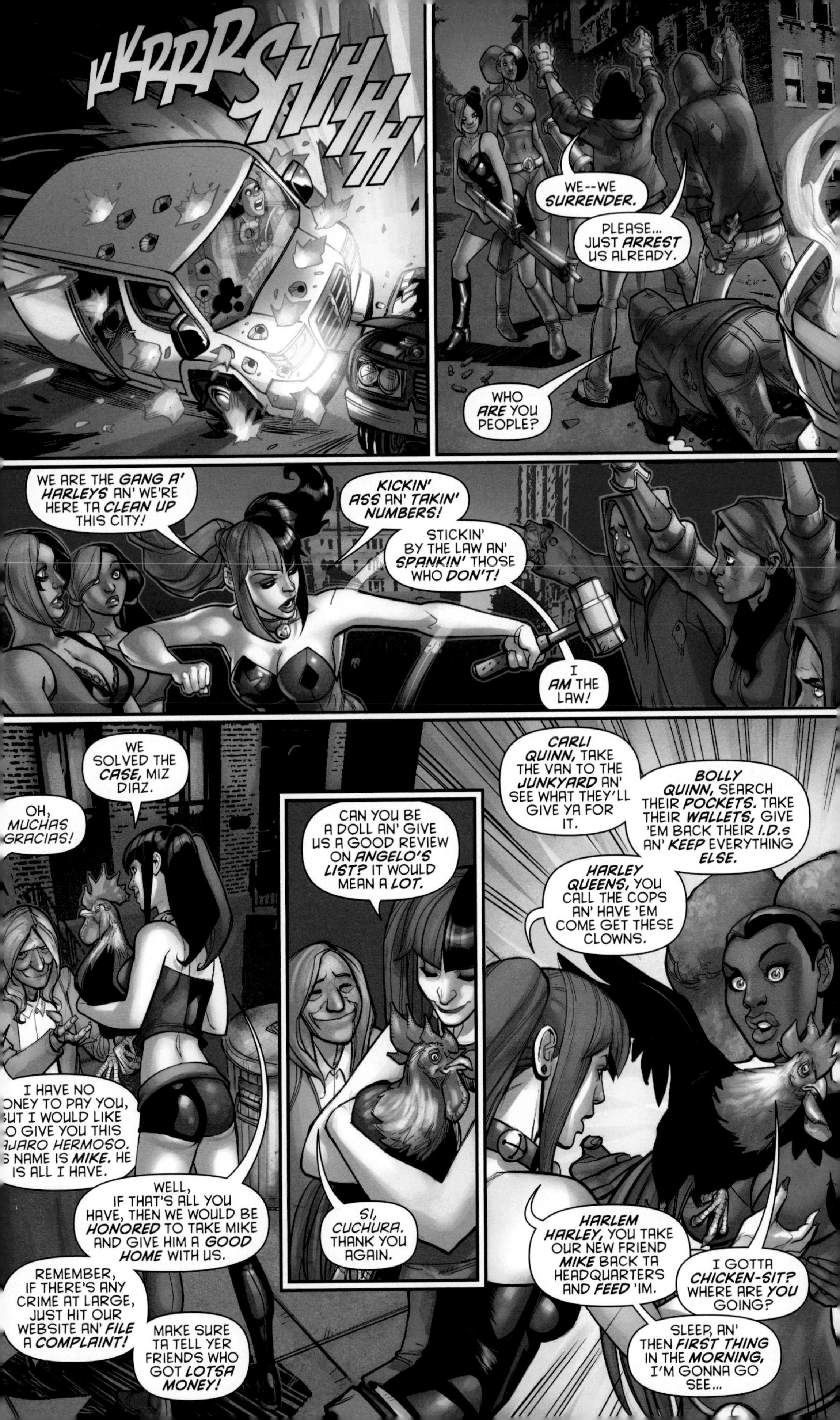
KKRRRSHHHH
WE--WE SURRENDER.
PLEASE... JUST ARREST US ALREADY.
WHO ARE YOU PEOPLE?
WE ARE THE GANG A' HARLEYS AN' WE'RE HERE TA CLEAN UP THIS CITY!
KICKIN' ASS AN' TAKIN' NUMBERS!
STICKIN' BY THE LAW AN' SPANKIN' THOSE WHO DON'T!
I AM THE LAW!
WE SOLVED THE CASE, MIZ DIAZ.
OH, MUCHAS GRACIAS!
I HAVE NO ONEY TO PAY YOU, UT I WOULD LIKE O GIVE YOU THIS AJARO HERMOSO. S NAME IS MIKE. HE IS ALL I HAVE.
WELL, IF THAT'S ALL YOU HAVE, THEN WE WOULD BE HONORED TO TAKE MIKE AND GIVE HIM A GOOD HOME WITH US.
REMEMBER, IF THERE'S ANY CRIME AT LARGE, JUST HIT OUR WEBSITE AN' FILE A COMPLAINT!
MAKE SURE TA TELL YER FRIENDS WHO GOT LOTSA MONEY!
CAN YOU BE A DOLL AN' GIVE US A GOOD REVIEW ON ANGELO'S LIST? IT WOULD MEAN A LOT.
SI, CUCHURA. THANK YOU AGAIN.
CARLI QUINN, TAKE THE VAN TO THE JUNKYARD AN' SEE WHAT THEY'LL GIVE YA FOR IT.
BOLLY QUINN, SEARCH THEIR POCKETS. TAKE THEIR WALLETS, GIVE 'EM BACK THEIR I.D.s AN' KEEP EVERYTHING ELSE.
HARLEY QUEENS, YOU CALL THE COPS AN' HAVE 'EM COME GET THESE CLOWNS.
HARLEM HARLEY, YOU TAKE OUR NEW FRIEND MIKE BACK TA HEADQUARTERS AND FEED 'IM.
I GOTTA CHICKEN-SIT? WHERE ARE YOU GOING?
SLEEP, AN' THEN FIRST THING IN THE MORNING, I'M GONNA GO SEE...

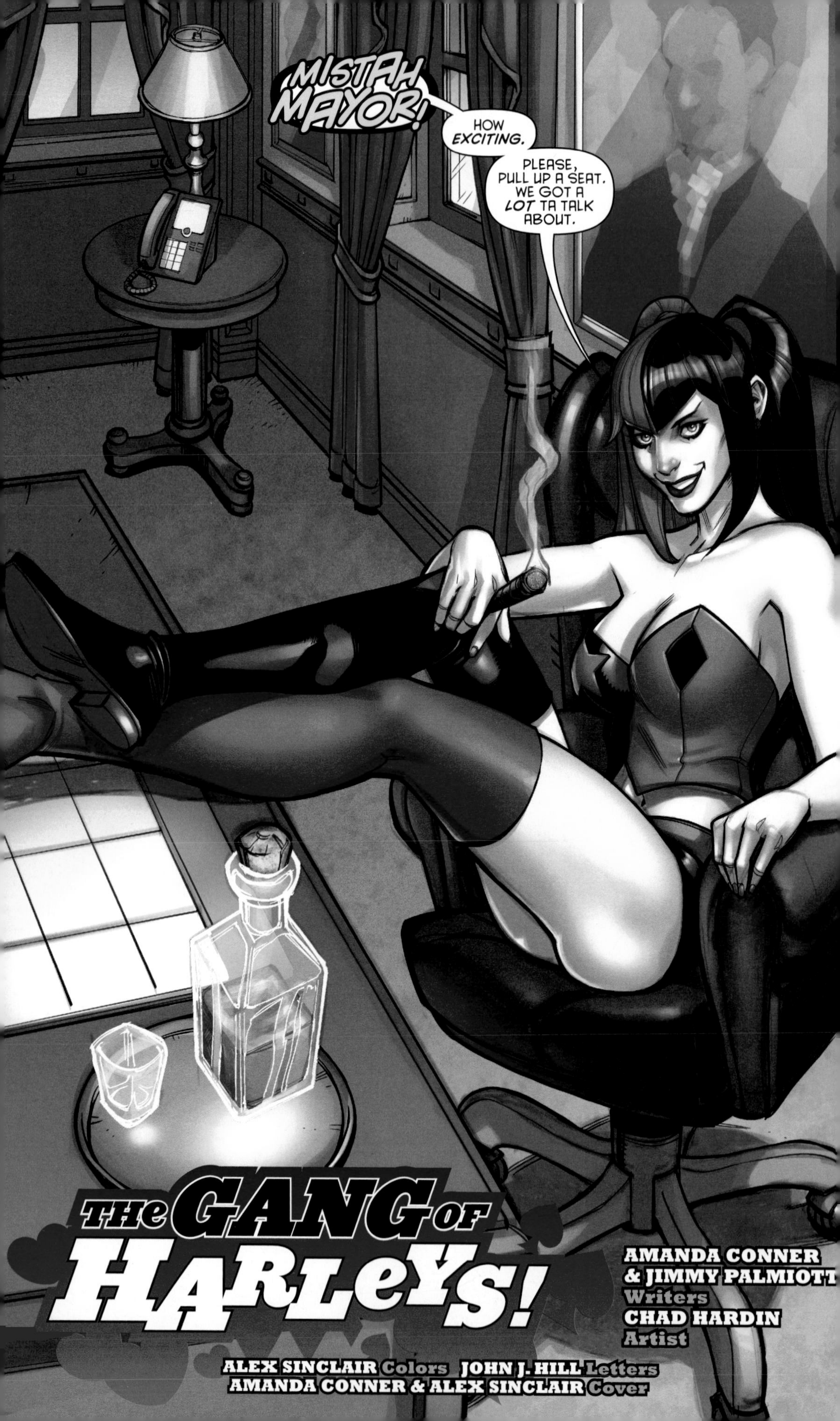
MISTAH MAYOR!
HOW EXCITING.
PLEASE, PULL UP A SEAT. WE GOT A LOT TA TALK ABOUT.
THE GANG OF HARLEYS!
AMANDA CONNER & JIMMY PALMIOTTI Writers
CHAD HARDIN Artist
ALEX SINCLAIR Colors JOHN J. HILL Letters
AMANDA CONNER & ALEX SINCLAIR Cover

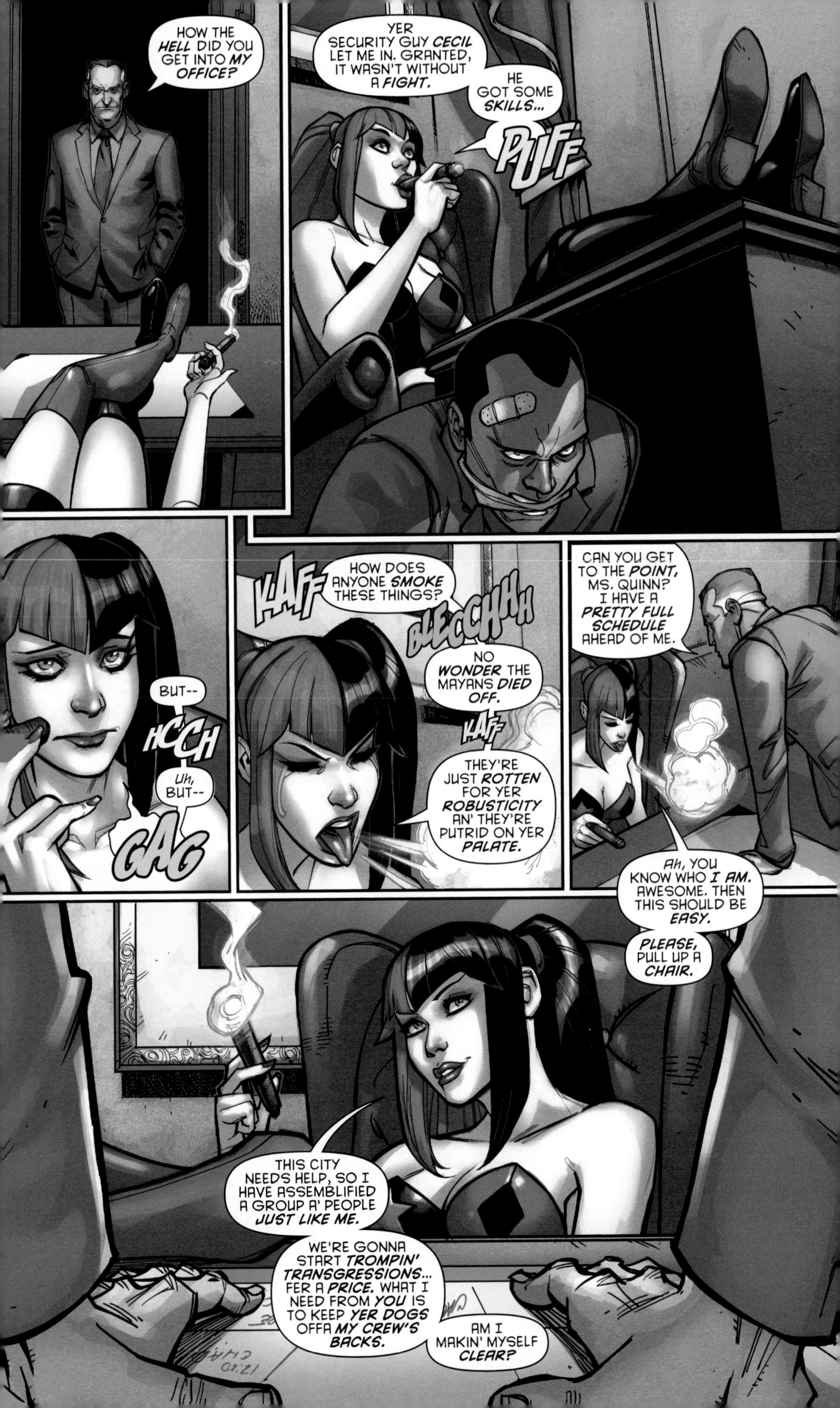
HOW THE HELL DID YOU GET INTO MY OFFICE?
YER SECURITY GUY CECIL LET ME IN. GRANTED, IT WASN'T WITHOUT A FIGHT.
HE GOT SOME SKILLS...
PUFF
BUT--
HCCH
UH, BUT--
GAG
KAFF
HOW DOES ANYONE SMOKE THESE THINGS?
BLECCHHHH
NO WONDER THE MAYANS DIED OFF.
KAFF
THEY'RE JUST ROTTEN FOR YER ROBUSTICITY AN' THEY'RE PUTRID ON YER PALATE.
CAN YOU GET TO THE POINT, MS. QUINN? I HAVE A PRETTY FULL SCHEDULE AHEAD OF ME.
AH, YOU KNOW WHO I AM. AWESOME. THEN THIS SHOULD BE EASY.
PLEASE, PULL UP A CHAIR.
THIS CITY NEEDS HELP, SO I HAVE ASSEMBLIFIED A GROUP A' PEOPLE JUST LIKE ME.
WE'RE GONNA START TROMPIN' TRANSGRESSIONS... FER A PRICE. WHAT I NEED FROM YOU IS TO KEEP YER DOGS OFFA MY CREW'S BACKS.
AM I MAKIN' MYSELF CLEAR?

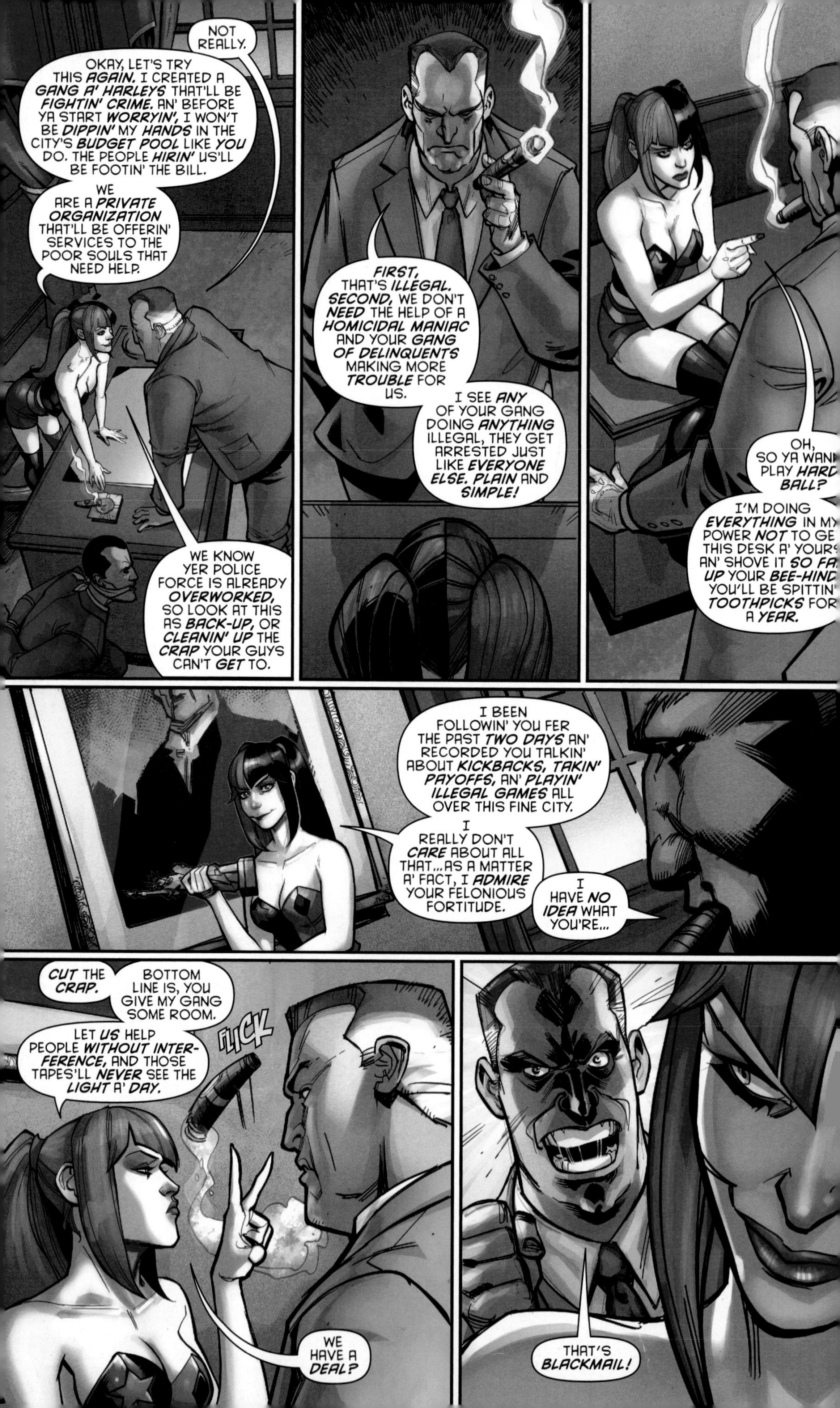
NOT REALLY.
OKAY, LET'S TRY THIS AGAIN. I CREATED A GANG A' HARLEYS THAT'LL BE FIGHTIN' CRIME. AN' BEFORE YA START WORRYIN', I WON'T BE DIPPIN' MY HANDS IN THE CITY'S BUDGET POOL LIKE YOU DO. THE PEOPLE HIRIN' US'LL BE FOOTIN' THE BILL.
WE ARE A PRIVATE ORGANIZATION THAT'LL BE OFFERIN' SERVICES TO THE POOR SOULS THAT NEED HELP.
WE KNOW YER POLICE FORCE IS ALREADY OVERWORKED, SO LOOK AT THIS AS BACK-UP, OR CLEANIN' UP THE CRAP YOUR GUYS CAN'T GET TO.
FIRST, THAT'S ILLEGAL. SECOND, WE DON'T NEED THE HELP OF A HOMICIDAL MANIAC AND YOUR GANG OF DELINQUENTS MAKING MORE TROUBLE FOR US.
I SEE ANY OF YOUR GANG DOING ANYTHING ILLEGAL, THEY GET ARRESTED JUST LIKE EVERYONE ELSE. PLAIN AND SIMPLE!
OH, SO YA WAN PLAY HARD BALL?
I'M DOING EVERYTHING IN MY POWER NOT TO GE THIS DESK A' YOURS AN' SHOVE IT SO FA UP YOUR BEE-HIND YOU'LL BE SPITTIN' TOOTHPICKS FOR A YEAR.
I BEEN FOLLOWIN' YOU FER THE PAST TWO DAYS AN' RECORDED YOU TALKIN' ABOUT KICKBACKS, TAKIN' PAYOFFS, AN' PLAYIN' ILLEGAL GAMES ALL OVER THIS FINE CITY.
I REALLY DON'T CARE ABOUT ALL THAT...AS A MATTER A' FACT, I ADMIRE YOUR FELONIOUS FORTITUDE.
I HAVE NO IDEA WHAT YOU'RE...
CUT THE CRAP.
BOTTOM LINE IS, YOU GIVE MY GANG SOME ROOM.
LET US HELP PEOPLE WITHOUT INTERFERENCE, AND THOSE TAPES'LL NEVER SEE THE LIGHT A' DAY.
FLICK
WE HAVE A DEAL?
THAT'S BLACKMAIL!

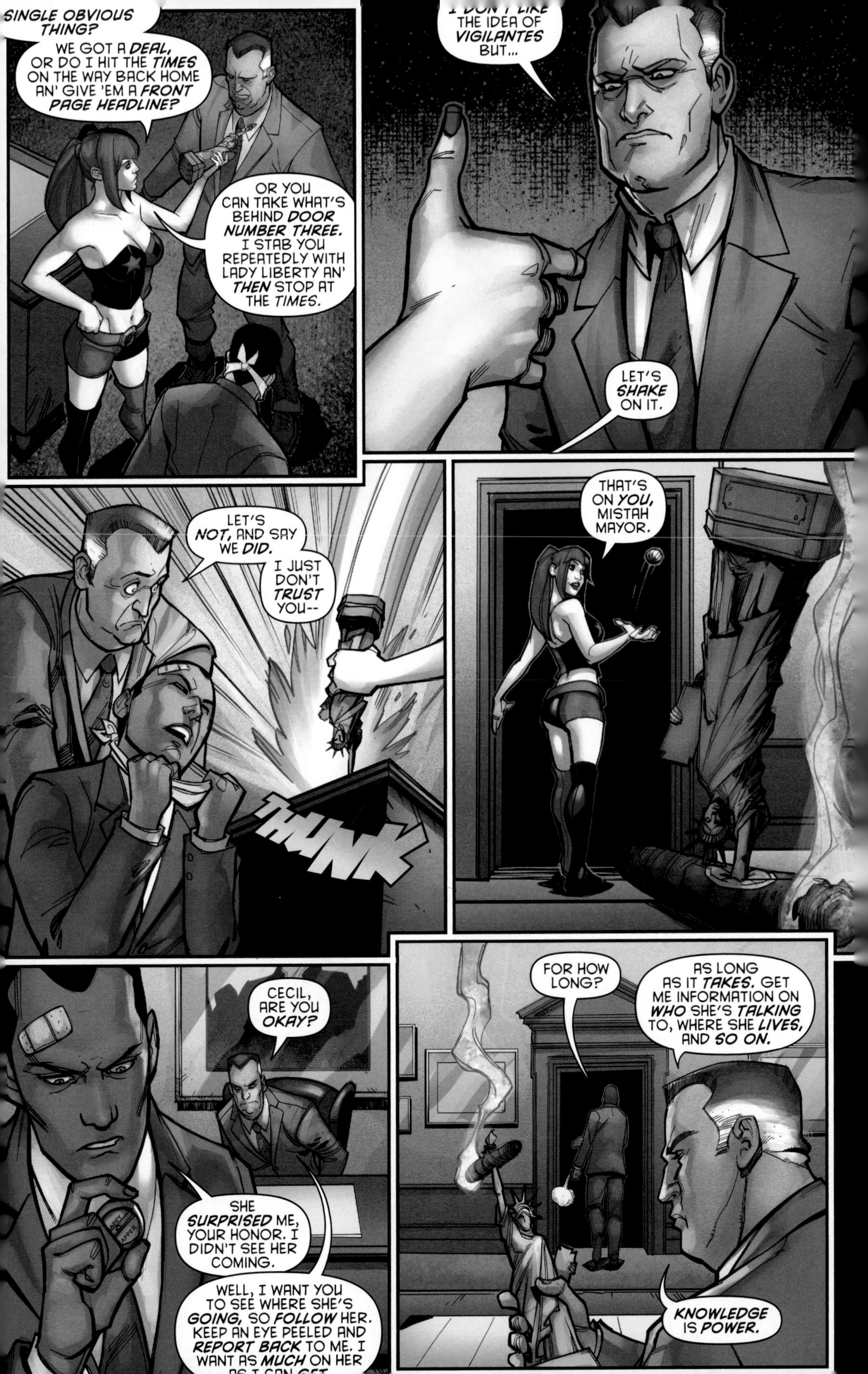
SINGLE OBVIOUS THING?
WE GOT A DEAL, OR DO I HIT THE TIMES ON THE WAY BACK HOME AN' GIVE 'EM A FRONT PAGE HEADLINE?
OR YOU CAN TAKE WHAT'S BEHIND DOOR NUMBER THREE. I STAB YOU REPEATEDLY WITH LADY LIBERTY AN' THEN STOP AT THE TIMES.
THE IDEA OF VIGILANTES BUT...
LET'S SHAKE ON IT.
LET'S NOT, AND SAY WE DID.
I JUST DON'T TRUST YOU--
THUNK
THAT'S ON YOU, MISTAH MAYOR.
CECIL, ARE YOU OKAY?
SHE SURPRISED ME, YOUR HONOR. I DIDN'T SEE HER COMING.
WELL, I WANT YOU TO SEE WHERE SHE'S GOING, SO FOLLOW HER. KEEP AN EYE PEELED AND REPORT BACK TO ME. I WANT AS MUCH ON HER
FOR HOW LONG?
AS LONG AS IT TAKES. GET ME INFORMATION ON WHO SHE'S TALKING TO, WHERE SHE LIVES, AND SO ON.
KNOWLEDGE IS POWER.

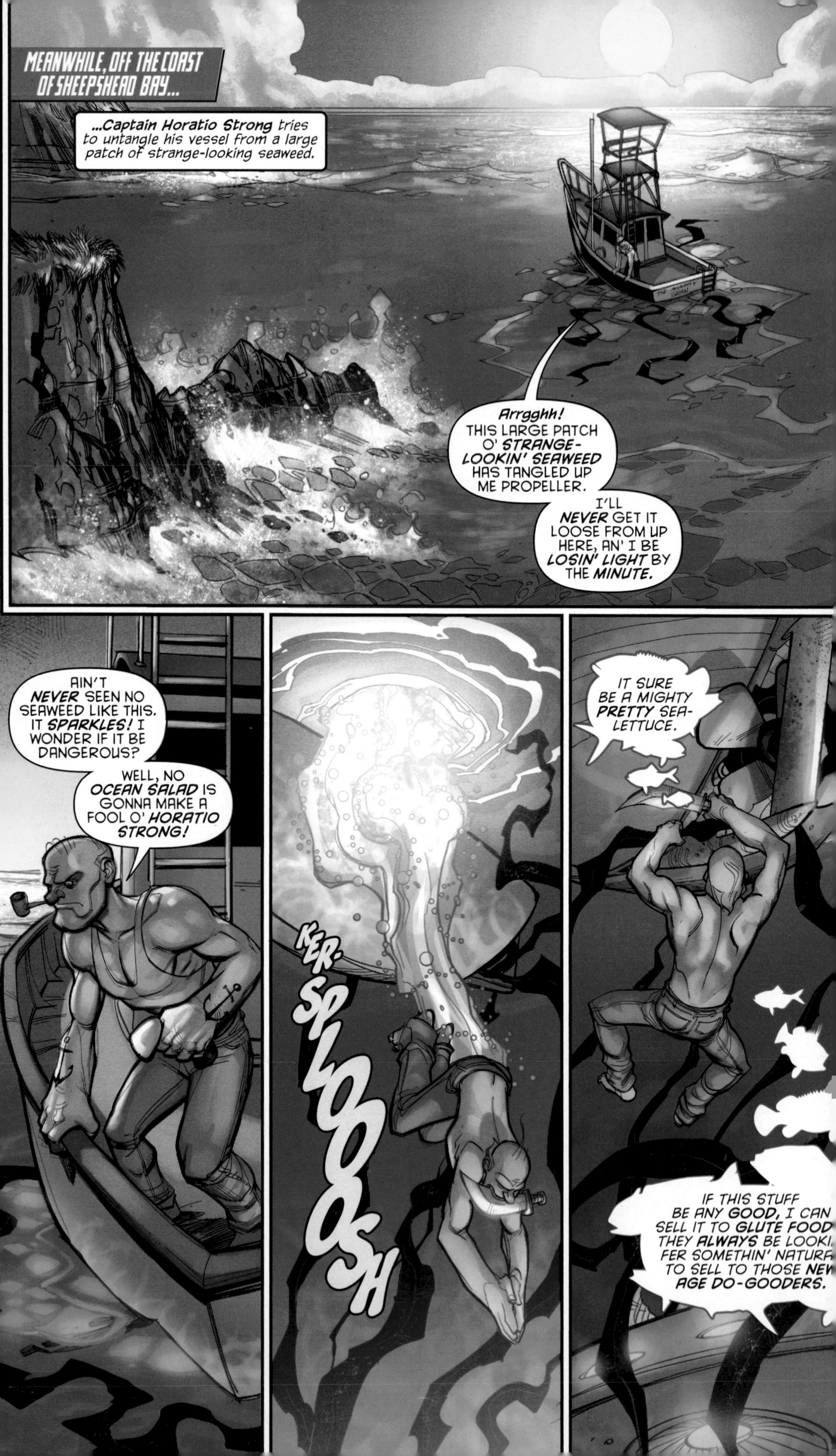
MEANWHILE, OFF THE COAST OF SHEEPSHEAD BAY...
...Captain Horatio Strong tries to untangle his vessel from a large patch of strange-looking seaweed.
Arrrgghh! THIS LARGE PATCH O' STRANGE-LOOKIN' SEAWEED HAS TANGLED UP ME PROPELLER.
I'LL NEVER GET IT LOOSE FROM UP HERE, AN' I BE LOSIN' LIGHT BY THE MINUTE.
AIN'T NEVER SEEN NO SEAWEED LIKE THIS. IT SPARKLES! I WONDER IF IT BE DANGEROUS?
WELL, NO OCEAN SALAD IS GONNA MAKE A FOOL O' HORATIO STRONG!
KER-SPLOOOOSH
IT SURE BE A MIGHTY PRETTY SEA-LETTUCE.
IF THIS STUFF BE ANY GOOD, I CAN SELL IT TO GLUTE FOOD THEY ALWAYS BE LOOKI FER SOMETHIN' NATURA TO SELL TO THOSE NEW AGE DO-GOODERS.

THE MURPHY SWAN

THAT OUGHTA DO THE TRICK. SEEMS LIKE THESE MARINE GREENS DON'T WANNA BE LETTIN' GO.

BE SMELLIN' LIKE A CROSS BETWEEN A GUTTED FISH AN' A MOLDY SHOE, WITH A WHIFF O' LICORICE.

WONDER HOW IT BE TASTIN'?

Hmmm, NOT BAD. NOT BAD AT ALL...

FEELIN' MIGHTY STRANGE...CAN'T FOCUS...CAN HEAR ME OWN BLOOD PUMPIN'--

AHOY!

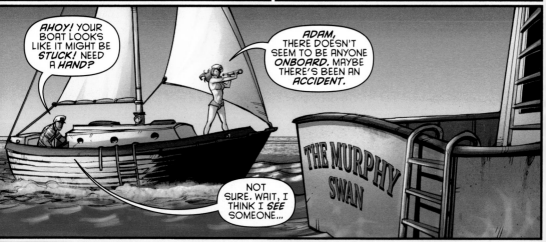

AHOY! YOUR BOAT LOOKS LIKE IT MIGHT BE STUCK! NEED A HAND?

ADAM, THERE DOESN'T SEEM TO BE ANYONE ONBOARD. MAYBE THERE'S BEEN AN ACCIDENT.

NOT SURE. WAIT, I THINK I SEE SOMEONE...

THE MURPHY SWAN

I--I BE RIGHT HERE...I BE FINE.

PLEASE... LEAVE ME BE...

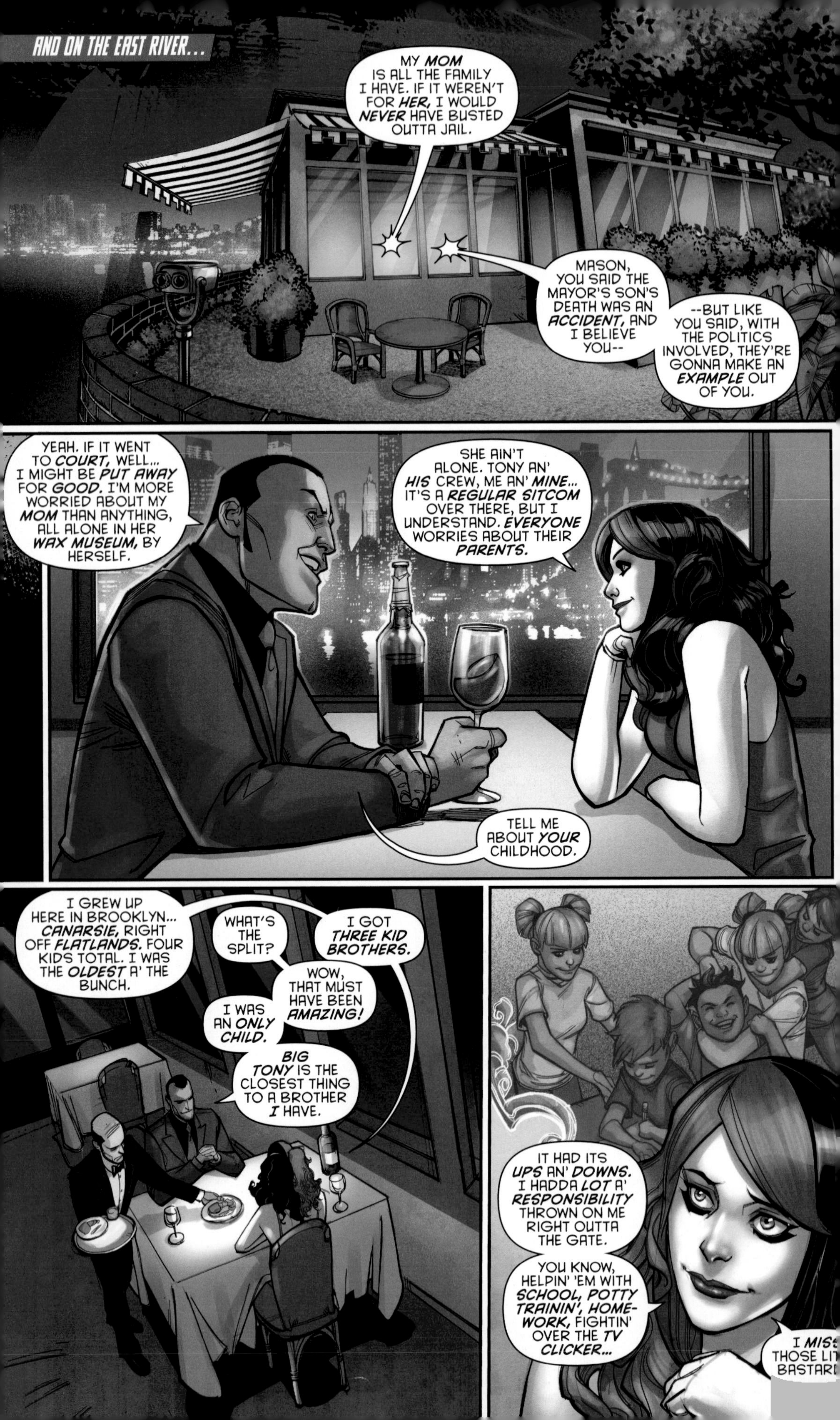
AND ON THE EAST RIVER...
MY MOM IS ALL THE FAMILY I HAVE. IF IT WEREN'T FOR HER, I WOULD NEVER HAVE BUSTED OUTTA JAIL.
MASON, YOU SAID THE MAYOR'S SON'S DEATH WAS AN ACCIDENT, AND I BELIEVE YOU--
--BUT LIKE YOU SAID, WITH THE POLITICS INVOLVED, THEY'RE GONNA MAKE AN EXAMPLE OUT OF YOU.
YEAH. IF IT WENT TO COURT, WELL... I MIGHT BE PUT AWAY FOR GOOD. I'M MORE WORRIED ABOUT MY MOM THAN ANYTHING, ALL ALONE IN HER WAX MUSEUM, BY HERSELF.
SHE AIN'T ALONE. TONY AN' HIS CREW, ME AN' MINE... IT'S A REGULAR SITCOM OVER THERE, BUT I UNDERSTAND. EVERYONE WORRIES ABOUT THEIR PARENTS.
TELL ME ABOUT YOUR CHILDHOOD.
I GREW UP HERE IN BROOKLYN... CANARSIE, RIGHT OFF FLATLANDS. FOUR KIDS TOTAL. I WAS THE OLDEST A' THE BUNCH.
WHAT'S THE SPLIT?
I GOT THREE KID BROTHERS.
WOW, THAT MUST HAVE BEEN AMAZING!
I WAS AN ONLY CHILD.
BIG TONY IS THE CLOSEST THING TO A BROTHER I HAVE.
IT HAD ITS UPS AN' DOWNS. I HADDA LOT A' RESPONSIBILITY THROWN ON ME RIGHT OUTTA THE GATE.
YOU KNOW, HELPIN' 'EM WITH SCHOOL, POTTY TRAININ', HOME-WORK, FIGHTIN' OVER THE TV CLICKER...
I MIS THOSE LI BASTAR

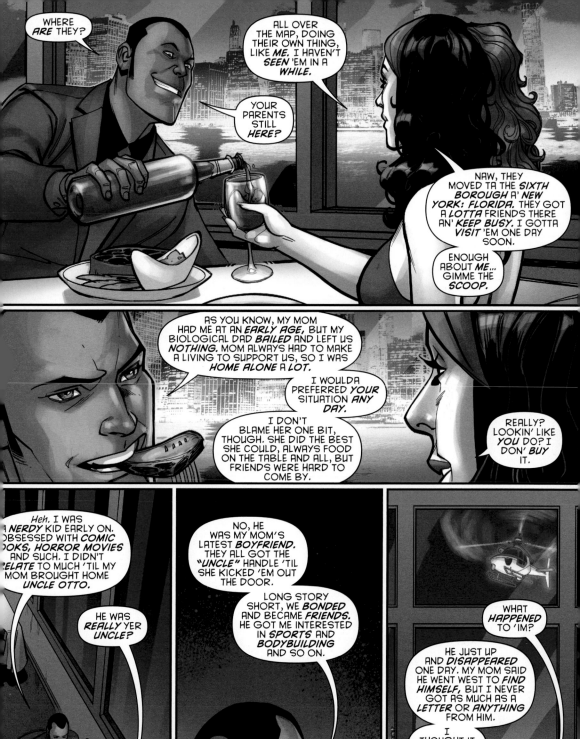

WHERE *ARE* THEY?

ALL OVER THE MAP, DOING THEIR OWN THING, LIKE *ME.* I HAVEN'T *SEEN* 'EM IN A *WHILE.*

YOUR PARENTS STILL *HERE?*

NAW, THEY MOVED TA THE *SIXTH BOROUGH A' NEW YORK: FLORIDA.* THEY GOT A *LOTTA* FRIENDS THERE AN' *KEEP BUSY.* I GOTTA *VISIT* 'EM ONE DAY SOON.

ENOUGH ABOUT *ME...* GIMME THE *SCOOP.*

AS YOU KNOW, MY MOM HAD ME AT AN *EARLY AGE,* BUT MY BIOLOGICAL DAD *BAILED* AND LEFT US *NOTHING.* MOM ALWAYS HAD TO MAKE A LIVING TO SUPPORT US, SO I WAS *HOME ALONE A LOT.*

I WOULDA PREFERRED *YOUR* SITUATION *ANY DAY.*

I DON'T BLAME HER ONE BIT, THOUGH. SHE DID THE BEST SHE COULD, ALWAYS FOOD ON THE TABLE AND ALL, BUT FRIENDS WERE HARD TO COME BY.

REALLY? LOOKIN' LIKE *YOU* DO? I DON' *BUY* IT.

Heh. I WAS A *NERDY* KID EARLY ON. OBSESSED WITH *COMIC BOOKS, HORROR MOVIES* AND SUCH. I DIDN'T *RELATE* TO MUCH 'TIL MY MOM BROUGHT HOME *UNCLE OTTO.*

HE WAS *REALLY* YER UNCLE?

NO, HE WAS MY MOM'S LATEST *BOYFRIEND.* THEY ALL GOT THE *"UNCLE"* HANDLE 'TIL SHE KICKED 'EM OUT THE DOOR.

LONG STORY SHORT, WE *BONDED* AND BECAME *FRIENDS.* HE GOT ME INTERESTED IN *SPORTS* AND *BODYBUILDING* AND SO ON.

WHAT *HAPPENED* TO 'IM?

HE JUST UP AND *DISAPPEARED* ONE DAY. MY MOM SAID HE WENT WEST TO *FIND HIMSELF,* BUT I NEVER GOT AS MUCH AS A *LETTER* OR *ANYTHING* FROM HIM.

I THOUGHT IT MIGHT'A BEEN BECAUSE OF *ME.*

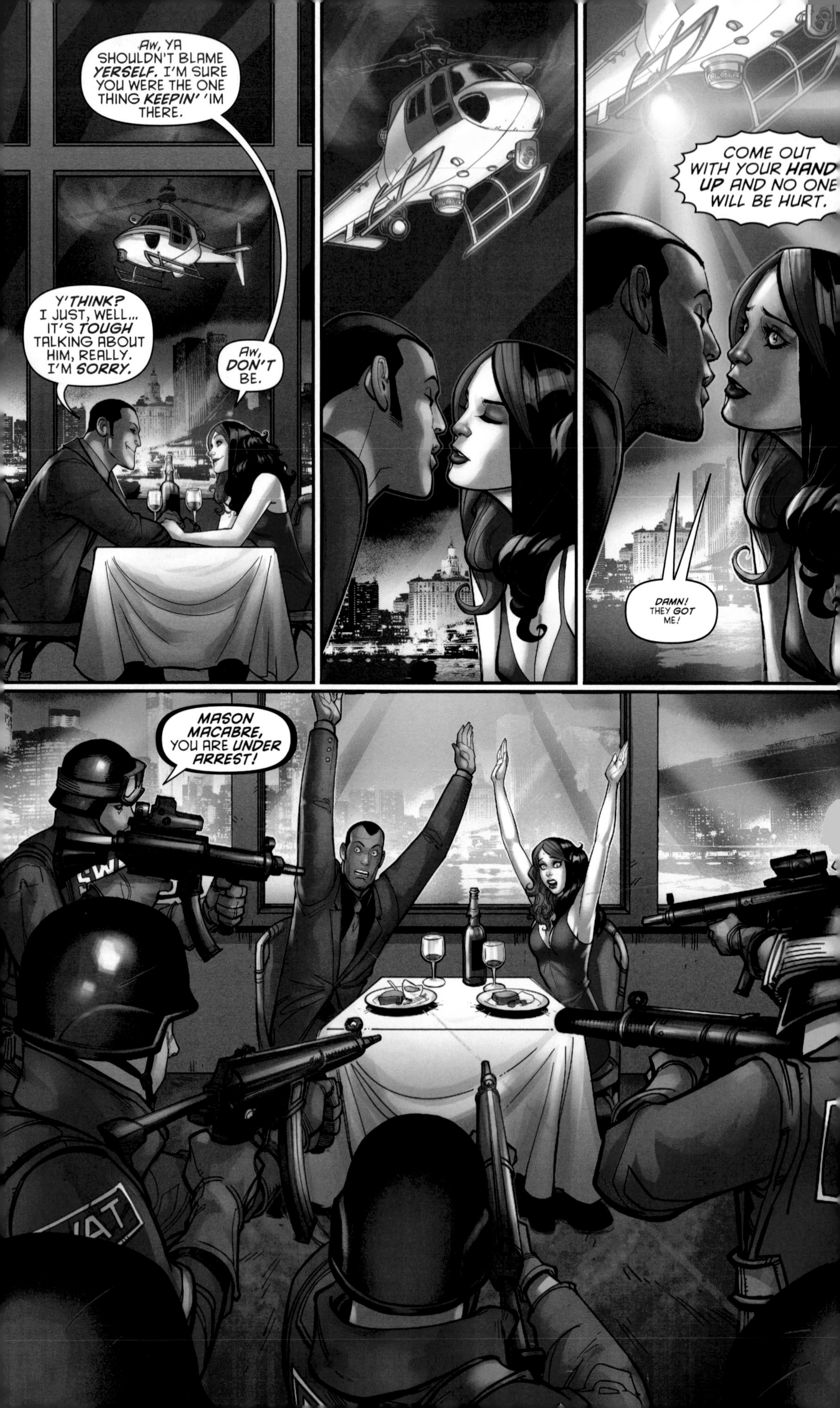
AW, YA SHOULDN'T BLAME YERSELF. I'M SURE YOU WERE THE ONE THING KEEPIN' 'IM THERE.
Y'THINK? I JUST, WELL... IT'S TOUGH TALKING ABOUT HIM, REALLY. I'M SORRY.
AW, DON'T BE.
COME OUT WITH YOUR HAND UP AND NO ONE WILL BE HURT.
DAMN! THEY GOT ME!
MASON MACABRE, YOU ARE UNDER ARREST!
SWAT

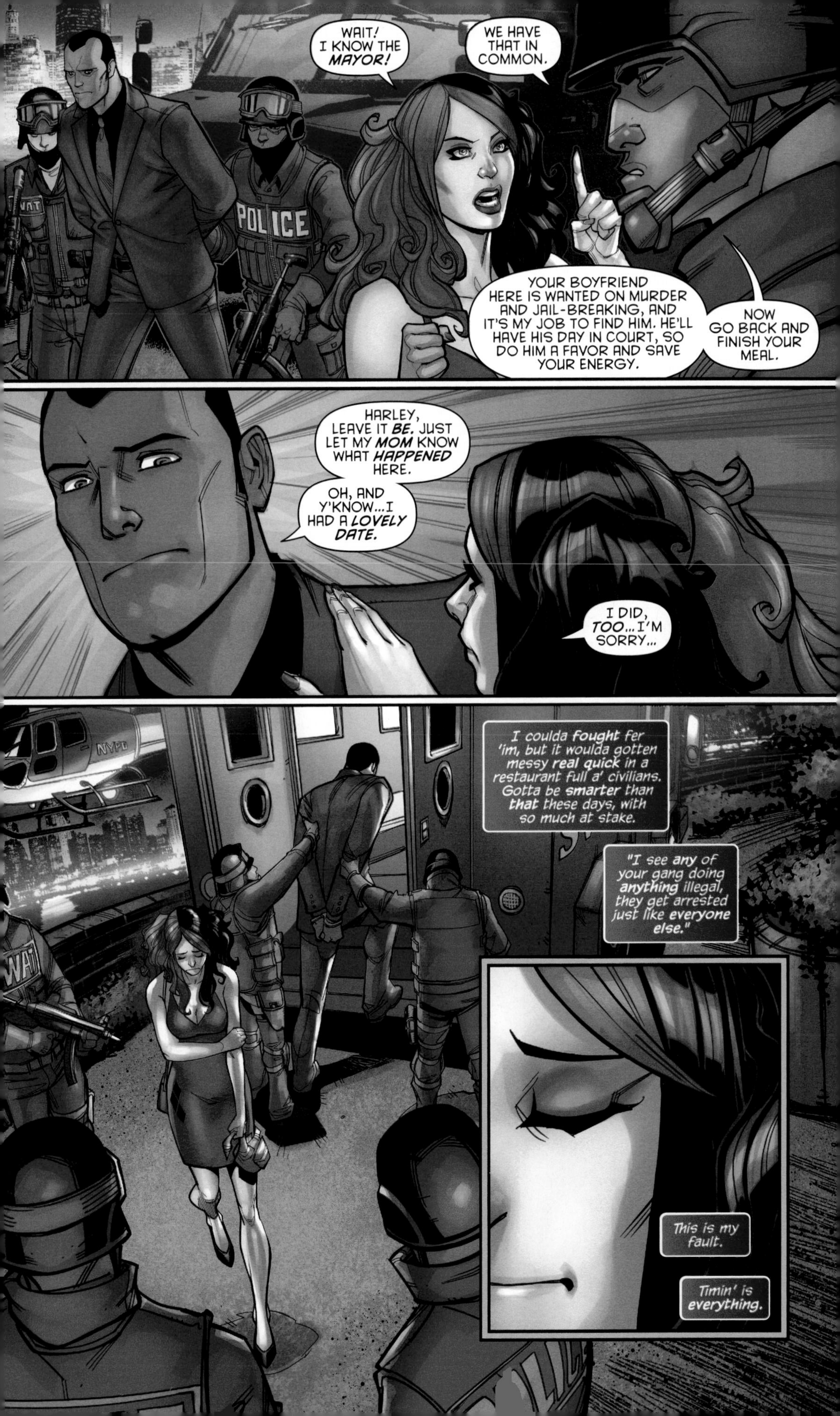
WAIT! I KNOW THE *MAYOR!*
WE HAVE THAT IN COMMON.
YOUR BOYFRIEND HERE IS WANTED ON MURDER AND JAIL-BREAKING, AND IT'S MY JOB TO FIND HIM. HE'LL HAVE HIS DAY IN COURT, SO DO HIM A FAVOR AND SAVE YOUR ENERGY.
NOW GO BACK AND FINISH YOUR MEAL.
HARLEY, LEAVE IT *BE.* JUST LET MY *MOM* KNOW WHAT *HAPPENED* HERE.
OH, AND Y'KNOW...I HAD A *LOVELY DATE.*
I DID, *TOO*...I'M SORRY...
I coulda **fought** fer 'im, but it woulda gotten messy **real quick** in a restaurant full a' civilians. Gotta be **smarter** than **that** these days, with so much at stake.
"I see **any** of your gang doing **anything** illegal, they get arrested just like **everyone** else."
This is my fault.
Timin' is **everything.**

Ughhh, I HATE HOW LAST NIGHT STARTED OUT AS A DREAM, AN' THEN TURNED INTO A BIG, FAT NIGHTMARE.

AIN'T THERE SOMETHIN' YOU OUGHTA BE DOING?

DIDN'CHA GET ENOUGH ATTENTION LAST NIGHT?

NOT ME... MASON'S MOM!

BZZZZTTT
BZZZZTTT

KNOCK KNOCK

YEAH, YEAH, I'M COMIN'.

HERE'S YOUR ORDER FROM THE PET STORE. A HUNDRED AN' FORTY PARAKEETS. SAYS YA BOUGHT 'EM TWO DAYS AGO.

OH, YEAH... CAN YOU BRING 'EM UP TO THE ROOF? JUST FOLLOW ME.

THE VIEW FROM HERE IS AMAZING.

WELL, IT AIN'T GONNA SPANK ITSELF.

WHAT? REALLY??

NO, NOT REALLY! YOU TALK TO YER MOTHER WITH THAT MOUTH?

HEY, IT'S A COMPLIMENT!

OKAY, TOILET MOUTH, OPEN THE BOX.

THEY'RE GONNA FLY AWAY!

THAT'S RIGHT. MY BIRDS NOW. OPEN IT UP.

YOU'RE FREE NOW! GO! FLY HOME, MY LITTLE FRIENDS!

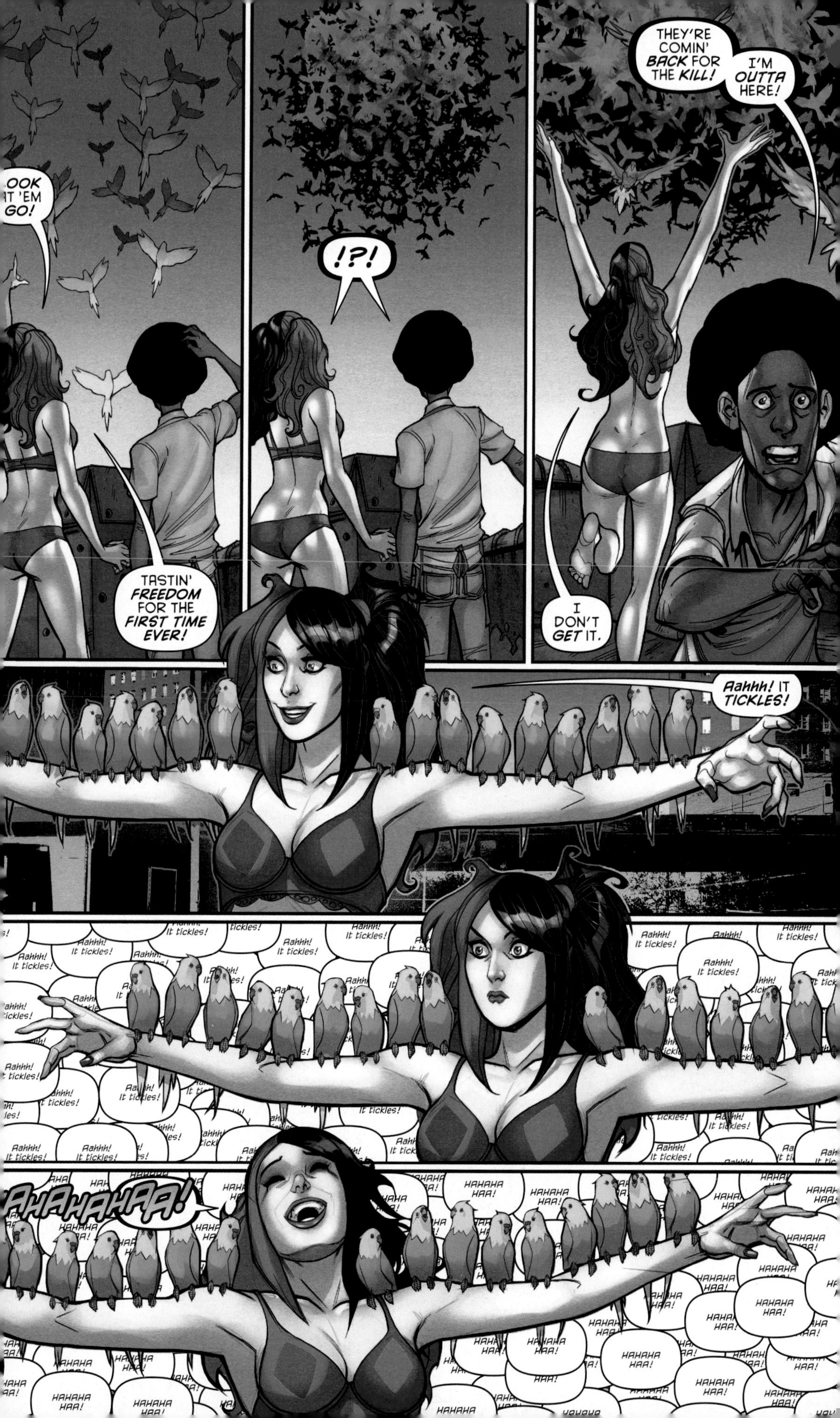

LOOK AT 'EM GO!
TASTIN' FREEDOM FOR THE FIRST TIME EVER!
!?!
THEY'RE COMIN' BACK FOR THE KILL!
I'M OUTTA HERE!
I DON'T GET IT.
Aahhh! IT TICKLES!
Aahhh! It tickles!
AHAHAHAA!
HAHAHA HAA!

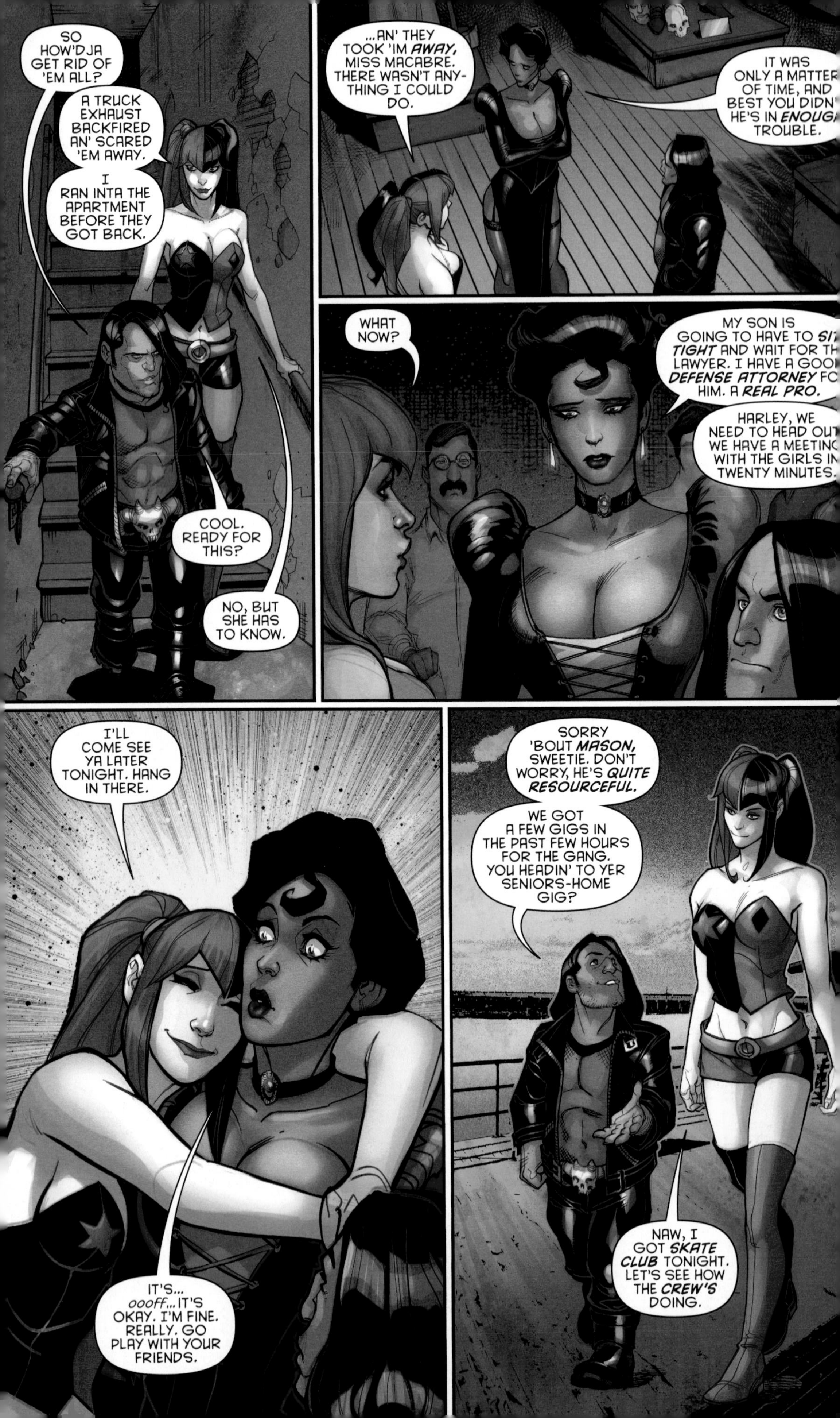

SO HOW'DJA GET RID OF 'EM ALL?
A TRUCK EXHAUST BACKFIRED AN' SCARED 'EM AWAY.
I RAN INTA THE APARTMENT BEFORE THEY GOT BACK.
COOL. READY FOR THIS?
NO, BUT SHE HAS TO KNOW.
...AN' THEY TOOK 'IM AWAY, MISS MACABRE. THERE WASN'T ANY-THING I COULD DO.
IT WAS ONLY A MATTER OF TIME, AND BEST YOU DIDN'T. HE'S IN ENOUGH TROUBLE.
WHAT NOW?
MY SON IS GOING TO HAVE TO SIT TIGHT AND WAIT FOR THE LAWYER. I HAVE A GOOD DEFENSE ATTORNEY FOR HIM. A REAL PRO.
HARLEY, WE NEED TO HEAD OUT. WE HAVE A MEETING WITH THE GIRLS IN TWENTY MINUTES.
I'LL COME SEE YA LATER TONIGHT. HANG IN THERE.
IT'S... oooff... IT'S OKAY. I'M FINE. REALLY. GO PLAY WITH YOUR FRIENDS.
SORRY 'BOUT MASON, SWEETIE. DON'T WORRY, HE'S QUITE RESOURCEFUL.
WE GOT A FEW GIGS IN THE PAST FEW HOURS FOR THE GANG. YOU HEADIN' TO YER SENIORS-HOME GIG?
NAW, I GOT SKATE CLUB TONIGHT. LET'S SEE HOW THE CREW'S DOING.

TRY TO NOT ONLY *BLOCK* MY ADVANCES, BUT *PLAN* YOUR *NEXT ASSAULT*.

THIS IS *SO MUCH FUN!*

OH, PLEASE.

IS THIS REALLY *HAPPENING?* AM I *TOTALLY* FIGHTING *HUMPTY DUMPTY?*

SIS, YOU GOTTA SEE SOMEONE ABOUT YOUR *PROBLEM.*

YOU'RE NOT MY MOM.

NO, I'M YOUR *SISTER* AND YOU SMELL LIKE *WILLIE NELSON'S BEARD.*

DUDE, I WONDER IF YOU CAN *SMOKE* THAT?

PON!

HEY, *COACH,* WHERE'S THE *REST* OF THE CREW?

WE GOT A MISSING-PERSONS CALL. SOME *FISHERMAN'S WIFE* WAS WORRIED ABOUT HER HUSBAND.

SHE SAID THE COPS WERE USELESS AND THE COAST GUARD WAS TOO *BUSY.*

DUDE... OOOWW.

SHE MAY BE *OVER-REACTING,* BUT SHE SAID SHE WOULD PAY *DOUBLE RATE* IF WE FOUND HIM.

HE'S OUT IN THE *ATLANTIC?*

WELL, *MAYBE,* BUT SHE WASN'T SURE. WE HAVE *HARLEM HARLEY* AND *HARVEY QUINN* CHECKING THE BARS AROUND WHERE HIS BOAT TOOK OFF IN *ROCKAWAY.*

THE OTHER GIRLS WENT *FOOD SHOPPING* SINCE THERE ISN'T MUCH HERE.

WAIT, *FISHERMEN'S* BARS? *THOSE* TWO? UH OH.

AHOY, YE CUSTOMERS OF HARPOON HANKS! I AM LOOKING FOR THE WHEREABOUTS OF A CERTAIN CAPTAIN HORATIO STRONG!

TELL ME WHAT I NEED TO KNOW, OTHERWISE I'M GONNA BURN THIS DUMP TO THE GROUND!

GET THE HELL DOWN FROM THERE! TALENT NIGHT ISN'T 'TIL NEXT WEDNESDAY.

WHAT? YOU HAVE A TALENT NIGHT??

WAIT, WAIT, I'M GETTING AWAY FROM MYSELF HERE...

FAR ROCKAWAY.

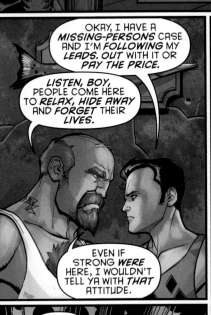

OKAY, I HAVE A MISSING-PERSONS CASE AND I'M FOLLOWING MY LEADS. OUT WITH IT OR PAY THE PRICE.

LISTEN, BOY, PEOPLE COME HERE TO RELAX, HIDE AWAY AND FORGET THEIR LIVES.

EVEN IF STRONG WERE HERE, I WOULDN'T TELL YA WITH THAT ATTITUDE.

LOOK, WITH ONE TUG I CAN DO WHAT WOULD TAKE A GALLON OF WAX, A ROLL OF TAPE, AND TWO KOREAN WOMEN HOURS TO DO, SO UNLESS YOU START TALKING...

YOU DON'T SCARE ME, YA FRUITY PUNK... FRUITY??

WHAT OF IT?

HIYAAAAAAAA

RIPPPP

YOU DONE?

HOW IS THIS POSSIBLE?

I'M A BARTENDER, A DRUNK, AND I GET HIGH ON MY OWN SUPPLY. I HAVEN'T FELT ANYTHING FROM MY NECK DOWN SINCE 1978.

YOU WON'T BE ABLE TO SAY THE SAME IN A FEW SECONDS.

HOW SO?

Whoooff!

KRASH

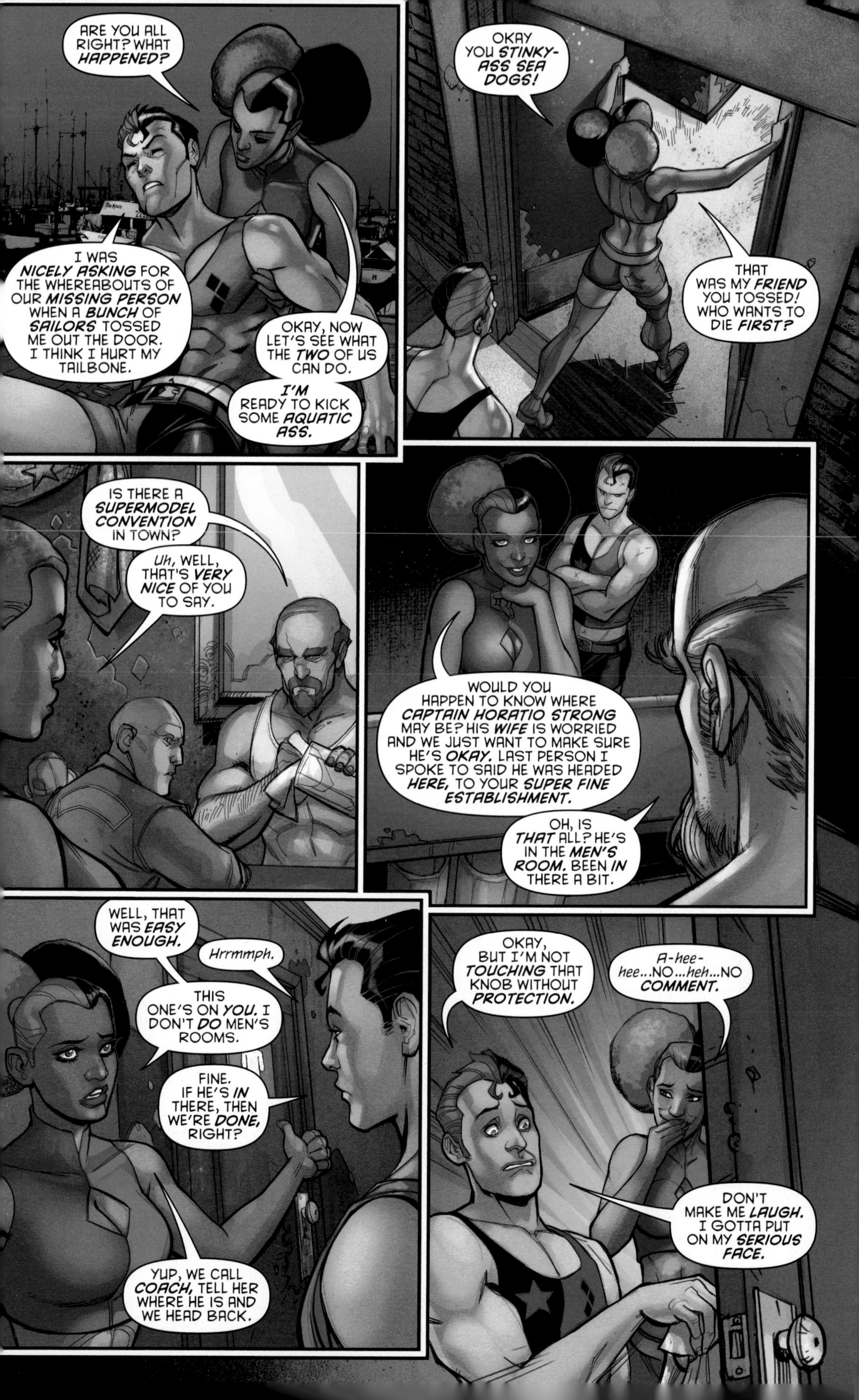

ARE YOU ALL RIGHT? WHAT HAPPENED?
I WAS NICELY ASKING FOR THE WHEREABOUTS OF OUR MISSING PERSON WHEN A BUNCH OF SAILORS TOSSED ME OUT THE DOOR. I THINK I HURT MY TAILBONE.
OKAY, NOW LET'S SEE WHAT THE TWO OF US CAN DO.
I'M READY TO KICK SOME AQUATIC ASS.
OKAY YOU STINKY-ASS SEA DOGS!
THAT WAS MY FRIEND YOU TOSSED! WHO WANTS TO DIE FIRST?
IS THERE A SUPERMODEL CONVENTION IN TOWN?
Uh, WELL, THAT'S VERY NICE OF YOU TO SAY.
WOULD YOU HAPPEN TO KNOW WHERE CAPTAIN HORATIO STRONG MAY BE? HIS WIFE IS WORRIED AND WE JUST WANT TO MAKE SURE HE'S OKAY. LAST PERSON I SPOKE TO SAID HE WAS HEADED HERE, TO YOUR SUPER FINE ESTABLISHMENT.
OH, IS THAT ALL? HE'S IN THE MEN'S ROOM. BEEN IN THERE A BIT.
WELL, THAT WAS EASY ENOUGH.
Hrrmmph.
THIS ONE'S ON YOU. I DON'T DO MEN'S ROOMS.
FINE. IF HE'S IN THERE, THEN WE'RE DONE, RIGHT?
YUP, WE CALL COACH, TELL HER WHERE HE IS AND WE HEAD BACK.
OKAY, BUT I'M NOT TOUCHING THAT KNOB WITHOUT PROTECTION.
A-hee-hee...NO...heh...NO COMMENT.
DON'T MAKE ME LAUGH. I GOTTA PUT ON MY SERIOUS FACE.

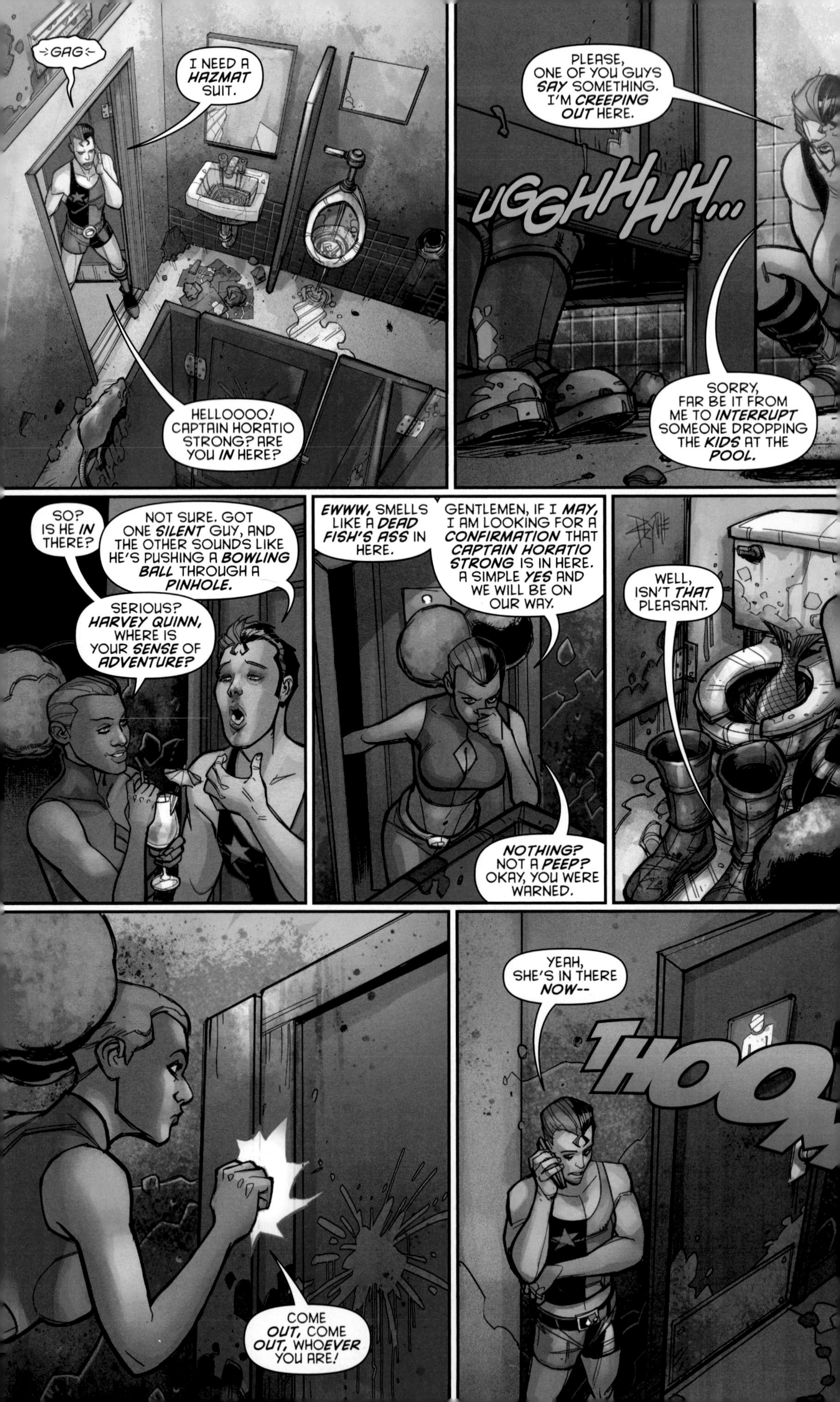
GAG
I NEED A *HAZMAT* SUIT.
HELLOOOO! CAPTAIN HORATIO STRONG? ARE YOU *IN* HERE?
PLEASE, ONE OF YOU GUYS *SAY* SOMETHING. I'M *CREEPING OUT* HERE.
UGGHHHH...
SORRY, FAR BE IT FROM ME TO *INTERRUPT* SOMEONE DROPPING THE *KIDS* AT THE *POOL.*
SO? IS HE *IN* THERE?
NOT SURE. GOT ONE *SILENT* GUY, AND THE OTHER SOUNDS LIKE HE'S PUSHING A *BOWLING BALL* THROUGH A *PINHOLE.*
SERIOUS? *HARVEY QUINN,* WHERE IS YOUR *SENSE* OF *ADVENTURE?*
EWWW, SMELLS LIKE A *DEAD FISH'S ASS* IN HERE.
GENTLEMEN, IF I *MAY,* I AM LOOKING FOR A *CONFIRMATION* THAT *CAPTAIN HORATIO STRONG* IS IN HERE. A SIMPLE *YES* AND WE WILL BE ON OUR WAY.
NOTHING? NOT A *PEEP?* OKAY, YOU WERE WARNED.
WELL, ISN'T *THAT* PLEASANT.
COME *OUT,* COME *OUT,* WHO*EVER* YOU ARE!
YEAH, SHE'S IN THERE *NOW--*
THOOM

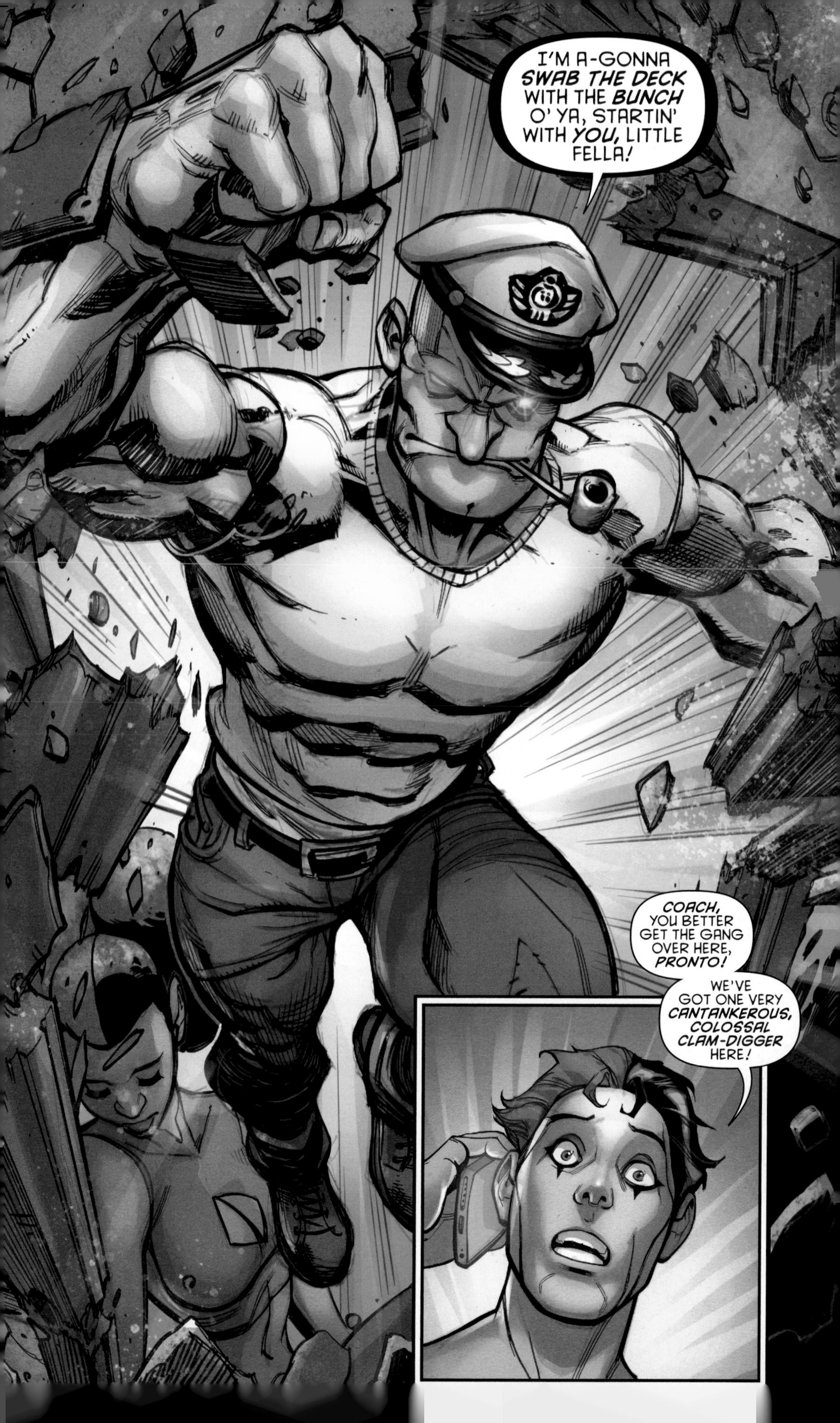
I'M A-GONNA SWAB THE DECK WITH THE BUNCH O' YA, STARTIN' WITH YOU, LITTLE FELLA!
COACH, YOU BETTER GET THE GANG OVER HERE, PRONTO!
WE'VE GOT ONE VERY CANTANKEROUS, COLOSSAL CLAM-DIGGER HERE!

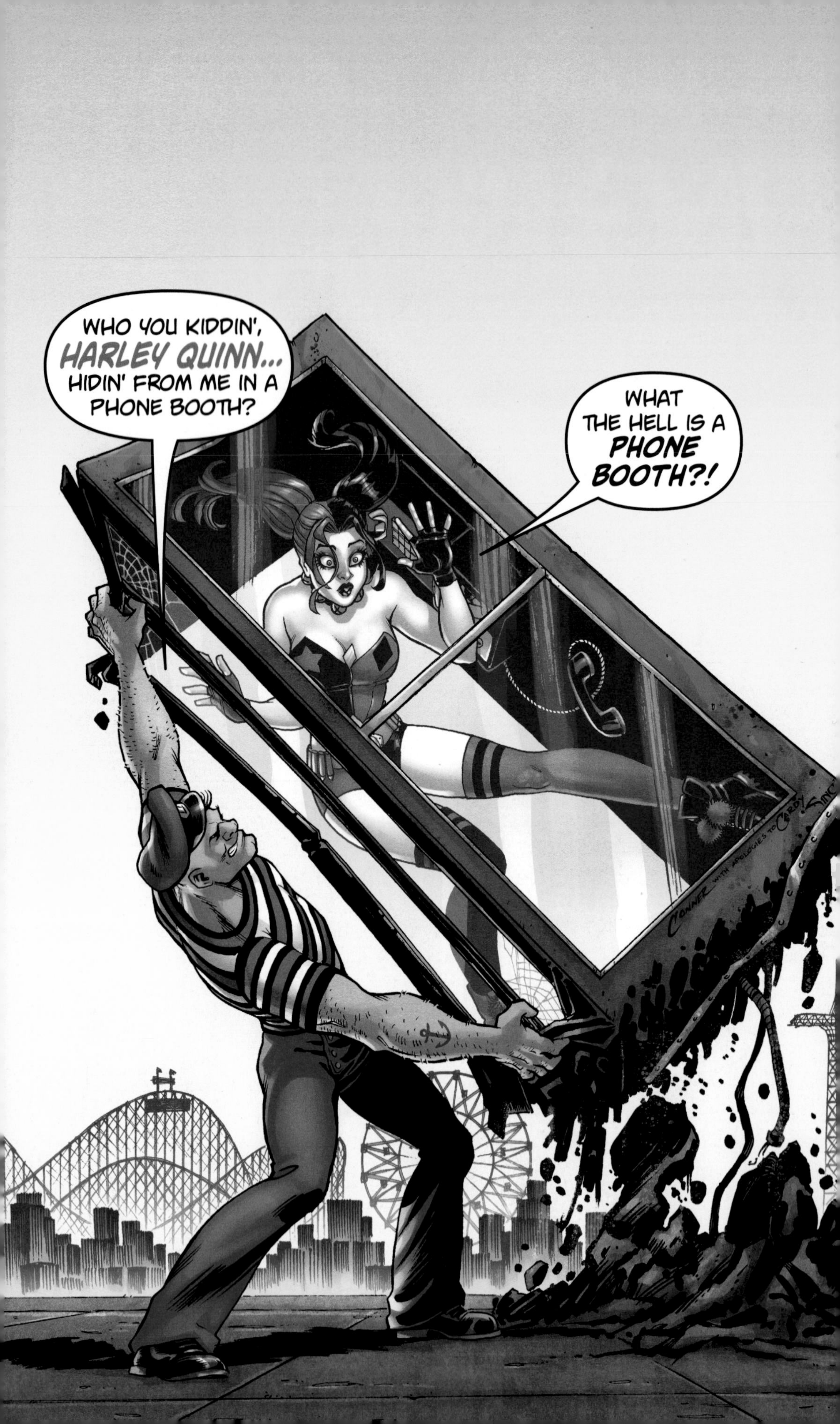
WHO YOU KIDDIN', HARLEY QUINN... HIDIN' FROM ME IN A PHONE BOOTH?
WHAT THE HELL IS A PHONE BOOTH?!

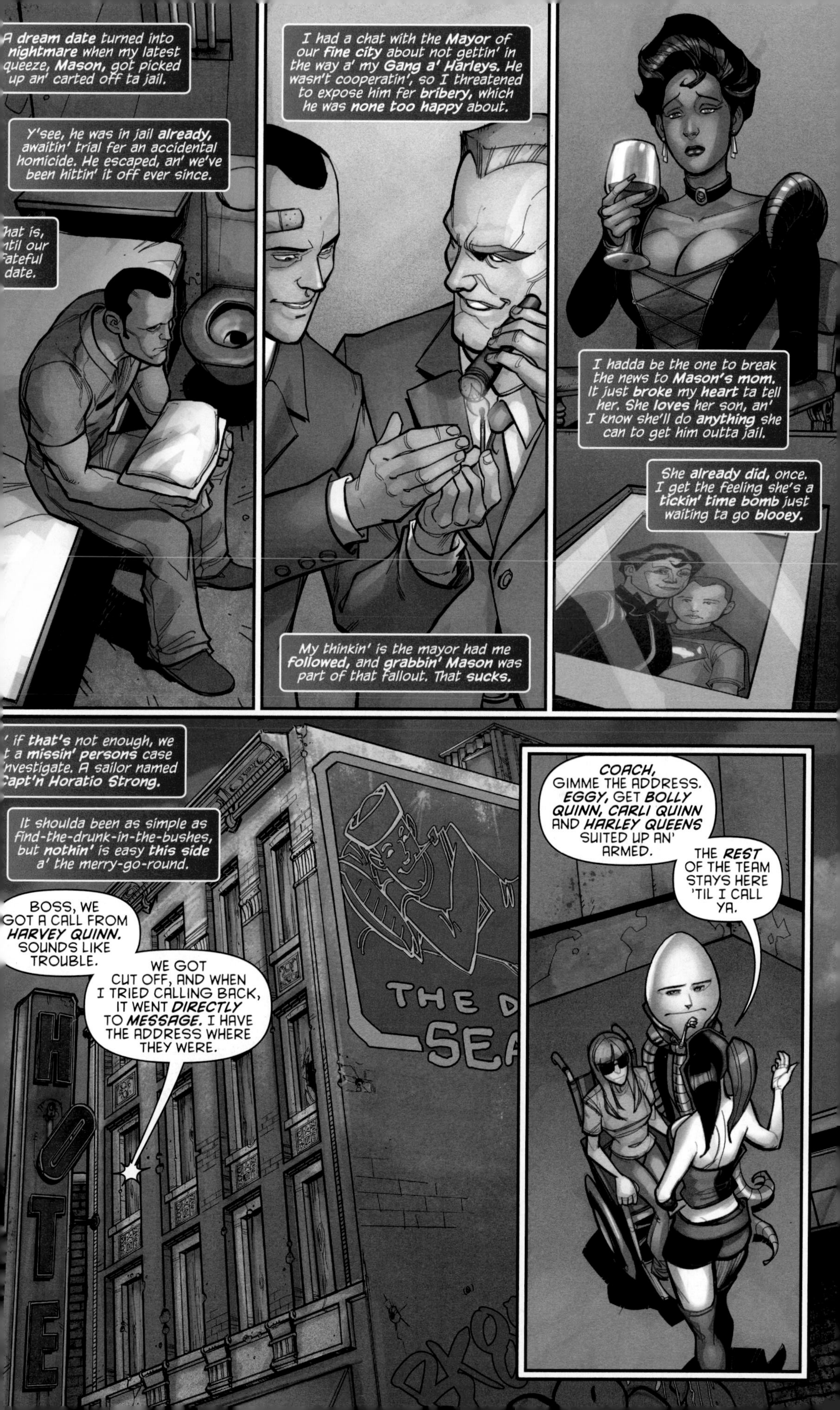

A dream date turned into nightmare when my latest queeze, Mason, got picked up an' carted off ta jail.
Y'see, he was in jail already, awaitin' trial fer an accidental homicide. He escaped, an' we've been hittin' it off ever since.
hat is, ntil our ateful date.
I had a chat with the Mayor of our fine city about not gettin' in the way a' my Gang a' Harleys. He wasn't cooperatin', so I threatened to expose him fer bribery, which he was none too happy about.
My thinkin' is the mayor had me followed, and grabbin' Mason was part of that fallout. That sucks.
I hadda be the one to break the news to Mason's mom. It just broke my heart ta tell her. She loves her son, an' I know she'll do anything she can to get him outta jail.
She already did, once. I get the feeling she's a tickin' time bomb just waiting ta go blooey.
' if that's not enough, we t a missin' persons case nvestigate. A sailor named Capt'n Horatio Strong.
It shoulda been as simple as find-the-drunk-in-the-bushes, but nothin' is easy this side a' the merry-go-round.
BOSS, WE GOT A CALL FROM HARVEY QUINN. SOUNDS LIKE TROUBLE.
WE GOT CUT OFF, AND WHEN I TRIED CALLING BACK, IT WENT DIRECTLY TO MESSAGE. I HAVE THE ADDRESS WHERE THEY WERE.
THE D
SEA
COACH, GIMME THE ADDRESS. EGGY, GET BOLLY QUINN, CARLI QUINN AND HARLEY QUEENS SUITED UP AN' ARMED.
THE REST OF THE TEAM STAYS HERE 'TIL I CALL YA.

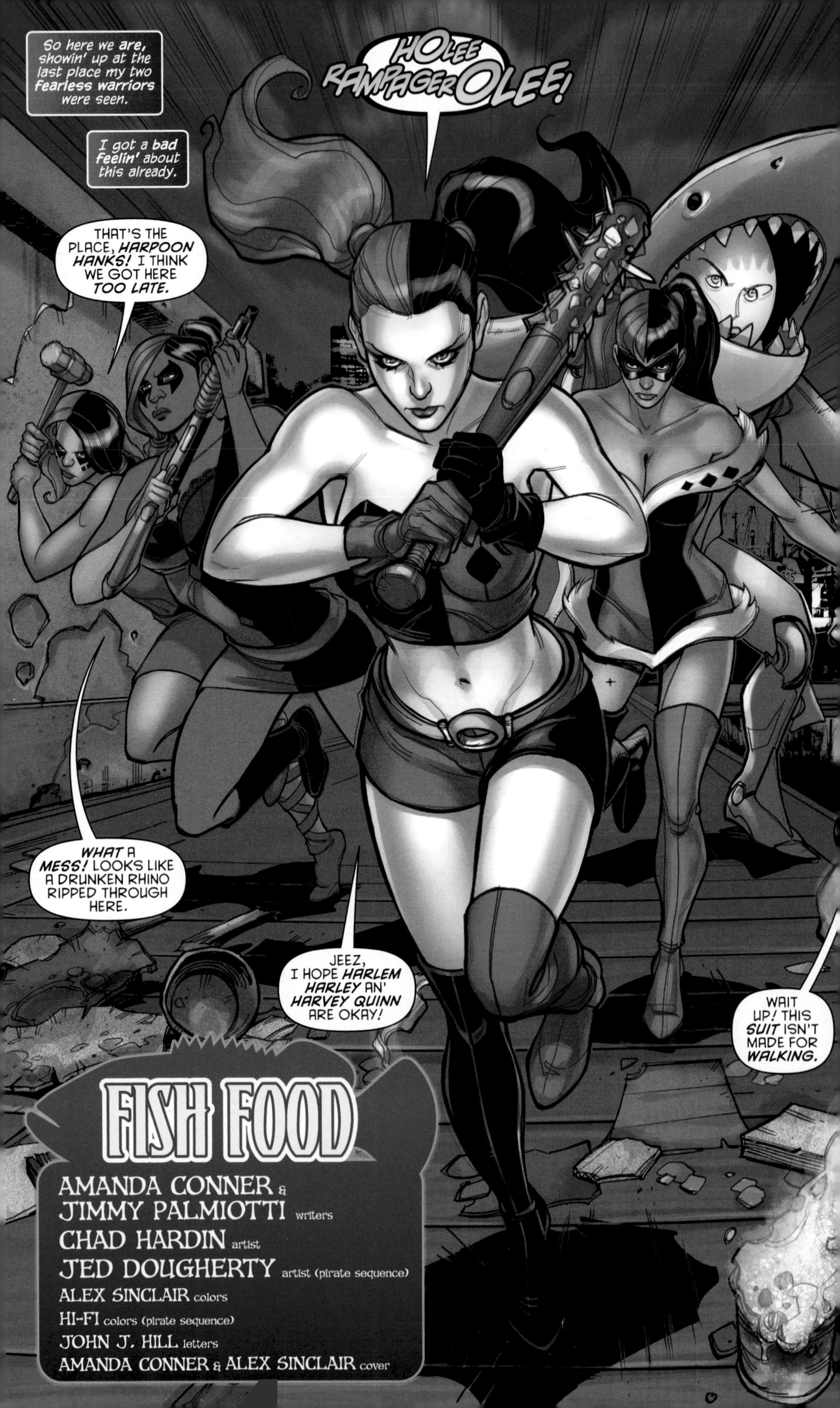

So here we are, showin' up at the last place my two fearless warriors were seen.
I got a bad feelin' about this already.
HOLEE RAMPAGEROLEE!
THAT'S THE PLACE, HARPOON HANKS! I THINK WE GOT HERE TOO LATE.
WHAT A MESS! LOOKS LIKE A DRUNKEN RHINO RIPPED THROUGH HERE.
JEEZ, I HOPE HARLEM HARLEY AN' HARVEY QUINN ARE OKAY!
WAIT UP! THIS SUIT ISN'T MADE FOR WALKING.
FISH FOOD
AMANDA CONNER & JIMMY PALMIOTTI writers
CHAD HARDIN artist
JED DOUGHERTY artist (pirate sequence)
ALEX SINCLAIR colors
HI-FI colors (pirate sequence)
JOHN J. HILL letters
AMANDA CONNER & ALEX SINCLAIR cover

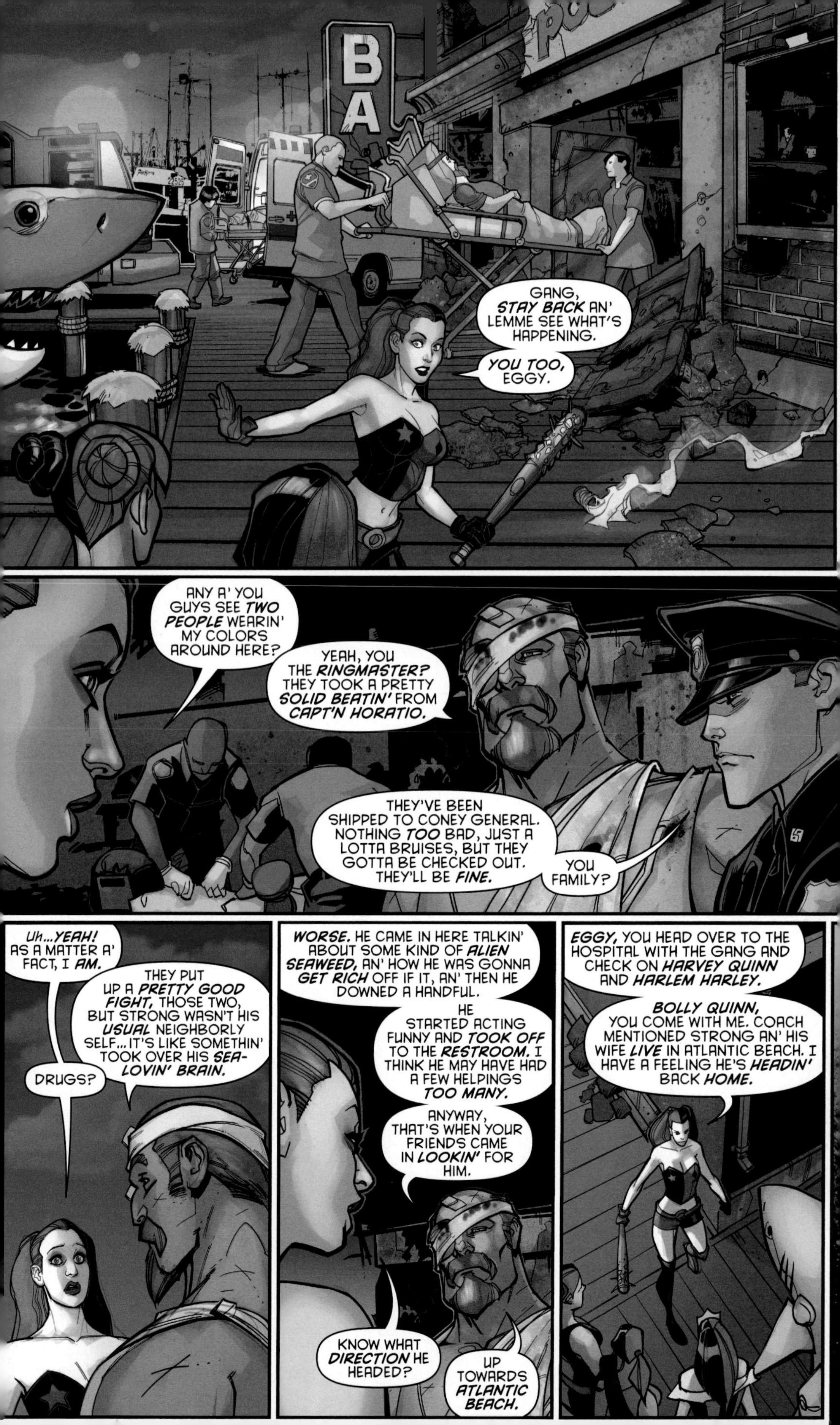

GANG, STAY BACK AN' LEMME SEE WHAT'S HAPPENING.
YOU TOO, EGGY.
ANY A' YOU GUYS SEE TWO PEOPLE WEARIN' MY COLORS AROUND HERE?
YEAH, YOU THE RINGMASTER? THEY TOOK A PRETTY SOLID BEATIN' FROM CAPT'N HORATIO.
THEY'VE BEEN SHIPPED TO CONEY GENERAL. NOTHING TOO BAD, JUST A LOTTA BRUISES, BUT THEY GOTTA BE CHECKED OUT. THEY'LL BE FINE.
YOU FAMILY?
Uh...YEAH! AS A MATTER A' FACT, I AM.
THEY PUT UP A PRETTY GOOD FIGHT, THOSE TWO, BUT STRONG WASN'T HIS USUAL NEIGHBORLY SELF... IT'S LIKE SOMETHIN' TOOK OVER HIS SEA-LOVIN' BRAIN.
DRUGS?
WORSE. HE CAME IN HERE TALKIN' ABOUT SOME KIND OF ALIEN SEAWEED, AN' HOW HE WAS GONNA GET RICH OFF IF IT, AN' THEN HE DOWNED A HANDFUL.
HE STARTED ACTING FUNNY AND TOOK OFF TO THE RESTROOM. I THINK HE MAY HAVE HAD A FEW HELPINGS TOO MANY.
ANYWAY, THAT'S WHEN YOUR FRIENDS CAME IN LOOKIN' FOR HIM.
KNOW WHAT DIRECTION HE HEADED?
UP TOWARDS ATLANTIC BEACH.
EGGY, YOU HEAD OVER TO THE HOSPITAL WITH THE GANG AND CHECK ON HARVEY QUINN AND HARLEM HARLEY.
BOLLY QUINN, YOU COME WITH ME. COACH MENTIONED STRONG AN' HIS WIFE LIVE IN ATLANTIC BEACH. I HAVE A FEELING HE'S HEADIN' BACK HOME.

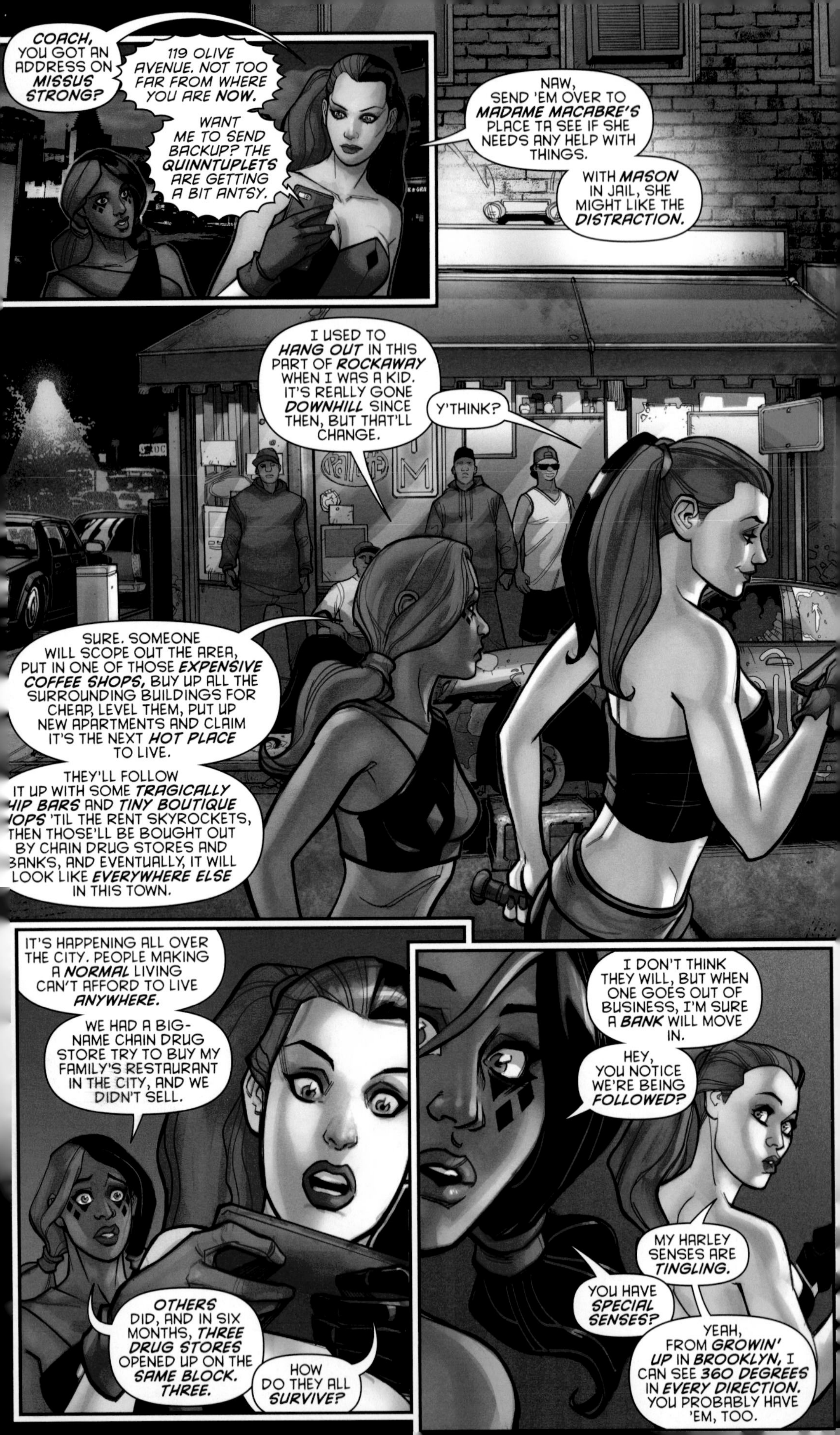
COACH, YOU GOT AN ADDRESS ON MISSUS STRONG?
119 OLIVE AVENUE. NOT TOO FAR FROM WHERE YOU ARE NOW.
WANT ME TO SEND BACKUP? THE QUINNTUPLETS ARE GETTING A BIT ANTSY.
NAW, SEND 'EM OVER TO MADAME MACABRE'S PLACE TA SEE IF SHE NEEDS ANY HELP WITH THINGS.
WITH MASON IN JAIL, SHE MIGHT LIKE THE DISTRACTION.
I USED TO HANG OUT IN THIS PART OF ROCKAWAY WHEN I WAS A KID. IT'S REALLY GONE DOWNHILL SINCE THEN, BUT THAT'LL CHANGE.
Y'THINK?
SURE. SOMEONE WILL SCOPE OUT THE AREA, PUT IN ONE OF THOSE EXPENSIVE COFFEE SHOPS, BUY UP ALL THE SURROUNDING BUILDINGS FOR CHEAP, LEVEL THEM, PUT UP NEW APARTMENTS AND CLAIM IT'S THE NEXT HOT PLACE TO LIVE.
THEY'LL FOLLOW IT UP WITH SOME TRAGICALLY HIP BARS AND TINY BOUTIQUE SHOPS 'TIL THE RENT SKYROCKETS, THEN THOSE'LL BE BOUGHT OUT BY CHAIN DRUG STORES AND BANKS, AND EVENTUALLY, IT WILL LOOK LIKE EVERYWHERE ELSE IN THIS TOWN.
IT'S HAPPENING ALL OVER THE CITY. PEOPLE MAKING A NORMAL LIVING CAN'T AFFORD TO LIVE ANYWHERE.
WE HAD A BIG-NAME CHAIN DRUG STORE TRY TO BUY MY FAMILY'S RESTAURANT IN THE CITY, AND WE DIDN'T SELL.
OTHERS DID, AND IN SIX MONTHS, THREE DRUG STORES OPENED UP ON THE SAME BLOCK. THREE.
HOW DO THEY ALL SURVIVE?
I DON'T THINK THEY WILL, BUT WHEN ONE GOES OUT OF BUSINESS, I'M SURE A BANK WILL MOVE IN.
HEY, YOU NOTICE WE'RE BEING FOLLOWED?
MY HARLEY SENSES ARE TINGLING.
YOU HAVE SPECIAL SENSES?
YEAH, FROM GROWIN' UP IN BROOKLYN, I CAN SEE 360 DEGREES IN EVERY DIRECTION. YOU PROBABLY HAVE 'EM, TOO.

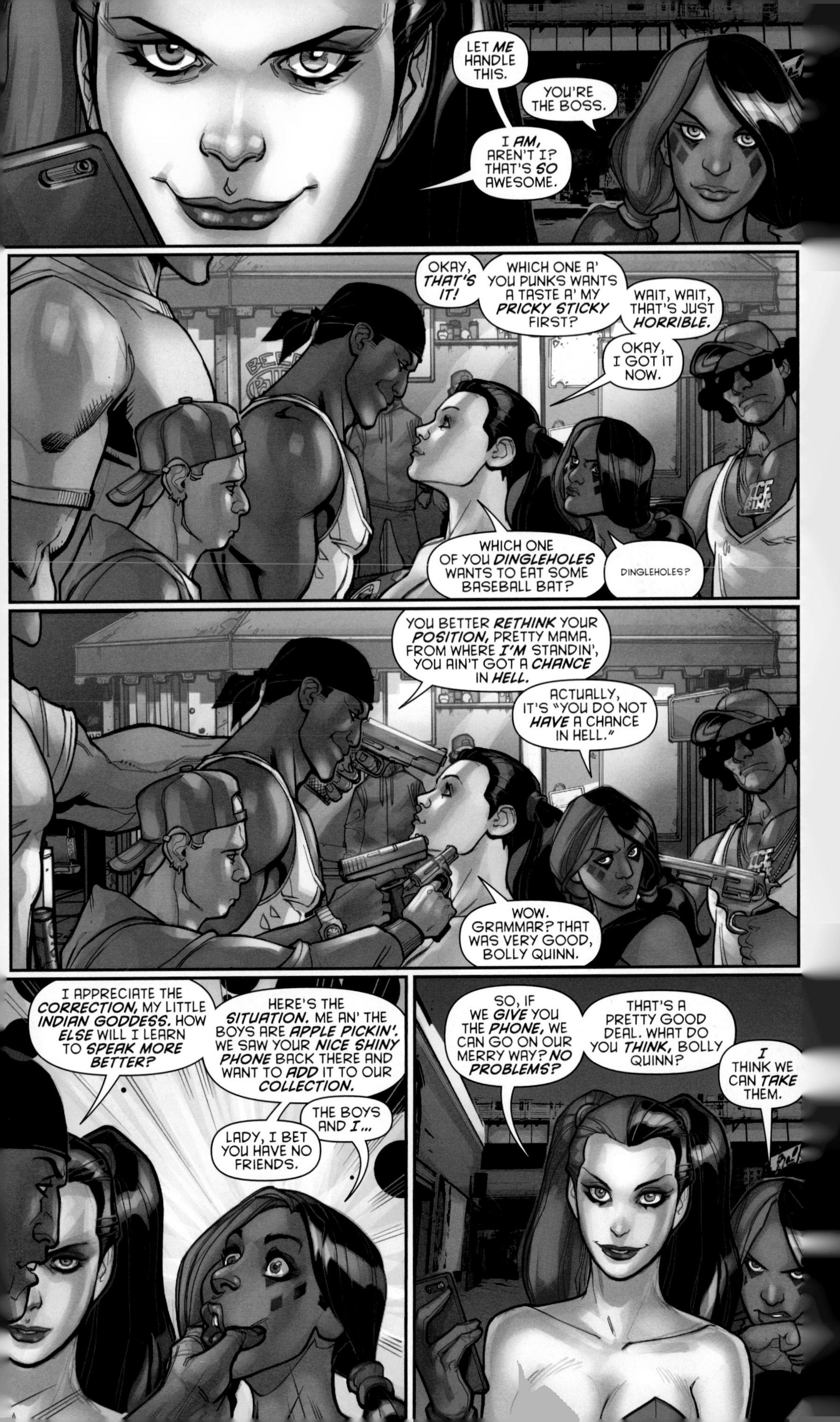
LET *ME* HANDLE THIS.
YOU'RE THE BOSS.
I *AM*, AREN'T I? THAT'S *SO* AWESOME.
OKAY, *THAT'S IT!*
WHICH ONE A' YOU PUNKS WANTS A TASTE A' MY *PRICKY STICKY* FIRST?
WAIT, WAIT, THAT'S JUST *HORRIBLE.*
OKAY, I GOT IT NOW.
WHICH ONE OF YOU *DINGLEHOLES* WANTS TO EAT SOME BASEBALL BAT?
DINGLEHOLES?
YOU BETTER *RETHINK* YOUR *POSITION*, PRETTY MAMA. FROM WHERE *I'M* STANDIN', YOU AIN'T GOT A *CHANCE* IN *HELL.*
ACTUALLY, IT'S "YOU DO NOT *HAVE* A CHANCE IN HELL."
WOW. GRAMMAR? THAT WAS VERY GOOD, BOLLY QUINN.
I APPRECIATE THE *CORRECTION*, MY LITTLE *INDIAN GODDESS.* HOW *ELSE* WILL I LEARN TO *SPEAK MORE BETTER?*
HERE'S THE *SITUATION.* ME AN' THE BOYS ARE *APPLE PICKIN'.* WE SAW YOUR *NICE SHINY PHONE* BACK THERE AND WANT TO *ADD* IT TO OUR *COLLECTION.*
THE BOYS AND *I*...
LADY, I BET YOU HAVE NO FRIENDS.
SO, IF WE *GIVE* YOU THE *PHONE*, WE CAN GO ON OUR MERRY WAY? *NO PROBLEMS?*
THAT'S A PRETTY GOOD DEAL. WHAT DO YOU *THINK*, BOLLY QUINN?
I THINK WE CAN *TAKE* THEM.

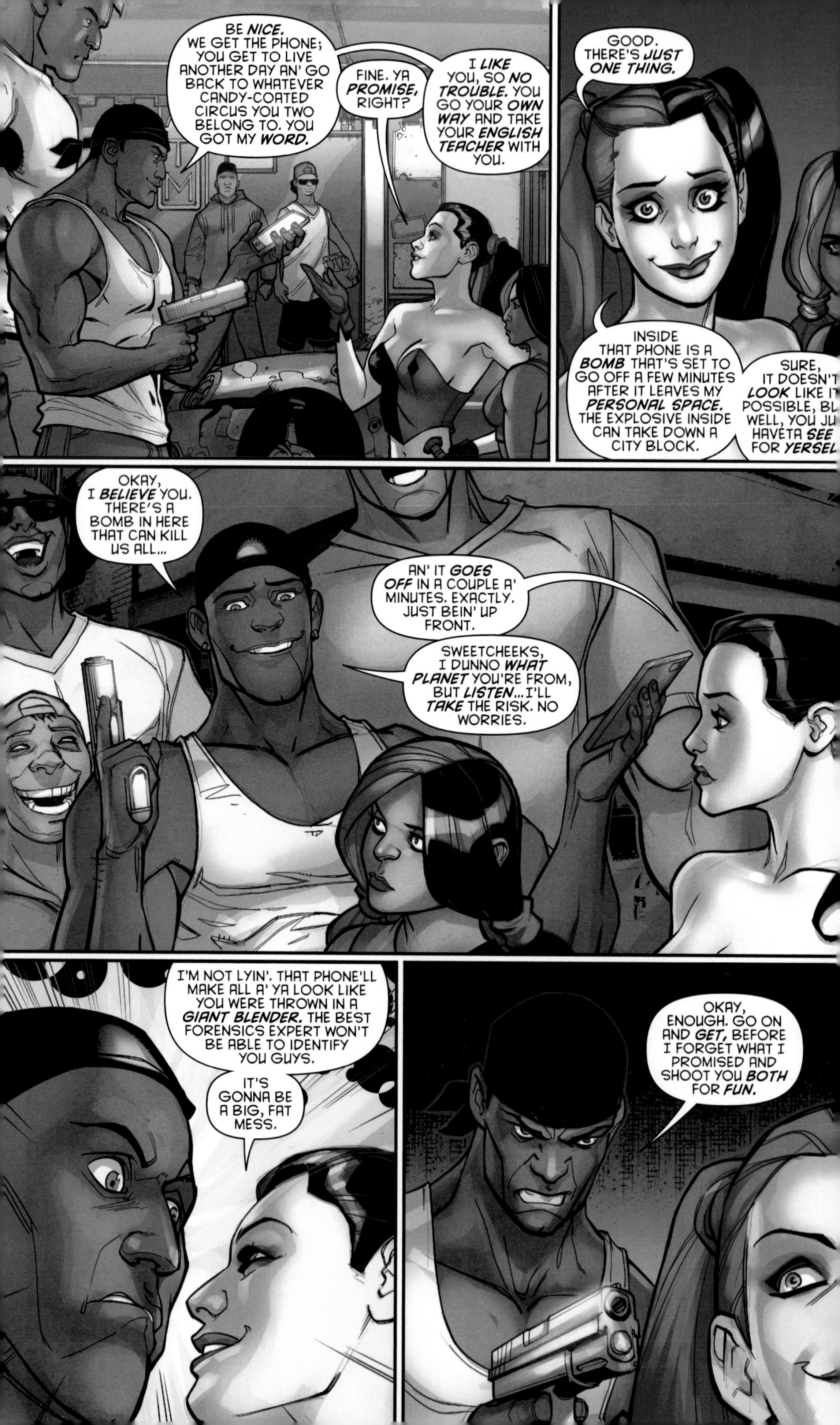

BE NICE. WE GET THE PHONE; YOU GET TO LIVE ANOTHER DAY AN' GO BACK TO WHATEVER CANDY-COATED CIRCUS YOU TWO BELONG TO. YOU GOT MY WORD.
FINE. YA PROMISE, RIGHT?
I LIKE YOU, SO NO TROUBLE. YOU GO YOUR OWN WAY AND TAKE YOUR ENGLISH TEACHER WITH YOU.
GOOD. THERE'S JUST ONE THING.
INSIDE THAT PHONE IS A BOMB THAT'S SET TO GO OFF A FEW MINUTES AFTER IT LEAVES MY PERSONAL SPACE. THE EXPLOSIVE INSIDE CAN TAKE DOWN A CITY BLOCK.
SURE, IT DOESN'T LOOK LIKE IT POSSIBLE, BL WELL, YOU JU HAVETA SEE FOR YERSEL
OKAY, I BELIEVE YOU. THERE'S A BOMB IN HERE THAT CAN KILL US ALL...
AN' IT GOES OFF IN A COUPLE A' MINUTES. EXACTLY. JUST BEIN' UP FRONT.
SWEETCHEEKS, I DUNNO WHAT PLANET YOU'RE FROM, BUT LISTEN...I'LL TAKE THE RISK. NO WORRIES.
I'M NOT LYIN'. THAT PHONE'LL MAKE ALL A' YA LOOK LIKE YOU WERE THROWN IN A GIANT BLENDER. THE BEST FORENSICS EXPERT WON'T BE ABLE TO IDENTIFY YOU GUYS.
IT'S GONNA BE A BIG, FAT MESS.
OKAY, ENOUGH. GO ON AND GET, BEFORE I FORGET WHAT I PROMISED AND SHOOT YOU BOTH FOR FUN.

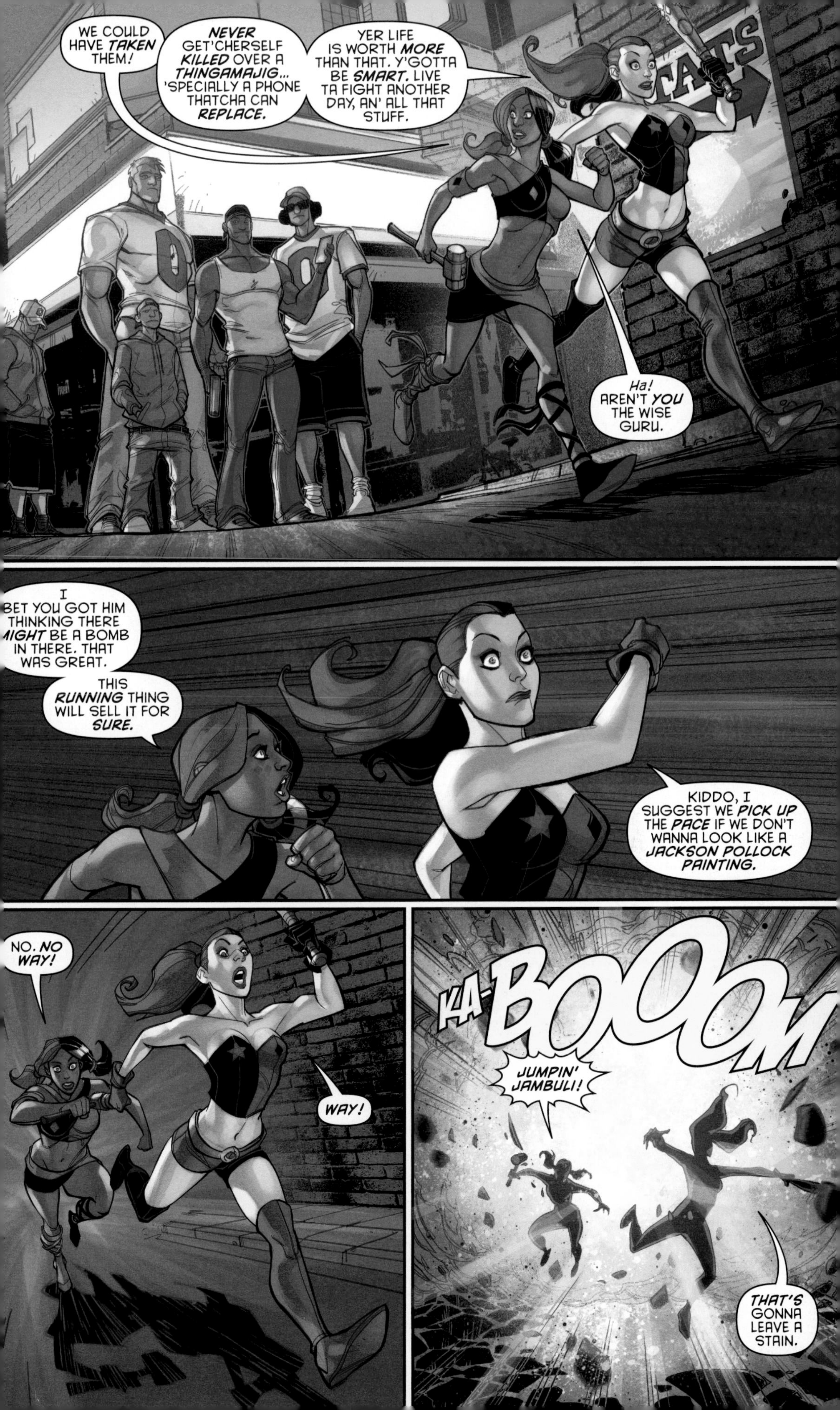

WE COULD HAVE TAKEN THEM!
NEVER GET'CHERSELF KILLED OVER A THINGAMAJIG... 'SPECIALLY A PHONE THATCHA CAN REPLACE.
YER LIFE IS WORTH MORE THAN THAT. Y'GOTTA BE SMART. LIVE TA FIGHT ANOTHER DAY, AN' ALL THAT STUFF.
Ha! AREN'T YOU THE WISE GURU.
I BET YOU GOT HIM THINKING THERE MIGHT BE A BOMB IN THERE. THAT WAS GREAT.
THIS RUNNING THING WILL SELL IT FOR SURE.
KIDDO, I SUGGEST WE PICK UP THE PACE IF WE DON'T WANNA LOOK LIKE A JACKSON POLLOCK PAINTING.
NO. NO WAY!
WAY!
KA-BOOOM
JUMPIN' JAMBULI!
THAT'S GONNA LEAVE A STAIN.

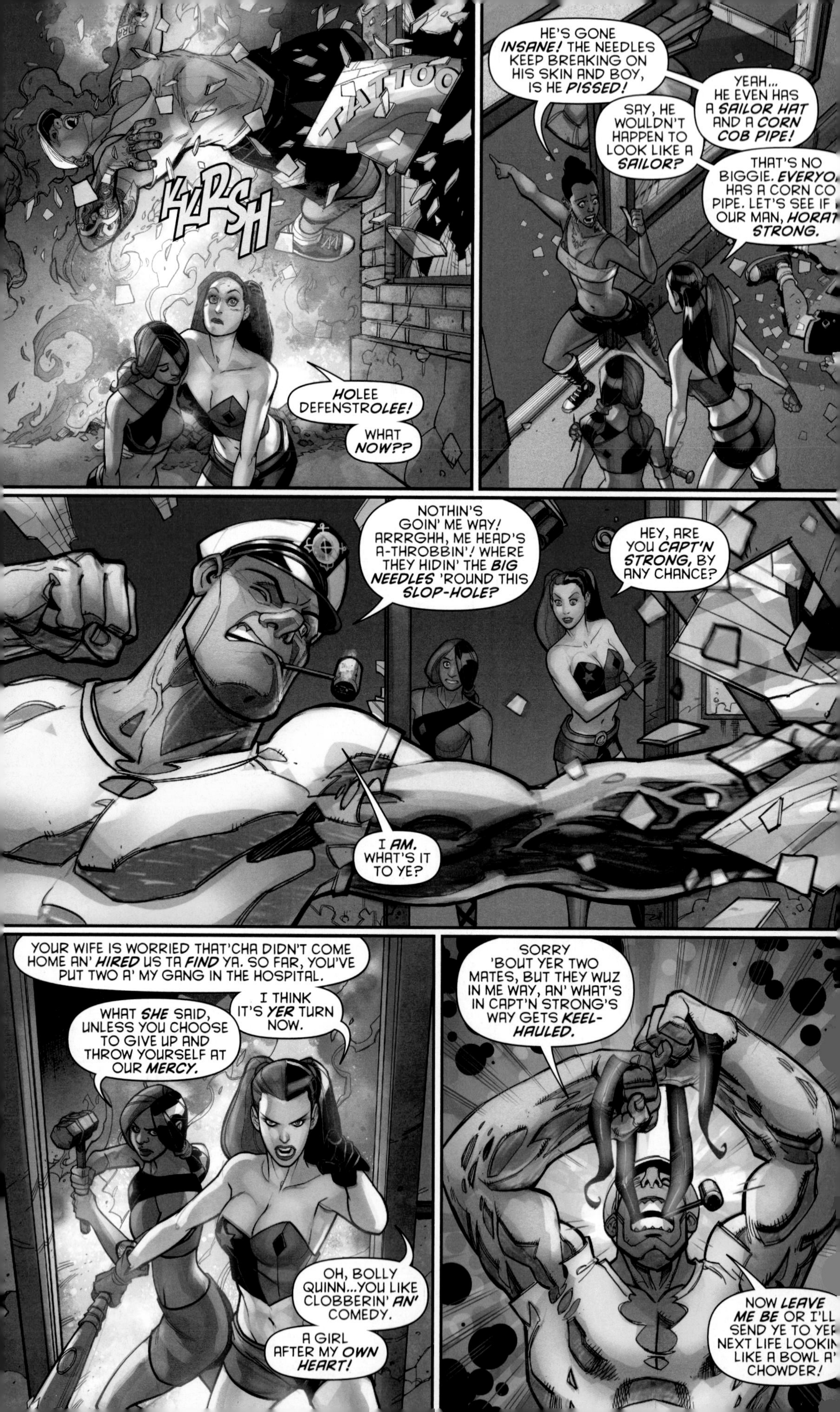
TATTOO
KRSH
HOLEE DEFENSTROLEE!
WHAT NOW??
HE'S GONE INSANE! THE NEEDLES KEEP BREAKING ON HIS SKIN AND BOY, IS HE PISSED!
SAY, HE WOULDN'T HAPPEN TO LOOK LIKE A SAILOR?
YEAH... HE EVEN HAS A SAILOR HAT AND A CORN COB PIPE!
THAT'S NO BIGGIE. EVERYO HAS A CORN CO PIPE. LET'S SEE IF OUR MAN, HORAT STRONG.
NOTHIN'S GOIN' ME WAY! ARRRGHH, ME HEAD'S A-THROBBIN'! WHERE THEY HIDIN' THE BIG NEEDLES 'ROUND THIS SLOP-HOLE?
HEY, ARE YOU CAPT'N STRONG, BY ANY CHANCE?
I AM. WHAT'S IT TO YE?
YOUR WIFE IS WORRIED THAT'CHA DIDN'T COME HOME AN' HIRED US TA FIND YA. SO FAR, YOU'VE PUT TWO A' MY GANG IN THE HOSPITAL.
I THINK IT'S YER TURN NOW.
WHAT SHE SAID, UNLESS YOU CHOOSE TO GIVE UP AND THROW YOURSELF AT OUR MERCY.
OH, BOLLY QUINN...YOU LIKE CLOBBERIN' AN' COMEDY.
A GIRL AFTER MY OWN HEART!
SORRY 'BOUT YER TWO MATES, BUT THEY WUZ IN ME WAY, AN' WHAT'S IN CAPT'N STRONG'S WAY GETS KEEL-HAULED.
NOW LEAVE ME BE OR I'LL SEND YE TO YER NEXT LIFE LOOKIN LIKE A BOWL A' CHOWDER!

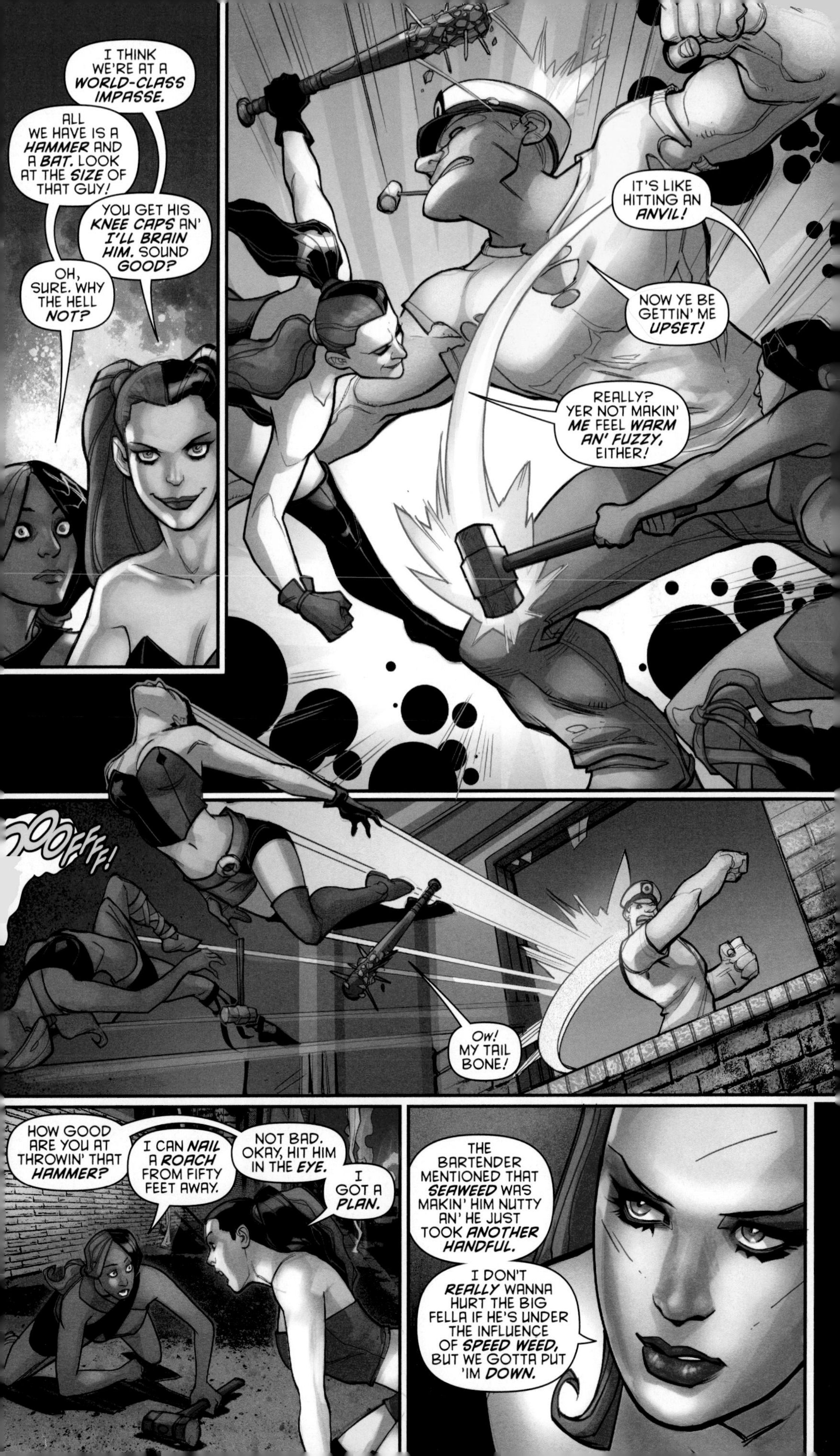
I THINK WE'RE AT A WORLD-CLASS IMPASSE.
ALL WE HAVE IS A HAMMER AND A BAT. LOOK AT THE SIZE OF THAT GUY!
YOU GET HIS KNEE CAPS AN' I'LL BRAIN HIM. SOUND GOOD?
OH, SURE. WHY THE HELL NOT?
IT'S LIKE HITTING AN ANVIL!
NOW YE BE GETTIN' ME UPSET!
REALLY? YER NOT MAKIN' ME FEEL WARM AN' FUZZY, EITHER!
OOOFFFF!
OW! MY TAIL BONE!
HOW GOOD ARE YOU AT THROWIN' THAT HAMMER?
I CAN NAIL A ROACH FROM FIFTY FEET AWAY.
NOT BAD. OKAY, HIT HIM IN THE EYE.
I GOT A PLAN.
THE BARTENDER MENTIONED THAT SEAWEED WAS MAKIN' HIM NUTTY AN' HE JUST TOOK ANOTHER HANDFUL.
I DON'T REALLY WANNA HURT THE BIG FELLA IF HE'S UNDER THE INFLUENCE OF SPEED WEED, BUT WE GOTTA PUT 'IM DOWN.

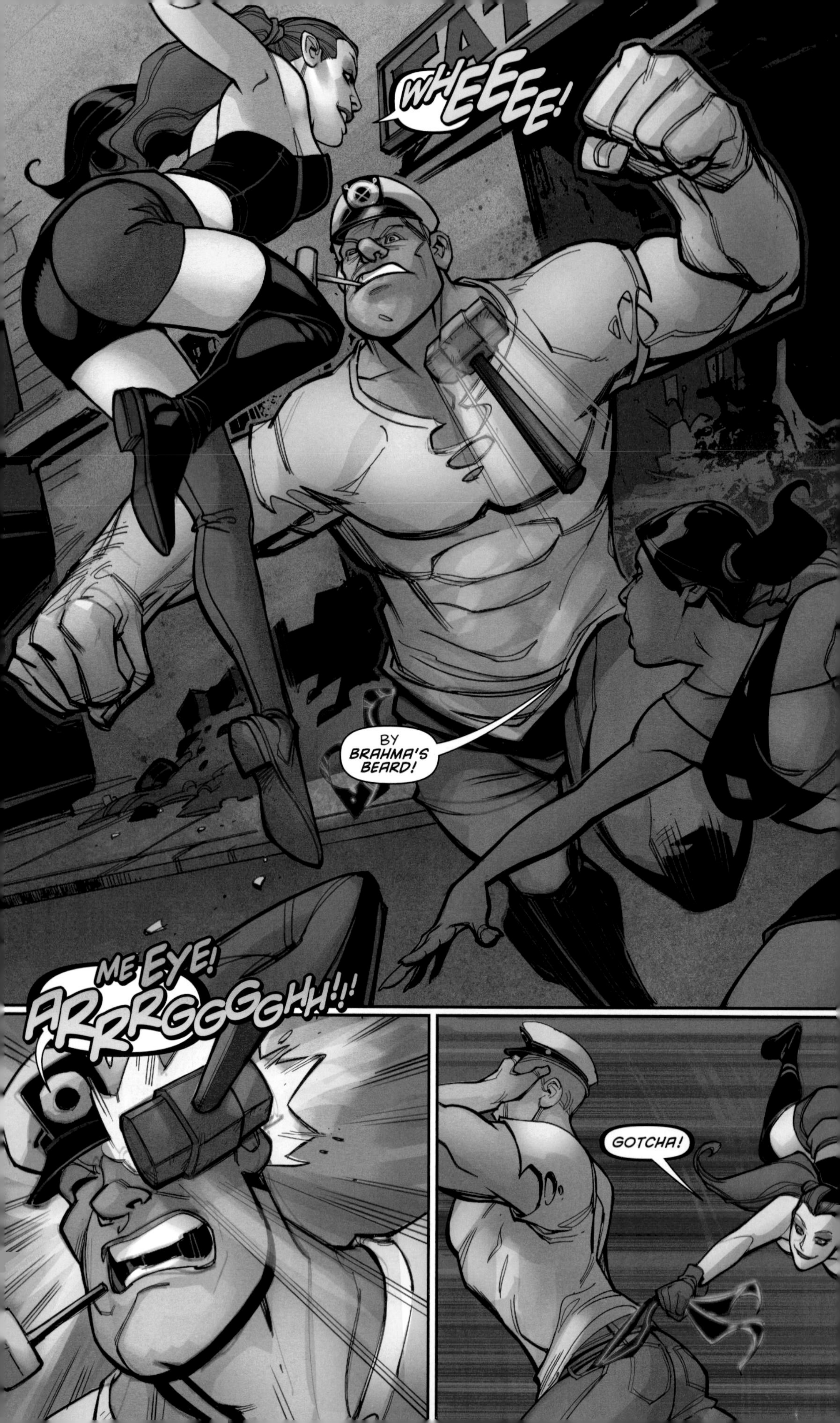
WHEEEEE!
BY BRAHMA'S BEARD!
ME EYE! ARRRGGGGHH!!!
GOTCHA!

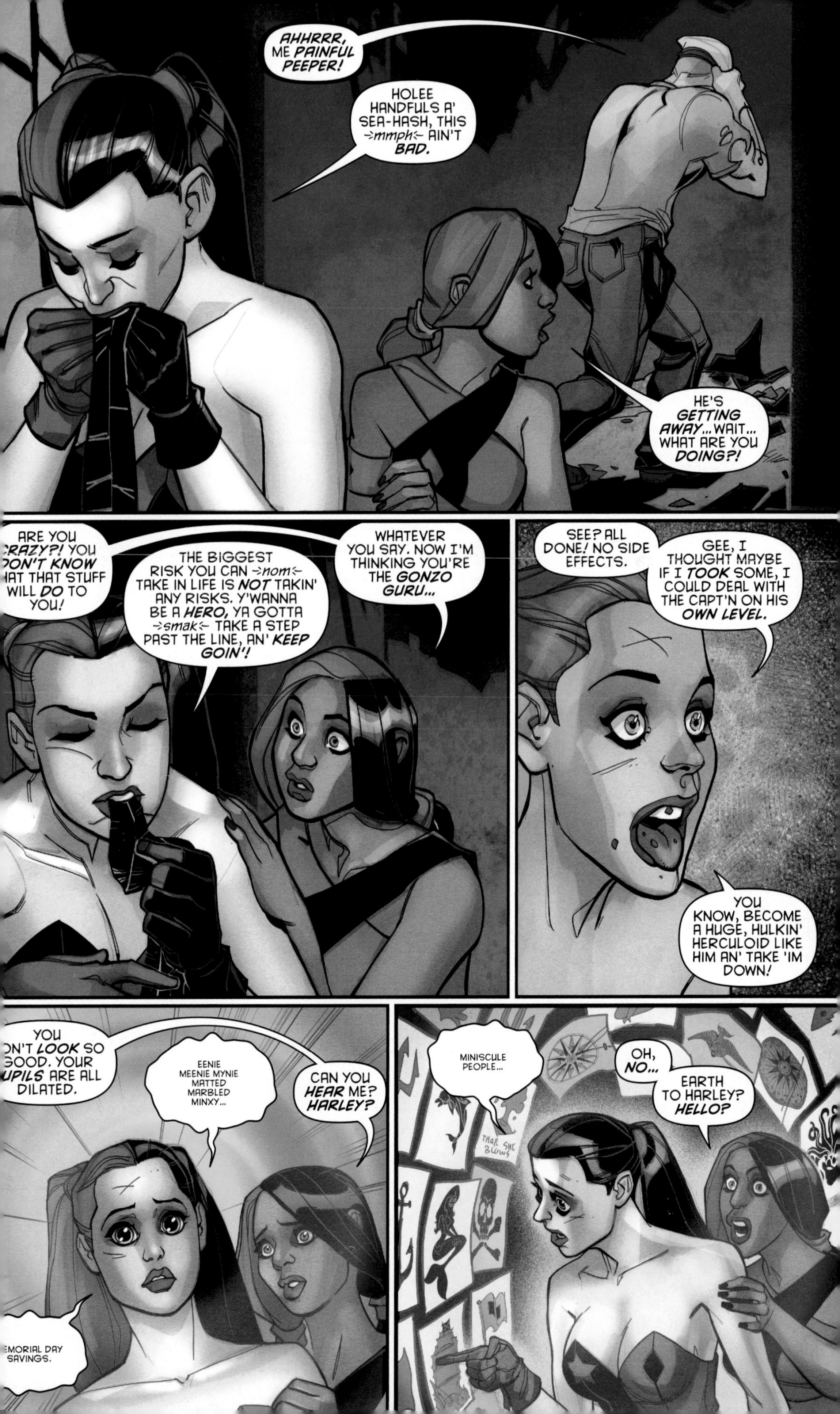
AHHRRR, ME PAINFUL PEEPER!
HOLEE HANDFULS A' SEA-HASH, THIS ->mmph<- AIN'T BAD.
HE'S GETTING AWAY... WAIT... WHAT ARE YOU DOING?!
ARE YOU CRAZY?! YOU DON'T KNOW WHAT THAT STUFF WILL DO TO YOU!
THE BIGGEST RISK YOU CAN ->nom<- TAKE IN LIFE IS NOT TAKIN' ANY RISKS. Y'WANNA BE A HERO, YA GOTTA ->smak<- TAKE A STEP PAST THE LINE, AN' KEEP GOIN'!
WHATEVER YOU SAY. NOW I'M THINKING YOU'RE THE GONZO GURU...
SEE? ALL DONE! NO SIDE EFFECTS.
GEE, I THOUGHT MAYBE IF I TOOK SOME, I COULD DEAL WITH THE CAPT'N ON HIS OWN LEVEL.
YOU KNOW, BECOME A HUGE, HULKIN' HERCULOID LIKE HIM AN' TAKE 'IM DOWN!
YOU DON'T LOOK SO GOOD. YOUR PUPILS ARE ALL DILATED.
EENIE MEENIE MYNIE MATTED MARBLED MINXY...
CAN YOU HEAR ME? HARLEY?
MEMORIAL DAY SAVINGS.
MINISCULE PEOPLE...
OH, NO...
EARTH TO HARLEY? HELLO?
THAR SHE BLOWS

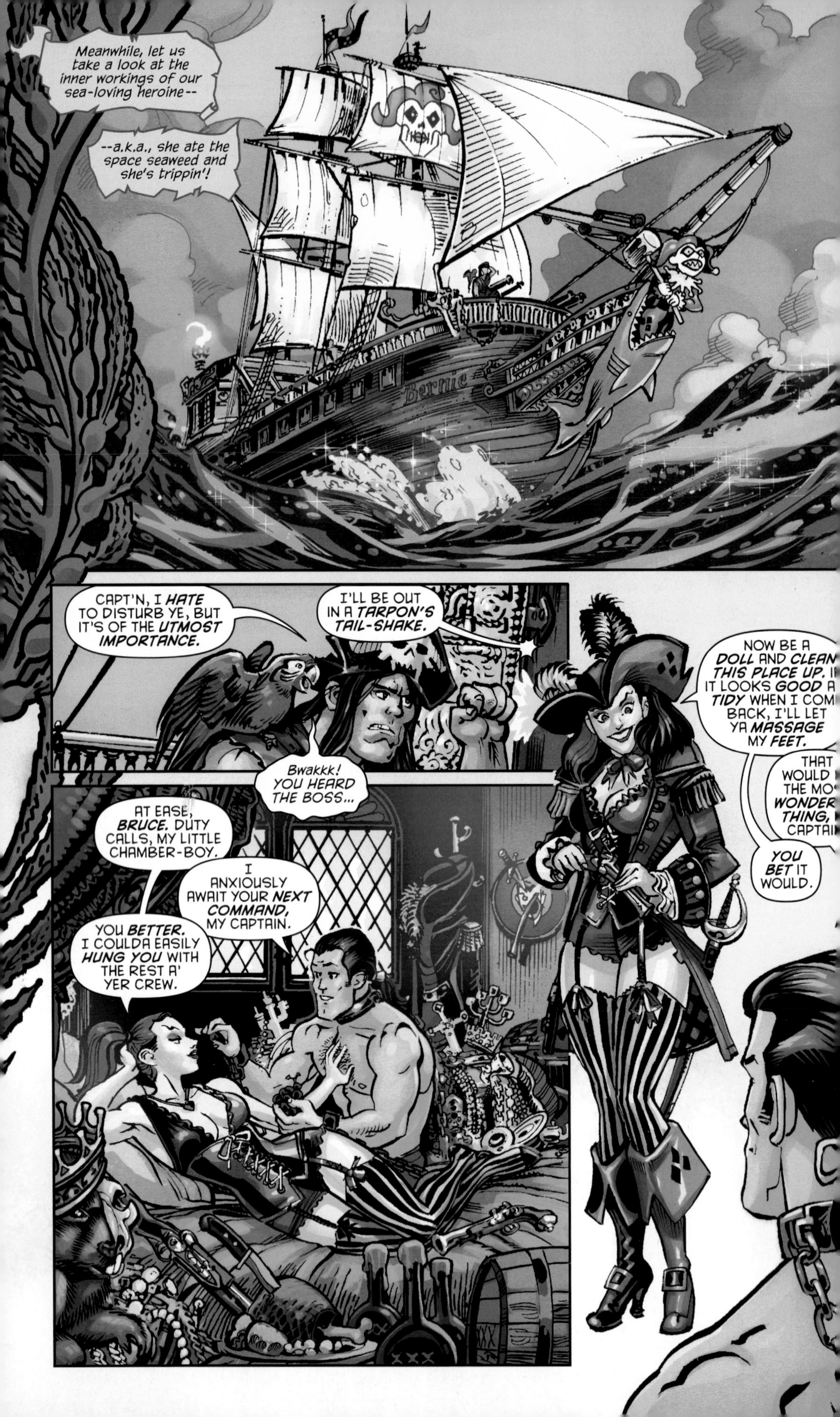
Meanwhile, let us take a look at the inner workings of our sea-loving heroine--
--a.k.a., she ate the space seaweed and she's trippin'!
Bernie
CAPT'N, I HATE TO DISTURB YE, BUT IT'S OF THE UTMOST IMPORTANCE.
I'LL BE OUT IN A TARPON'S TAIL-SHAKE.
Bwakkk! YOU HEARD THE BOSS...
AT EASE, BRUCE. DUTY CALLS, MY LITTLE CHAMBER-BOY.
I ANXIOUSLY AWAIT YOUR NEXT COMMAND, MY CAPTAIN.
YOU BETTER. I COULDA EASILY HUNG YOU WITH THE REST A' YER CREW.
NOW BE A DOLL AND CLEAN THIS PLACE UP. IF IT LOOKS GOOD AND TIDY WHEN I COME BACK, I'LL LET YA MASSAGE MY FEET.
THAT WOULD BE THE MOST WONDERFUL THING, CAPTAIN.
YOU BET IT WOULD.

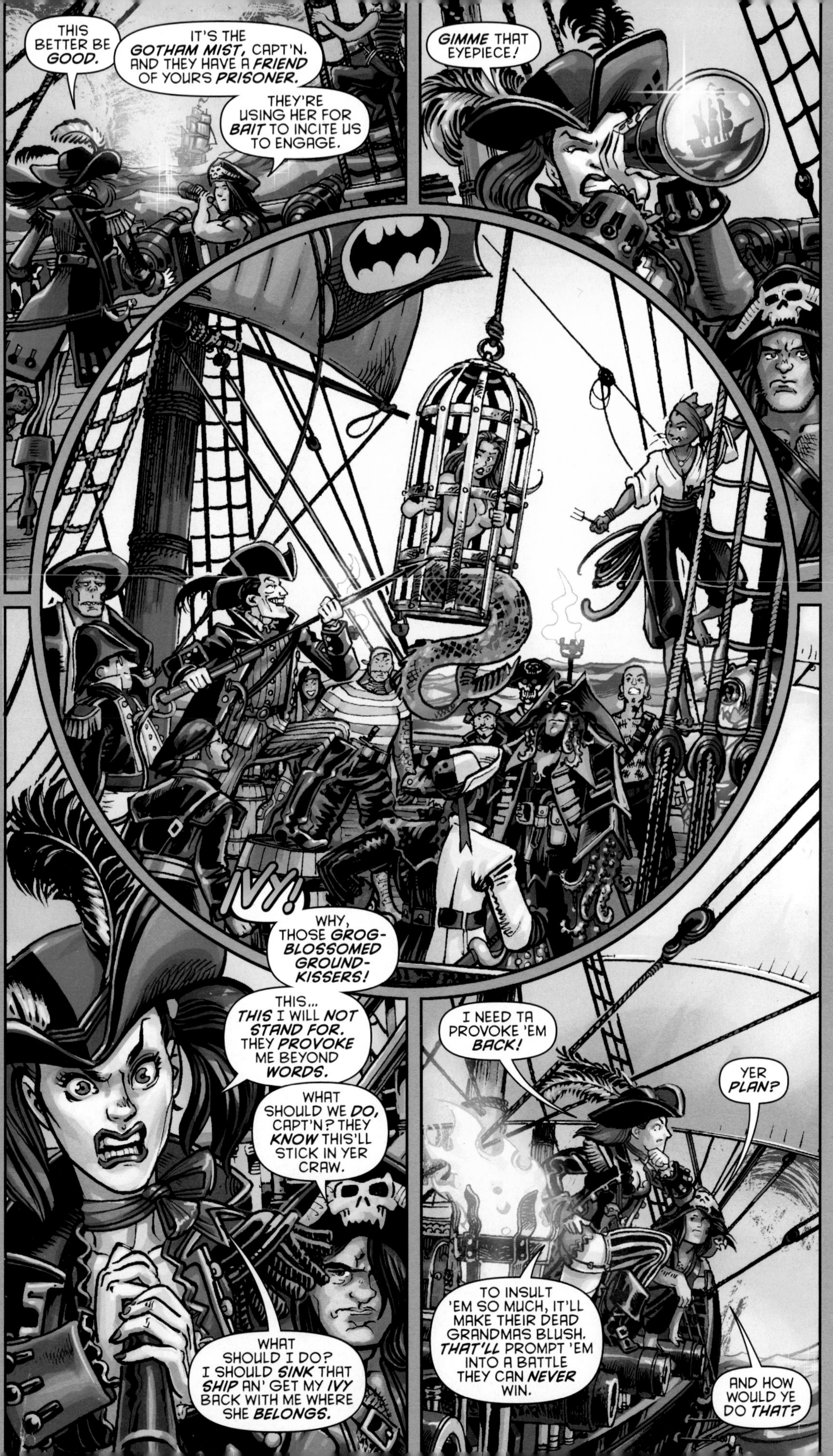
THIS BETTER BE GOOD.
IT'S THE GOTHAM MIST, CAPT'N. AND THEY HAVE A FRIEND OF YOURS PRISONER.
THEY'RE USING HER FOR BAIT TO INCITE US TO ENGAGE.
GIMME THAT EYEPIECE!
IVY!
WHY, THOSE GROG-BLOSSOMED GROUND-KISSERS!
THIS... THIS I WILL NOT STAND FOR. THEY PROVOKE ME BEYOND WORDS.
WHAT SHOULD WE DO, CAPT'N? THEY KNOW THIS'LL STICK IN YER CRAW.
WHAT SHOULD I DO? I SHOULD SINK THAT SHIP AN' GET MY IVY BACK WITH ME WHERE SHE BELONGS.
I NEED TA PROVOKE 'EM BACK!
YER PLAN?
TO INSULT 'EM SO MUCH, IT'LL MAKE THEIR DEAD GRANDMAS BLUSH. THAT'LL PROMPT 'EM INTO A BATTLE THEY CAN NEVER WIN.
AND HOW WOULD YE DO THAT?

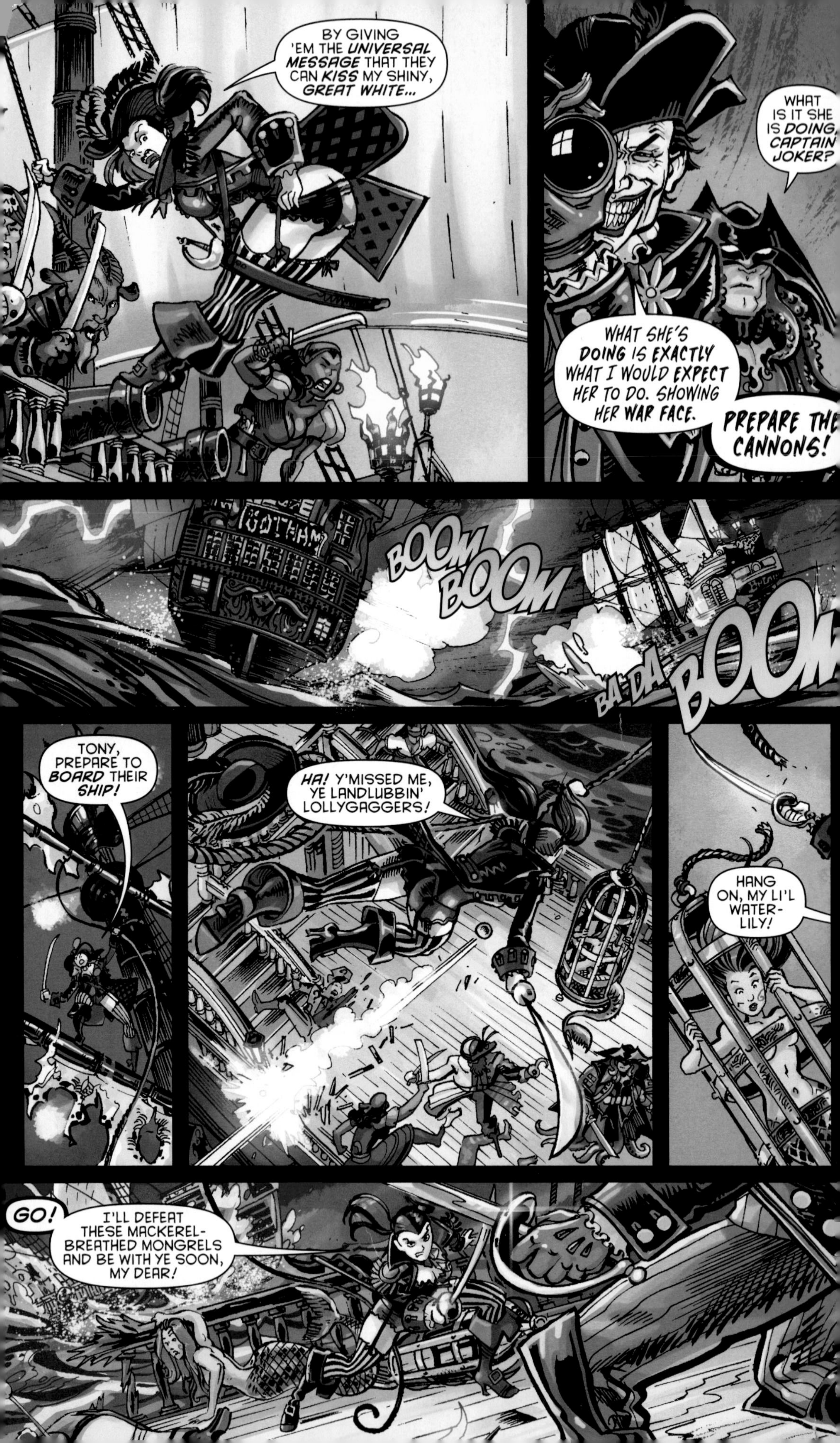

BY GIVING 'EM THE UNIVERSAL MESSAGE THAT THEY CAN KISS MY SHINY, GREAT WHITE...
WHAT IS IT SHE IS DOING, CAPTAIN JOKER?
WHAT SHE'S DOING IS EXACTLY WHAT I WOULD EXPECT HER TO DO. SHOWING HER WAR FACE.
PREPARE THE CANNONS!
GOTHAM
BOOM BOOM
BA-DA BOOM
TONY, PREPARE TO BOARD THEIR SHIP!
HA! Y'MISSED ME, YE LANDLUBBIN' LOLLYGAGGERS!
HANG ON, MY LI'L WATER-LILY!
GO!
I'LL DEFEAT THESE MACKEREL-BREATHED MONGRELS AND BE WITH YE SOON, MY DEAR!

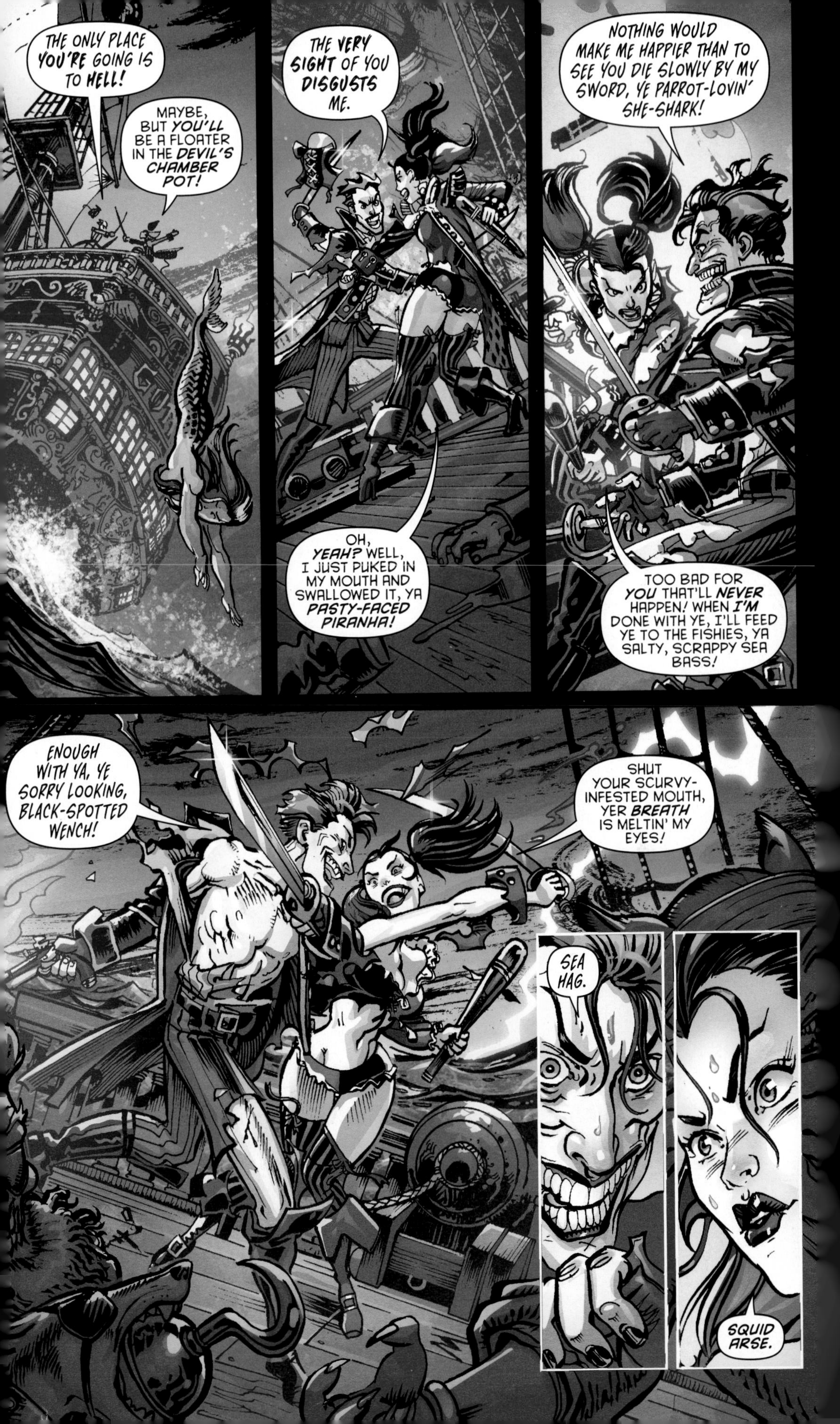
THE ONLY PLACE YOU'RE GOING IS TO HELL!
MAYBE, BUT YOU'LL BE A FLOATER IN THE DEVIL'S CHAMBER POT!
THE VERY SIGHT OF YOU DISGUSTS ME.
OH, YEAH? WELL, I JUST PUKED IN MY MOUTH AND SWALLOWED IT, YA PASTY-FACED PIRANHA!
NOTHING WOULD MAKE ME HAPPIER THAN TO SEE YOU DIE SLOWLY BY MY SWORD, YE PARROT-LOVIN' SHE-SHARK!
TOO BAD FOR YOU THAT'LL NEVER HAPPEN! WHEN I'M DONE WITH YE, I'LL FEED YE TO THE FISHIES, YA SALTY, SCRAPPY SEA BASS!
ENOUGH WITH YA, YE SORRY LOOKING, BLACK-SPOTTED WENCH!
SHUT YOUR SCURVY-INFESTED MOUTH, YER BREATH IS MELTIN' MY EYES!
SEA HAG.
SQUID ARSE.

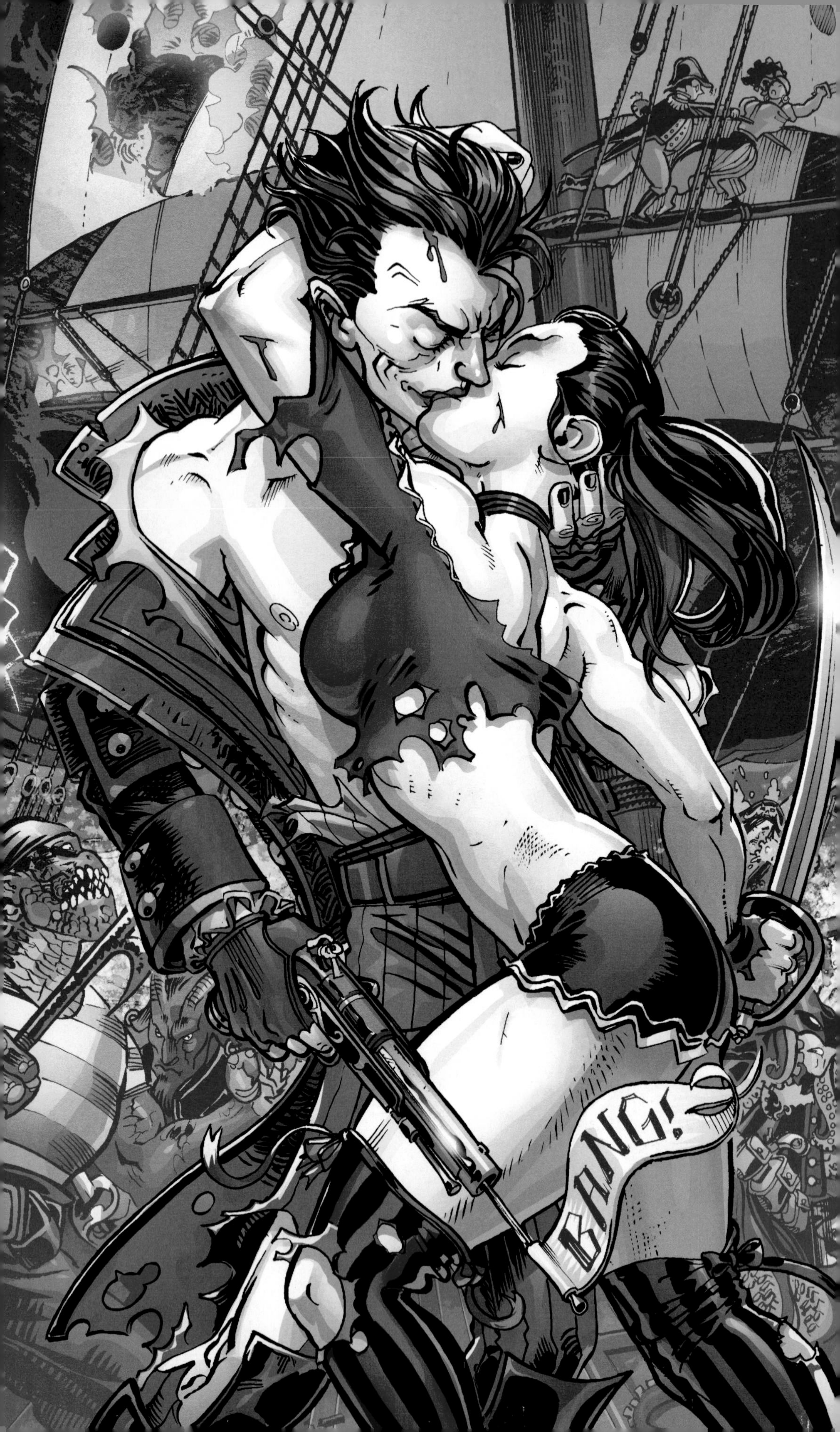
BANG!

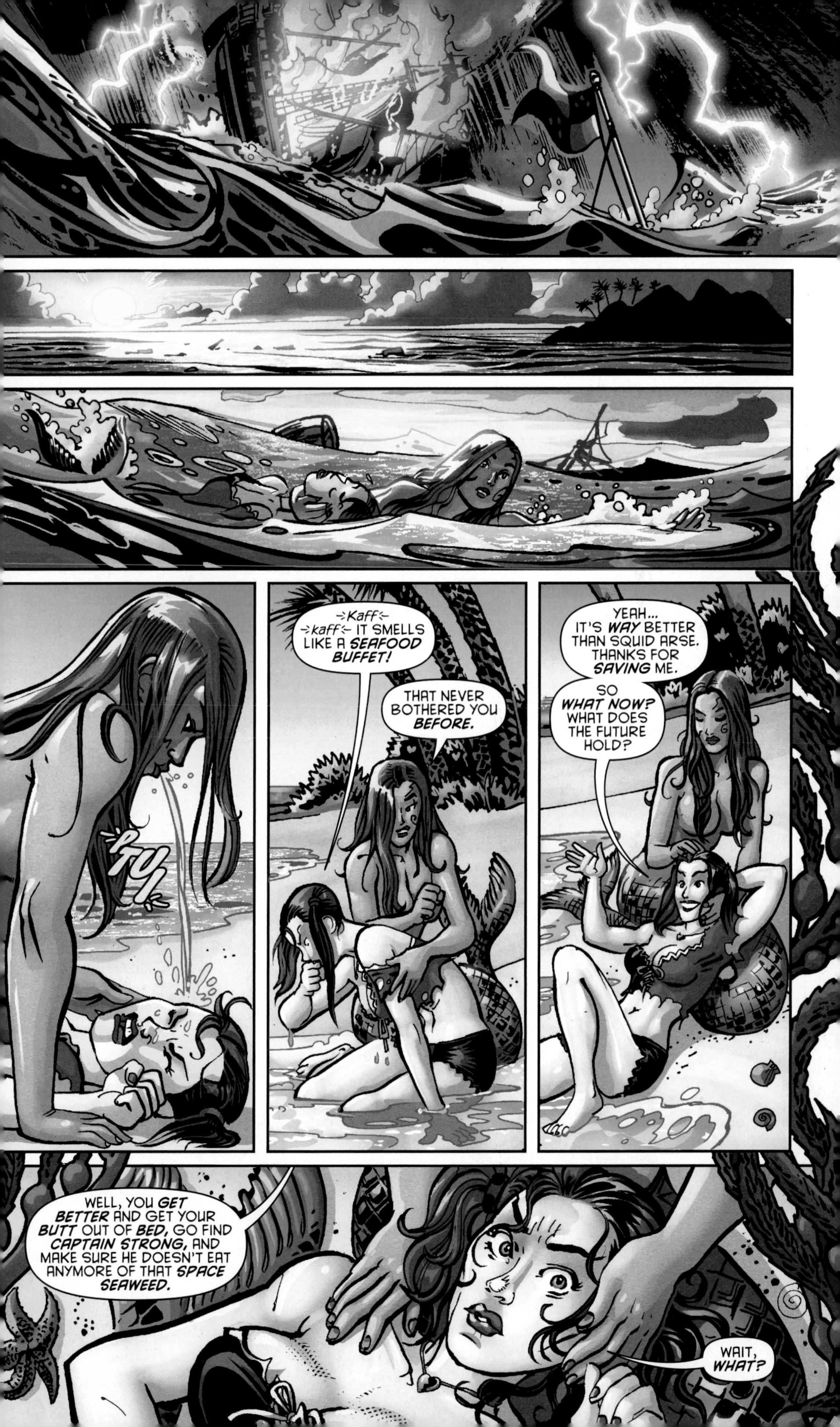

PTUI
-Kaff- -kaff- IT SMELLS LIKE A SEAFOOD BUFFET!
THAT NEVER BOTHERED YOU BEFORE.
YEAH... IT'S WAY BETTER THAN SQUID ARSE. THANKS FOR SAVING ME.
SO WHAT NOW? WHAT DOES THE FUTURE HOLD?
WELL, YOU GET BETTER AND GET YOUR BUTT OUT OF BED, GO FIND CAPTAIN STRONG, AND MAKE SURE HE DOESN'T EAT ANYMORE OF THAT SPACE SEAWEED.
WAIT, WHAT?

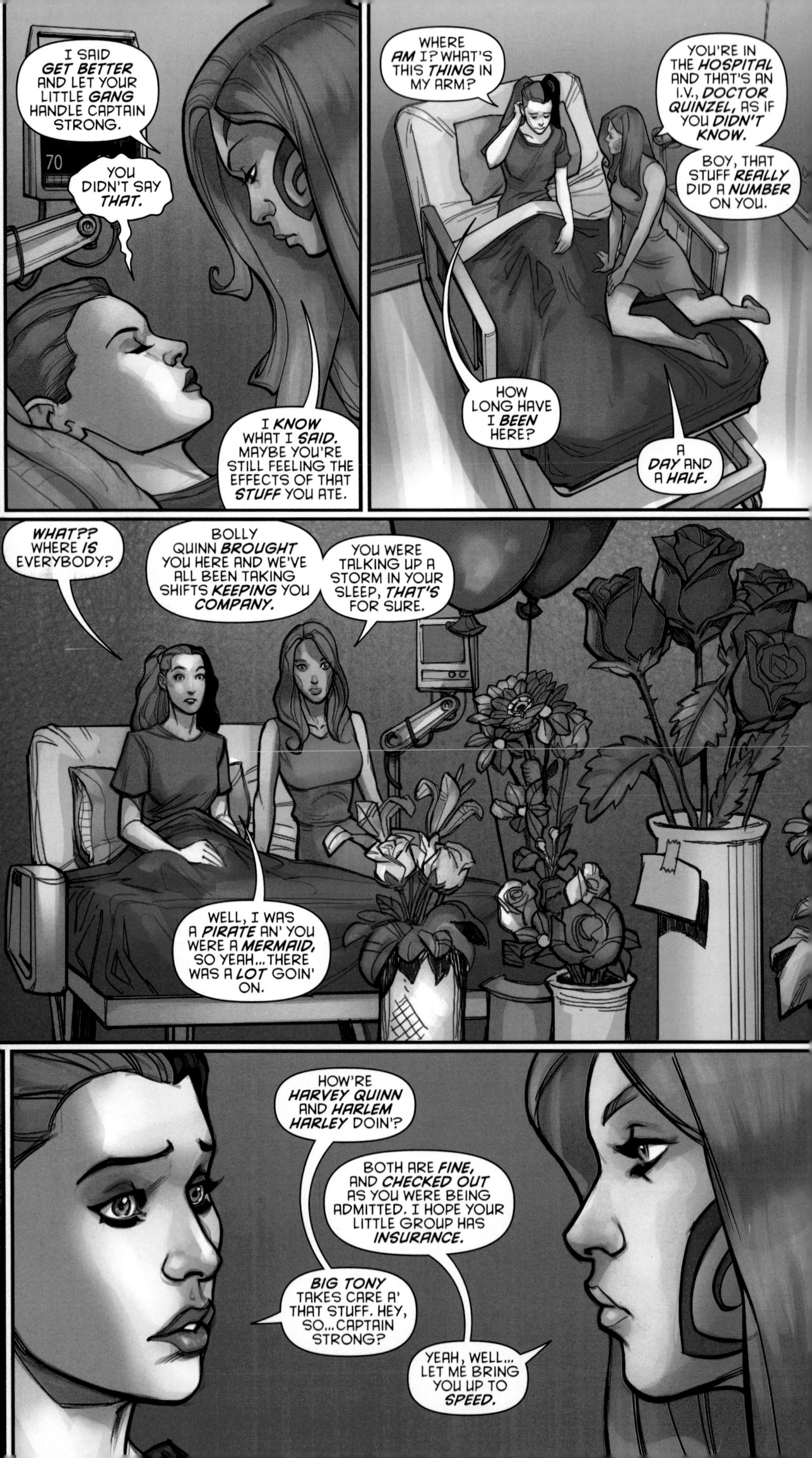
I SAID GET BETTER AND LET YOUR LITTLE GANG HANDLE CAPTAIN STRONG.
YOU DIDN'T SAY THAT.
I KNOW WHAT I SAID. MAYBE YOU'RE STILL FEELING THE EFFECTS OF THAT STUFF YOU ATE.
WHERE AM I? WHAT'S THIS THING IN MY ARM?
YOU'RE IN THE HOSPITAL AND THAT'S AN I.V., DOCTOR QUINZEL, AS IF YOU DIDN'T KNOW.
BOY, THAT STUFF REALLY DID A NUMBER ON YOU.
HOW LONG HAVE I BEEN HERE?
A DAY AND A HALF.
WHAT?? WHERE IS EVERYBODY?
BOLLY QUINN BROUGHT YOU HERE AND WE'VE ALL BEEN TAKING SHIFTS KEEPING YOU COMPANY.
YOU WERE TALKING UP A STORM IN YOUR SLEEP, THAT'S FOR SURE.
WELL, I WAS A PIRATE AN' YOU WERE A MERMAID, SO YEAH... THERE WAS A LOT GOIN' ON.
HOW'RE HARVEY QUINN AND HARLEM HARLEY DOIN'?
BOTH ARE FINE, AND CHECKED OUT AS YOU WERE BEING ADMITTED. I HOPE YOUR LITTLE GROUP HAS INSURANCE.
BIG TONY TAKES CARE A' THAT STUFF. HEY, SO... CAPTAIN STRONG?
YEAH, WELL... LET ME BRING YOU UP TO SPEED.

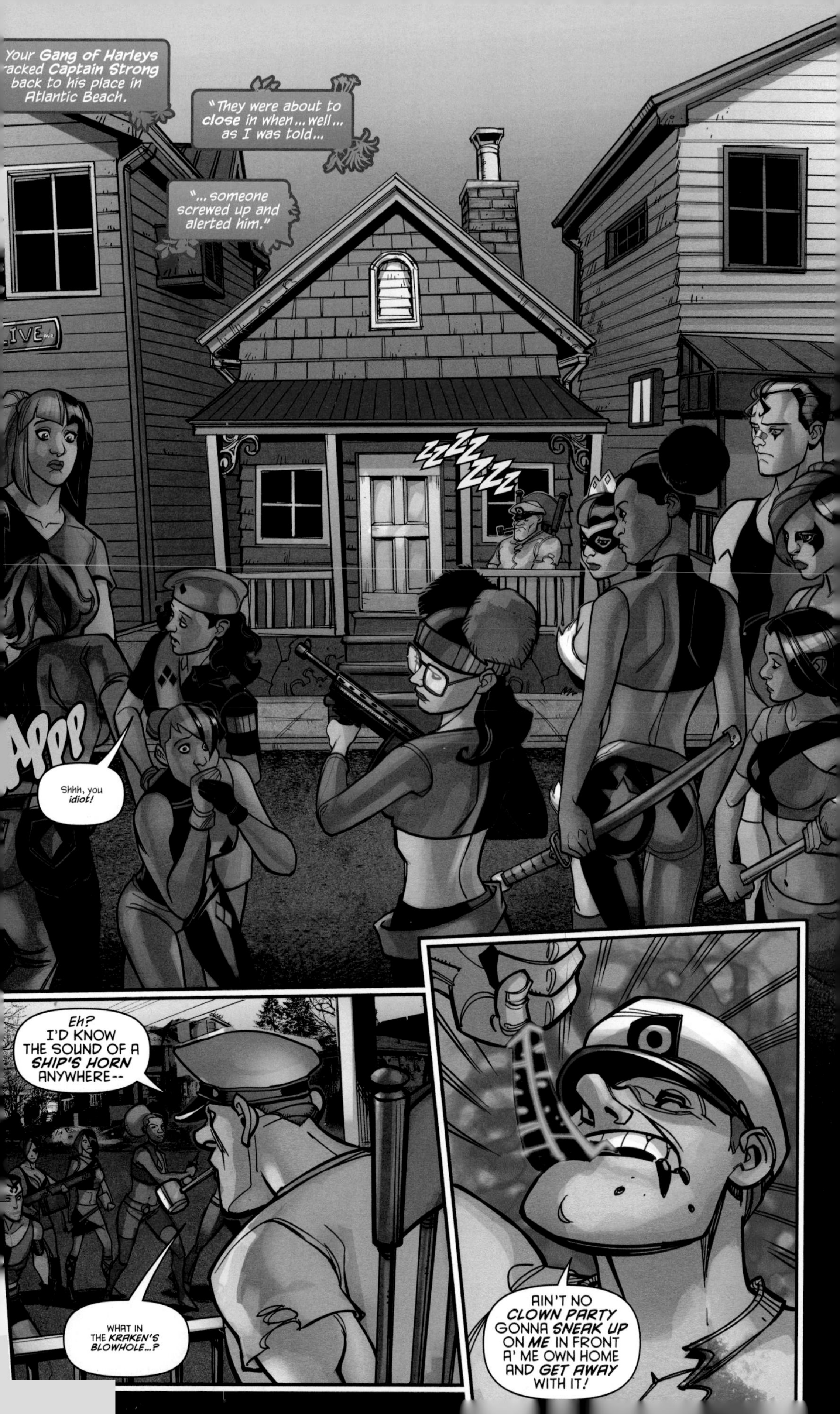

Your Gang of Harleys tracked Captain Strong back to his place in Atlantic Beach.
"They were about to close in when... well... as I was told...
"...someone screwed up and alerted him."
LIVE AVE
ZZZZZZ
APPP
Shhh, you idiot!
Eh? I'D KNOW THE SOUND OF A SHIP'S HORN ANYWHERE--
WHAT IN THE KRAKEN'S BLOWHOLE...?
AIN'T NO CLOWN PARTY GONNA SNEAK UP ON ME IN FRONT A' ME OWN HOME AND GET AWAY WITH IT!

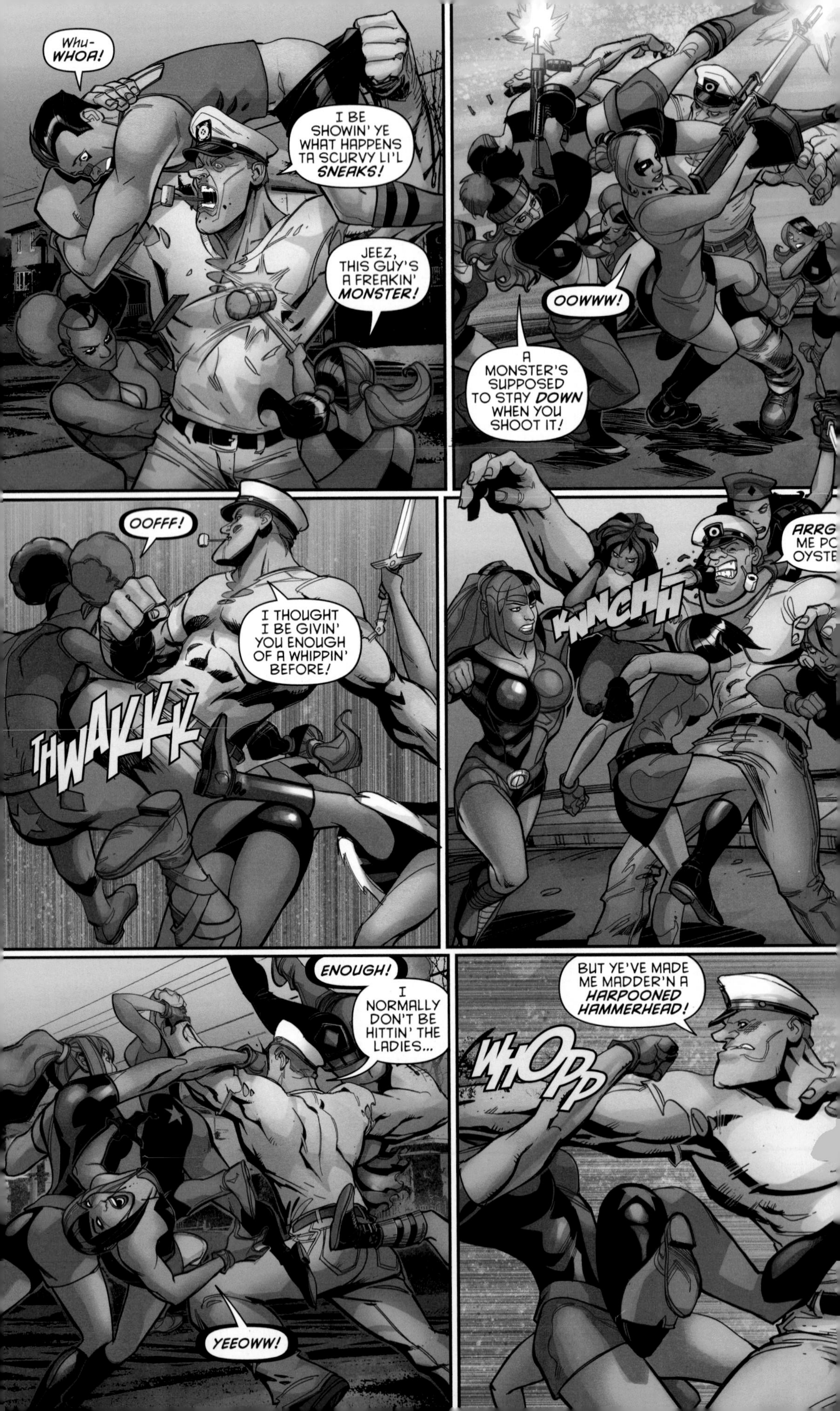
Whu-WHOA!
I BE SHOWIN' YE WHAT HAPPENS TA SCURVY LI'L SNEAKS!
JEEZ, THIS GUY'S A FREAKIN' MONSTER!
OOWWW!
A MONSTER'S SUPPOSED TO STAY DOWN WHEN YOU SHOOT IT!
OOFFF!
I THOUGHT I BE GIVIN' YOU ENOUGH OF A WHIPPIN' BEFORE!
THWAKKK
KNNCHH
ARRG
ME PO
OYSTE
ENOUGH!
I NORMALLY DON'T BE HITTIN' THE LADIES...
YEEOWW!
BUT YE'VE MADE ME MADDER'N A HARPOONED HAMMERHEAD!
WHOPP

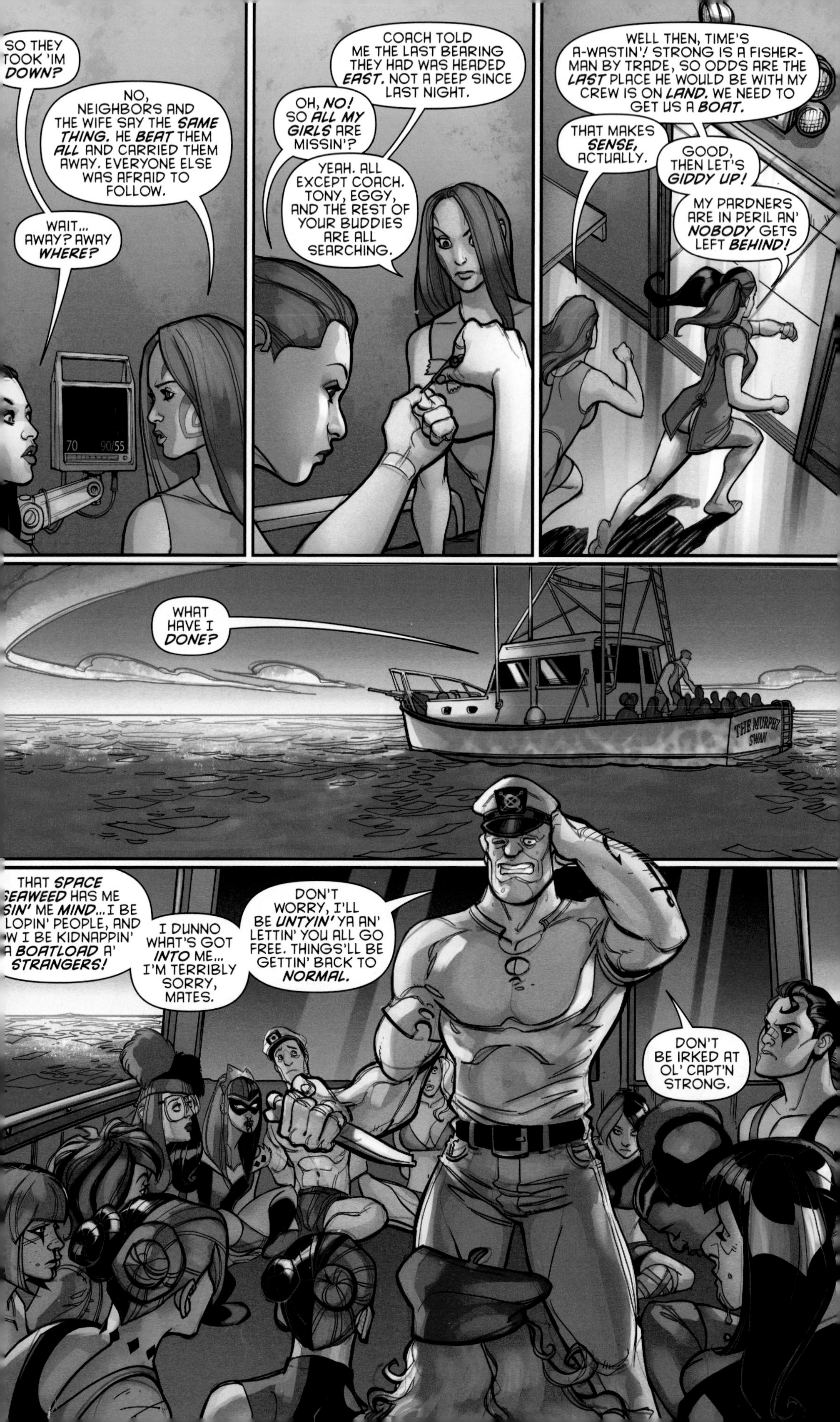
SO THEY TOOK 'IM DOWN?
NO, NEIGHBORS AND THE WIFE SAY THE SAME THING. HE BEAT THEM ALL AND CARRIED THEM AWAY. EVERYONE ELSE WAS AFRAID TO FOLLOW.
WAIT... AWAY? AWAY WHERE?
70 90/55
COACH TOLD ME THE LAST BEARING THEY HAD WAS HEADED EAST. NOT A PEEP SINCE LAST NIGHT.
OH, NO! SO ALL MY GIRLS ARE MISSIN'?
YEAH. ALL EXCEPT COACH. TONY, EGGY, AND THE REST OF YOUR BUDDIES ARE ALL SEARCHING.
WELL THEN, TIME'S A-WASTIN'! STRONG IS A FISHERMAN BY TRADE, SO ODDS ARE THE LAST PLACE HE WOULD BE WITH MY CREW IS ON LAND. WE NEED TO GET US A BOAT.
THAT MAKES SENSE, ACTUALLY.
GOOD, THEN LET'S GIDDY UP!
MY PARDNERS ARE IN PERIL AN' NOBODY GETS LEFT BEHIND!
WHAT HAVE I DONE?
THE MURPHY SWAN
THAT SPACE SEAWEED HAS ME SIN' ME MIND...I BE LOPIN' PEOPLE, AND W I BE KIDNAPPIN' A BOATLOAD A' STRANGERS!
I DUNNO WHAT'S GOT INTO ME... I'M TERRIBLY SORRY, MATES.
DON'T WORRY, I'LL BE UNTYIN' YA AN' LETTIN' YOU ALL GO FREE. THINGS'LL BE GETTIN' BACK TO NORMAL.
DON'T BE IRKED AT OL' CAPT'N STRONG.

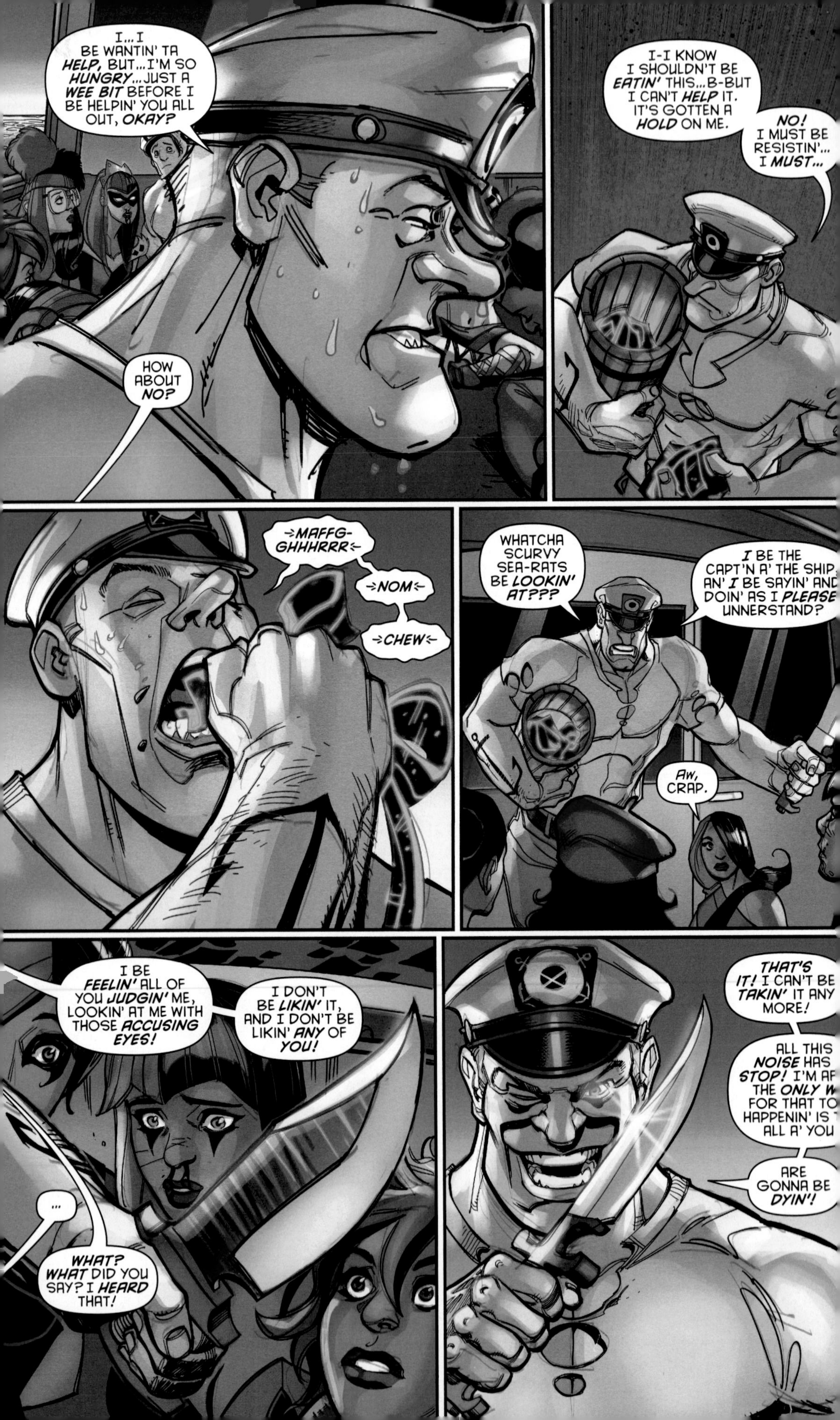
I...I BE WANTIN' TA HELP, BUT...I'M SO HUNGRY...JUST A WEE BIT BEFORE I BE HELPIN' YOU ALL OUT, OKAY?
HOW ABOUT NO?
I-I KNOW I SHOULDN'T BE EATIN' THIS...B-BUT I CAN'T HELP IT. IT'S GOTTEN A HOLD ON ME.
NO! I MUST BE RESISTIN'... I MUST...
MAFFG-GHHHRRR
NOM
CHEW
WHATCHA SCURVY SEA-RATS BE LOOKIN' AT???
I BE THE CAPT'N A' THE SHIP, AN' I BE SAYIN' AND DOIN' AS I PLEASE. UNNERSTAND?
AW, CRAP.
I BE FEELIN' ALL OF YOU JUDGIN' ME, LOOKIN' AT ME WITH THOSE ACCUSING EYES!
I DON'T BE LIKIN' IT, AND I DON'T BE LIKIN' ANY OF YOU!
...
WHAT? WHAT DID YOU SAY? I HEARD THAT!
THAT'S IT! I CAN'T BE TAKIN' IT ANY MORE!
ALL THIS NOISE HAS STOP! I'M AF THE ONLY W FOR THAT TO HAPPENIN' IS ALL A' YOU
ARE GONNA BE DYIN'!

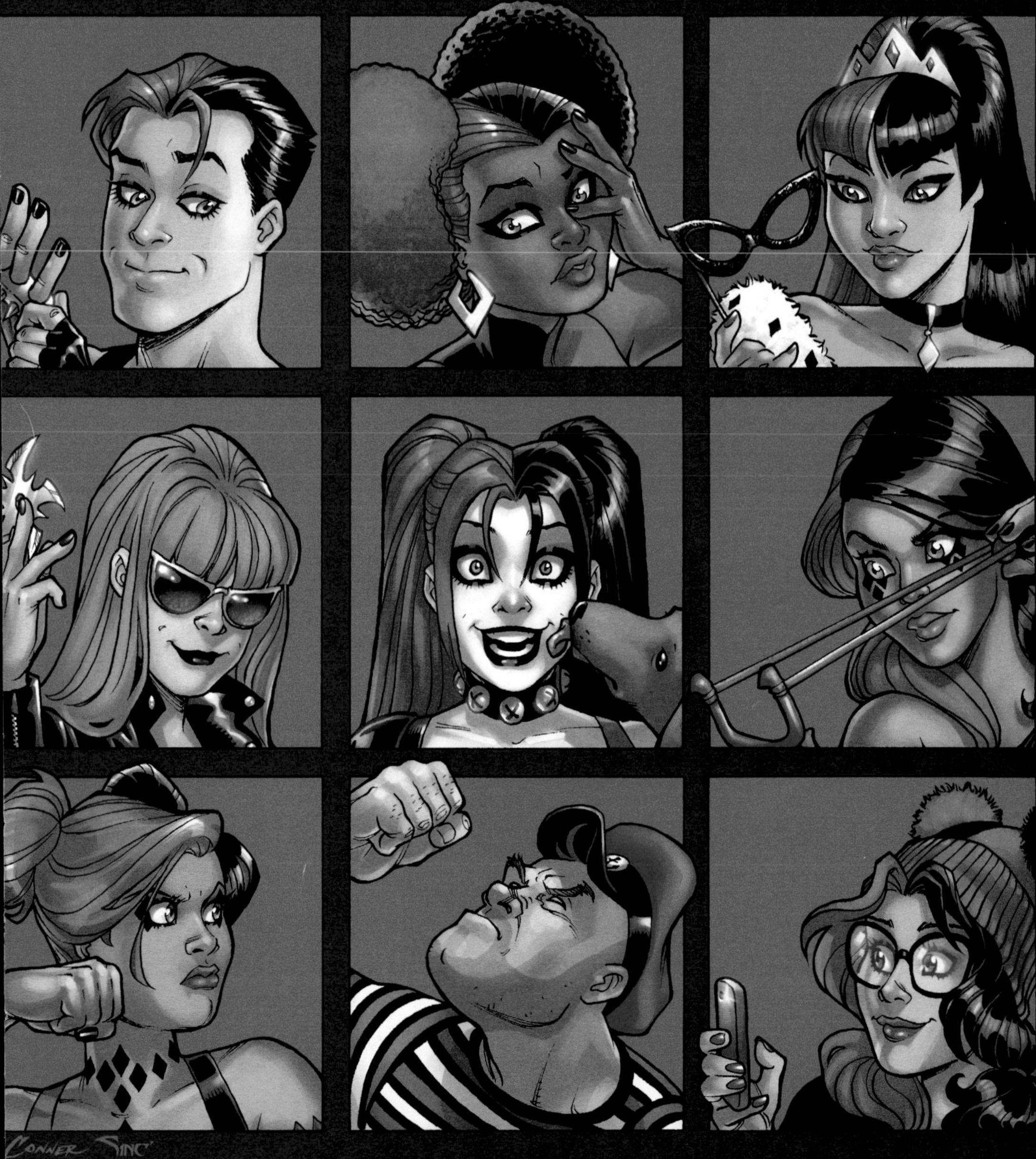
CONNER

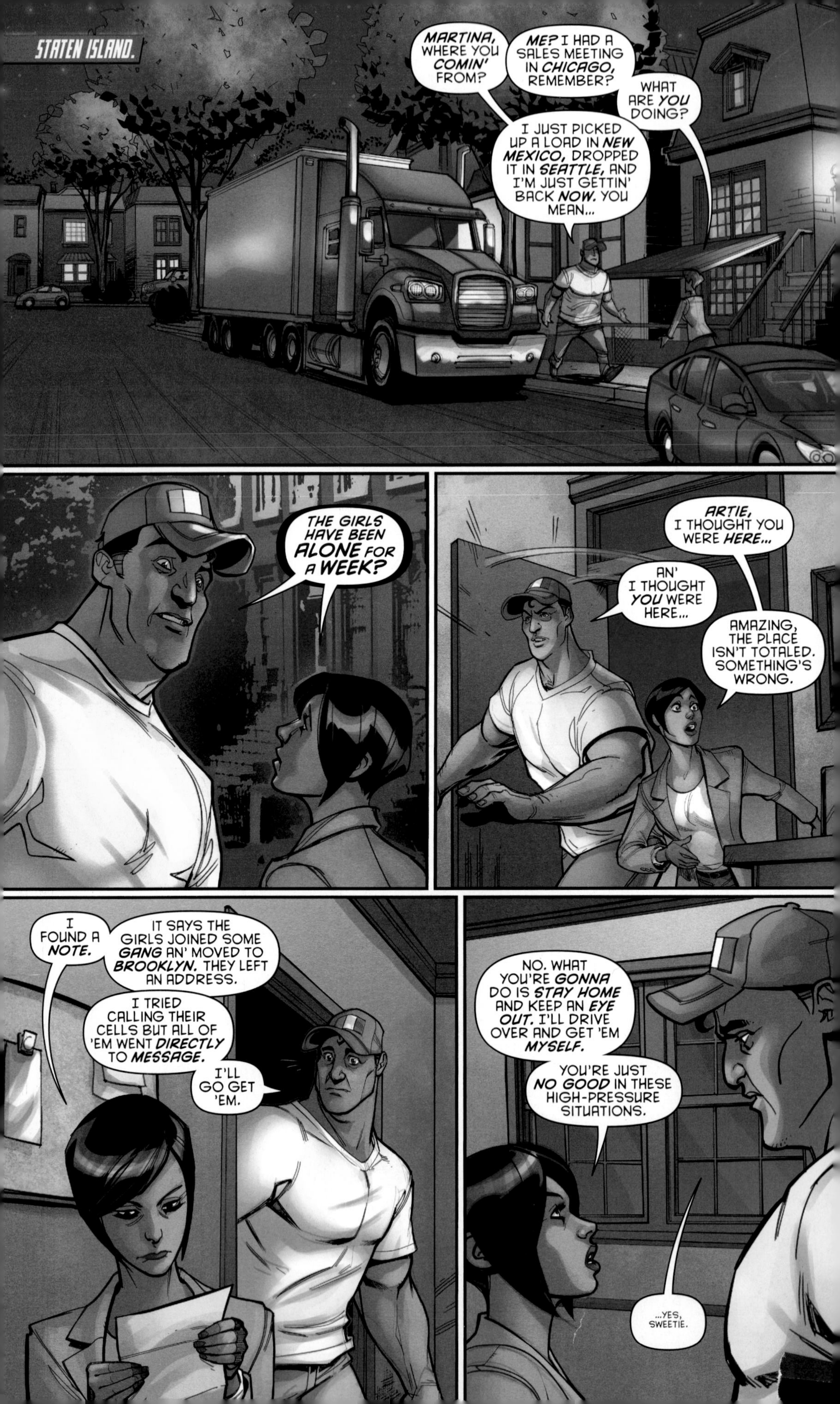
STATEN ISLAND.
MARTINA, WHERE YOU COMIN' FROM?
ME? I HAD A SALES MEETING IN CHICAGO, REMEMBER?
WHAT ARE YOU DOING?
I JUST PICKED UP A LOAD IN NEW MEXICO, DROPPED IT IN SEATTLE, AND I'M JUST GETTIN' BACK NOW. YOU MEAN...
THE GIRLS HAVE BEEN ALONE FOR A WEEK?
ARTIE, I THOUGHT YOU WERE HERE...
AN' I THOUGHT YOU WERE HERE...
AMAZING, THE PLACE ISN'T TOTALED. SOMETHING'S WRONG.
I FOUND A NOTE.
IT SAYS THE GIRLS JOINED SOME GANG AN' MOVED TO BROOKLYN. THEY LEFT AN ADDRESS.
I TRIED CALLING THEIR CELLS BUT ALL OF 'EM WENT DIRECTLY TO MESSAGE.
I'LL GO GET 'EM.
NO. WHAT YOU'RE GONNA DO IS STAY HOME AND KEEP AN EYE OUT. I'LL DRIVE OVER AND GET 'EM MYSELF.
YOU'RE JUST NO GOOD IN THESE HIGH-PRESSURE SITUATIONS.
...YES, SWEETIE.

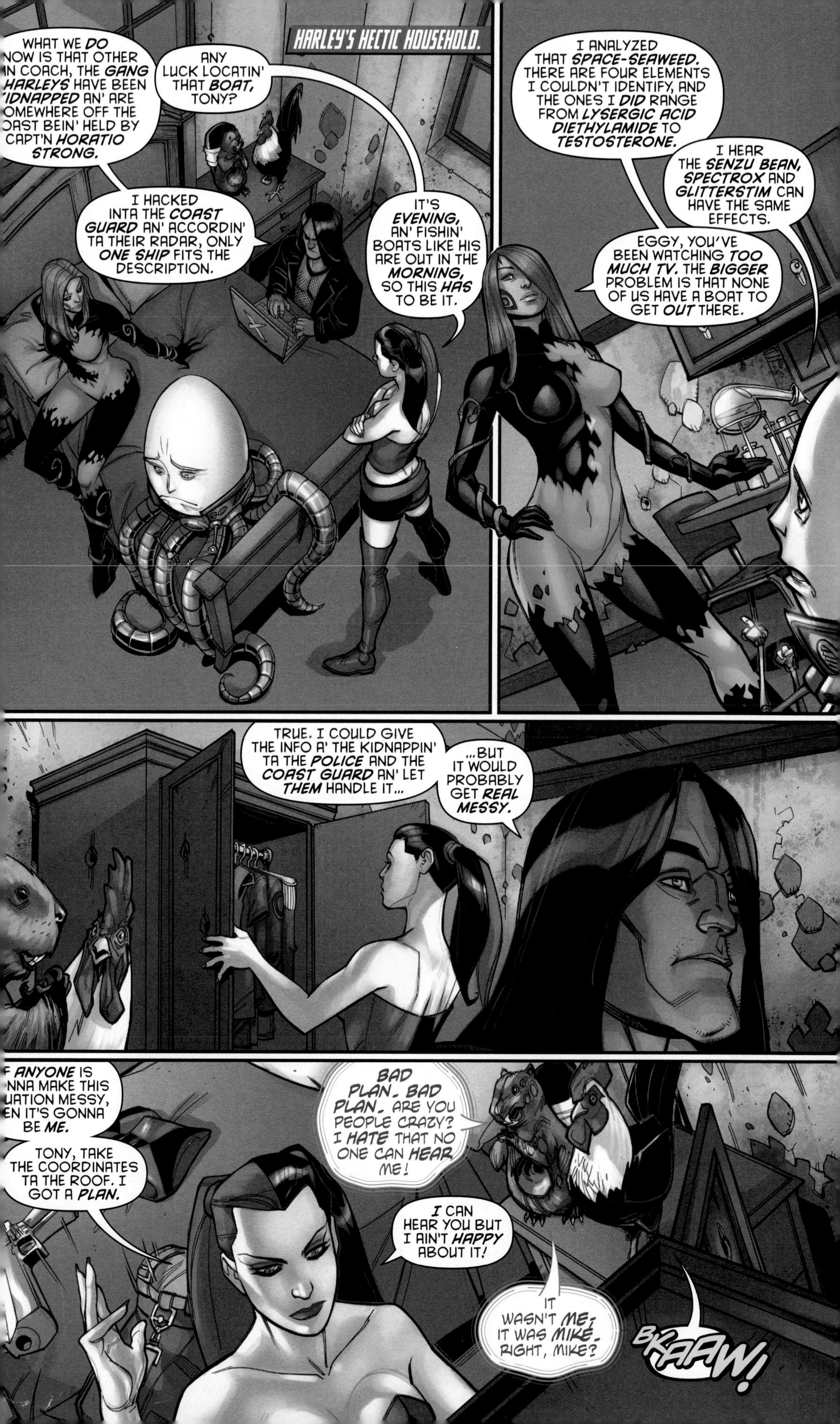
HARLEY'S HECTIC HOUSEHOLD.
WHAT WE DO NOW IS THAT OTHER IN COACH, THE GANG HARLEYS HAVE BEEN KIDNAPPED AN' ARE SOMEWHERE OFF THE COAST BEIN' HELD BY CAPT'N HORATIO STRONG.
ANY LUCK LOCATIN' THAT BOAT, TONY?
I HACKED INTA THE COAST GUARD AN' ACCORDIN' TA THEIR RADAR, ONLY ONE SHIP FITS THE DESCRIPTION.
IT'S EVENING, AN' FISHIN' BOATS LIKE HIS ARE OUT IN THE MORNING, SO THIS HAS TO BE IT.
I ANALYZED THAT SPACE-SEAWEED. THERE ARE FOUR ELEMENTS I COULDN'T IDENTIFY, AND THE ONES I DID RANGE FROM LYSERGIC ACID DIETHYLAMIDE TO TESTOSTERONE.
I HEAR THE SENZU BEAN, SPECTROX AND GLITTERSTIM CAN HAVE THE SAME EFFECTS.
EGGY, YOU'VE BEEN WATCHING TOO MUCH TV. THE BIGGER PROBLEM IS THAT NONE OF US HAVE A BOAT TO GET OUT THERE.
TRUE. I COULD GIVE THE INFO A' THE KIDNAPPIN' TA THE POLICE AND THE COAST GUARD AN' LET THEM HANDLE IT...
...BUT IT WOULD PROBABLY GET REAL MESSY.
F ANYONE IS NNA MAKE THIS UATION MESSY, EN IT'S GONNA BE ME.
TONY, TAKE THE COORDINATES TA THE ROOF. I GOT A PLAN.
BAD PLAN. BAD PLAN. ARE YOU PEOPLE CRAZY? I HATE THAT NO ONE CAN HEAR ME!
I CAN HEAR YOU BUT I AIN'T HAPPY ABOUT IT!
IT WASN'T ME. IT WAS MIKE. RIGHT, MIKE?
BKAAAW!

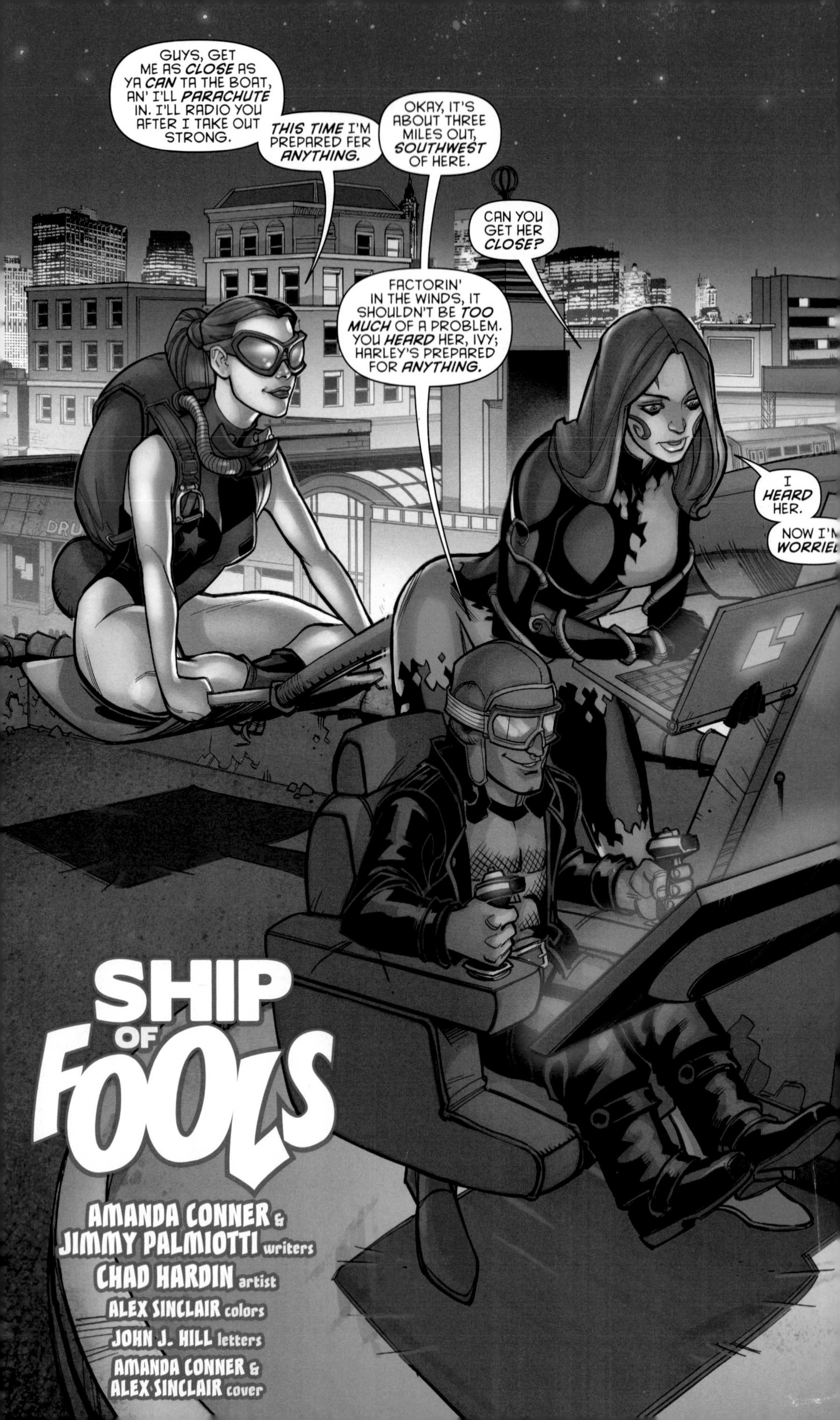
GUYS, GET ME AS CLOSE AS YA CAN TA THE BOAT, AN' I'LL PARACHUTE IN. I'LL RADIO YOU AFTER I TAKE OUT STRONG.
THIS TIME I'M PREPARED FER ANYTHING.
OKAY, IT'S ABOUT THREE MILES OUT, SOUTHWEST OF HERE.
CAN YOU GET HER CLOSE?
FACTORIN' IN THE WINDS, IT SHOULDN'T BE TOO MUCH OF A PROBLEM. YOU HEARD HER, IVY; HARLEY'S PREPARED FOR ANYTHING.
I HEARD HER.
NOW I'M WORRIED
SHIP OF FOOLS
AMANDA CONNER & JIMMY PALMIOTTI writers
CHAD HARDIN artist
ALEX SINCLAIR colors
JOHN J. HILL letters
AMANDA CONNER & ALEX SINCLAIR cover

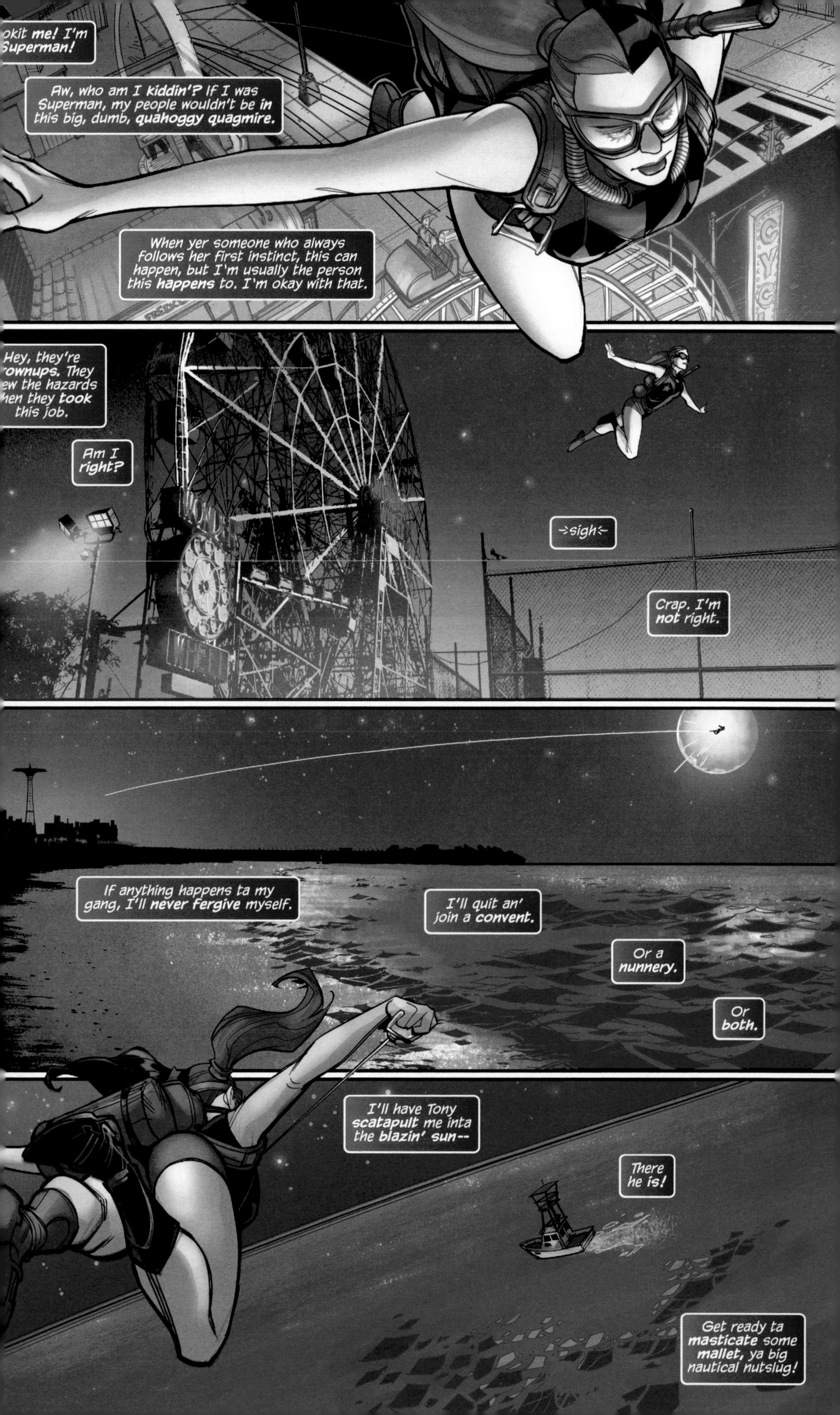
okit me! I'm Superman!
Aw, who am I kiddin'? If I was Superman, my people wouldn't be in this big, dumb, quahoggy quagmire.
When yer someone who always follows her first instinct, this can happen, but I'm usually the person this happens to. I'm okay with that.
Hey, they're rownups. They ew the hazards hen they took this job.
Am I right?
sigh
Crap. I'm not right.
If anything happens ta my gang, I'll never fergive myself.
I'll quit an' join a convent.
Or a nunnery.
Or both.
I'll have Tony scatapult me inta the blazin' sun--
There he is!
Get ready ta masticate some mallet, ya big nautical nutslug!

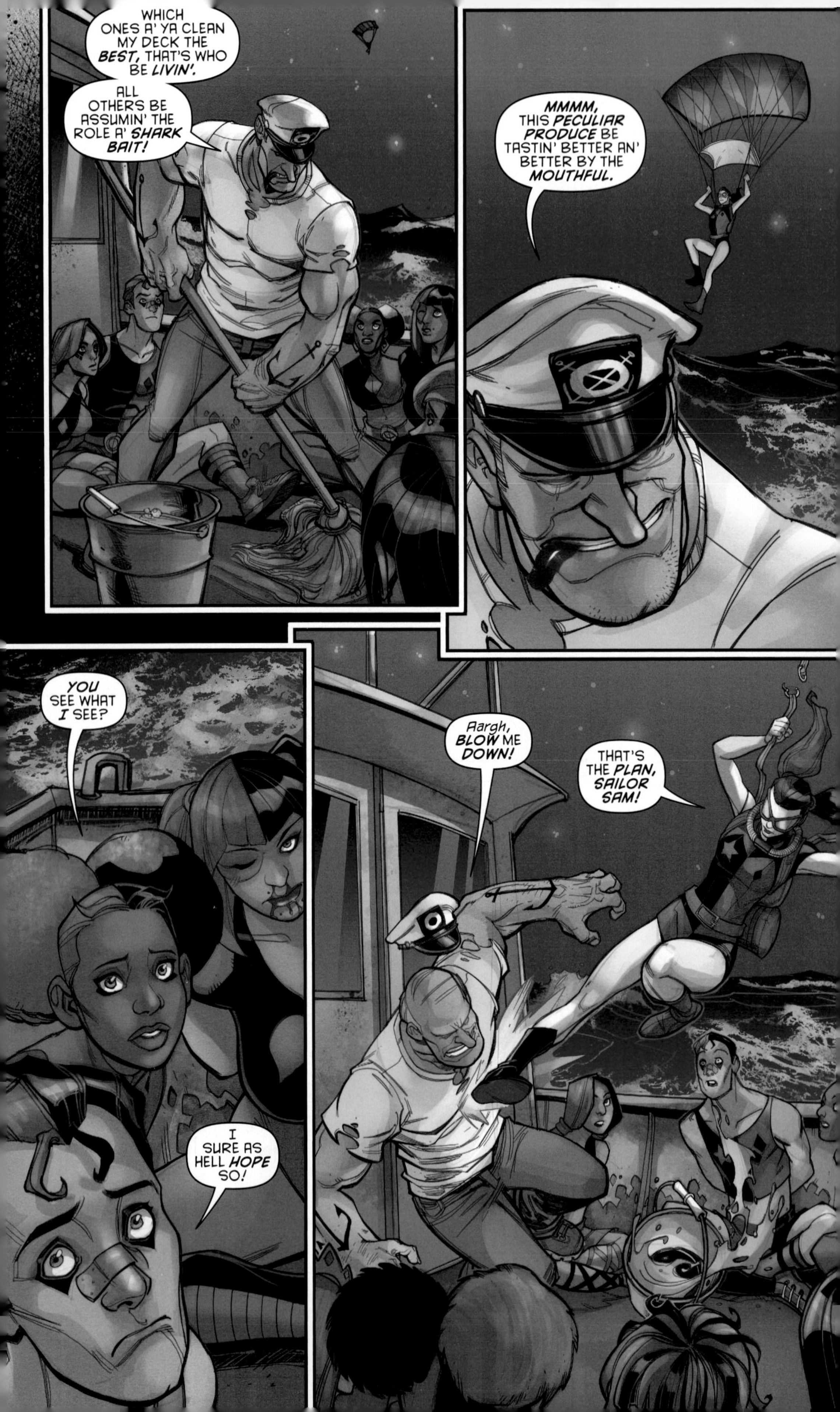
WHICH ONES A' YA CLEAN MY DECK THE BEST, THAT'S WHO BE LIVIN'.
ALL OTHERS BE ASSUMIN' THE ROLE A' SHARK BAIT!
MMMM, THIS PECULIAR PRODUCE BE TASTIN' BETTER AN' BETTER BY THE MOUTHFUL.
YOU SEE WHAT I SEE?
I SURE AS HELL HOPE SO!
Aargh, BLOW ME DOWN!
THAT'S THE PLAN, SAILOR SAM!

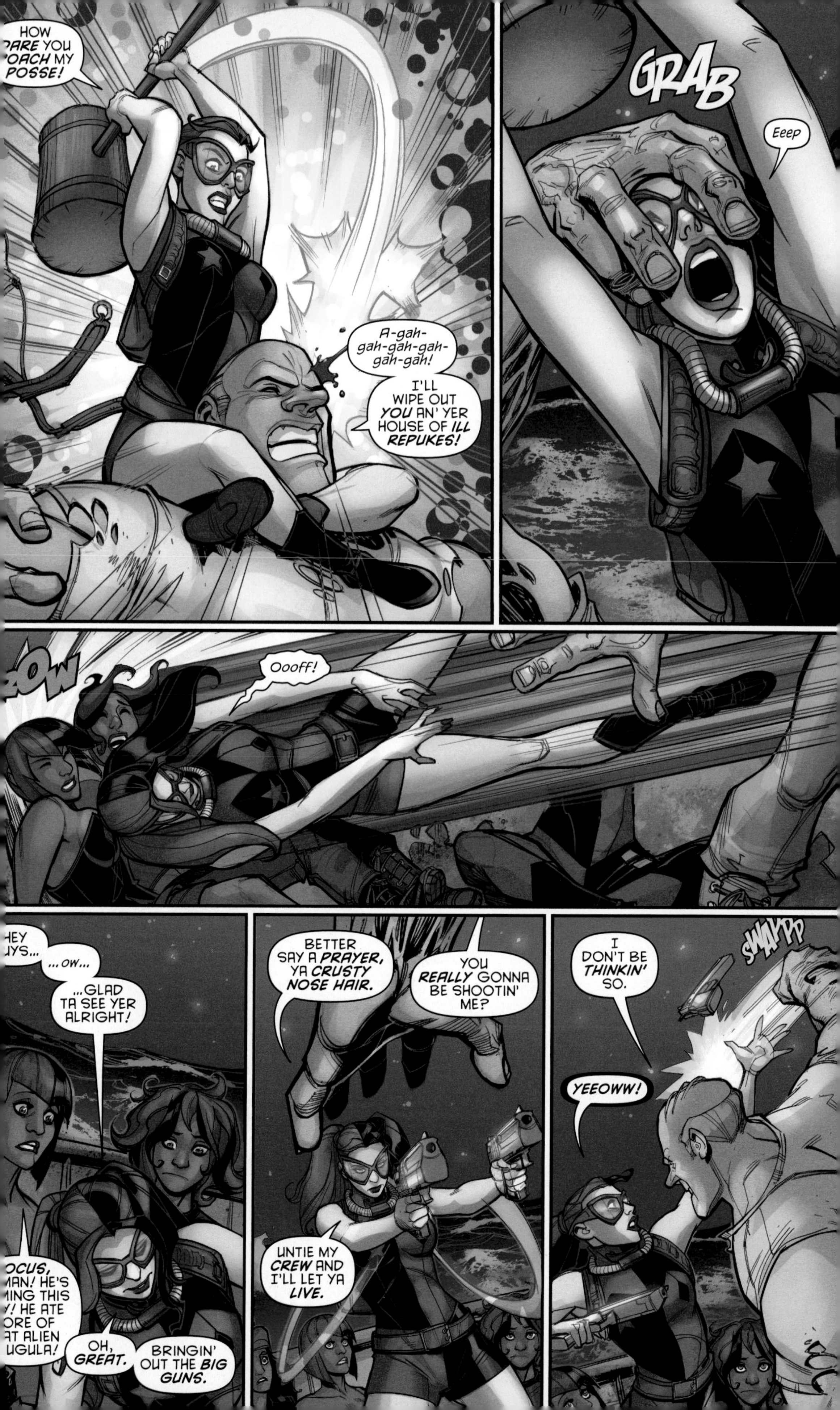
HOW
ARE YOU
OACH MY
POSSE!
A-gah-gah-gah-gah-gah-gah!
I'LL WIPE OUT YOU AN' YER HOUSE OF ILL REPUKES!
GRAB
Eeep
Oooff!
HEY
UYS...
...OW...
...GLAD TA SEE YER ALRIGHT!
OCUS,
MAN! HE'S
MING THIS
! HE ATE
ORE OF
AT ALIEN
UGULA!
OH, GREAT.
BRINGIN' OUT THE BIG GUNS.
BETTER SAY A PRAYER, YA CRUSTY NOSE HAIR.
YOU REALLY GONNA BE SHOOTIN' ME?
UNTIE MY CREW AND I'LL LET YA LIVE.
I DON'T BE THINKIN' SO.
YEEOWW!

THAT'S IT, YA OVERCOOKED *SEA STONER!*

POT BANG

Heh. Heh heh.

HA HAHA HA!

THAT... *HAHAHA!* I CAN'T...

HAHAHA HAHA!!!

OKAY, IT'S NOT *THAT* FUNNY.

HAHAHA... I CAN'T... HAHAHAHA!

YA CAN'T *WHAT?*

JUST *TELL* US, ALREADY!

I CAN'T...I NO CONTROLLIN

GRRGG

nnn... uhh...

HEY! WHERE YA GOIN'?

GRRLLP

FRRAPPPPPP

ARRGGGHHHH!!

IS IT TOO SOON FOR *POOP DEC* JOKE?

NO?

THAT WAS THE *NASTIEST NOISE* I EVER HEARD.

WORK IN AN INDIAN RESTAURANT.

BELIEVE ME, YOU HEAR THINGS YOU'LL NEVER *UN-HEAR.*

HURRY, I DUNNO HOW LONG CAPT'N CRAPALOT IS GONNA STAY DOWN THERE.

SO WHAT'S THE *PLAN?*

FIRST, MAKE SURE HE'S *DOWN* FER THE COUNT.

THEN, TAKE THE BOAT BACK TA *CONEY ISLAND.*

THEN, WE GET *HORATIO* THE *HULKING HERB-HOUND* INTO A TWELVE-STEP PROGRAM A' SOME SORT.

SO, WHO'S GONNA GO DOWN AND CHECK HIS *STATUS?*

WELL, SINCE *I'M* THE *BOSS*...

...I CHOOSE THE ONLY *OTHER* MAN ON THE SHIP...

...*HARVEY QUINN.*

OH THANK GOD.

ME?!

NO FRIGGIN' WAY! WHAT DOES ME BEING A *MAN* HAVE TO DO WITH IT?

WELL, HE MIGHT HAVE HIS *PANTS DOWN.*

SO, I HAVE TO *DESCEND* INTO THE *FOG* OF *FOULNESS* BELOW AND SPY HIS *BABY BELUGA* IN THE NAME OF *JUSTICE?*

I *CAN'T DO IT.*

YO, *I'LL DO IT.*

I FRIED MY SENSE OF SMELL WHEN I PUT TOGETHER A MODEL KIT WITH AIRPLANE GLUE.

IT TOOK ME FOUR YEARS TO PUT IT TOGETHER.

WAIT...*WHAT* AM I S'POSED BE DOING AGAIN?

THANKS, GNARLY. SEE IF THE CAPT'N IS PASSED OUT ON THE BOWL OR NOT.

IF HE *IS,* COME BACK UP AND TELL US.

IF HE *ISN'T,* WELL, JUST SCREAM REAL LOUD.

EASY-PEEZY.

IT WAS NICE *KNOWING* YOU.

YOU'RE MY *HERO.*

CAN I HAVE YOUR BED?

I'LL LET MOM AND DAD KNOW YOU WENT OUT A *WARRIOR.*

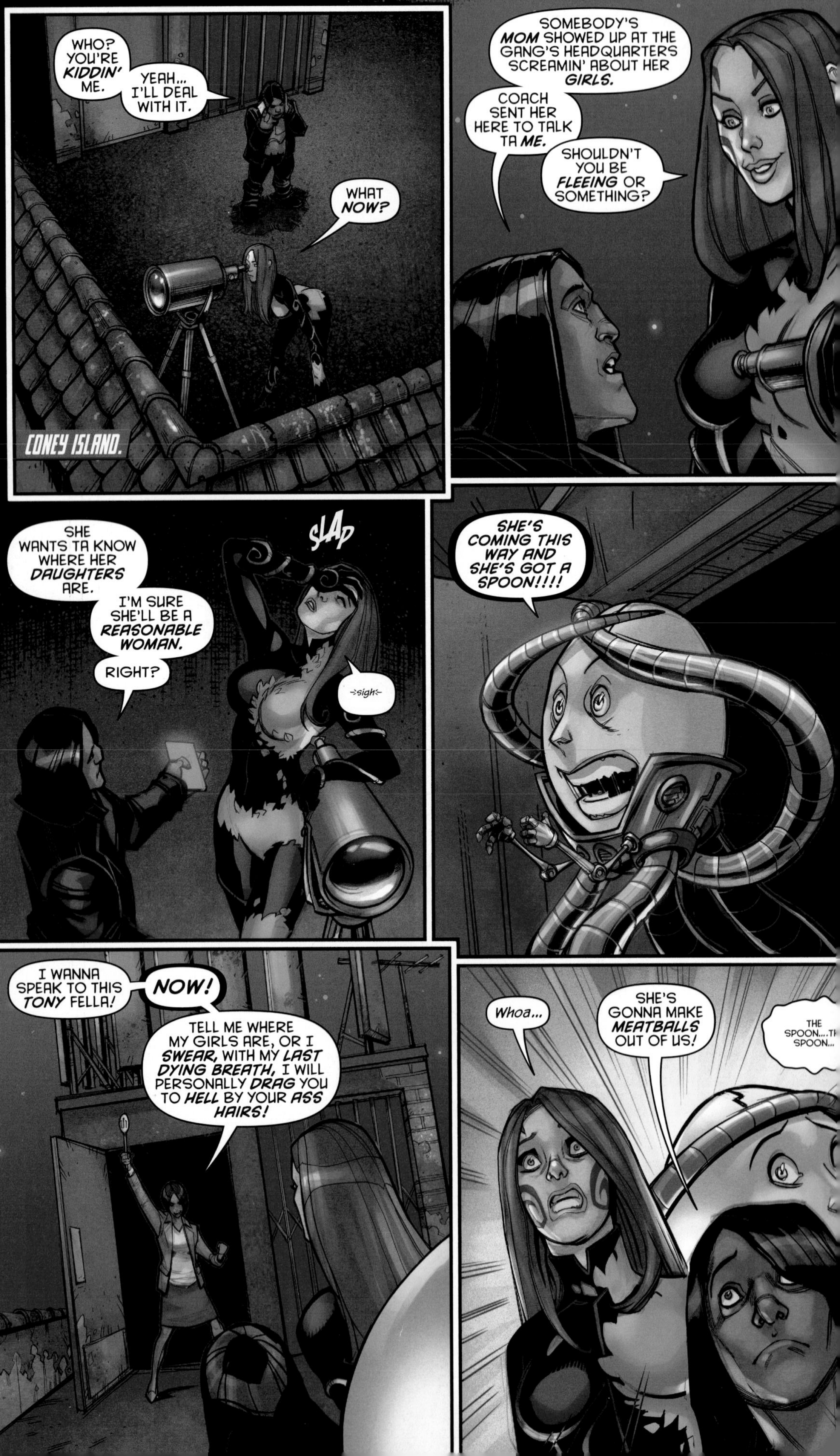
WHO? YOU'RE KIDDIN' ME.
YEAH... I'LL DEAL WITH IT.
WHAT NOW?
CONEY ISLAND.
SOMEBODY'S MOM SHOWED UP AT THE GANG'S HEADQUARTERS SCREAMIN' ABOUT HER GIRLS.
COACH SENT HER HERE TO TALK TA ME.
SHOULDN'T YOU BE FLEEING OR SOMETHING?
SHE WANTS TA KNOW WHERE HER DAUGHTERS ARE.
I'M SURE SHE'LL BE A REASONABLE WOMAN.
RIGHT?
SLAP
sigh
SHE'S COMING THIS WAY AND SHE'S GOT A SPOON!!!!
I WANNA SPEAK TO THIS TONY FELLA!
NOW!
TELL ME WHERE MY GIRLS ARE, OR I SWEAR, WITH MY LAST DYING BREATH, I WILL PERSONALLY DRAG YOU TO HELL BY YOUR ASS HAIRS!
Whoa...
SHE'S GONNA MAKE MEATBALLS OUT OF US!
THE SPOON....T
SPOON...

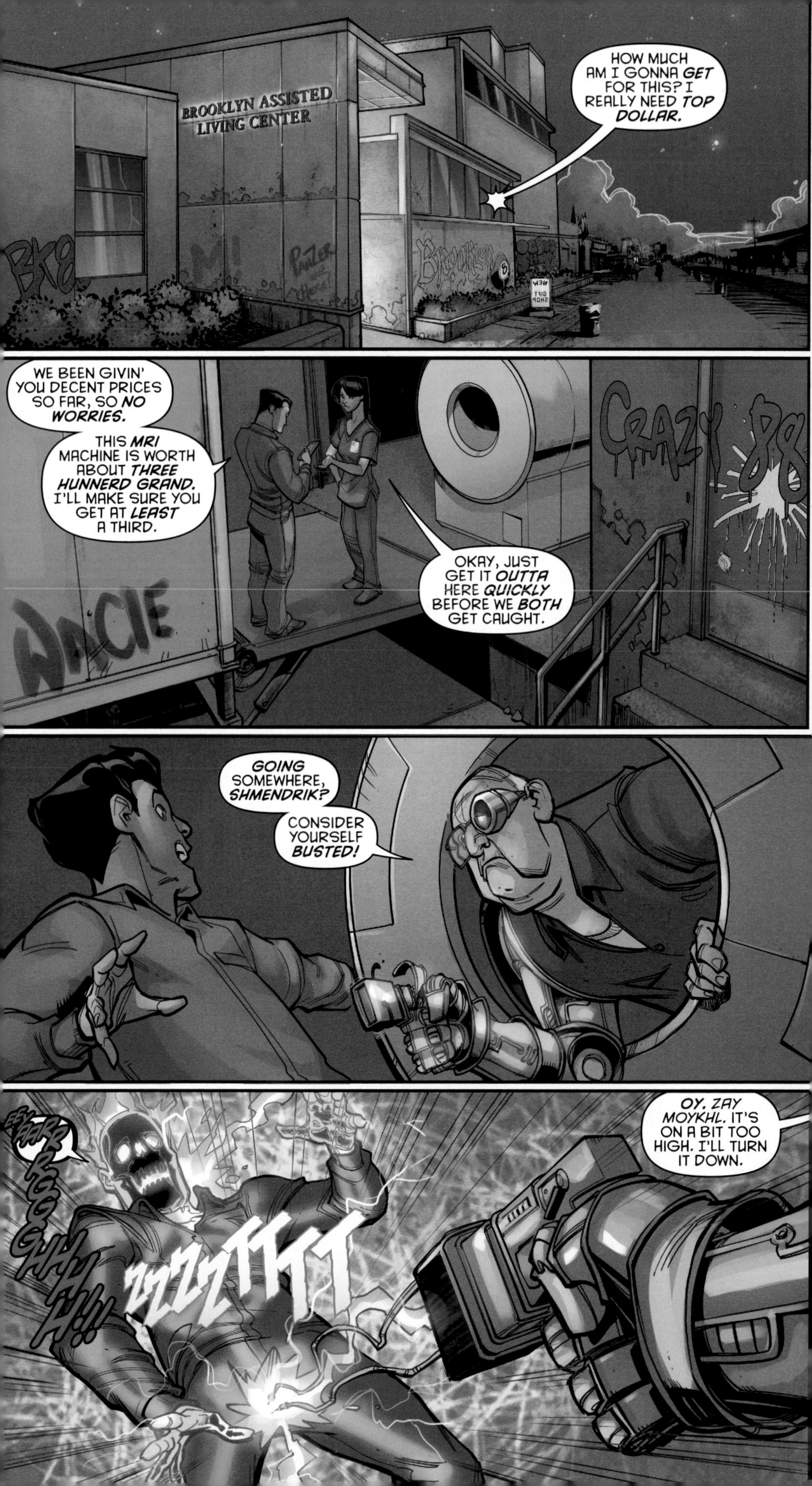
BROOKLYN ASSISTED LIVING CENTER
HOW MUCH AM I GONNA GET FOR THIS? I REALLY NEED TOP DOLLAR.
WE BEEN GIVIN' YOU DECENT PRICES SO FAR, SO NO WORRIES.
THIS MRI MACHINE IS WORTH ABOUT THREE HUNNERD GRAND. I'LL MAKE SURE YOU GET AT LEAST A THIRD.
OKAY, JUST GET IT OUTTA HERE QUICKLY BEFORE WE BOTH GET CAUGHT.
CRAZY 88
GOING SOMEWHERE, SHMENDRIK?
CONSIDER YOURSELF BUSTED!
EEYAARRRGGGHHHH!!!
ZZZZTTTT
OY. ZAY MOYKHL. IT'S ON A BIT TOO HIGH. I'LL TURN IT DOWN.

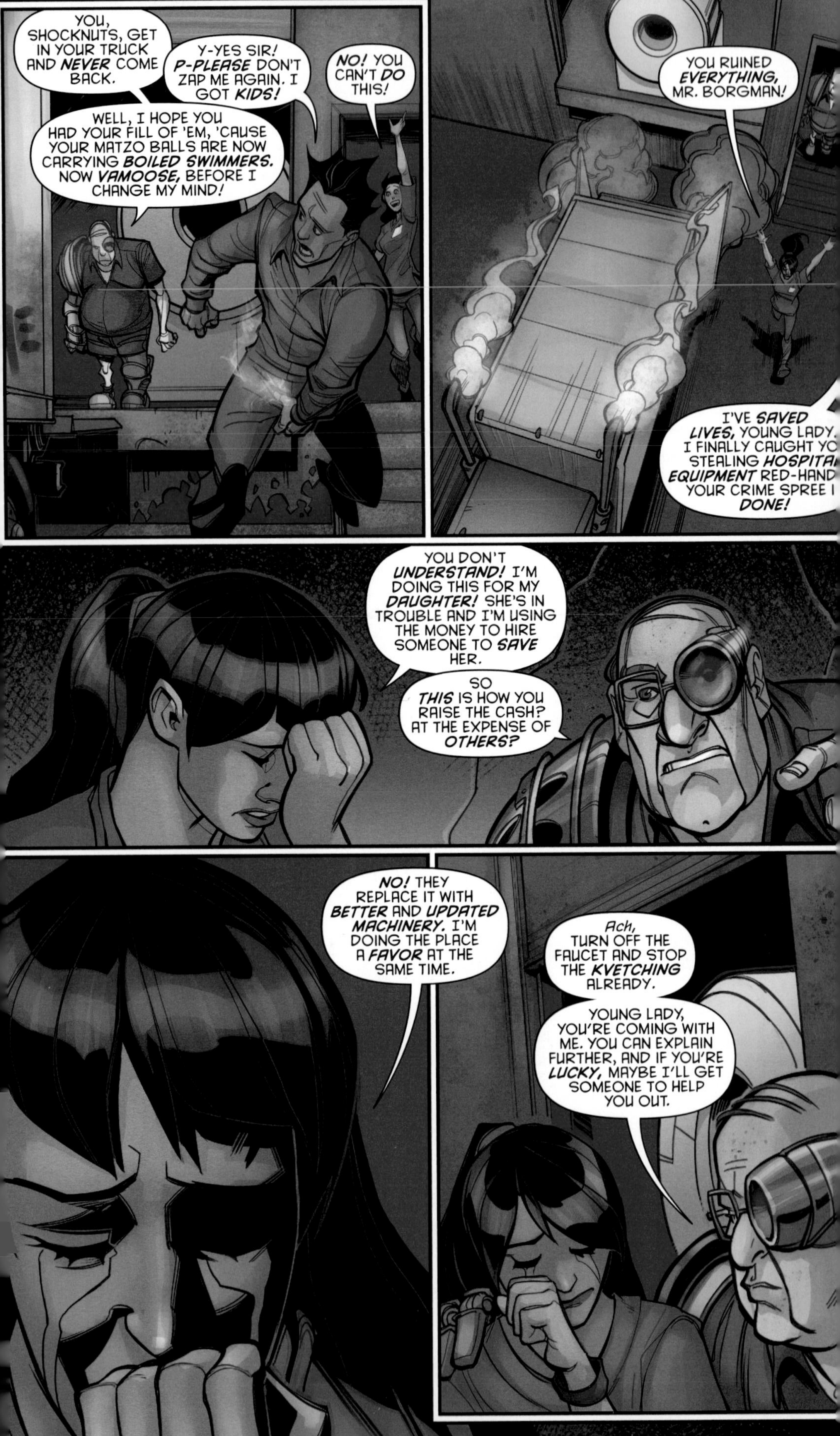
YOU, SHOCKNUTS, GET IN YOUR TRUCK AND NEVER COME BACK.
Y-YES SIR! P-PLEASE DON'T ZAP ME AGAIN. I GOT KIDS!
WELL, I HOPE YOU HAD YOUR FILL OF 'EM, 'CAUSE YOUR MATZO BALLS ARE NOW CARRYING BOILED SWIMMERS. NOW VAMOOSE, BEFORE I CHANGE MY MIND!
NO! YOU CAN'T DO THIS!
YOU RUINED EVERYTHING, MR. BORGMAN!
I'VE SAVED LIVES, YOUNG LADY. I FINALLY CAUGHT YO STEALING HOSPITA EQUIPMENT RED-HAND YOUR CRIME SPREE I DONE!
YOU DON'T UNDERSTAND! I'M DOING THIS FOR MY DAUGHTER! SHE'S IN TROUBLE AND I'M USING THE MONEY TO HIRE SOMEONE TO SAVE HER.
SO THIS IS HOW YOU RAISE THE CASH? AT THE EXPENSE OF OTHERS?
NO! THEY REPLACE IT WITH BETTER AND UPDATED MACHINERY. I'M DOING THE PLACE A FAVOR AT THE SAME TIME.
Ach, TURN OFF THE FAUCET AND STOP THE KVETCHING ALREADY.
YOUNG LADY, YOU'RE COMING WITH ME. YOU CAN EXPLAIN FURTHER, AND IF YOU'RE LUCKY, MAYBE I'LL GET SOMEONE TO HELP YOU OUT.

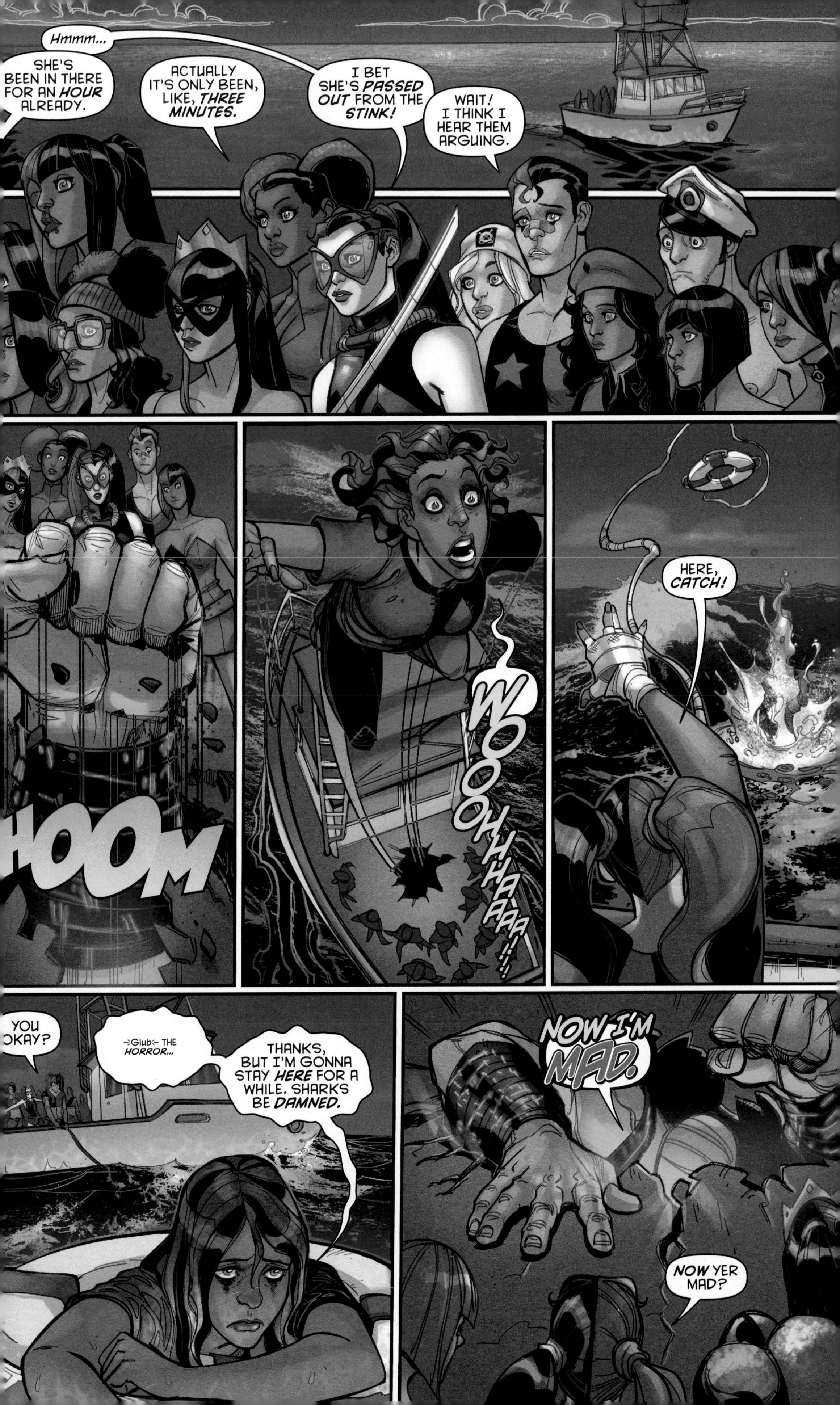
Hmmm...
SHE'S BEEN IN THERE FOR AN HOUR ALREADY.
ACTUALLY IT'S ONLY BEEN, LIKE, THREE MINUTES.
I BET SHE'S PASSED OUT FROM THE STINK!
WAIT! I THINK I HEAR THEM ARGUING.
HOOM
WOOOOHHAAAA!!!
HERE, CATCH!
YOU OKAY?
Glub THE HORROR...
THANKS, BUT I'M GONNA STAY HERE FOR A WHILE. SHARKS BE DAMNED.
NOW I'M MAD.
NOW YER MAD?

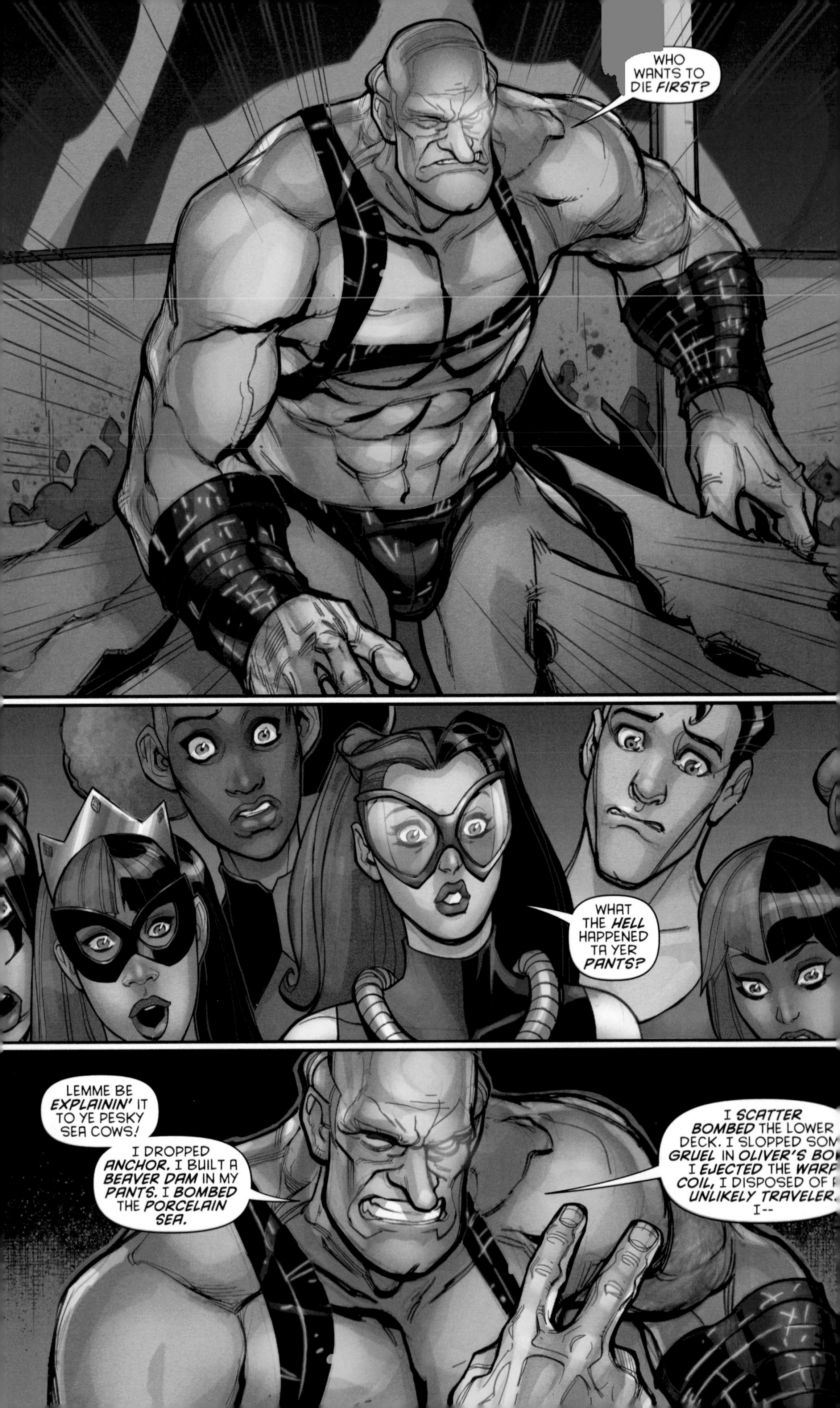
WHO WANTS TO DIE FIRST?
WHAT THE HELL HAPPENED TA YER PANTS?
LEMME BE EXPLAININ' IT TO YE PESKY SEA COWS!
I DROPPED ANCHOR. I BUILT A BEAVER DAM IN MY PANTS. I BOMBED THE PORCELAIN SEA.
I SCATTER BOMBED THE LOWER DECK. I SLOPPED SOM GRUEL IN OLIVER'S BO I EJECTED THE WARP COIL, I DISPOSED OF UNLIKELY TRAVELER. I--

WELL, YOU'RE ABOUT TA MAKE ALL OF US PAINT THE BOAT DECK WITH PIZZA. DO A CHEEKTOWAGA SCREAM.

DRIVE THE *BUICK* TA EUROPE. HAVE AN OUTTA-STOMACH EXPERIENCE.

HOCK A *FURBALL.* CHUCK UP SOME *NEW ENGLAND CLAM CHOWDER.* HOLLER AT THE *ANTS.*

MAKE US *TECHNICOLOR YODEL.* SPEW A *THUNDER-CHUNDER RAINBOW PARFAIT.* WHISTLE *BEER...*

ENOUGH. YOU WANT A *FIGHT,* YOUNG LADIES? THEN LET'S BE *FIGHTIN'.*

TACKLE 'IM, TEAM!

ARRGGHHH!!!!!

WHAT THE--?

BUDDA BUDDA BUDDABUDDA BUDDA

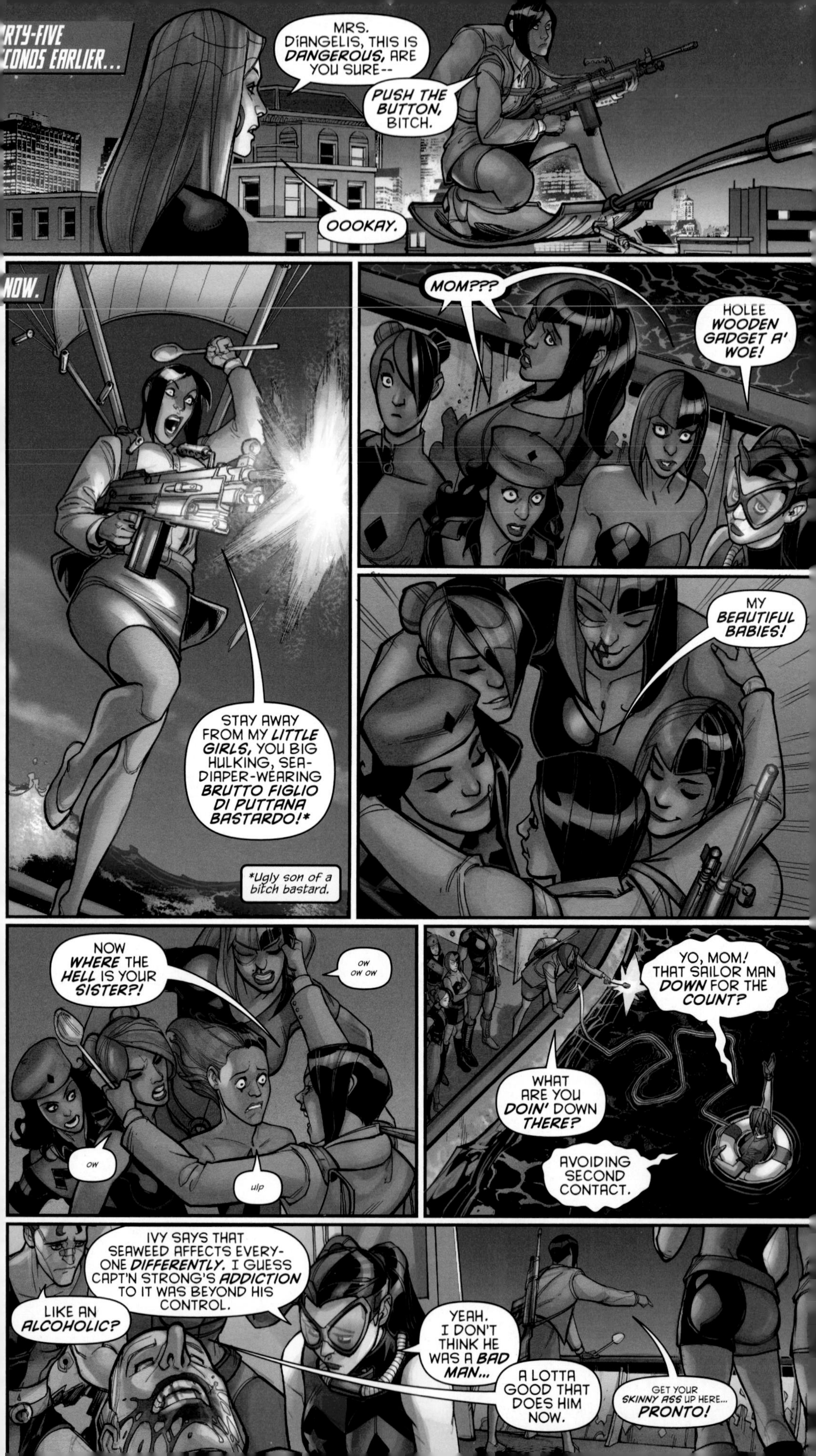
RTY-FIVE
CONDS EARLIER...
MRS. DIANGELIS, THIS IS DANGEROUS, ARE YOU SURE--
PUSH THE BUTTON, BITCH.
OOOKAY.
NOW.
STAY AWAY FROM MY LITTLE GIRLS, YOU BIG HULKING, SEA-DIAPER-WEARING BRUTTO FIGLIO DI PUTTANA BASTARDO!*
*Ugly son of a bitch bastard.
MOM???
HOLEE WOODEN GADGET A' WOE!
MY BEAUTIFUL BABIES!
NOW WHERE THE HELL IS YOUR SISTER?!
OW OW OW
OW
ulp
YO, MOM! THAT SAILOR MAN DOWN FOR THE COUNT?
WHAT ARE YOU DOIN' DOWN THERE?
AVOIDING SECOND CONTACT.
IVY SAYS THAT SEAWEED AFFECTS EVERY-ONE DIFFERENTLY. I GUESS CAPT'N STRONG'S ADDICTION TO IT WAS BEYOND HIS CONTROL.
LIKE AN ALCOHOLIC?
YEAH. I DON'T THINK HE WAS A BAD MAN...
A LOTTA GOOD THAT DOES HIM NOW.
GET YOUR SKINNY ASS UP HERE... PRONTO!

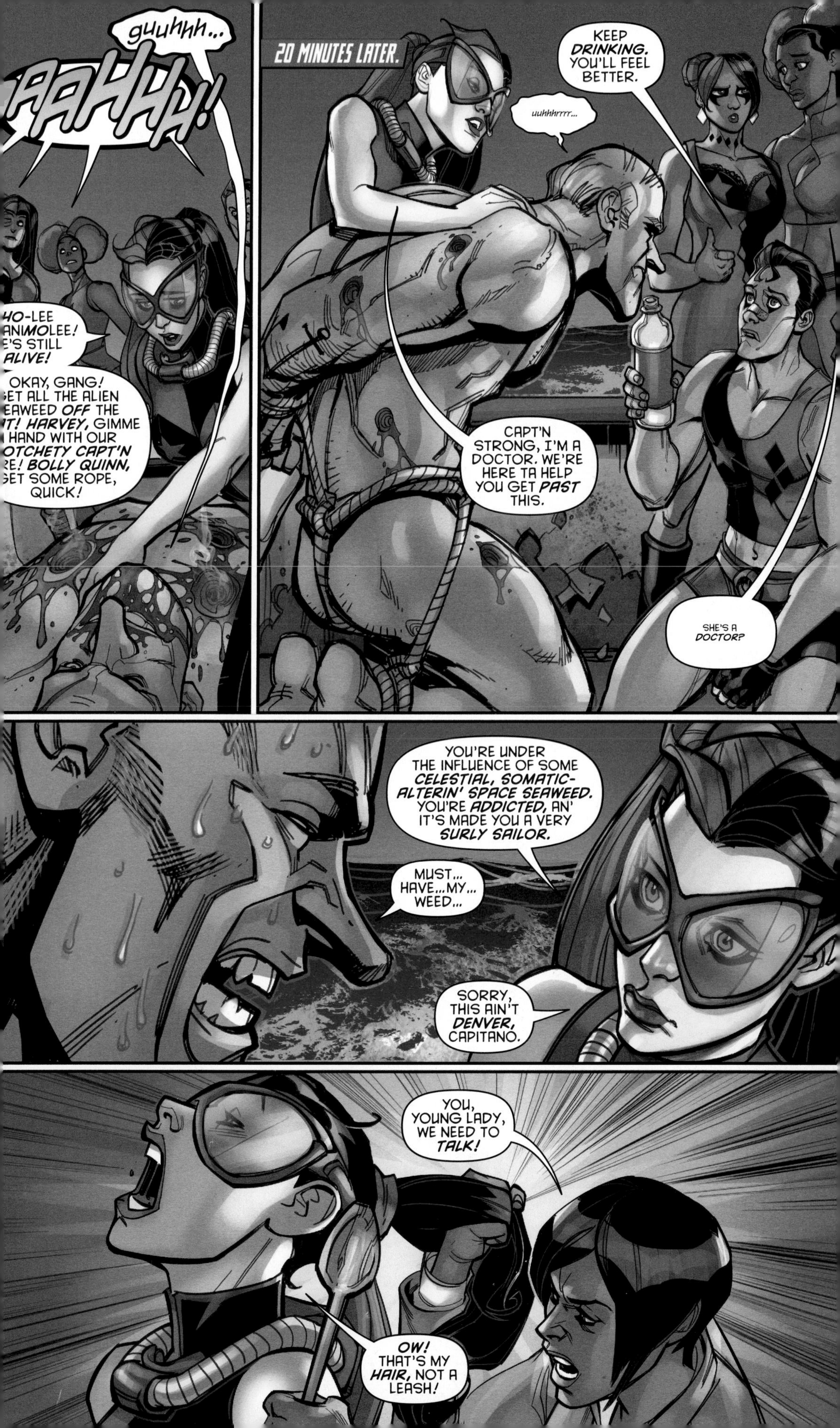
guuhhh...
AAHHHH!
HO-LEE ANIMOLEE! E'S STILL ALIVE!
OKAY, GANG! ET ALL THE ALIEN EAWEED OFF THE T! HARVEY, GIMME HAND WITH OUR OTCHETY CAPT'N E! BOLLY QUINN, ET SOME ROPE, QUICK!
20 MINUTES LATER.
uuhhhrrrr...
KEEP DRINKING. YOU'LL FEEL BETTER.
CAPT'N STRONG, I'M A DOCTOR. WE'RE HERE TA HELP YOU GET PAST THIS.
SHE'S A DOCTOR?
YOU'RE UNDER THE INFLUENCE OF SOME CELESTIAL, SOMATIC-ALTERIN' SPACE SEAWEED. YOU'RE ADDICTED, AN' IT'S MADE YOU A VERY SURLY SAILOR.
MUST... HAVE...MY... WEED...
SORRY, THIS AIN'T DENVER, CAPITANO.
YOU, YOUNG LADY, WE NEED TO TALK!
OW! THAT'S MY HAIR, NOT A LEASH!

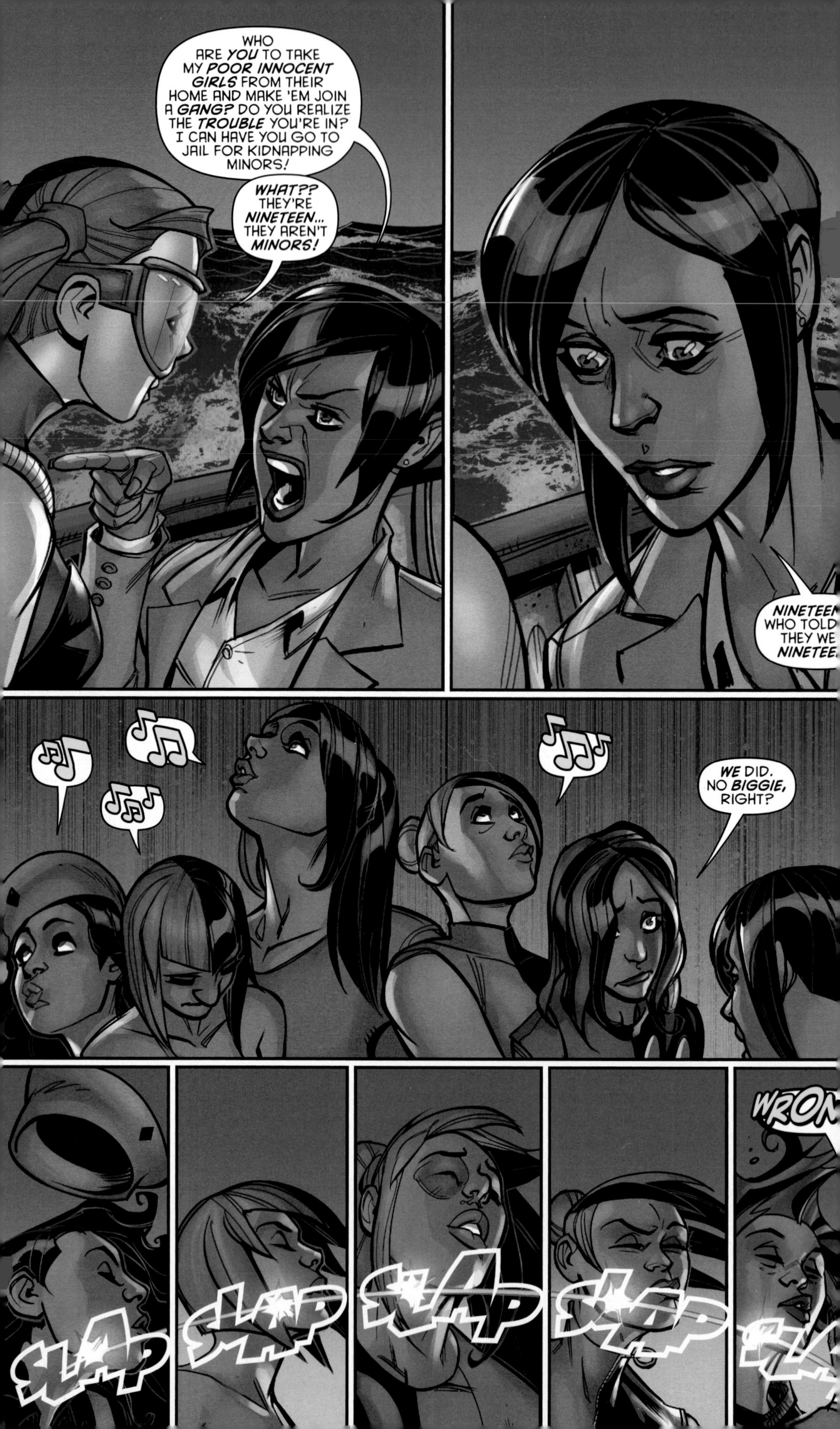
WHO ARE *YOU* TO TAKE MY *POOR INNOCENT GIRLS* FROM THEIR HOME AND MAKE 'EM JOIN A *GANG?* DO YOU REALIZE THE *TROUBLE* YOU'RE IN? I CAN HAVE YOU GO TO JAIL FOR KIDNAPPING MINORS!
WHAT?? THEY'RE *NINETEEN*... THEY AREN'T *MINORS!*
NINETEEN WHO TOLD THEY WE *NINETEE*
WE DID. NO *BIGGIE,* RIGHT?
SLAP
SLAP
SLAP
SLAP
WRON

THESE GIRLS ARE ONLY *FOURTEEN* YEARS OLD!

FOURTEEN YEARS OLD?!?

LY CRAP, I NO IDEA! M *REALLY* SORRY!

SERIOUSLY, I WOULD *NEVER* PUT THE GIRLS IN ANY DANGER IF I KNEW THEIR AGE!

LOOK AT THE BIGGER PICTURE. YER GIRLS JOINED SO WE COULD HELP PEOPLE WITH PROBLEMS. THEY HAVE SUCH *BIG HEARTS* TA GO ALONG WITH THEIR *GIGANTIC* SELVES.

WHAT I'M TRYIN' TA SAY IS, YA BROUGHT UP *GREAT KIDS*, AN' THEY'RE GONNA DO *GREAT THINGS* IN THE FUTURE.

HONEST, MA! HARLEY *SAVED* US! WE WERE ALMOST OUTTA *FOOD*!

YEAH, 'CAUSE *ALEX* HERE EATS *EVERYTHING*!

HEY, YA *SNOOZE*, YA *LOSE*.

AND THE *MATTEO* BOYS CAME SNIFF AROUND, TOO! S *RESCUED* US FRO THEIR *BIG GROP* PAWS!

YAY HARLE

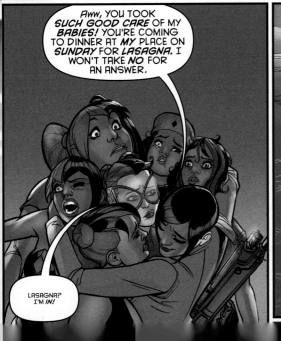

AWW, YOU TOOK *SUCH GOOD CARE* OF MY *BABIES*! YOU'RE COMING TO DINNER AT *MY* PLACE ON *SUNDAY* FOR *LASAGNA*. I WON'T TAKE *NO* FOR AN ANSWER.

LASAGNA? I'M *IN*!

NOW LET'S GET *SKIPPER THE TRIPPER* BACK HOME AN' CALL IT A NIGHT.

SAY, *MIZ DIANGELIS*, I MEAN NO *DISRESPECT*, BUT LOOK AT YOU!

HOW CAN *YOU* HAVE POSSIBLY GIVEN BIRTH TA *THOSE GREAT BIG GIRLS*?

WHAT, IS YER HUSBAND *PAUL BUNYAN* OR SOMETHIN'?

MY HUSBAND IS A *VERY LARGE MAN*, IF THAT'S WHAT YOU'RE ASKING.

MAZEL TOV!

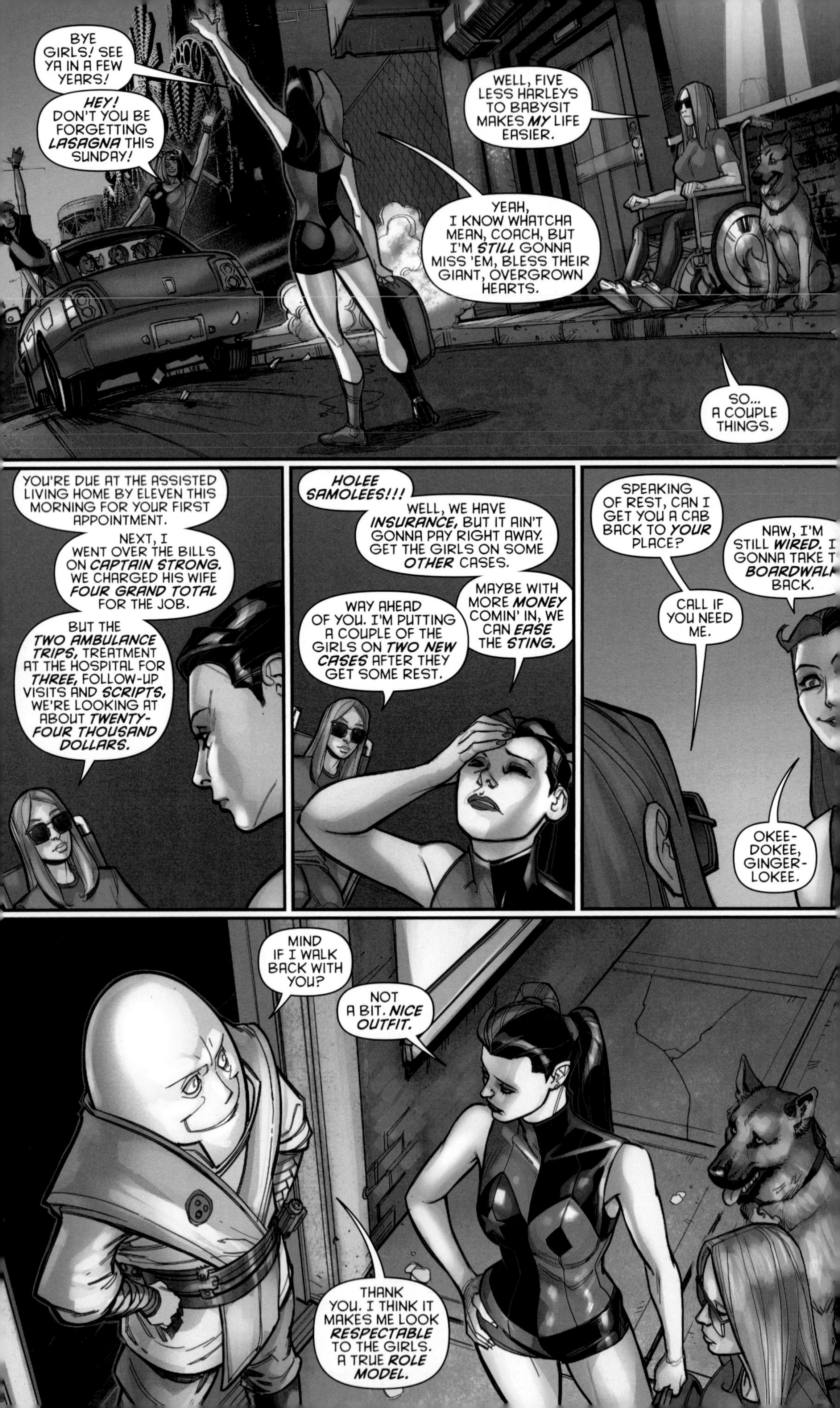

BYE GIRLS! SEE YA IN A FEW YEARS!
HEY! DON'T YOU BE FORGETTING LASAGNA THIS SUNDAY!
WELL, FIVE LESS HARLEYS TO BABYSIT MAKES MY LIFE EASIER.
YEAH, I KNOW WHATCHA MEAN, COACH, BUT I'M STILL GONNA MISS 'EM, BLESS THEIR GIANT, OVERGROWN HEARTS.
SO... A COUPLE THINGS.
YOU'RE DUE AT THE ASSISTED LIVING HOME BY ELEVEN THIS MORNING FOR YOUR FIRST APPOINTMENT.
NEXT, I WENT OVER THE BILLS ON CAPTAIN STRONG. WE CHARGED HIS WIFE FOUR GRAND TOTAL FOR THE JOB.
BUT THE TWO AMBULANCE TRIPS, TREATMENT AT THE HOSPITAL FOR THREE, FOLLOW-UP VISITS AND SCRIPTS, WE'RE LOOKING AT ABOUT TWENTY-FOUR THOUSAND DOLLARS.
HOLEE SAMOLEES!!!
WELL, WE HAVE INSURANCE, BUT IT AIN'T GONNA PAY RIGHT AWAY. GET THE GIRLS ON SOME OTHER CASES.
WAY AHEAD OF YOU. I'M PUTTING A COUPLE OF THE GIRLS ON TWO NEW CASES AFTER THEY GET SOME REST.
MAYBE WITH MORE MONEY COMIN' IN, WE CAN EASE THE STING.
SPEAKING OF REST, CAN I GET YOU A CAB BACK TO YOUR PLACE?
NAW, I'M STILL WIRED. I GONNA TAKE T BOARDWAL BACK.
CALL IF YOU NEED ME.
OKEE-DOKEE, GINGER-LOKEE.
MIND IF I WALK BACK WITH YOU?
NOT A BIT. NICE OUTFIT.
THANK YOU. I THINK IT MAKES ME LOOK RESPECTABLE TO THE GIRLS. A TRUE ROLE MODEL.

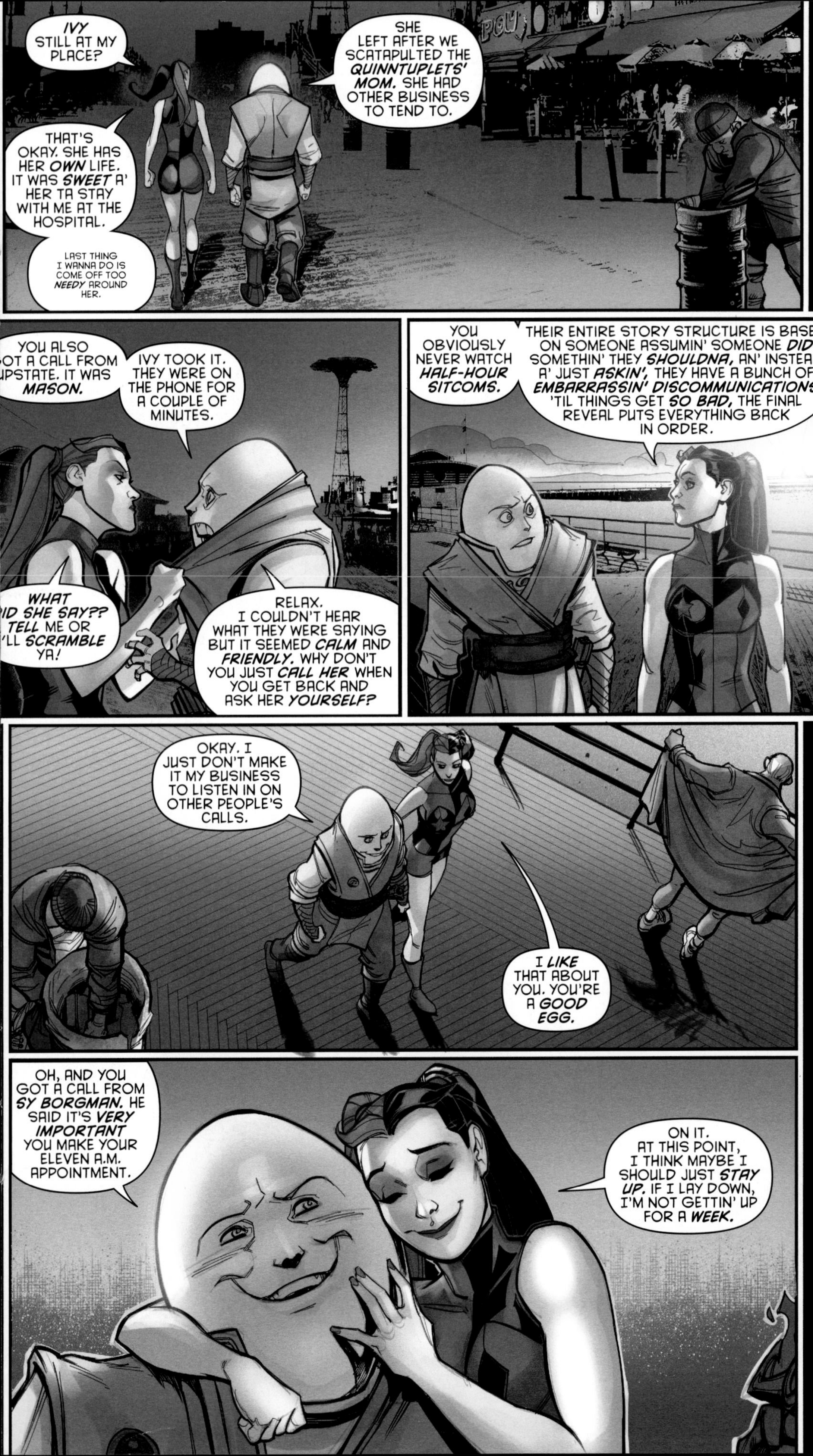

IVY STILL AT MY PLACE?
SHE LEFT AFTER WE SCATAPULTED THE QUINNTUPLETS' MOM. SHE HAD OTHER BUSINESS TO TEND TO.
THAT'S OKAY. SHE HAS HER OWN LIFE. IT WAS SWEET A' HER TA STAY WITH ME AT THE HOSPITAL.
LAST THING I WANNA DO IS COME OFF TOO NEEDY AROUND HER.
YOU ALSO GOT A CALL FROM UPSTATE. IT WAS MASON.
IVY TOOK IT. THEY WERE ON THE PHONE FOR A COUPLE OF MINUTES.
WHAT DID SHE SAY?? TELL ME OR I'LL SCRAMBLE YA!
RELAX. I COULDN'T HEAR WHAT THEY WERE SAYING BUT IT SEEMED CALM AND FRIENDLY. WHY DON'T YOU JUST CALL HER WHEN YOU GET BACK AND ASK HER YOURSELF?
YOU OBVIOUSLY NEVER WATCH HALF-HOUR SITCOMS.
THEIR ENTIRE STORY STRUCTURE IS BASED ON SOMEONE ASSUMIN' SOMEONE DID SOMETHIN' THEY SHOULDNA, AN' INSTEAD A' JUST ASKIN', THEY HAVE A BUNCH OF EMBARRASSIN' DISCOMMUNICATIONS 'TIL THINGS GET SO BAD, THE FINAL REVEAL PUTS EVERYTHING BACK IN ORDER.
OKAY. I JUST DON'T MAKE IT MY BUSINESS TO LISTEN IN ON OTHER PEOPLE'S CALLS.
I LIKE THAT ABOUT YOU. YOU'RE A GOOD EGG.
OH, AND YOU GOT A CALL FROM SY BORGMAN. HE SAID IT'S VERY IMPORTANT YOU MAKE YOUR ELEVEN A.M. APPOINTMENT.
ON IT. AT THIS POINT, I THINK MAYBE I SHOULD JUST STAY UP. IF I LAY DOWN, I'M NOT GETTIN' UP FOR A WEEK.

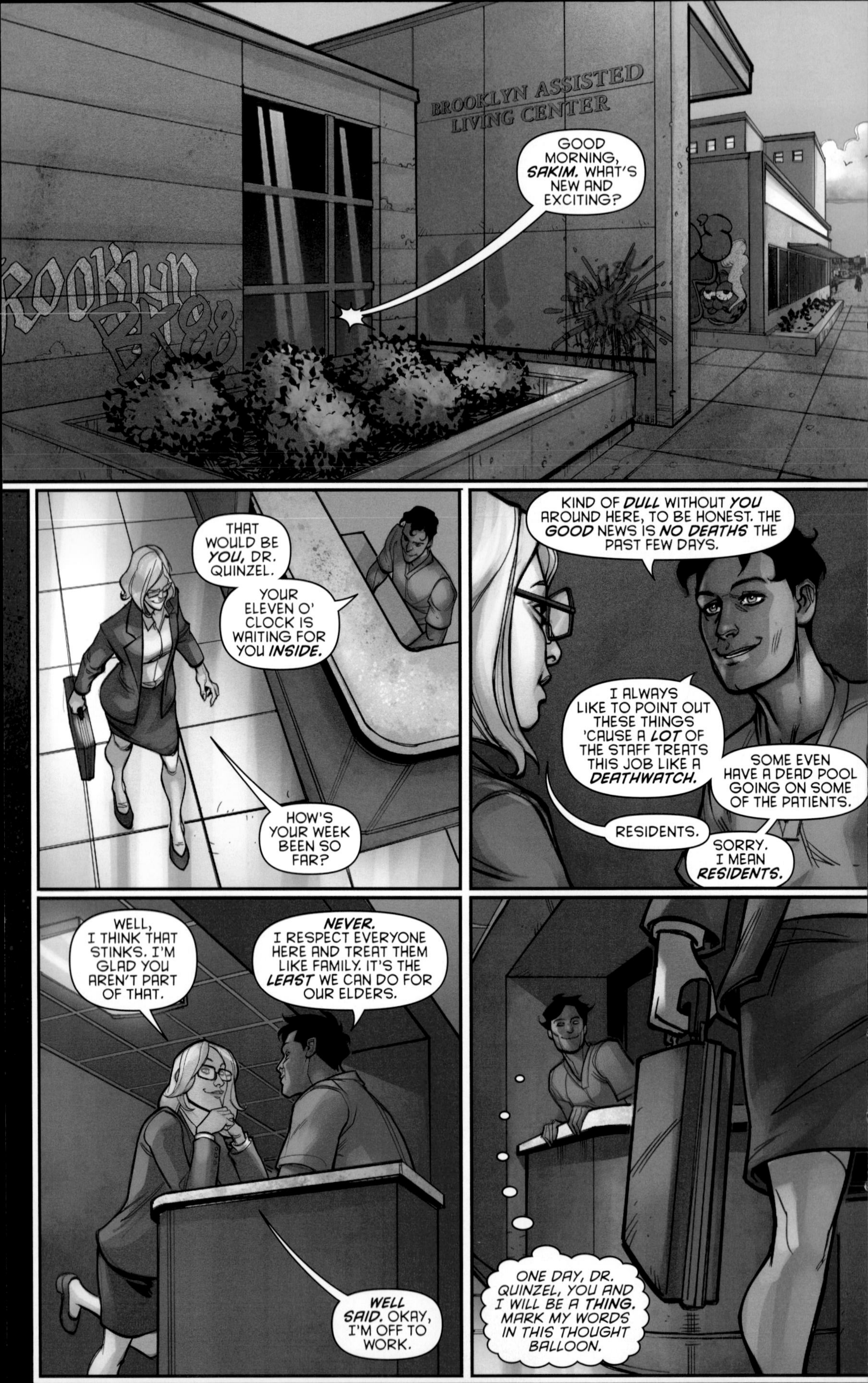
BROOKLYN ASSISTED LIVING CENTER
GOOD MORNING, SAKIM. WHAT'S NEW AND EXCITING?
THAT WOULD BE YOU, DR. QUINZEL.
YOUR ELEVEN O' CLOCK IS WAITING FOR YOU INSIDE.
HOW'S YOUR WEEK BEEN SO FAR?
KIND OF DULL WITHOUT YOU AROUND HERE, TO BE HONEST. THE GOOD NEWS IS NO DEATHS THE PAST FEW DAYS.
I ALWAYS LIKE TO POINT OUT THESE THINGS 'CAUSE A LOT OF THE STAFF TREATS THIS JOB LIKE A DEATHWATCH.
SOME EVEN HAVE A DEAD POOL GOING ON SOME OF THE PATIENTS.
RESIDENTS.
SORRY. I MEAN RESIDENTS.
WELL, I THINK THAT STINKS. I'M GLAD YOU AREN'T PART OF THAT.
NEVER. I RESPECT EVERYONE HERE AND TREAT THEM LIKE FAMILY. IT'S THE LEAST WE CAN DO FOR OUR ELDERS.
WELL SAID. OKAY, I'M OFF TO WORK.
ONE DAY, DR. QUINZEL, YOU AND I WILL BE A THING. MARK MY WORDS IN THIS THOUGHT BALLOON.

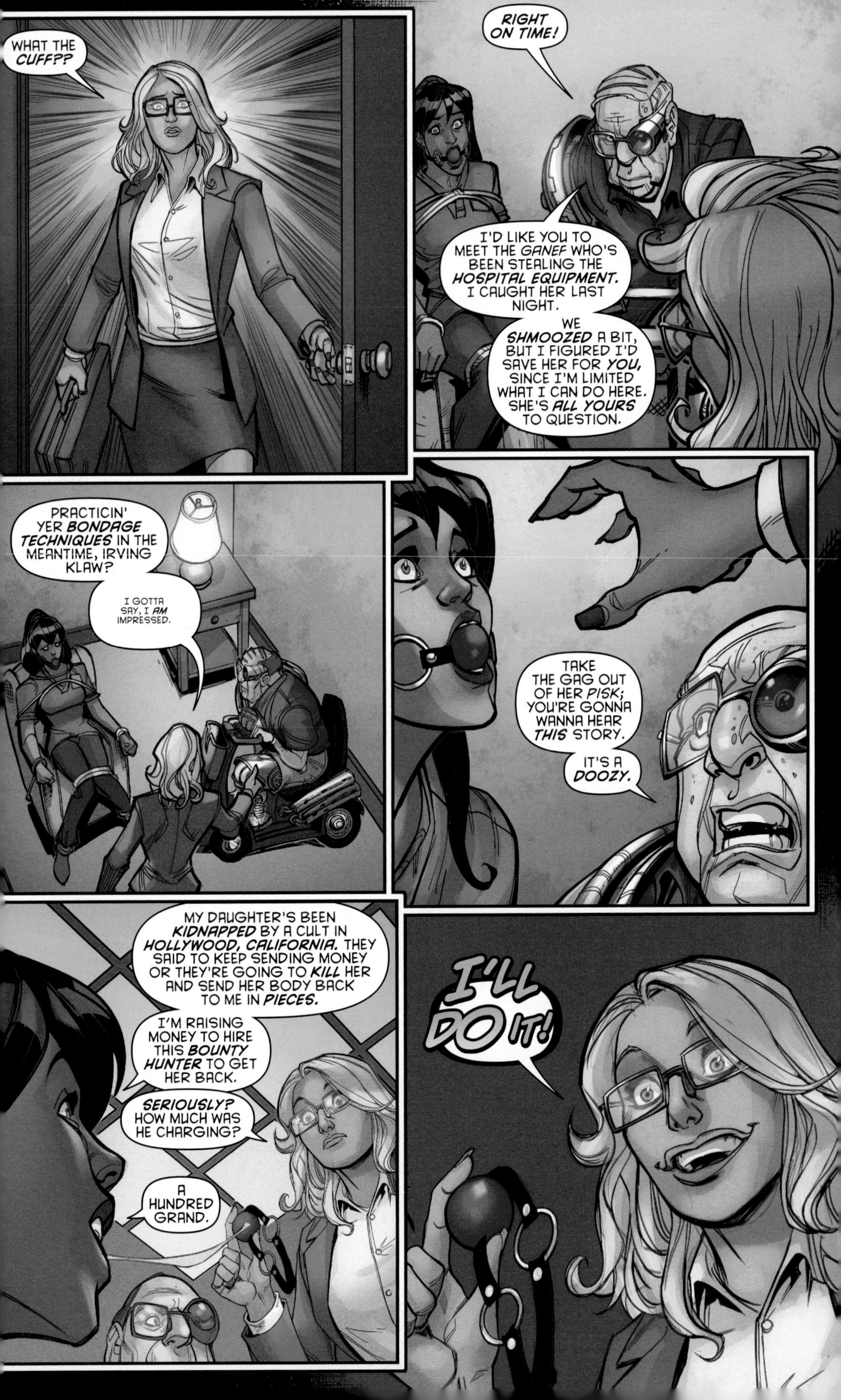
WHAT THE *CUFF??*
RIGHT ON TIME!
I'D LIKE YOU TO MEET THE *GANEF* WHO'S BEEN STEALING THE ***HOSPITAL EQUIPMENT.*** I CAUGHT HER LAST NIGHT.
WE ***SHMOOZED*** A BIT, BUT I FIGURED I'D SAVE HER FOR ***YOU,*** SINCE I'M LIMITED WHAT I CAN DO HERE. SHE'S ***ALL YOURS*** TO QUESTION.
PRACTICIN' YER ***BONDAGE TECHNIQUES*** IN THE MEANTIME, IRVING KLAW?
I GOTTA SAY, I ***AM*** IMPRESSED.
TAKE THE GAG OUT OF HER *PISK*; YOU'RE GONNA WANNA HEAR ***THIS*** STORY.
IT'S A ***DOOZY.***
MY DAUGHTER'S BEEN ***KIDNAPPED*** BY A CULT IN ***HOLLYWOOD, CALIFORNIA.*** THEY SAID TO KEEP SENDING MONEY OR THEY'RE GOING TO ***KILL*** HER AND SEND HER BODY BACK TO ME IN ***PIECES.***
I'M RAISING MONEY TO HIRE THIS ***BOUNTY HUNTER*** TO GET HER BACK.
SERIOUSLY? HOW MUCH WAS HE CHARGING?
A HUNDRED GRAND.
I'LL DO IT!

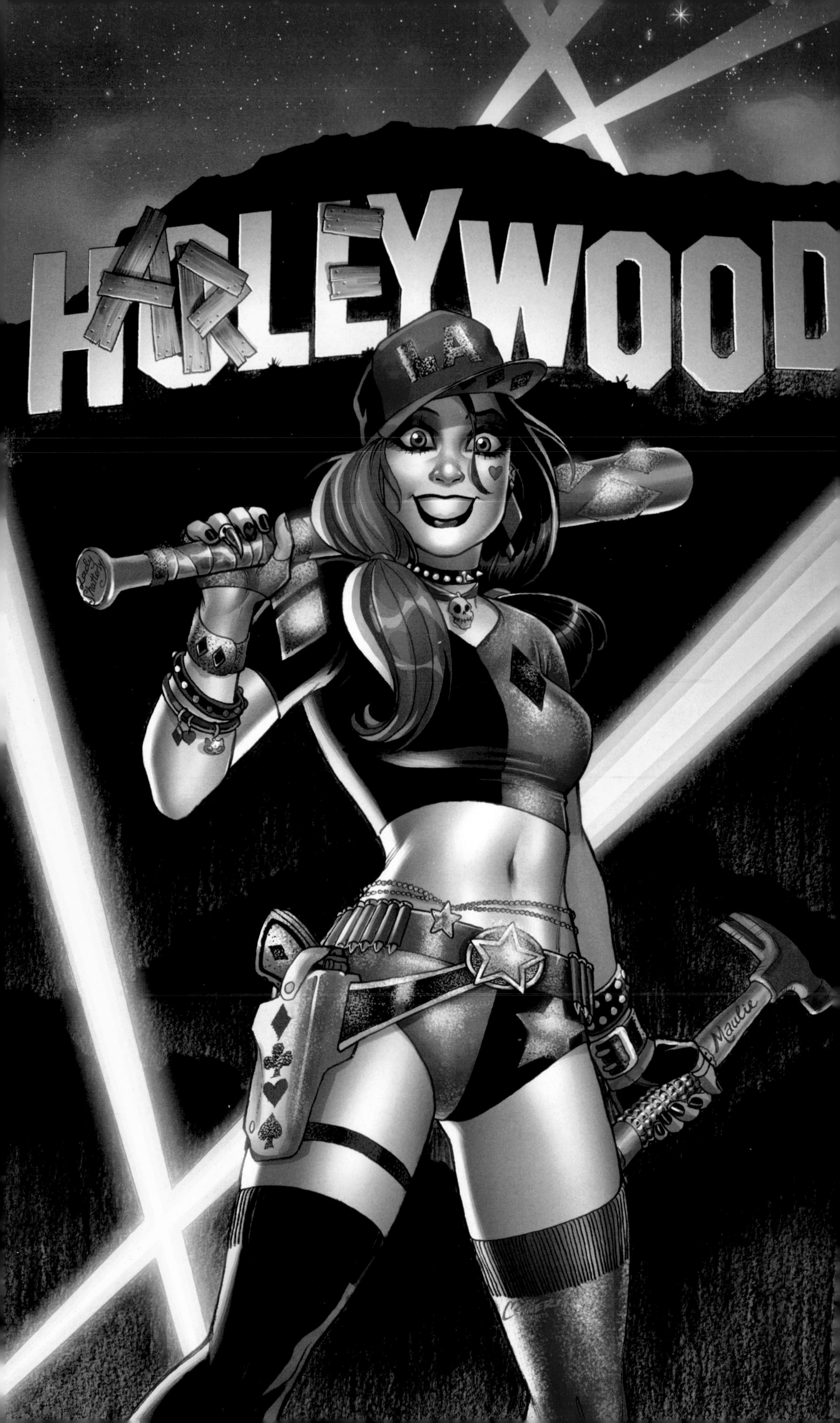
HARLEYWOOD
LA
Lady Shattery
Maulie

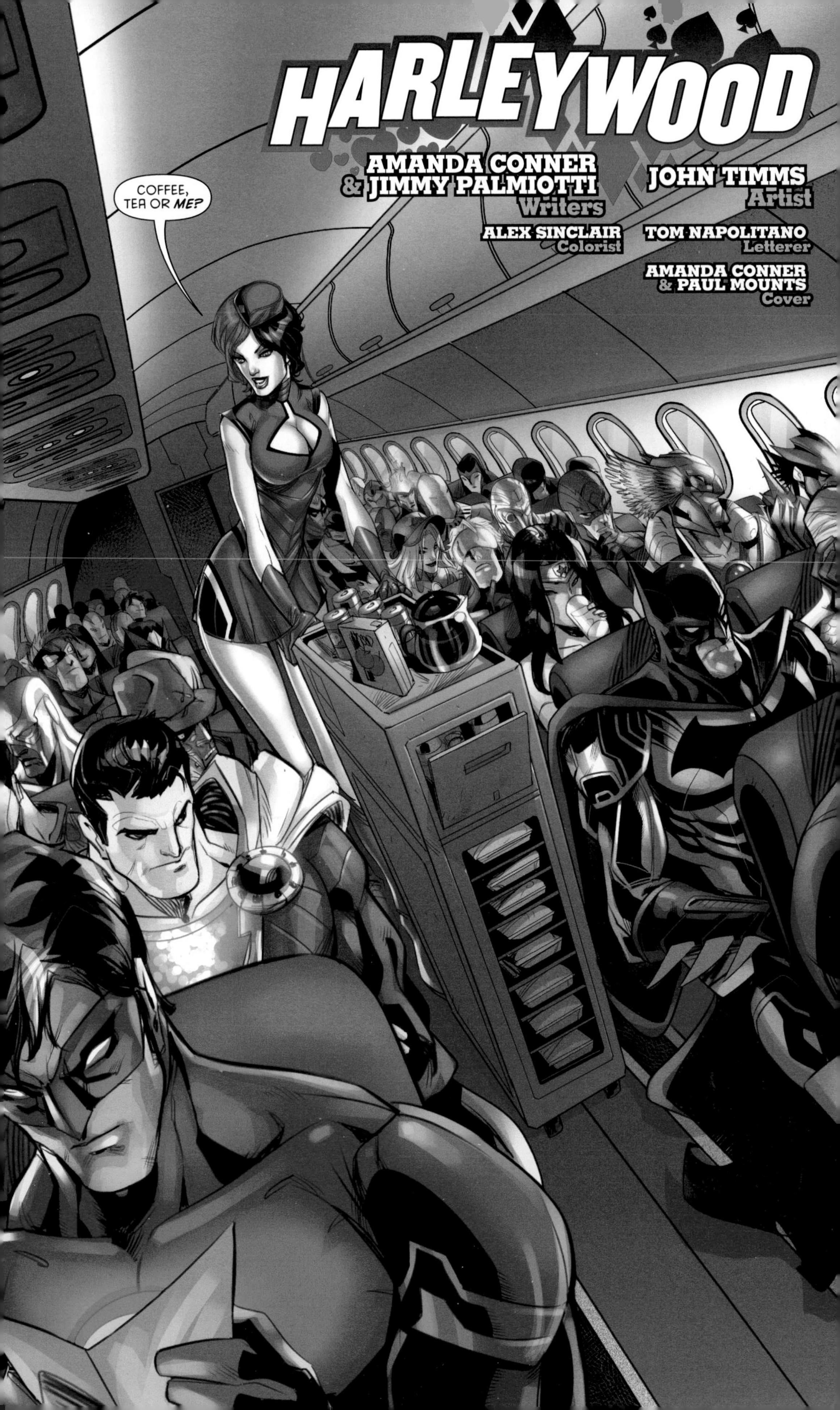

HARLEYWOOD
AMANDA CONNER & JIMMY PALMIOTTI Writers
JOHN TIMMS Artist
ALEX SINCLAIR Colorist
TOM NAPOLITANO Letterer
AMANDA CONNER & PAUL MOUNTS Cover
COFFEE, TEA OR ME?

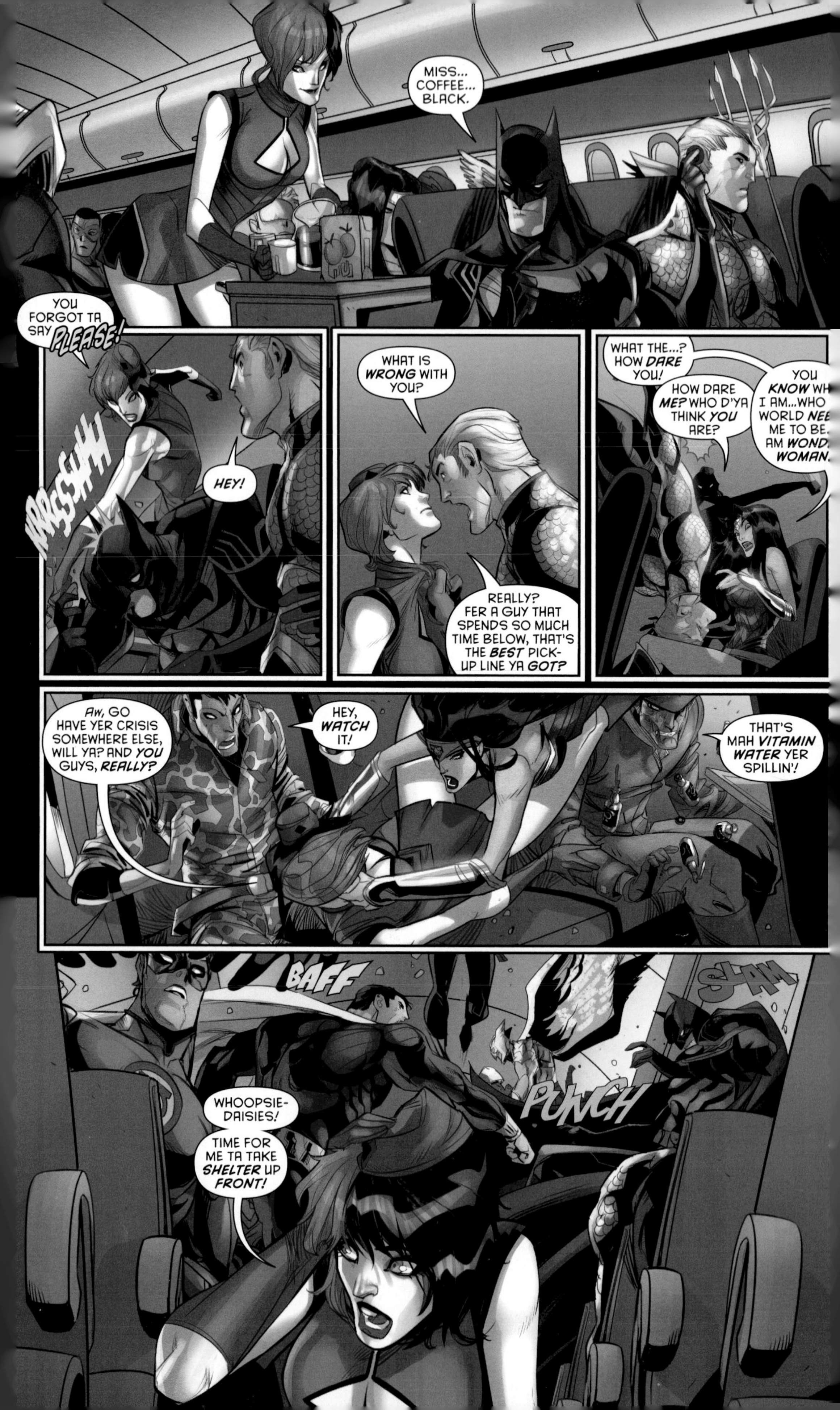

MISS... COFFEE... BLACK.
YOU FORGOT TA SAY PLEASE!
KRRSSHHH
HEY!
WHAT IS WRONG WITH YOU?
REALLY? FER A GUY THAT SPENDS SO MUCH TIME BELOW, THAT'S THE BEST PICK-UP LINE YA GOT?
WHAT THE...? HOW DARE YOU!
HOW DARE ME? WHO D'YA THINK YOU ARE?
AW, GO HAVE YER CRISIS SOMEWHERE ELSE, WILL YA? AND YOU GUYS, REALLY?
HEY, WATCH IT!
THAT'S MAH VITAMIN WATER YER SPILLIN'!
BAFF
SLAM
PUNCH
WHOOPSIE-DAISIES!
TIME FOR ME TA TAKE SHELTER UP FRONT!

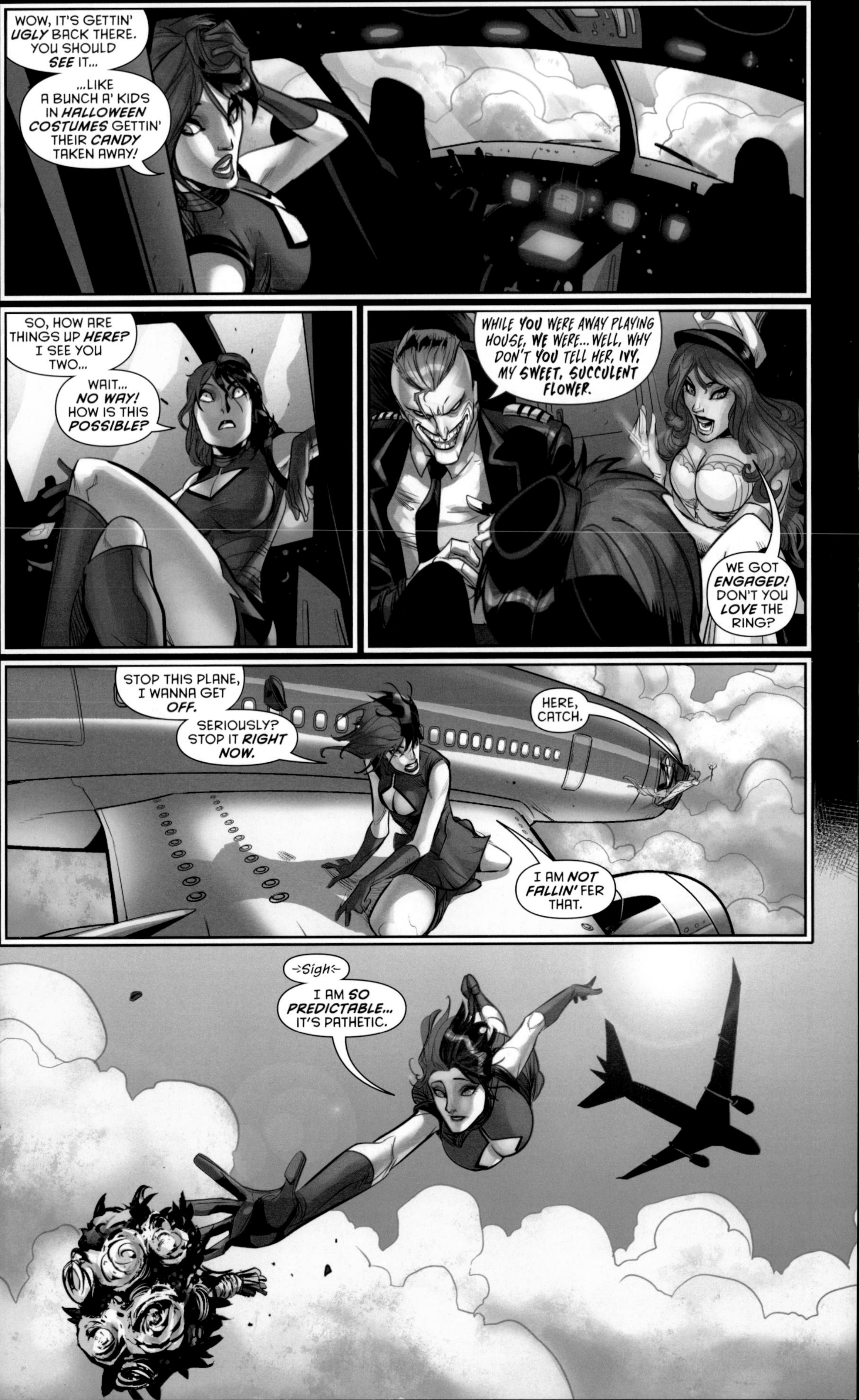
WOW, IT'S GETTIN' UGLY BACK THERE. YOU SHOULD SEE IT...
...LIKE A BUNCH A' KIDS IN HALLOWEEN COSTUMES GETTIN' THEIR CANDY TAKEN AWAY!
SO, HOW ARE THINGS UP HERE? I SEE YOU TWO...
WAIT... NO WAY! HOW IS THIS POSSIBLE?
WHILE YOU WERE AWAY PLAYING HOUSE, WE WERE... WELL, WHY DON'T YOU TELL HER, IVY, MY SWEET, SUCCULENT FLOWER.
WE GOT ENGAGED! DON'T YOU LOVE THE RING?
STOP THIS PLANE, I WANNA GET OFF.
SERIOUSLY? STOP IT RIGHT NOW.
HERE, CATCH.
I AM NOT FALLIN' FER THAT.
Sigh
I AM SO PREDICTABLE... IT'S PATHETIC.

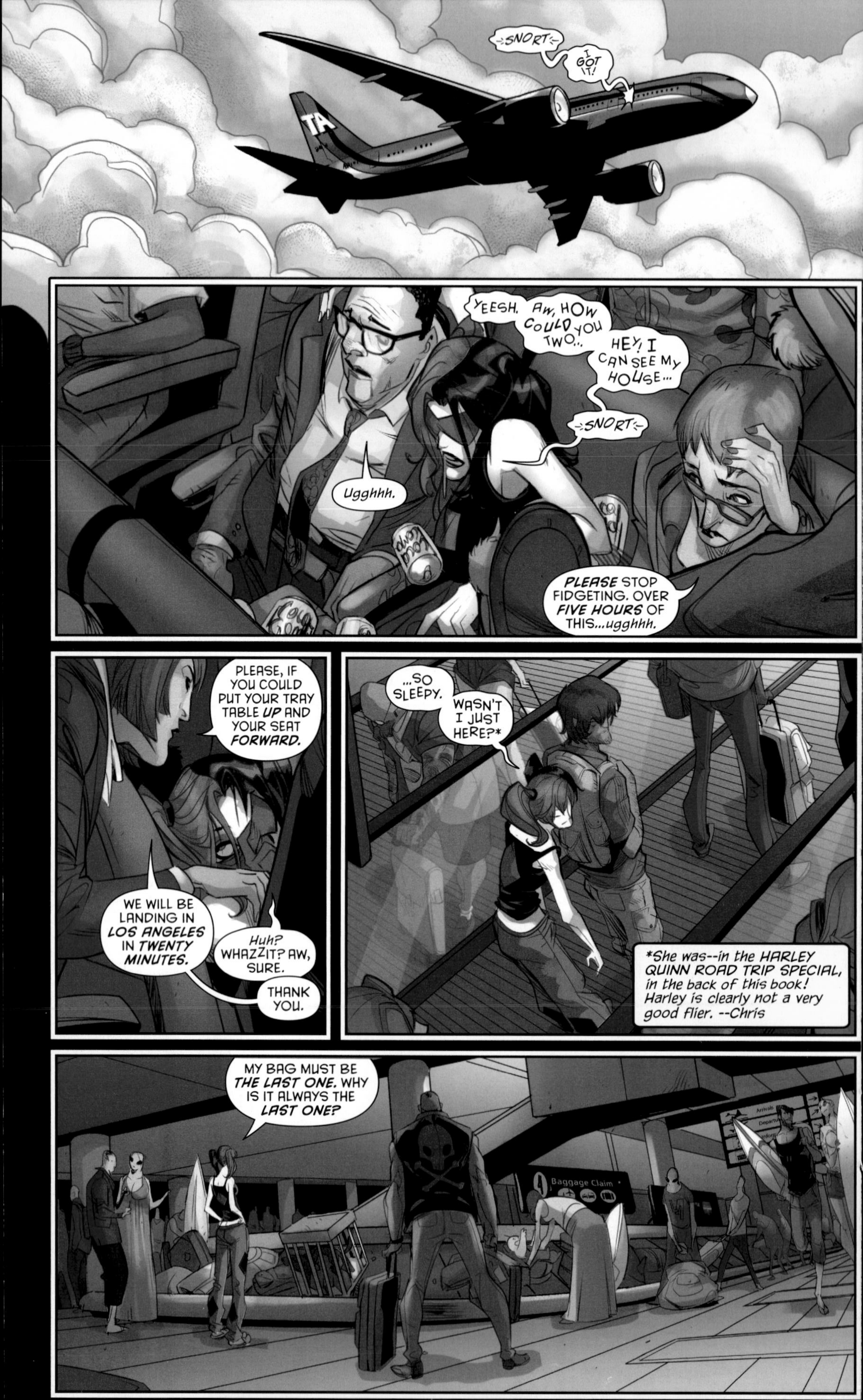

SNORT
I GOT IT!
YEESH.
AW, HOW COULD YOU TWO...
HEY! I CAN SEE MY HOUSE...
SNORT
Ugghhh.
PLEASE STOP FIDGETING. OVER FIVE HOURS OF THIS...ugghhh.
PLEASE, IF YOU COULD PUT YOUR TRAY TABLE UP AND YOUR SEAT FORWARD.
WE WILL BE LANDING IN LOS ANGELES IN TWENTY MINUTES.
Huh? WHAZZIT? AW, SURE.
THANK YOU.
...SO SLEEPY.
WASN'T I JUST HERE?*
*She was--in the HARLEY QUINN ROAD TRIP SPECIAL, in the back of this book! Harley is clearly not a very good flier. --Chris
MY BAG MUST BE THE LAST ONE. WHY IS IT ALWAYS THE LAST ONE?
Baggage Claim

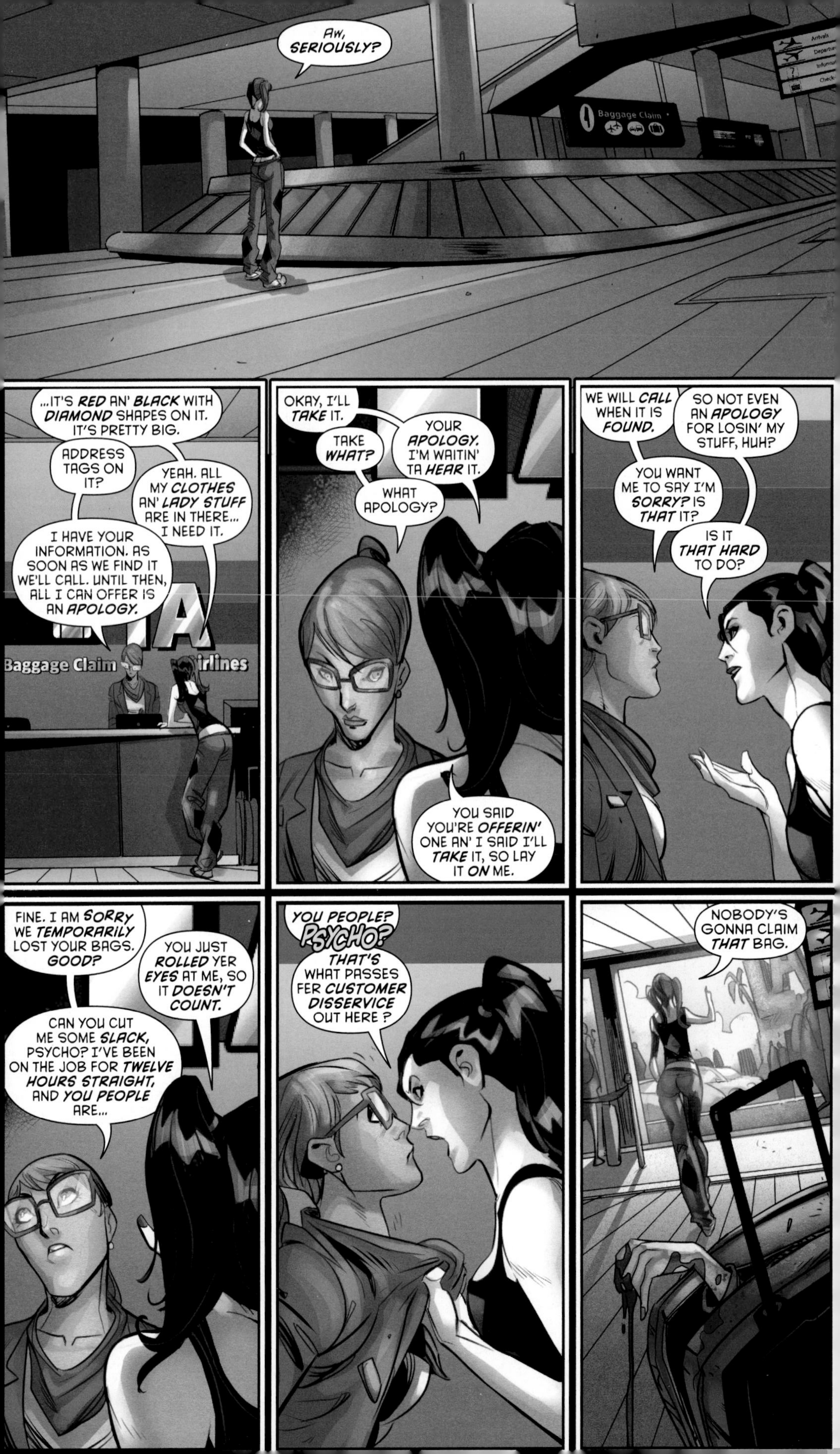

AW, SERIOUSLY?
Baggage Claim
...IT'S RED AN' BLACK WITH DIAMOND SHAPES ON IT. IT'S PRETTY BIG.
ADDRESS TAGS ON IT?
YEAH. ALL MY CLOTHES AN' LADY STUFF ARE IN THERE... I NEED IT.
I HAVE YOUR INFORMATION. AS SOON AS WE FIND IT WE'LL CALL. UNTIL THEN, ALL I CAN OFFER IS AN APOLOGY.
Baggage Claim
OKAY, I'LL TAKE IT.
TAKE WHAT?
YOUR APOLOGY. I'M WAITIN' TA HEAR IT.
WHAT APOLOGY?
YOU SAID YOU'RE OFFERIN' ONE AN' I SAID I'LL TAKE IT, SO LAY IT ON ME.
WE WILL CALL WHEN IT IS FOUND.
SO NOT EVEN AN APOLOGY FOR LOSIN' MY STUFF, HUH?
YOU WANT ME TO SAY I'M SORRY? IS THAT IT?
IS IT THAT HARD TO DO?
FINE. I AM SORRY WE TEMPORARILY LOST YOUR BAGS. GOOD?
YOU JUST ROLLED YER EYES AT ME, SO IT DOESN'T COUNT.
CAN YOU CUT ME SOME SLACK, PSYCHO? I'VE BEEN ON THE JOB FOR TWELVE HOURS STRAIGHT, AND YOU PEOPLE ARE...
YOU PEOPLE? PSYCHO? THAT'S WHAT PASSES FER CUSTOMER DISSERVICE OUT HERE ?
NOBODY'S GONNA CLAIM THAT BAG.

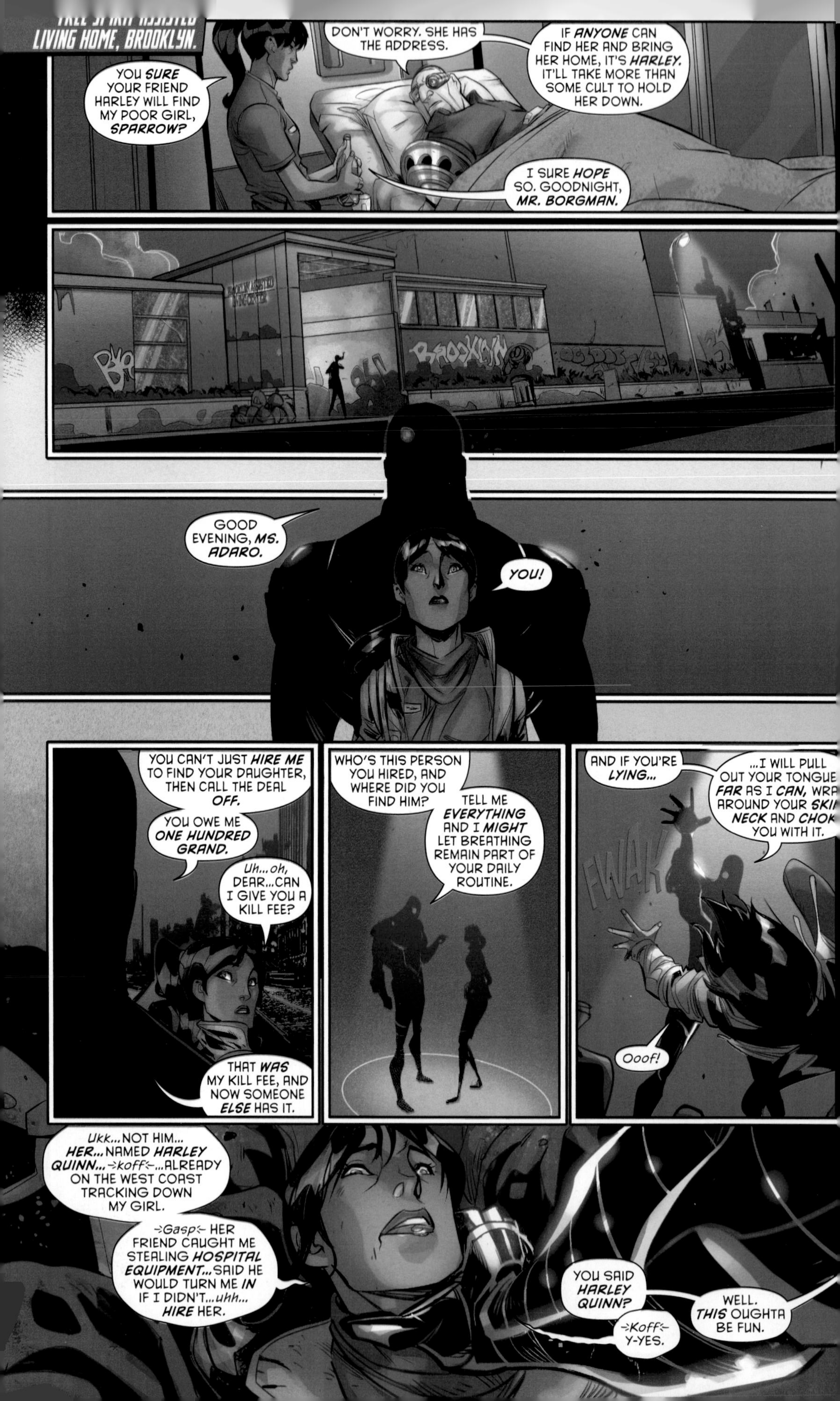

LIVING HOME, BROOKLYN.
YOU SURE YOUR FRIEND HARLEY WILL FIND MY POOR GIRL, SPARROW?
DON'T WORRY. SHE HAS THE ADDRESS.
IF ANYONE CAN FIND HER AND BRING HER HOME, IT'S HARLEY. IT'LL TAKE MORE THAN SOME CULT TO HOLD HER DOWN.
I SURE HOPE SO. GOODNIGHT, MR. BORGMAN.
GOOD EVENING, MS. ADARO.
YOU!
YOU CAN'T JUST HIRE ME TO FIND YOUR DAUGHTER, THEN CALL THE DEAL OFF.
YOU OWE ME ONE HUNDRED GRAND.
Uh...oh, DEAR...CAN I GIVE YOU A KILL FEE?
THAT WAS MY KILL FEE, AND NOW SOMEONE ELSE HAS IT.
WHO'S THIS PERSON YOU HIRED, AND WHERE DID YOU FIND HIM?
TELL ME EVERYTHING AND I MIGHT LET BREATHING REMAIN PART OF YOUR DAILY ROUTINE.
AND IF YOU'RE LYING...
...I WILL PULL OUT YOUR TONGUE FAR AS I CAN, WRA AROUND YOUR SKI NECK AND CHOK YOU WITH IT.
FWAK
Ooof!
Ukk...NOT HIM... HER...NAMED HARLEY QUINN...›koff‹...ALREADY ON THE WEST COAST TRACKING DOWN MY GIRL.
›Gasp‹ HER FRIEND CAUGHT ME STEALING HOSPITAL EQUIPMENT...SAID HE WOULD TURN ME IN IF I DIDN'T...uhh... HIRE HER.
YOU SAID HARLEY QUINN?
›Koff‹ Y-YES.
WELL. THIS OUGHTA BE FUN.

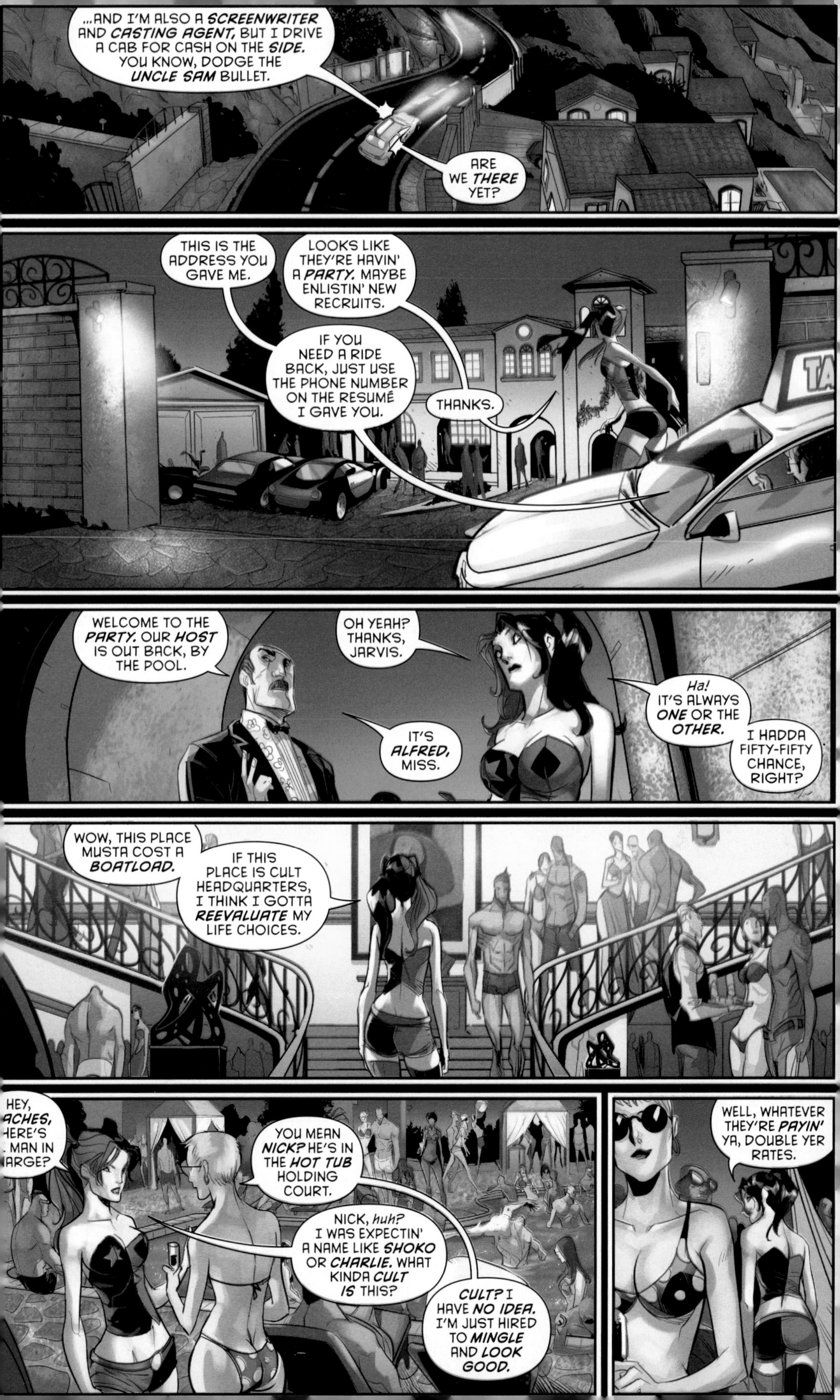

...AND I'M ALSO A SCREENWRITER AND CASTING AGENT, BUT I DRIVE A CAB FOR CASH ON THE SIDE. YOU KNOW, DODGE THE UNCLE SAM BULLET.
ARE WE THERE YET?
THIS IS THE ADDRESS YOU GAVE ME.
LOOKS LIKE THEY'RE HAVIN' A PARTY. MAYBE ENLISTIN' NEW RECRUITS.
IF YOU NEED A RIDE BACK, JUST USE THE PHONE NUMBER ON THE RESUMÉ I GAVE YOU.
THANKS.
WELCOME TO THE PARTY. OUR HOST IS OUT BACK, BY THE POOL.
OH YEAH? THANKS, JARVIS.
IT'S ALFRED, MISS.
Ha! IT'S ALWAYS ONE OR THE OTHER.
I HADDA FIFTY-FIFTY CHANCE, RIGHT?
WOW, THIS PLACE MUSTA COST A BOATLOAD.
IF THIS PLACE IS CULT HEADQUARTERS, I THINK I GOTTA REEVALUATE MY LIFE CHOICES.
HEY, ACHES, HERE'S MAN IN ARGE?
YOU MEAN NICK? HE'S IN THE HOT TUB HOLDING COURT.
NICK, huh? I WAS EXPECTIN' A NAME LIKE SHOKO OR CHARLIE. WHAT KINDA CULT IS THIS?
CULT? I HAVE NO IDEA. I'M JUST HIRED TO MINGLE AND LOOK GOOD.
WELL, WHATEVER THEY'RE PAYIN' YA, DOUBLE YER RATES.

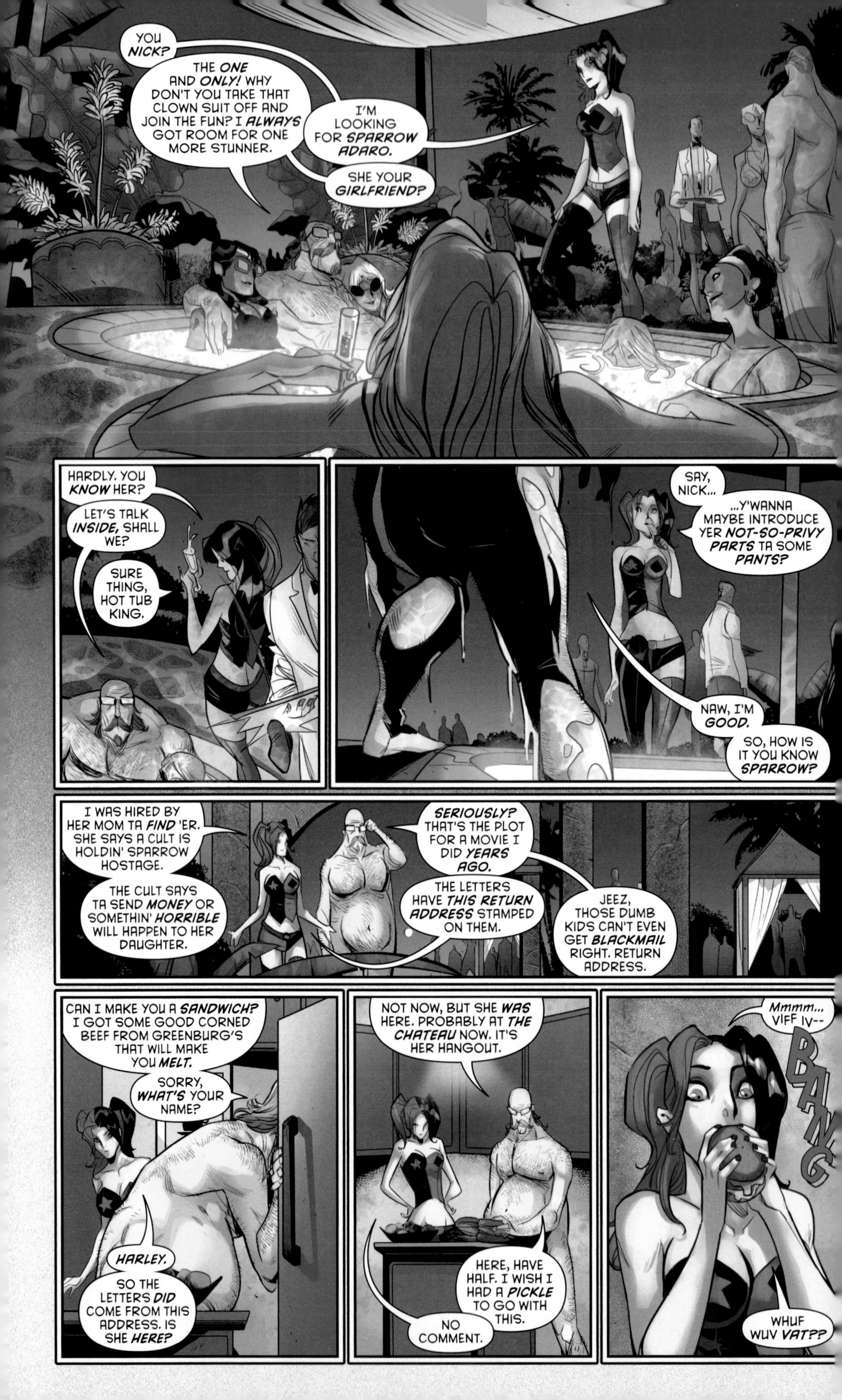
YOU NICK?
THE ONE AND ONLY! WHY DON'T YOU TAKE THAT CLOWN SUIT OFF AND JOIN THE FUN? I ALWAYS GOT ROOM FOR ONE MORE STUNNER.
I'M LOOKING FOR SPARROW ADARO.
SHE YOUR GIRLFRIEND?
HARDLY. YOU KNOW HER?
LET'S TALK INSIDE, SHALL WE?
SURE THING, HOT TUB KING.
SAY, NICK...
...Y'WANNA MAYBE INTRODUCE YER NOT-SO-PRIVY PARTS TA SOME PANTS?
NAW, I'M GOOD.
SO, HOW IS IT YOU KNOW SPARROW?
I WAS HIRED BY HER MOM TA FIND 'ER. SHE SAYS A CULT IS HOLDIN' SPARROW HOSTAGE.
THE CULT SAYS TA SEND MONEY OR SOMETHIN' HORRIBLE WILL HAPPEN TO HER DAUGHTER.
SERIOUSLY? THAT'S THE PLOT FOR A MOVIE I DID YEARS AGO.
THE LETTERS HAVE THIS RETURN ADDRESS STAMPED ON THEM.
JEEZ, THOSE DUMB KIDS CAN'T EVEN GET BLACKMAIL RIGHT. RETURN ADDRESS.
CAN I MAKE YOU A SANDWICH? I GOT SOME GOOD CORNED BEEF FROM GREENBURG'S THAT WILL MAKE YOU MELT.
SORRY, WHAT'S YOUR NAME?
HARLEY.
SO THE LETTERS DID COME FROM THIS ADDRESS. IS SHE HERE?
NOT NOW, BUT SHE WAS HERE. PROBABLY AT THE CHATEAU NOW. IT'S HER HANGOUT.
HERE, HAVE HALF. I WISH I HAD A PICKLE TO GO WITH THIS.
NO COMMENT.
Mmmm... VIFF IV--
BANG
WHUF WUV VAT??

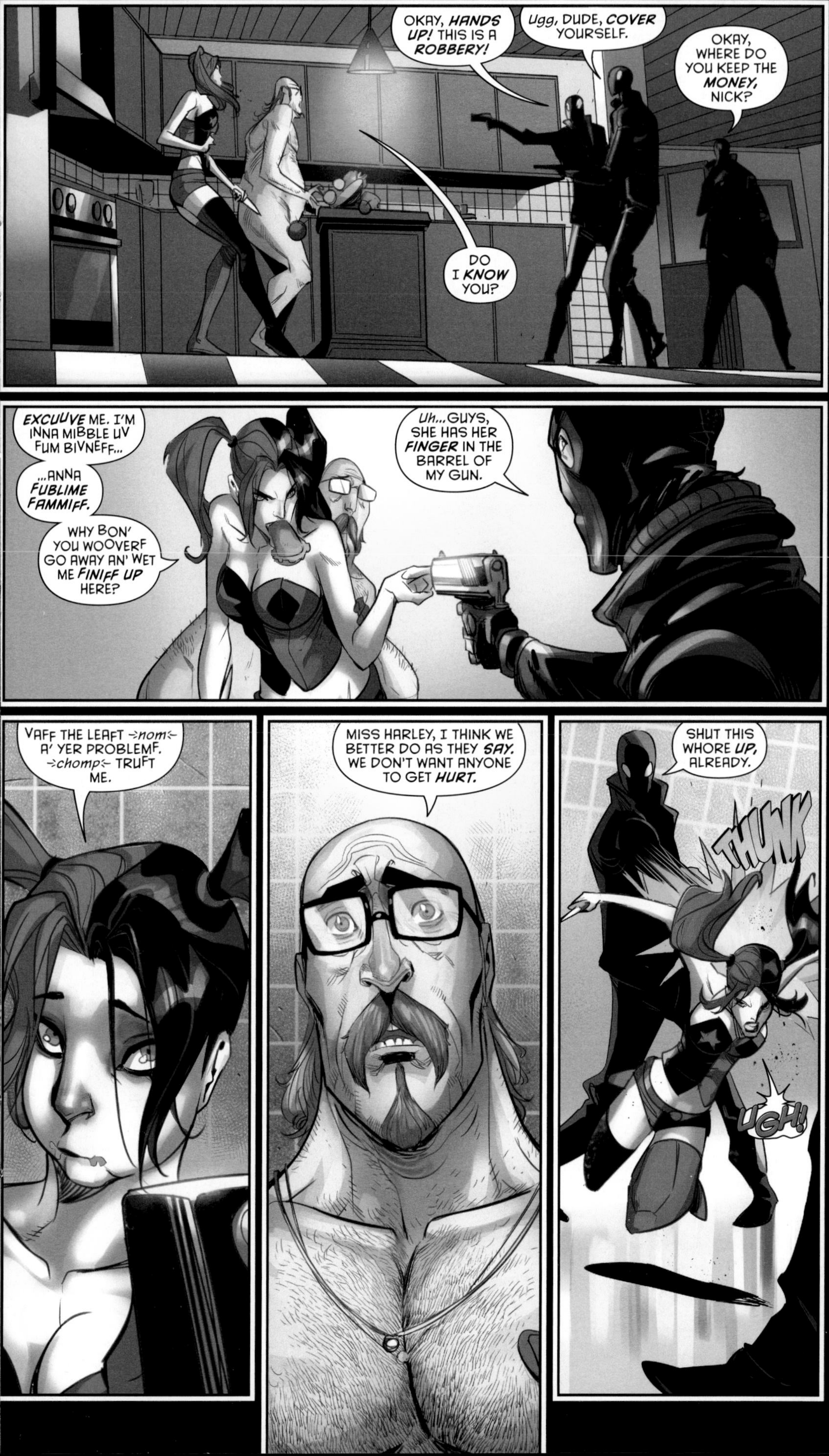
OKAY, HANDS UP! THIS IS A ROBBERY!
Ugg, DUDE, COVER YOURSELF.
OKAY, WHERE DO YOU KEEP THE MONEY, NICK?
DO I KNOW YOU?
EXCUUVE ME. I'M INNA MIBBLE UV FUM BIVNEFF...
...ANNA FUBLIME FAMMIFF.
WHY BON' YOU WOOVERF GO AWAY AN' WET ME FINIFF UP HERE?
Uh...GUYS, SHE HAS HER FINGER IN THE BARREL OF MY GUN.
VAFF THE LEAFT ⇒nom⇐ A' YER PROBLEMF. ⇒chomp⇐ TRUFT ME.
MISS HARLEY, I THINK WE BETTER DO AS THEY SAY. WE DON'T WANT ANYONE TO GET HURT.
SHUT THIS WHORE UP, ALREADY.
THUNK
UGH!

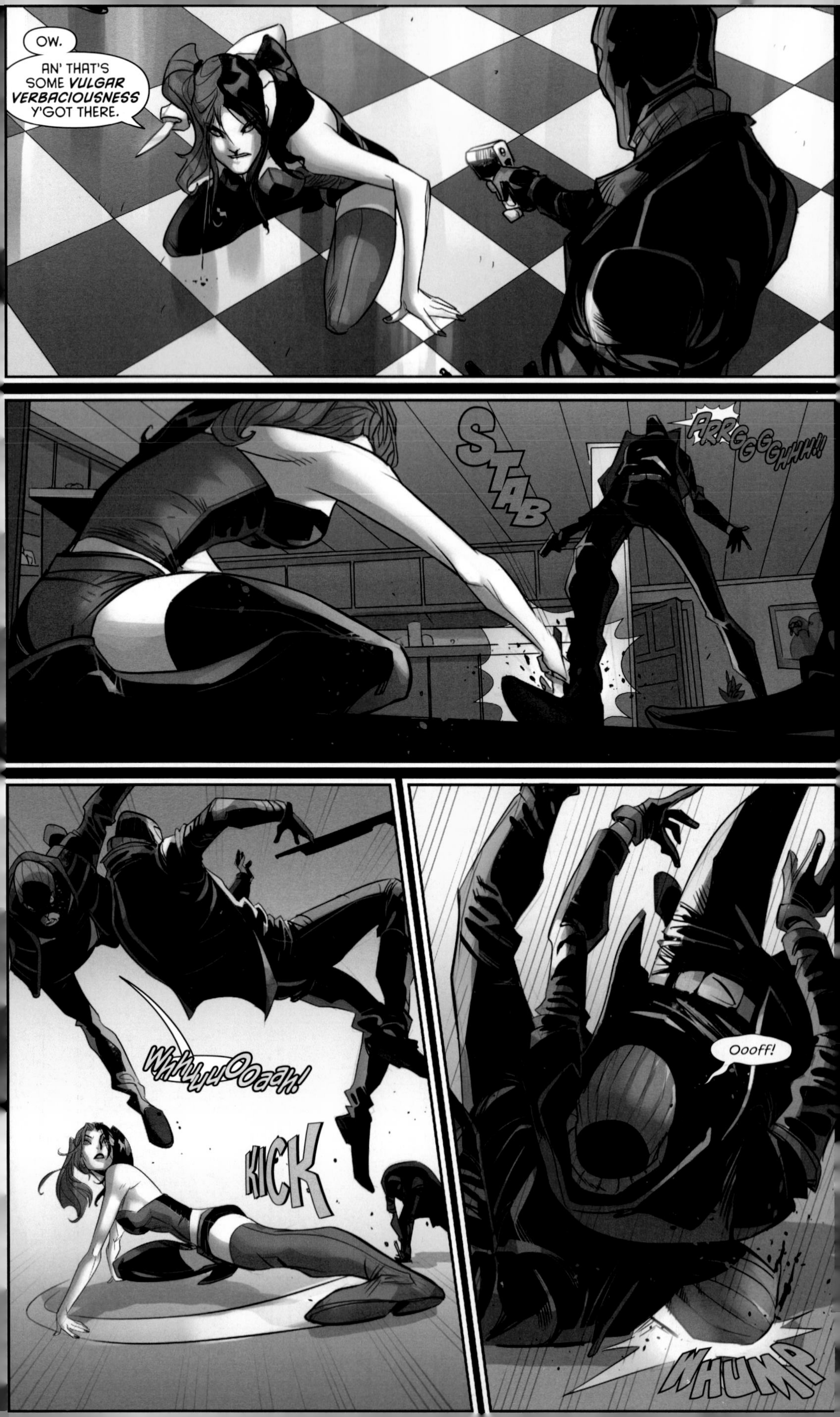
OW.
AN' THAT'S SOME VULGAR VERBACIOUSNESS Y'GOT THERE.
STAB
ARRGGGGHHH!!
WHHUUUOOAAH!
KICK
Oooff!
WHUMP

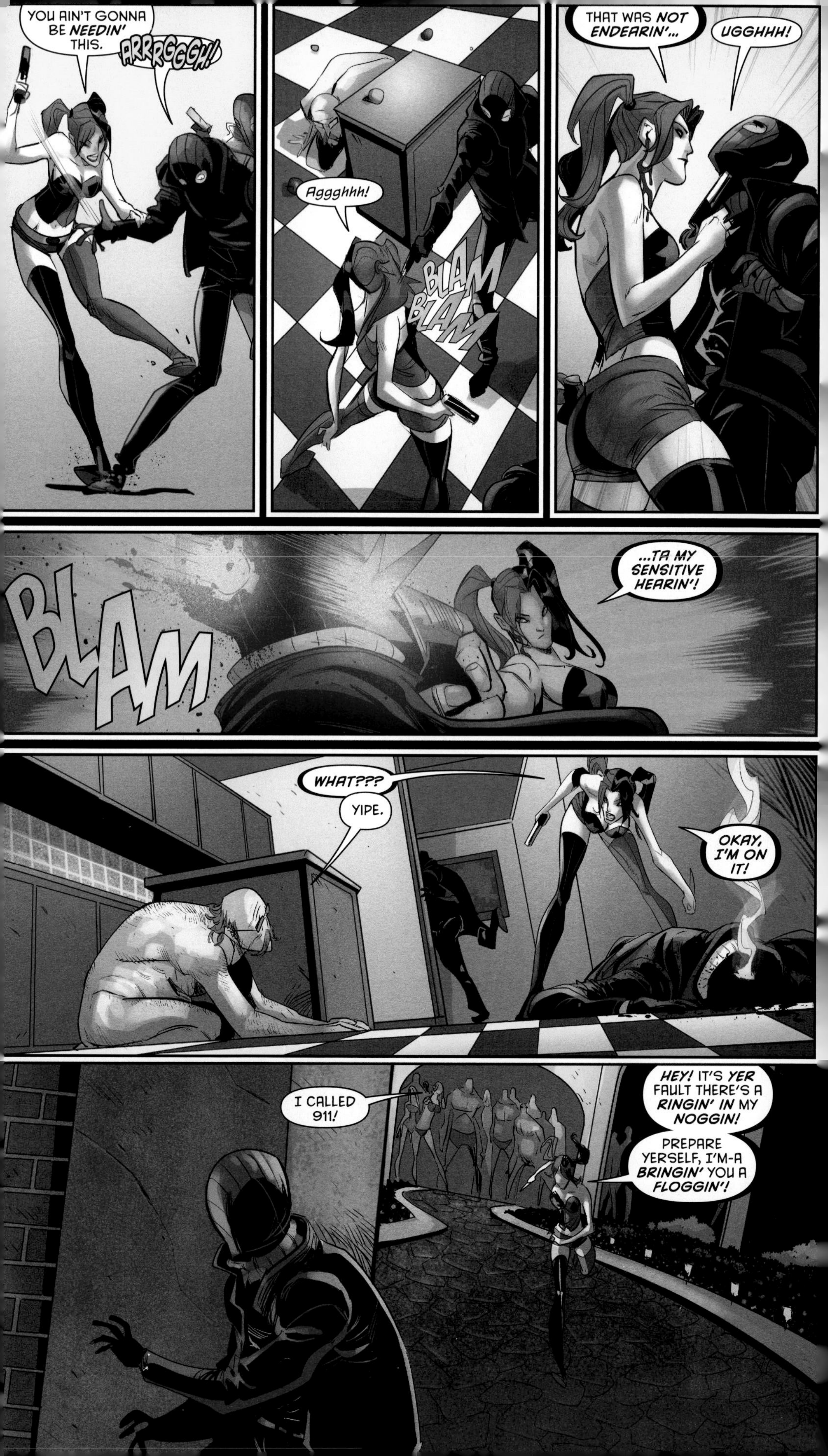

YOU AIN'T GONNA BE NEEDIN' THIS.
ARRRGGGH!
Aggghhh!
BLAM BLAM
THAT WAS NOT ENDEARIN'...
UGGHHH!
BLAM
...TA MY SENSITIVE HEARIN'!
WHAT???
YIPE.
OKAY, I'M ON IT!
I CALLED 911!
HEY! IT'S YER FAULT THERE'S A RINGIN' IN MY NOGGIN!
PREPARE YERSELF, I'M-A BRINGIN' YOU A FLOGGIN'!

STAY *AWAY* FROM ME! I'M JUST AN *ACTOR*!!!

EVERYONE OUT HERE IS!

SCREECH

VA-THUMP

AAA-AAAA-AAA...

SPLUTCH

FREEZE OR WE SHOOT!

HO!

FROZEN! ALL CHILLED OUT!

DROP THE KNIFE!

Oh, *THIS* LITTLE THING?

HAPPY NOW?

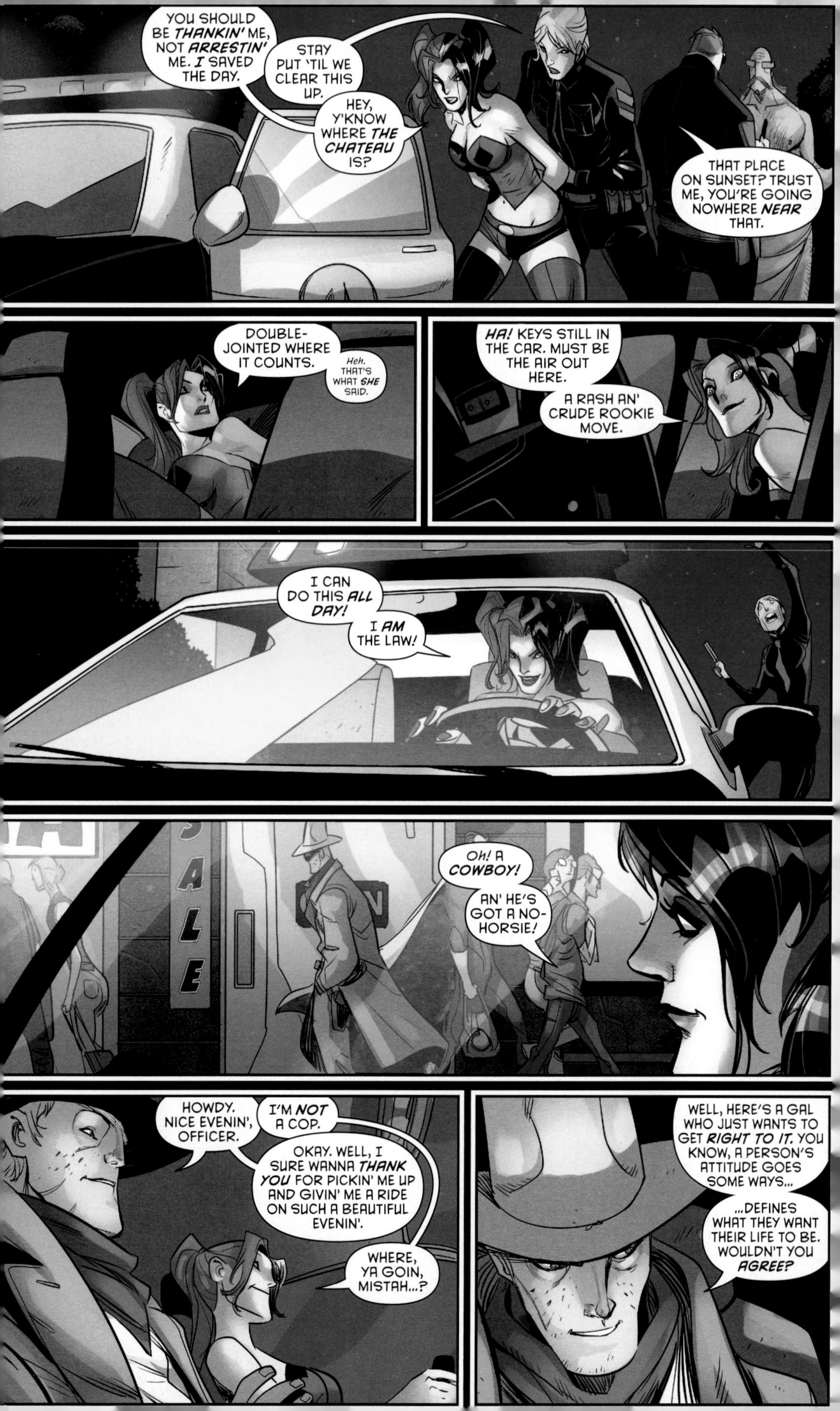
YOU SHOULD BE THANKIN' ME, NOT ARRESTIN' ME. I SAVED THE DAY.
STAY PUT 'TIL WE CLEAR THIS UP.
HEY, Y'KNOW WHERE THE CHATEAU IS?
THAT PLACE ON SUNSET? TRUST ME, YOU'RE GOING NOWHERE NEAR THAT.
DOUBLE-JOINTED WHERE IT COUNTS.
Heh. THAT'S WHAT SHE SAID.
HA! KEYS STILL IN THE CAR. MUST BE THE AIR OUT HERE.
A RASH AN' CRUDE ROOKIE MOVE.
I CAN DO THIS ALL DAY!
I AM THE LAW!
SALE
Oh! A COWBOY!
AN' HE'S GOT A NO-HORSIE!
HOWDY. NICE EVENIN', OFFICER.
I'M NOT A COP.
OKAY. WELL, I SURE WANNA THANK YOU FOR PICKIN' ME UP AND GIVIN' ME A RIDE ON SUCH A BEAUTIFUL EVENIN'.
WHERE, YA GOIN, MISTAH...?
WELL, HERE'S A GAL WHO JUST WANTS TO GET RIGHT TO IT. YOU KNOW, A PERSON'S ATTITUDE GOES SOME WAYS...
...DEFINES WHAT THEY WANT THEIR LIFE TO BE. WOULDN'T YOU AGREE?

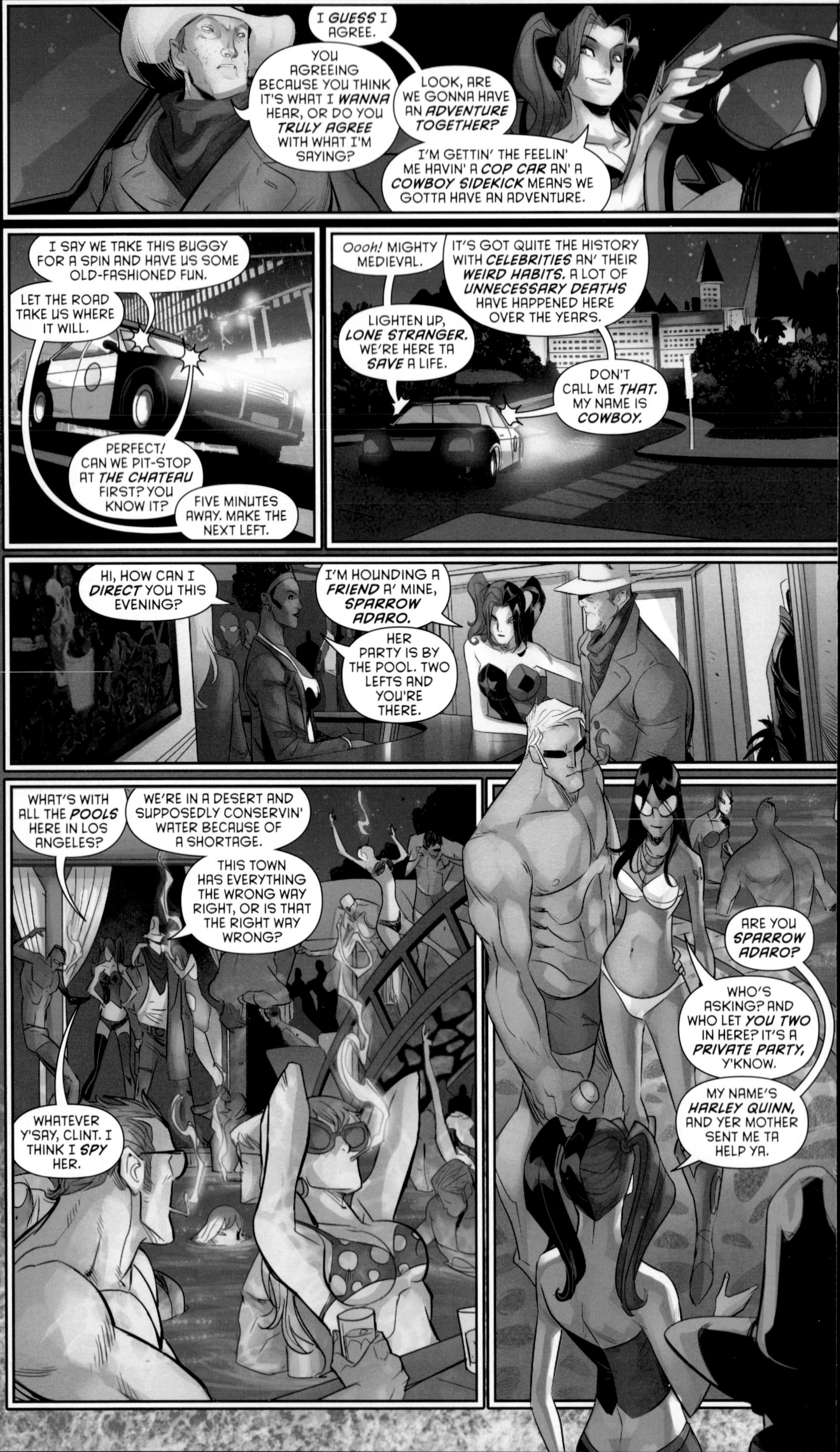

I GUESS I AGREE.
YOU AGREEING BECAUSE YOU THINK IT'S WHAT I WANNA HEAR, OR DO YOU TRULY AGREE WITH WHAT I'M SAYING?
LOOK, ARE WE GONNA HAVE AN ADVENTURE TOGETHER?
I'M GETTIN' THE FEELIN' ME HAVIN' A COP CAR AN' A COWBOY SIDEKICK MEANS WE GOTTA HAVE AN ADVENTURE.
I SAY WE TAKE THIS BUGGY FOR A SPIN AND HAVE US SOME OLD-FASHIONED FUN.
LET THE ROAD TAKE US WHERE IT WILL.
PERFECT! CAN WE PIT-STOP AT THE CHATEAU FIRST? YOU KNOW IT?
FIVE MINUTES AWAY. MAKE THE NEXT LEFT.
Oooh! MIGHTY MEDIEVAL.
IT'S GOT QUITE THE HISTORY WITH CELEBRITIES AN' THEIR WEIRD HABITS. A LOT OF UNNECESSARY DEATHS HAVE HAPPENED HERE OVER THE YEARS.
LIGHTEN UP, LONE STRANGER. WE'RE HERE TA SAVE A LIFE.
DON'T CALL ME THAT. MY NAME IS COWBOY.
HI, HOW CAN I DIRECT YOU THIS EVENING?
I'M HOUNDING A FRIEND A' MINE, SPARROW ADARO.
HER PARTY IS BY THE POOL. TWO LEFTS AND YOU'RE THERE.
WHAT'S WITH ALL THE POOLS HERE IN LOS ANGELES?
WE'RE IN A DESERT AND SUPPOSEDLY CONSERVIN' WATER BECAUSE OF A SHORTAGE.
THIS TOWN HAS EVERYTHING THE WRONG WAY RIGHT, OR IS THAT THE RIGHT WAY WRONG?
WHATEVER Y'SAY, CLINT. I THINK I SPY HER.
ARE YOU SPARROW ADARO?
WHO'S ASKING? AND WHO LET YOU TWO IN HERE? IT'S A PRIVATE PARTY, Y'KNOW.
MY NAME'S HARLEY QUINN, AND YER MOTHER SENT ME TA HELP YA.

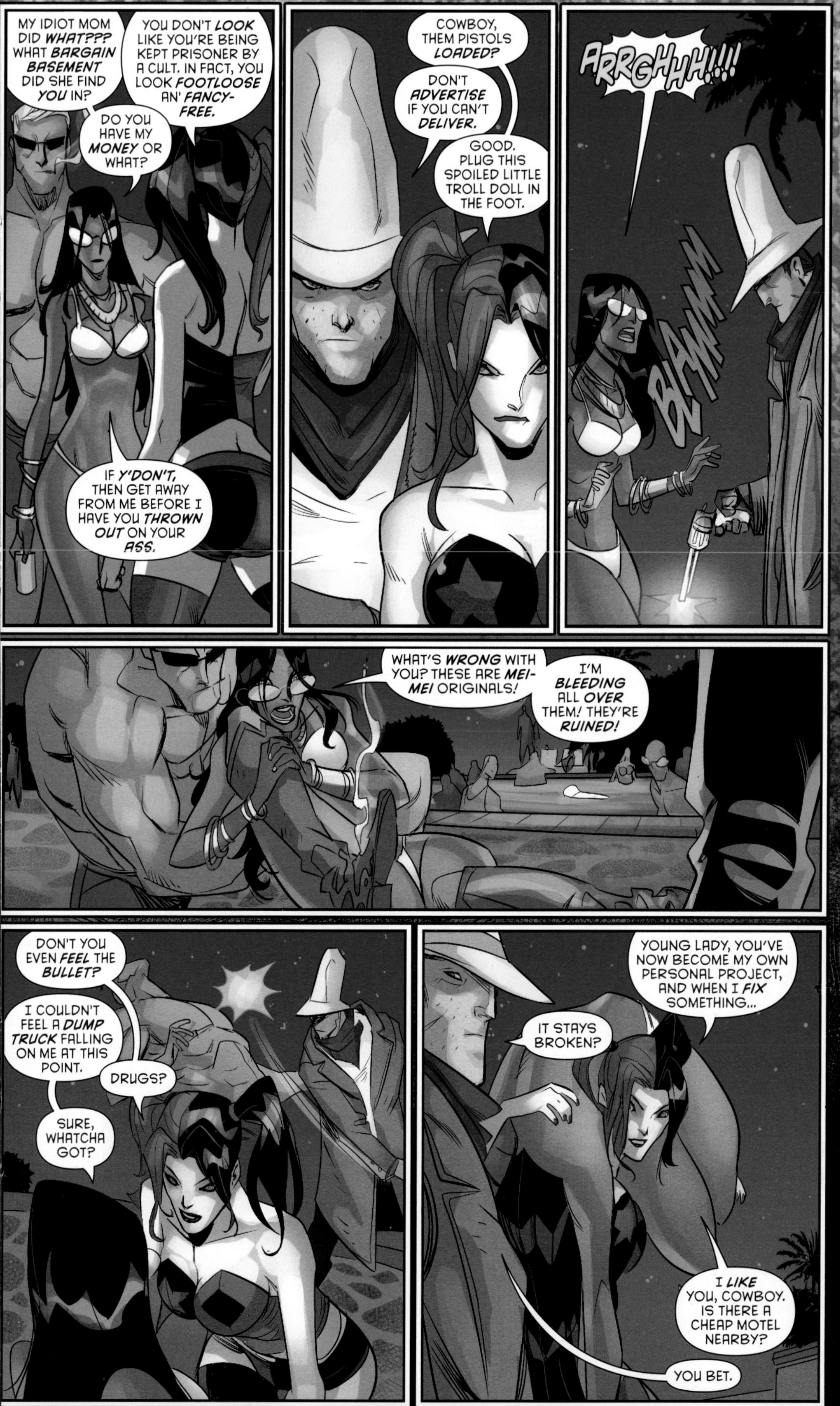

MY IDIOT MOM DID WHAT??? WHAT BARGAIN BASEMENT DID SHE FIND YOU IN?
YOU DON'T LOOK LIKE YOU'RE BEING KEPT PRISONER BY A CULT. IN FACT, YOU LOOK FOOTLOOSE AN' FANCY-FREE.
DO YOU HAVE MY MONEY OR WHAT?
IF Y'DON'T, THEN GET AWAY FROM ME BEFORE I HAVE YOU THROWN OUT ON YOUR ASS.
COWBOY, THEM PISTOLS LOADED?
DON'T ADVERTISE IF YOU CAN'T DELIVER.
GOOD. PLUG THIS SPOILED LITTLE TROLL DOLL IN THE FOOT.
ARRGHHHH!!!!
BLAMMM
WHAT'S WRONG WITH YOU? THESE ARE MEI-MEI ORIGINALS!
I'M BLEEDING ALL OVER THEM! THEY'RE RUINED!
DON'T YOU EVEN FEEL THE BULLET?
I COULDN'T FEEL A DUMP TRUCK FALLING ON ME AT THIS POINT.
DRUGS?
SURE, WHATCHA GOT?
YOUNG LADY, YOU'VE NOW BECOME MY OWN PERSONAL PROJECT, AND WHEN I FIX SOMETHING...
IT STAYS BROKEN?
I LIKE YOU, COWBOY. IS THERE A CHEAP MOTEL NEARBY?
YOU BET.

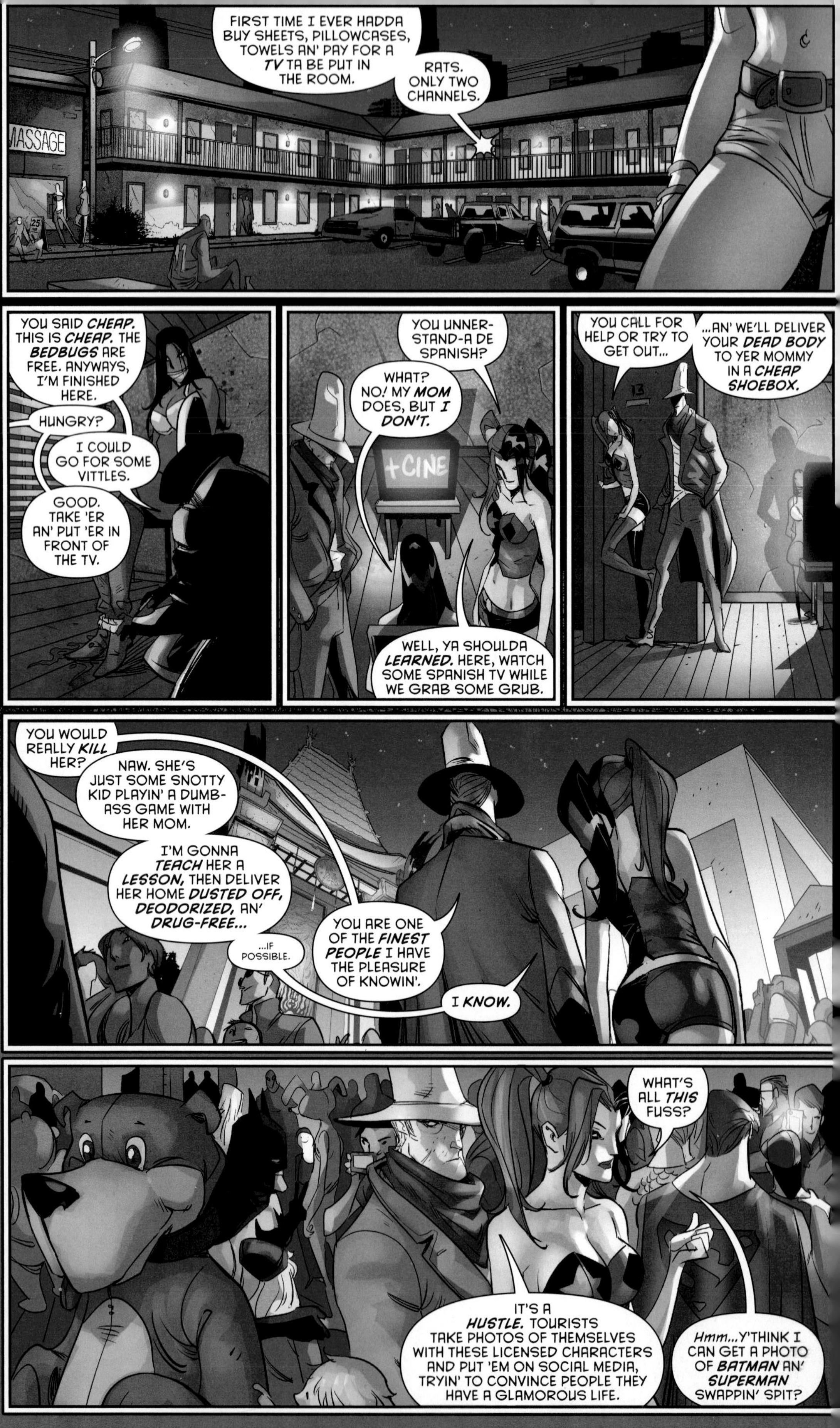
FIRST TIME I EVER HADDA BUY SHEETS, PILLOWCASES, TOWELS AN' PAY FOR A TV TA BE PUT IN THE ROOM.
RATS. ONLY TWO CHANNELS.
MASSAGE
YOU SAID CHEAP. THIS IS CHEAP. THE BEDBUGS ARE FREE. ANYWAYS, I'M FINISHED HERE.
HUNGRY?
I COULD GO FOR SOME VITTLES.
GOOD. TAKE 'ER AN' PUT 'ER IN FRONT OF THE TV.
YOU UNNER-STAND-A DE SPANISH?
WHAT? NO! MY MOM DOES, BUT I DON'T.
+CINE
WELL, YA SHOULDA LEARNED. HERE, WATCH SOME SPANISH TV WHILE WE GRAB SOME GRUB.
YOU CALL FOR HELP OR TRY TO GET OUT...
...AN' WE'LL DELIVER YOUR DEAD BODY TO YER MOMMY IN A CHEAP SHOEBOX.
YOU WOULD REALLY KILL HER?
NAW. SHE'S JUST SOME SNOTTY KID PLAYIN' A DUMB-ASS GAME WITH HER MOM.
I'M GONNA TEACH HER A LESSON, THEN DELIVER HER HOME DUSTED OFF, DEODORIZED, AN' DRUG-FREE...
...IF POSSIBLE.
YOU ARE ONE OF THE FINEST PEOPLE I HAVE THE PLEASURE OF KNOWIN'.
I KNOW.
WHAT'S ALL THIS FUSS?
IT'S A HUSTLE. TOURISTS TAKE PHOTOS OF THEMSELVES WITH THESE LICENSED CHARACTERS AND PUT 'EM ON SOCIAL MEDIA, TRYIN' TO CONVINCE PEOPLE THEY HAVE A GLAMOROUS LIFE.
Hmm...Y'THINK I CAN GET A PHOTO OF BATMAN AN' SUPERMAN SWAPPIN' SPIT?

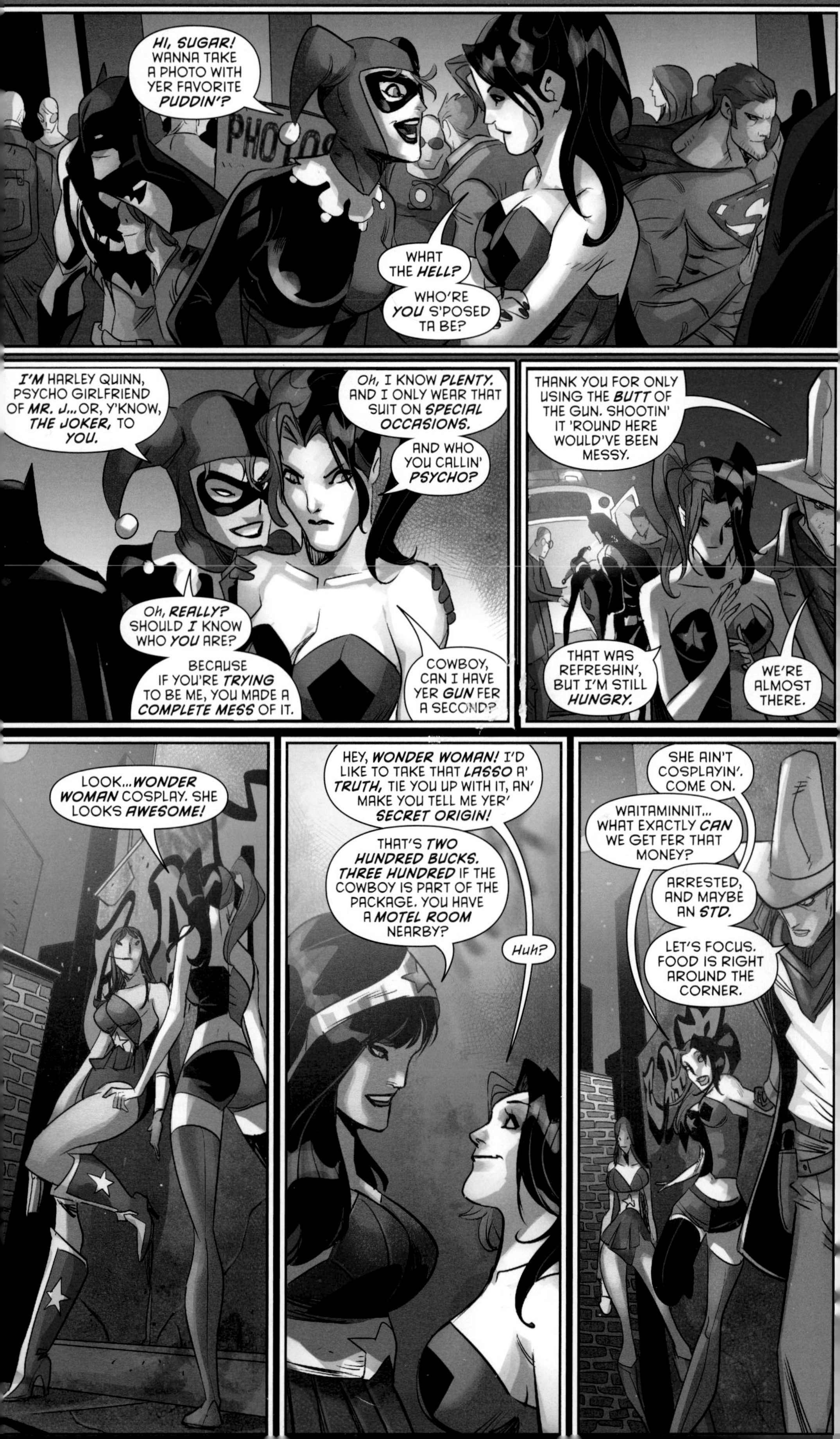
HI, SUGAR! WANNA TAKE A PHOTO WITH YER FAVORITE PUDDIN'?
PHOTOS
WHAT THE HELL?
WHO'RE YOU S'POSED TA BE?
I'M HARLEY QUINN, PSYCHO GIRLFRIEND OF MR. J...OR, Y'KNOW, THE JOKER, TO YOU.
Oh, I KNOW PLENTY. AND I ONLY WEAR THAT SUIT ON SPECIAL OCCASIONS.
AND WHO YOU CALLIN' PSYCHO?
Oh, REALLY? SHOULD I KNOW WHO YOU ARE?
BECAUSE IF YOU'RE TRYING TO BE ME, YOU MADE A COMPLETE MESS OF IT.
COWBOY, CAN I HAVE YER GUN FER A SECOND?
THANK YOU FOR ONLY USING THE BUTT OF THE GUN. SHOOTIN' IT 'ROUND HERE WOULD'VE BEEN MESSY.
THAT WAS REFRESHIN', BUT I'M STILL HUNGRY.
WE'RE ALMOST THERE.
LOOK...WONDER WOMAN COSPLAY. SHE LOOKS AWESOME!
HEY, WONDER WOMAN! I'D LIKE TO TAKE THAT LASSO A' TRUTH, TIE YOU UP WITH IT, AN' MAKE YOU TELL ME YER' SECRET ORIGIN!
THAT'S TWO HUNDRED BUCKS. THREE HUNDRED IF THE COWBOY IS PART OF THE PACKAGE. YOU HAVE A MOTEL ROOM NEARBY?
Huh?
SHE AIN'T COSPLAYIN'. COME ON.
WAITAMINNIT... WHAT EXACTLY CAN WE GET FER THAT MONEY?
ARRESTED, AND MAYBE AN STD.
LET'S FOCUS. FOOD IS RIGHT AROUND THE CORNER.

THIS WAY.

ARE YOU *KIDDIN'?*

THIS IS THE ALLEY IN COMIC BOOKS WHERE THE GIRL GETS ATTACKED AN' SOME *LAME SUPERHERO* COMES TA *RESCUE* HER AN' SHE WINDS UP *KISSIN'* HIM WHEN HE'S SWINGIN' UPSIDE DOWN IN A RAINSTORM THAT WETS THE...

...OKAY. *SOLD.* LET'S GO.

HOW'DJA KNOW THIS IS *HERE?*

PINKY TEXTS WHERE SHE'S GONNA SET UP, AND WE FOLLOW. WE ARE ALL DISCIPLES OF THE PINK.

IT SMELLS *HEAVENLY,* BUT THAT *LINE...*

THE COWBOY WAITS FOR *NO ONE.*

PINKY, TWO *HANDWARMERS* AND A COUPLE OF *ROCKETSAUCES.*

EAT IT FROM THE ENDS. SHOVING YOUR *FACE* INTO IT IS JUST *UNCOUTH.*

NO ONE'S EVER →nom← COMPLAINED BEFORE.

MAYBE THAT'S EAST COAST STYLE. MY APOLOGIES. SO *TELL* ME ABOUT YOURSELF...

YOU COULD SAY I'M A CRUSADER A' JUSTICE. I SEE SOMETHIN' I THINK IS *WRONG* AN' I DO MY BEST TA *FIX* IT.

HOW'S THAT GOIN' SO FAR?

MIXED RESULTS, BUT *NOBODY* LIKES A *QUITTER.* HOW'S 'BOUT *YOU?*

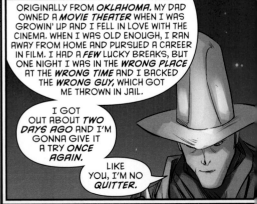

ORIGINALLY FROM *OKLAHOMA.* MY DAD OWNED A *MOVIE THEATER* WHEN I WAS GROWIN' UP AND I FELL IN LOVE WITH THE CINEMA. WHEN I WAS OLD ENOUGH, I RAN AWAY FROM HOME AND PURSUED A CAREER IN FILM. I HAD A *FEW* LUCKY BREAKS, BUT ONE NIGHT I WAS IN THE *WRONG PLACE* AT THE *WRONG TIME* AND I BACKED THE *WRONG GUY,* WHICH GOT ME THROWN IN JAIL.

I GOT OUT ABOUT *TWO DAYS AGO* AND I'M GONNA GIVE IT A TRY *ONCE AGAIN.*

LIKE YOU, I'M NO *QUITTER.*

WHAT'S WITH THE COWBOY SUIT... I LOVE IT, BUT WHAT'S IT FOR?

JUST SOMETHING TO MAKE ME BLEND IN. WEIRD IS NORMAL OUT HERE, IF YOU HAVEN'T NOTICED BY NOW.

IT'S YOU FER' SURE. WHEN YOU SAY YOU GOT OUTTA JAIL, IS THAT FER TIME SERVED?

I FEEL I SERVED ENOUGH TIME. THEY TOOK AWAY A HUGE CHUNK OF MY LIFE. I MISSED ENOUGH MOVIES--

I SEE. YOU BROKE OUT?

ARE YOU GONNA TURN ME IN?

I FEEL IF YOU THINK YOU SERVED THE RIGHT AMOUNT A' TIME, THEN I'M COOL WITH IT.

I HAVE A FRIEND OUT EAST WHO'S SERVIN' TIME FOR AN ACCIDENTAL HOMICIDE. AS SOON AS I GET BACK, I'M GONNA HELP HIM WITH HIS CASE.

FILE IN HIS BIRTHDAY CAKE?

HAND GRENADE. IT'S A PRETTY TOUGH PRISON UP THE HUDSON.

HEY! WATCH WHERE YER GOIN'!

THAT'S MY SPOT, BIMBO. GET UP BEFORE I CALL THE REST OF MY CREW OVER HERE TO KICK YOUR ASS.

THIS IS A PUBLIC PLACE! GO FRENCH KISS A LITTER BOX, FURBALL!

LAST CHANCE, SIZZLE FACE!

SERIOUSLY?

MOVE IT, OR I'LL BREAK YOU INTO UGLY LITTLE PIECES.

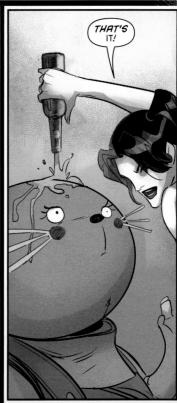

THAT'S IT!

Ooofff!

ALL RIGHT, LADY, YOU'RE *DONE* FOR.

YOU'VE MANAGED TO PISS OFF THE MOST WELL-CONNECTED *KITTY* IN THIS *CITY,* AND THAT COMES WITH A *PRICE!* YOU'RE GONNA--

Ahh, *STOP* YER *SCREECHIN'!*

PAFF

...AND *THIS* FAMOUS AREA OF HOLLYWOOD FEATURES THE WALK OF FAME, FEATURING FOOTPRINTS AND HANDPRINTS FROM THE STARS OF TODAY AND YESTERYEAR!

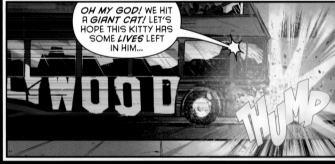

OH MY GOD! WE HIT A *GIANT CAT!* LET'S HOPE THIS KITTY HAS SOME *LIVES* LEFT IN HIM...

THUMP

GOOD-BYE, KITTY!

Ha! GOOD ONE.

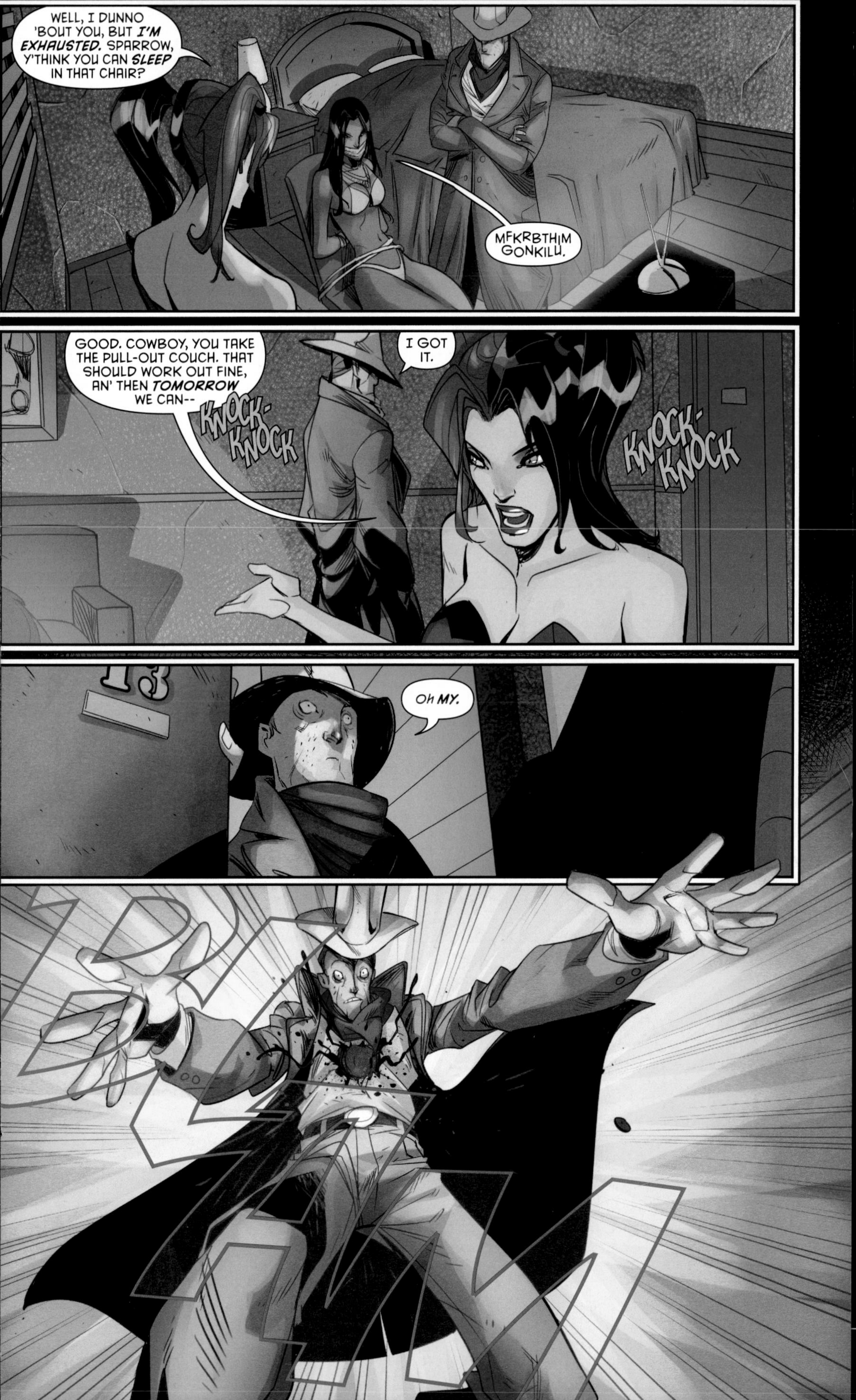
WELL, I DUNNO 'BOUT YOU, BUT *I'M EXHAUSTED.* SPARROW, Y'THINK YOU CAN *SLEEP* IN THAT CHAIR?
MFKRBTHIM GONKILU.
GOOD. COWBOY, YOU TAKE THE PULL-OUT COUCH. THAT SHOULD WORK OUT FINE, AN' THEN *TOMORROW* WE CAN--
I GOT IT.
KNOCK-KNOCK
KNOCK-KNOCK
13
Oh *MY.*

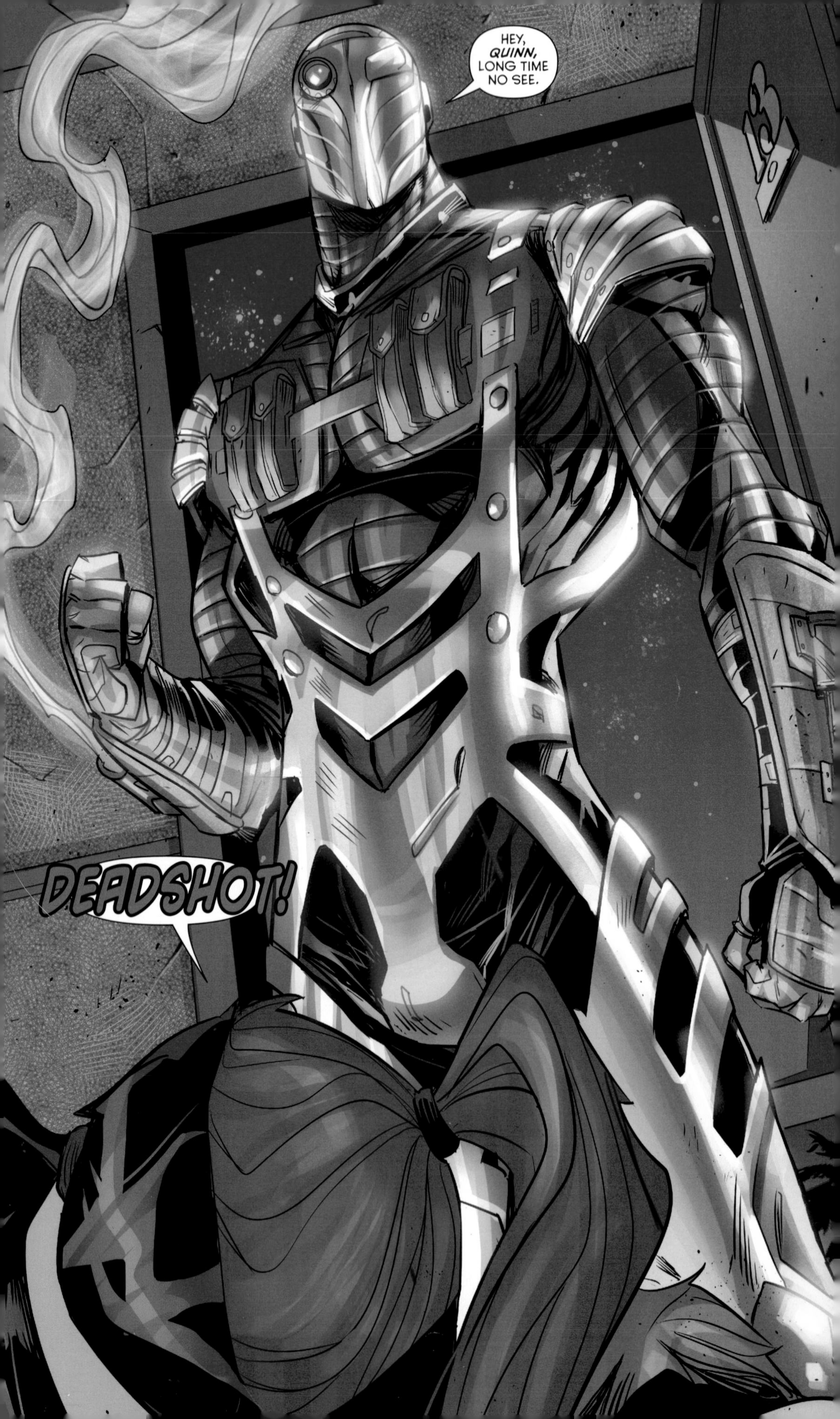
HEY, QUINN, LONG TIME NO SEE.
DEADSHOT!

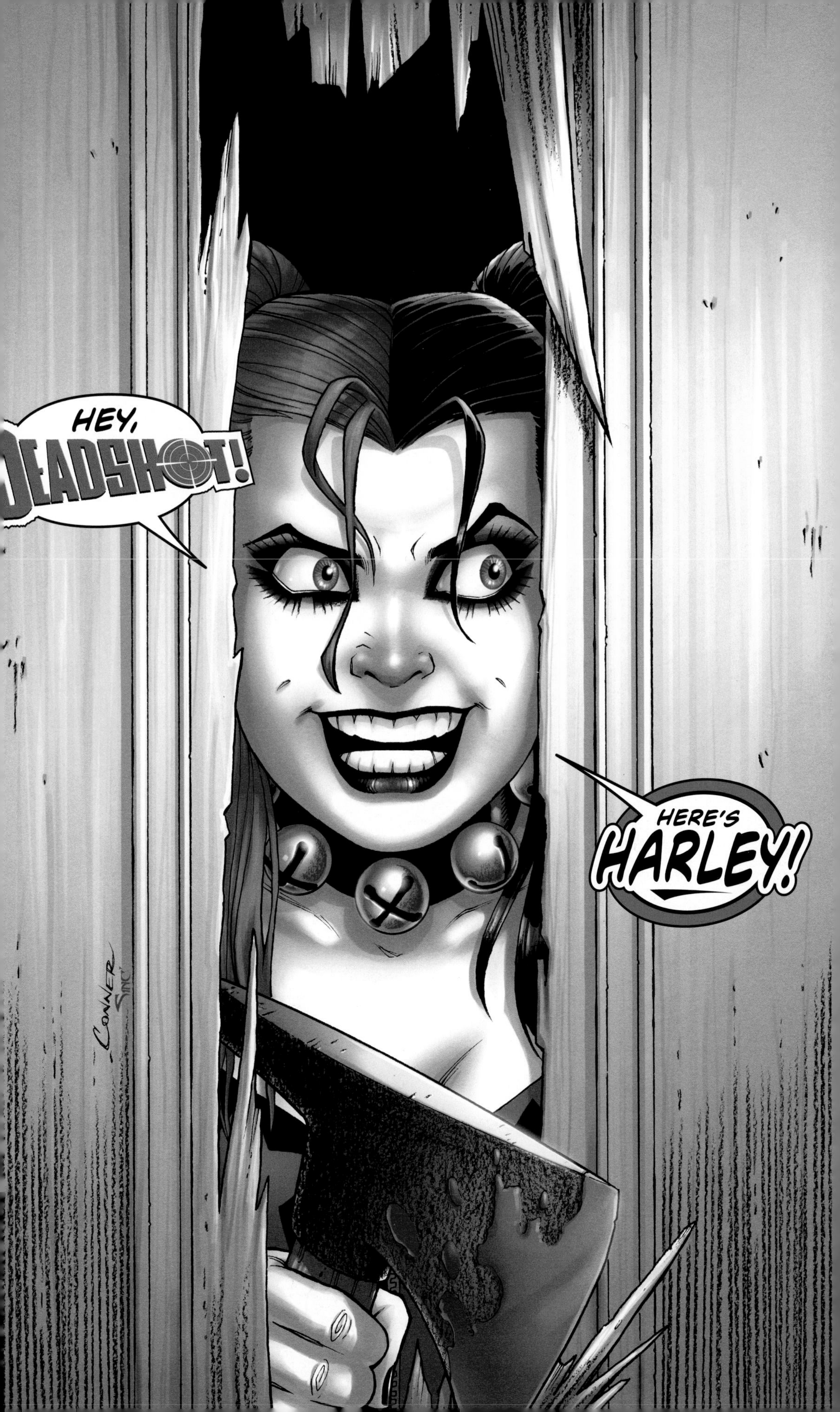
HEY, DEADSHOT!
HERE'S HARLEY!

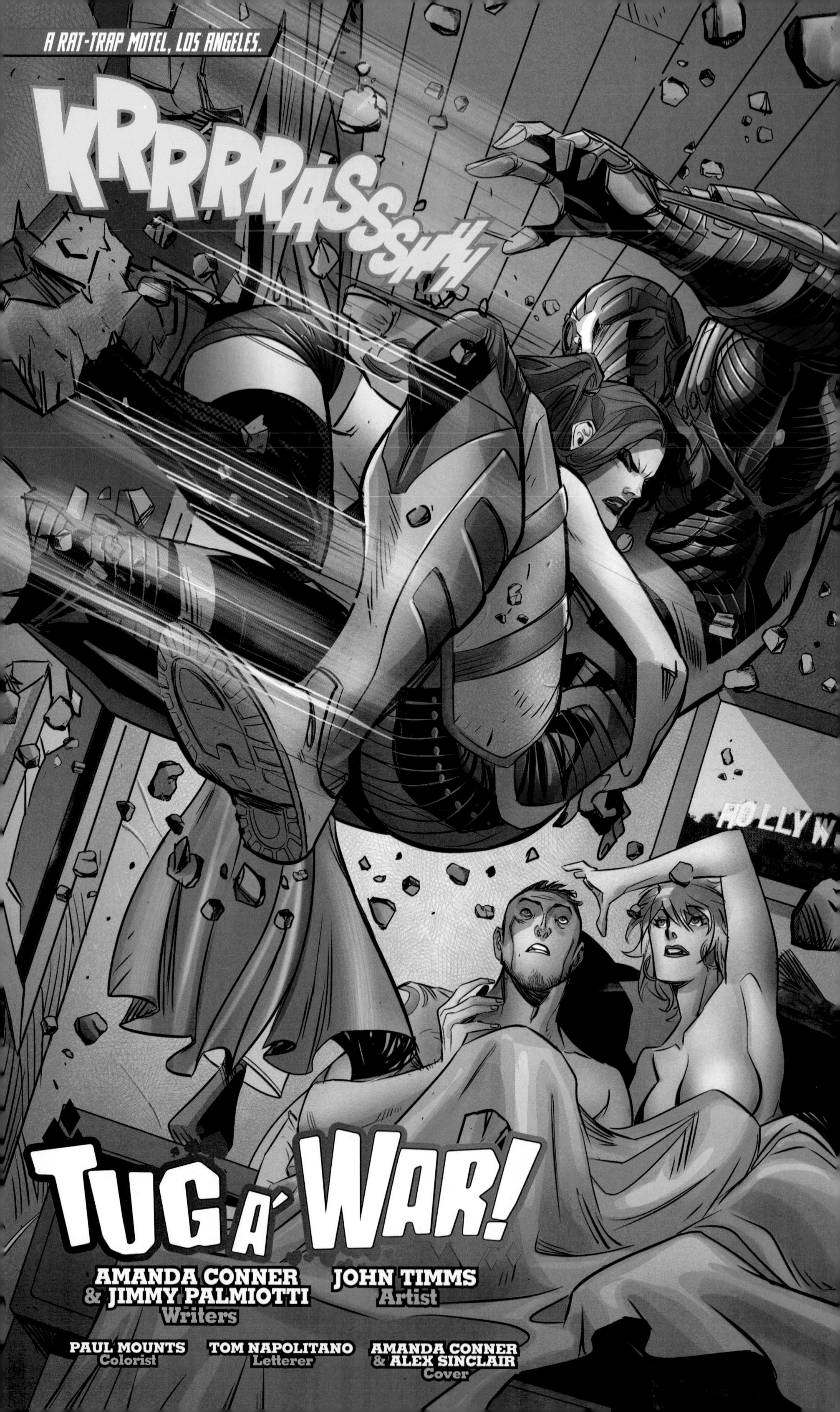

A RAT-TRAP MOTEL, LOS ANGELES.
KRRRRASSSHH
HOLLYW
TUG A' WAR!
AMANDA CONNER & JIMMY PALMIOTTI Writers
JOHN TIMMS Artist
PAUL MOUNTS Colorist
TOM NAPOLITANO Letterer
AMANDA CONNER & ALEX SINCLAIR Cover

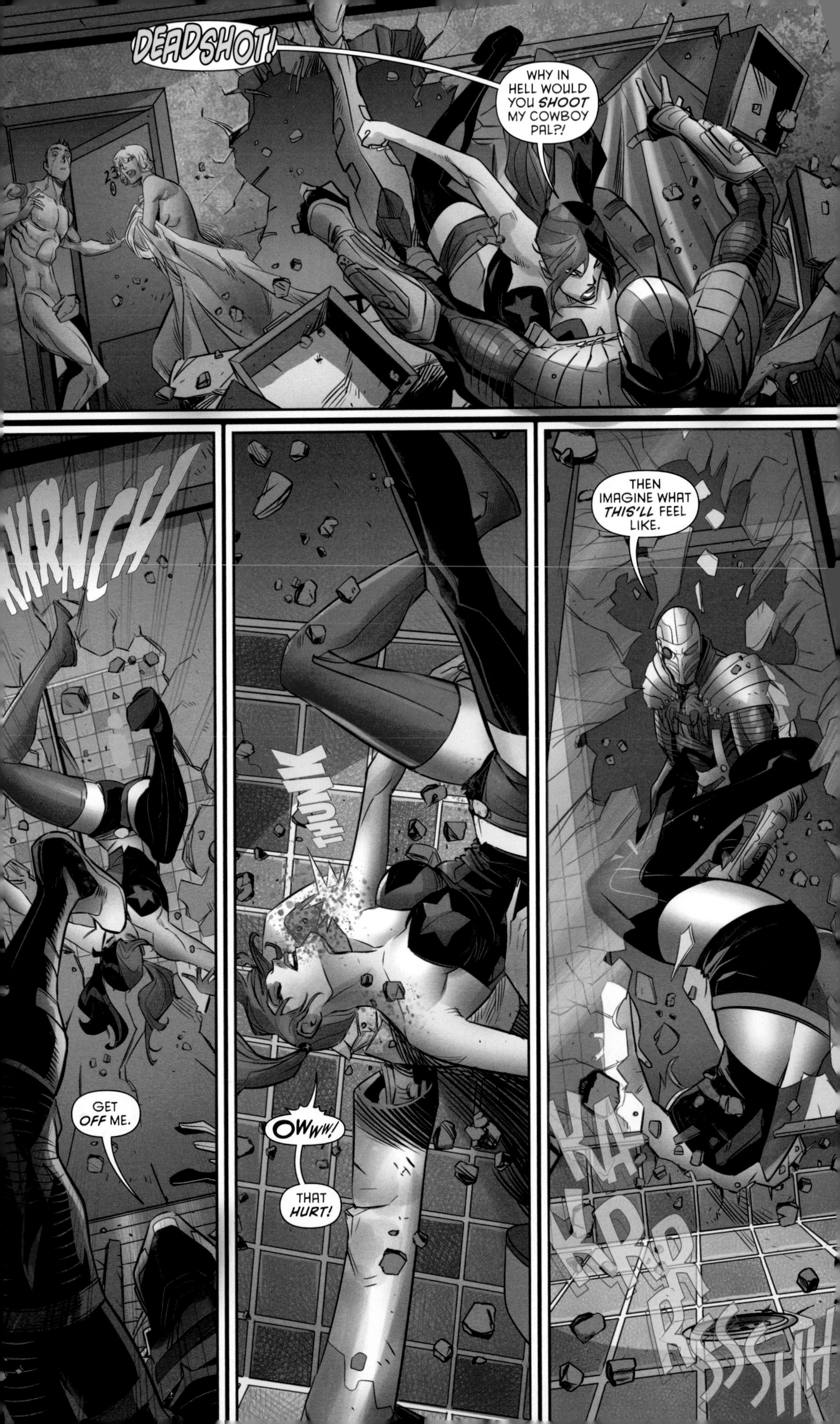
DEADSHOT!
WHY IN HELL WOULD YOU SHOOT MY COWBOY PAL?!
KRRNCH
GET OFF ME.
THUNK
OWWW!
THAT HURT!
THEN IMAGINE WHAT THIS'LL FEEL LIKE.
KA KRR RISSSHH

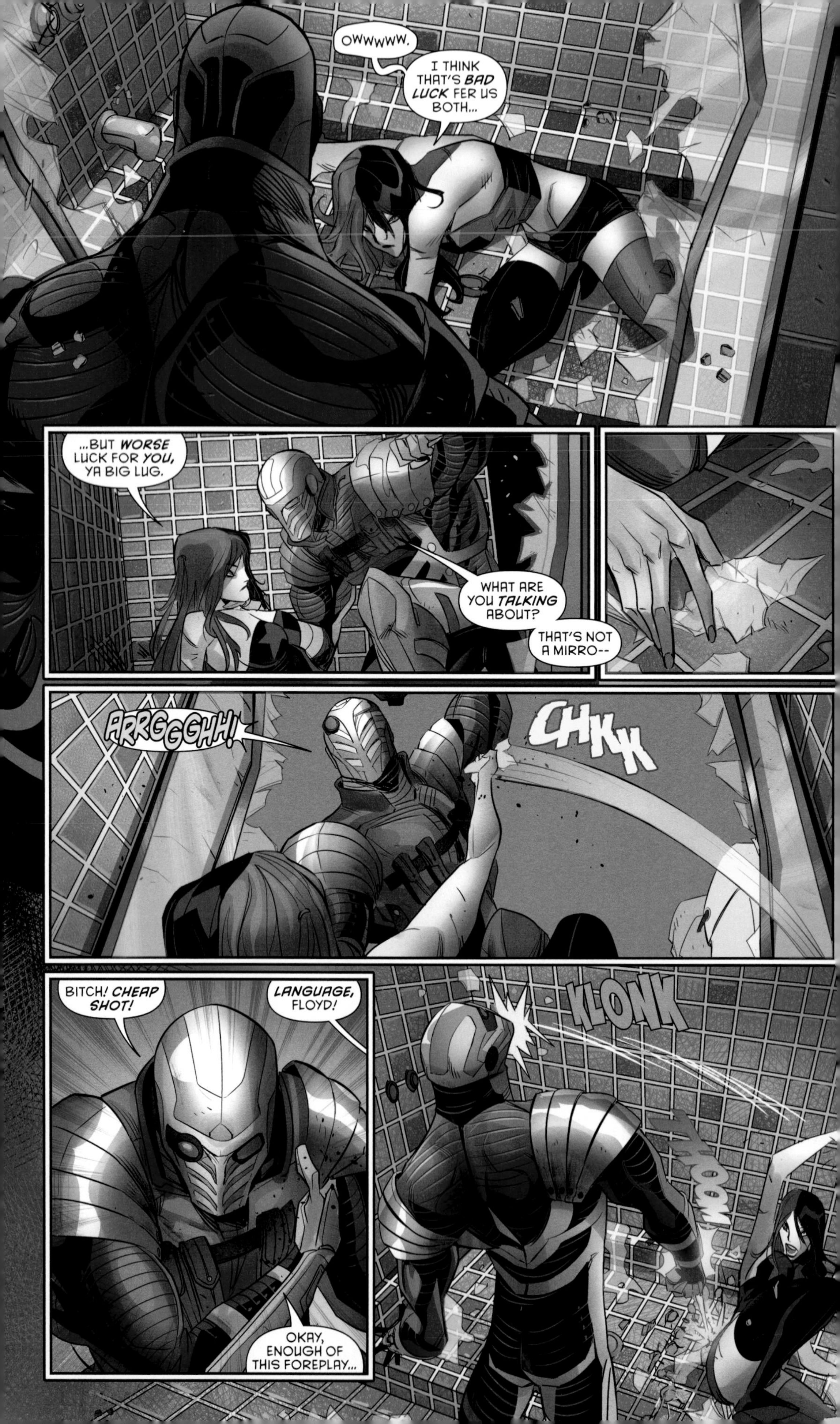
OWWWWW.
I THINK THAT'S *BAD LUCK* FER US BOTH...
...BUT *WORSE* LUCK FOR *YOU*, YA BIG LUG.
WHAT ARE YOU *TALKING* ABOUT?
THAT'S NOT A MIRRO--
ARRGGGHH!
CHKKK
BITCH! *CHEAP SHOT!*
LANGUAGE, FLOYD!
KLONK
OKAY, ENOUGH OF THIS FOREPLAY...

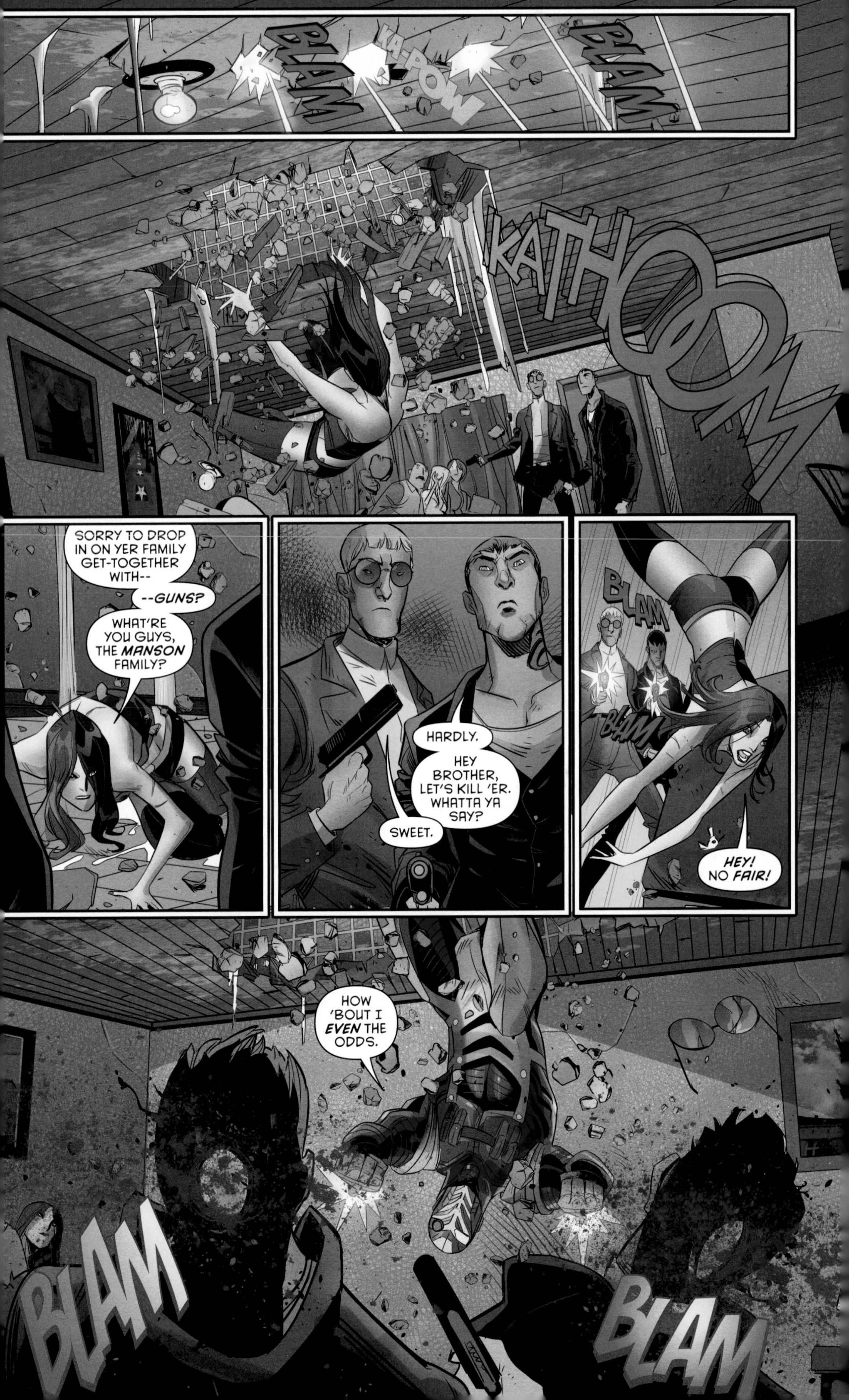
BLAM
KA-POW
BLAM
KATHOOM
SORRY TO DROP IN ON YER FAMILY GET-TOGETHER WITH--
--GUNS?
WHAT'RE YOU GUYS, THE MANSON FAMILY?
HARDLY.
HEY BROTHER, LET'S KILL 'ER. WHATTA YA SAY?
SWEET.
BLAM
BLAM
HEY! NO FAIR!
HOW 'BOUT I EVEN THE ODDS.
BLAM
BLAM

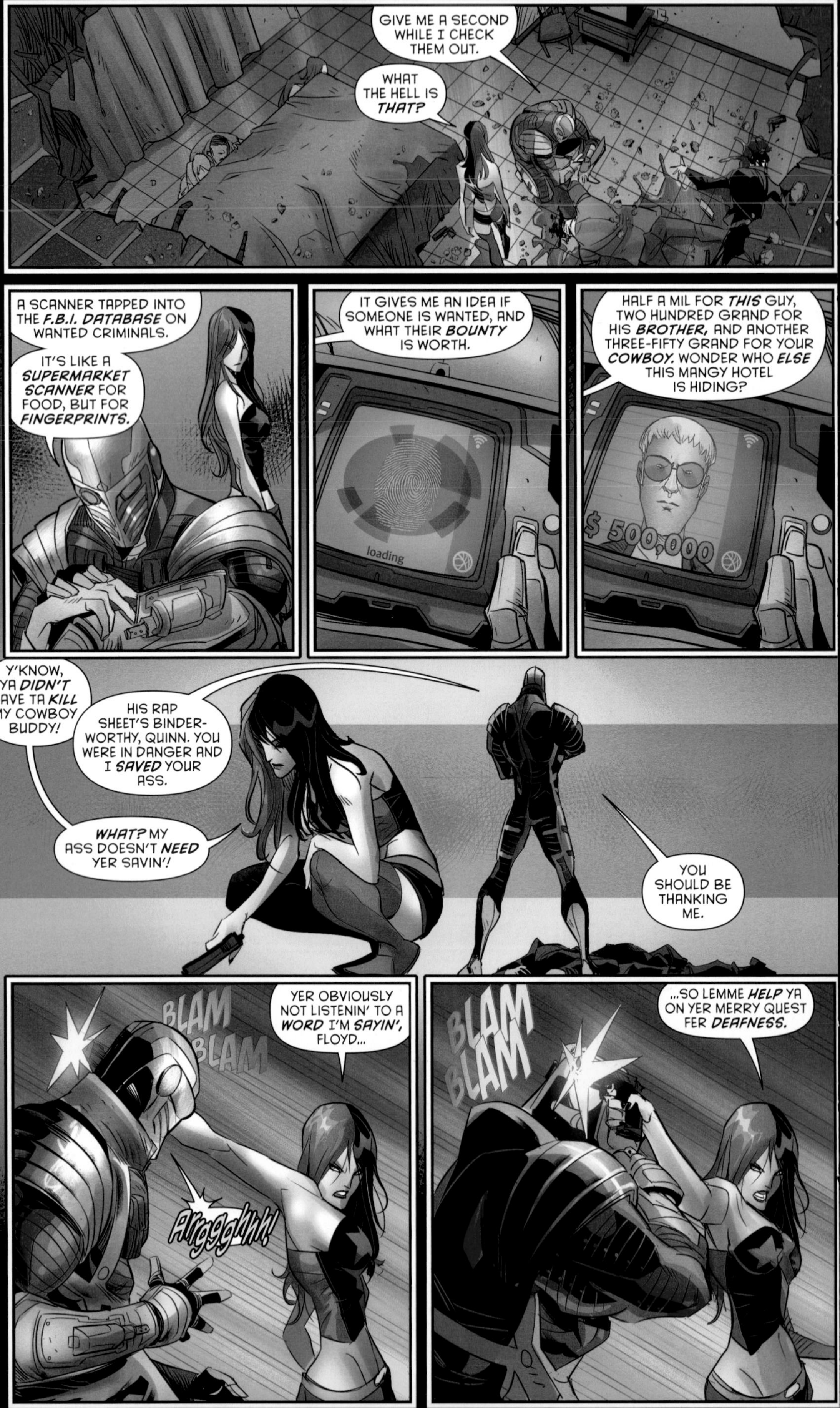
GIVE ME A SECOND WHILE I CHECK THEM OUT.
WHAT THE HELL IS *THAT?*
A SCANNER TAPPED INTO THE *F.B.I. DATABASE* ON WANTED CRIMINALS.
IT'S LIKE A *SUPERMARKET SCANNER* FOR FOOD, BUT FOR *FINGERPRINTS.*
IT GIVES ME AN IDEA IF SOMEONE IS WANTED, AND WHAT THEIR *BOUNTY* IS WORTH.
loading
HALF A MIL FOR *THIS* GUY, TWO HUNDRED GRAND FOR HIS *BROTHER,* AND ANOTHER THREE-FIFTY GRAND FOR YOUR *COWBOY.* WONDER WHO *ELSE* THIS MANGY HOTEL IS HIDING?
$ 500,000
Y'KNOW, YA *DIDN'T* HAVE TA *KILL* MY COWBOY BUDDY!
HIS RAP SHEET'S BINDER-WORTHY, QUINN. YOU WERE IN DANGER AND I *SAVED* YOUR ASS.
WHAT? MY ASS DOESN'T *NEED* YER SAVIN'!
YOU SHOULD BE THANKING ME.
BLAM BLAM
YER OBVIOUSLY NOT LISTENIN' TO A *WORD* I'M *SAYIN',* FLOYD...
Arrggghhh!
BLAM BLAM
...SO LEMME *HELP* YA ON YER MERRY QUEST FER *DEAFNESS.*

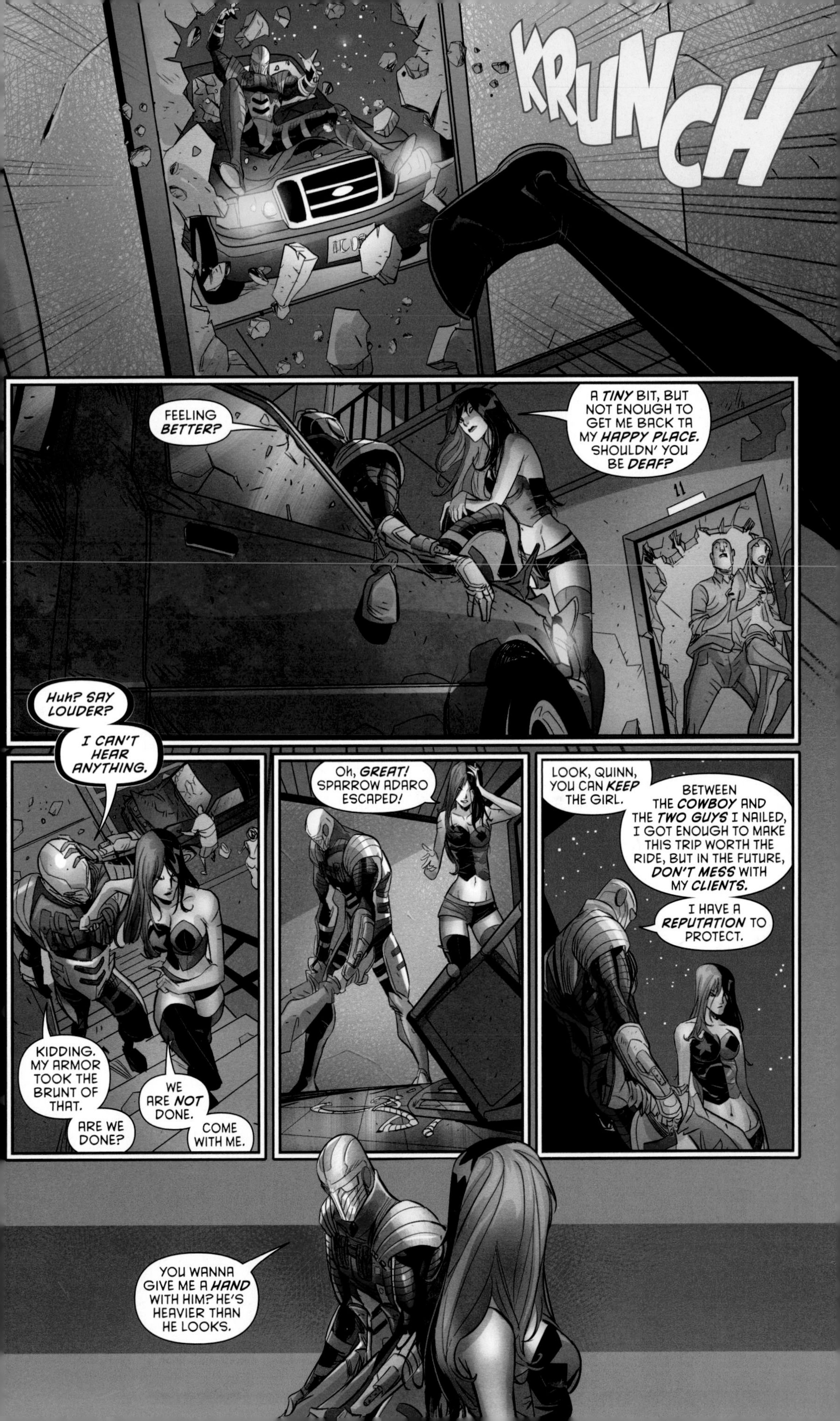
KRUNCH
FEELING BETTER?
A TINY BIT, BUT NOT ENOUGH TO GET ME BACK TA MY HAPPY PLACE. SHOULDN' YOU BE DEAF?
Huh? SAY LOUDER?
I CAN'T HEAR ANYTHING.
KIDDING. MY ARMOR TOOK THE BRUNT OF THAT.
ARE WE DONE?
WE ARE NOT DONE.
COME WITH ME.
Oh, GREAT! SPARROW ADARO ESCAPED!
LOOK, QUINN, YOU CAN KEEP THE GIRL.
BETWEEN THE COWBOY AND THE TWO GUYS I NAILED, I GOT ENOUGH TO MAKE THIS TRIP WORTH THE RIDE, BUT IN THE FUTURE, DON'T MESS WITH MY CLIENTS.
I HAVE A REPUTATION TO PROTECT.
YOU WANNA GIVE ME A HAND WITH HIM? HE'S HEAVIER THAN HE LOOKS.

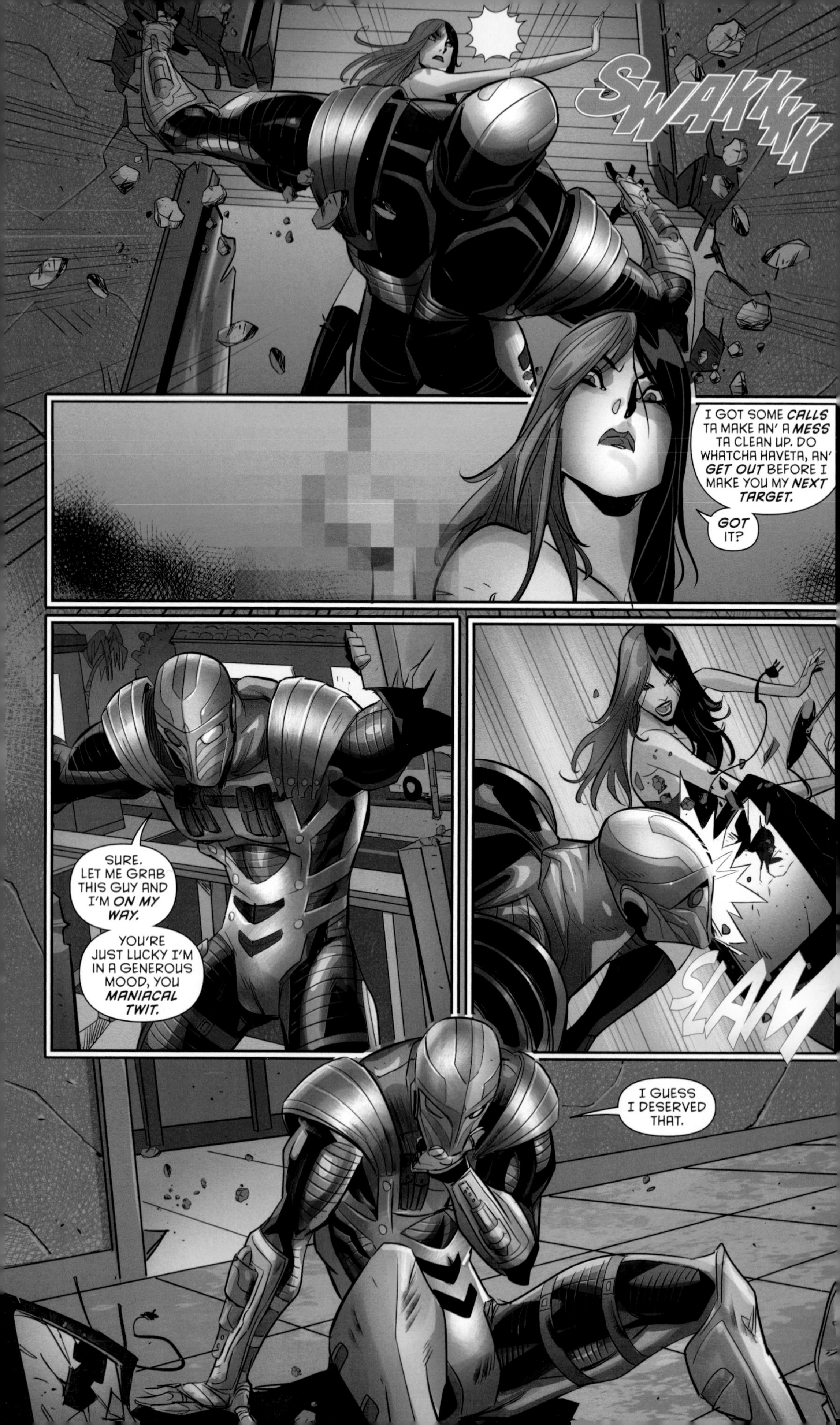
SWAKKKKK
I GOT SOME CALLS TA MAKE AN' A MESS TA CLEAN UP. DO WHATCHA HAVETA, AN' GET OUT BEFORE I MAKE YOU MY NEXT TARGET.
GOT IT?
SURE. LET ME GRAB THIS GUY AND I'M ON MY WAY.
YOU'RE JUST LUCKY I'M IN A GENEROUS MOOD, YOU MANIACAL TWIT.
SLAM
I GUESS I DESERVED THAT.

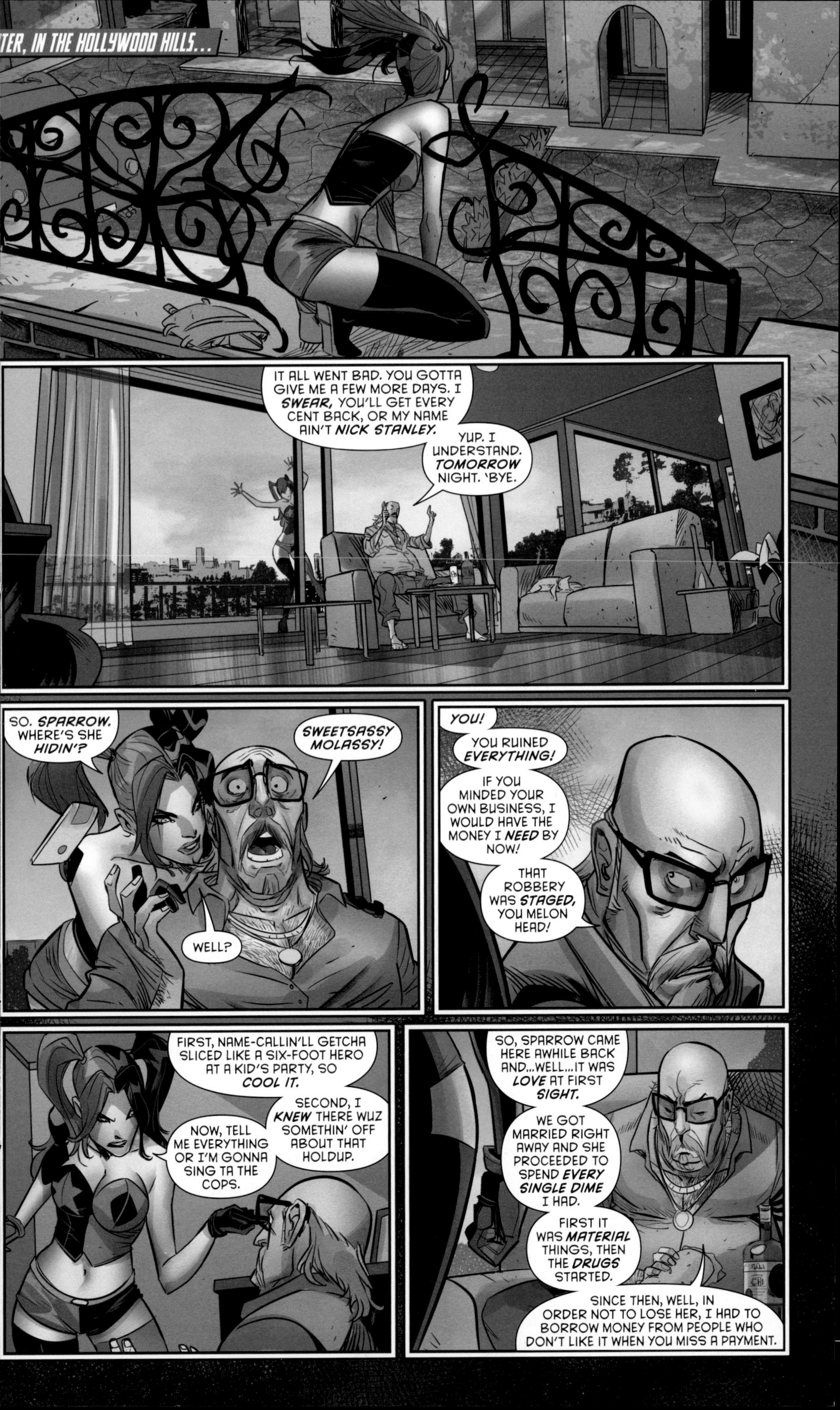

TER, IN THE HOLLYWOOD HILLS...
IT ALL WENT BAD. YOU GOTTA GIVE ME A FEW MORE DAYS. I SWEAR, YOU'LL GET EVERY CENT BACK, OR MY NAME AIN'T NICK STANLEY.
YUP. I UNDERSTAND. TOMORROW NIGHT. 'BYE.
SO. SPARROW. WHERE'S SHE HIDIN'?
SWEETSASSY MOLASSY!
WELL?
YOU!
YOU RUINED EVERYTHING!
IF YOU MINDED YOUR OWN BUSINESS, I WOULD HAVE THE MONEY I NEED BY NOW!
THAT ROBBERY WAS STAGED, YOU MELON HEAD!
FIRST, NAME-CALLIN'LL GETCHA SLICED LIKE A SIX-FOOT HERO AT A KID'S PARTY, SO COOL IT.
SECOND, I KNEW THERE WUZ SOMETHIN' OFF ABOUT THAT HOLDUP.
NOW, TELL ME EVERYTHING OR I'M GONNA SING TA THE COPS.
SO, SPARROW CAME HERE AWHILE BACK AND...WELL...IT WAS LOVE AT FIRST SIGHT.
WE GOT MARRIED RIGHT AWAY AND SHE PROCEEDED TO SPEND EVERY SINGLE DIME I HAD.
FIRST IT WAS MATERIAL THINGS, THEN THE DRUGS STARTED.
SINCE THEN, WELL, IN ORDER NOT TO LOSE HER, I HAD TO BORROW MONEY FROM PEOPLE WHO DON'T LIKE IT WHEN YOU MISS A PAYMENT.

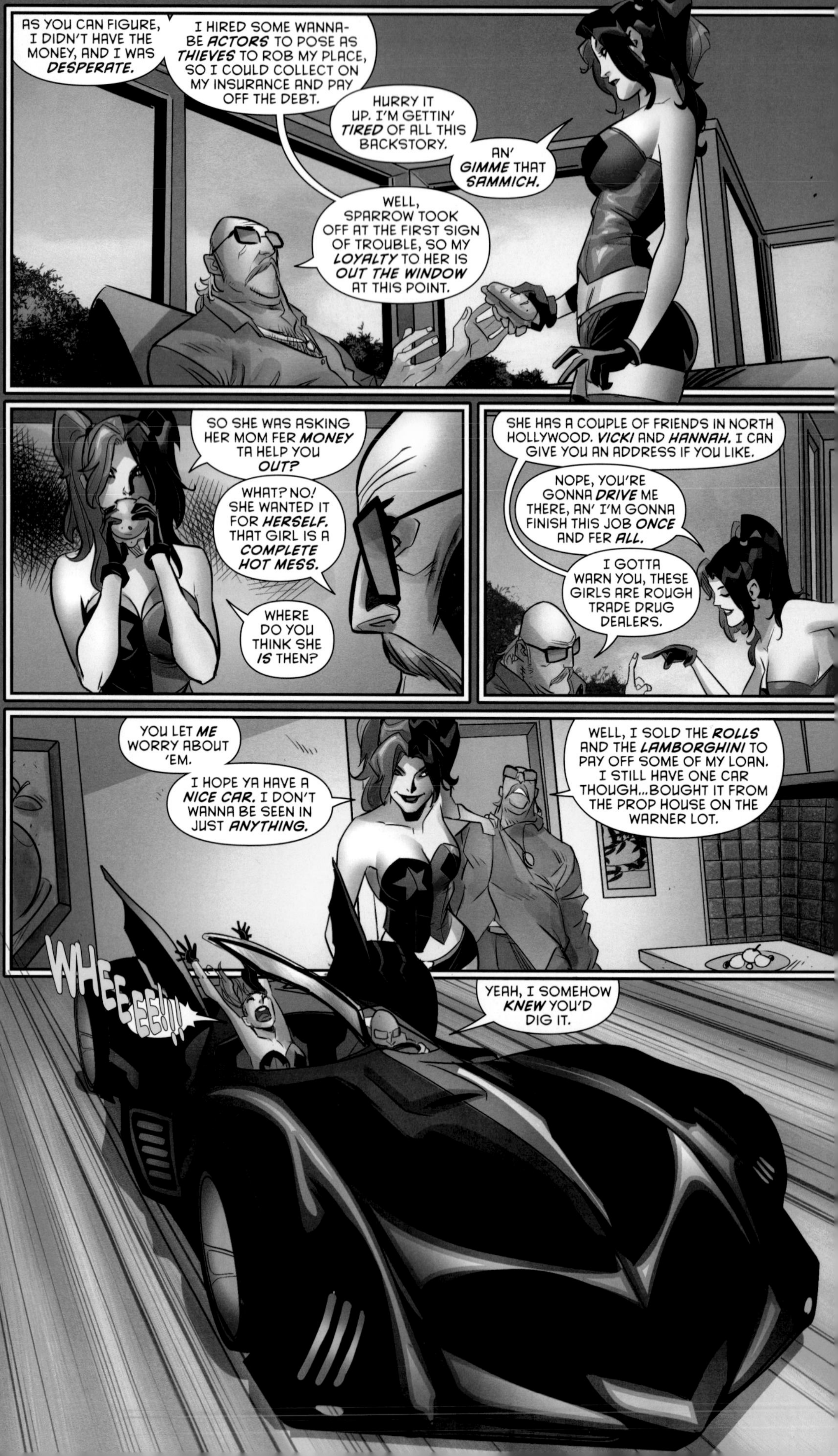
AS YOU CAN FIGURE, I DIDN'T HAVE THE MONEY, AND I WAS DESPERATE.
I HIRED SOME WANNA-BE ACTORS TO POSE AS THIEVES TO ROB MY PLACE, SO I COULD COLLECT ON MY INSURANCE AND PAY OFF THE DEBT.
HURRY IT UP. I'M GETTIN' TIRED OF ALL THIS BACKSTORY.
AN' GIMME THAT SAMMICH.
WELL, SPARROW TOOK OFF AT THE FIRST SIGN OF TROUBLE, SO MY LOYALTY TO HER IS OUT THE WINDOW AT THIS POINT.
SO SHE WAS ASKING HER MOM FER MONEY TA HELP YOU OUT?
WHAT? NO! SHE WANTED IT FOR HERSELF. THAT GIRL IS A COMPLETE HOT MESS.
WHERE DO YOU THINK SHE IS THEN?
SHE HAS A COUPLE OF FRIENDS IN NORTH HOLLYWOOD. VICKI AND HANNAH. I CAN GIVE YOU AN ADDRESS IF YOU LIKE.
NOPE, YOU'RE GONNA DRIVE ME THERE, AN' I'M GONNA FINISH THIS JOB ONCE AND FER ALL.
I GOTTA WARN YOU, THESE GIRLS ARE ROUGH TRADE DRUG DEALERS.
YOU LET ME WORRY ABOUT 'EM.
I HOPE YA HAVE A NICE CAR. I DON'T WANNA BE SEEN IN JUST ANYTHING.
WELL, I SOLD THE ROLLS AND THE LAMBORGHINI TO PAY OFF SOME OF MY LOAN. I STILL HAVE ONE CAR THOUGH...BOUGHT IT FROM THE PROP HOUSE ON THE WARNER LOT.
WHEEEEE!!!!
YEAH, I SOMEHOW KNEW YOU'D DIG IT.

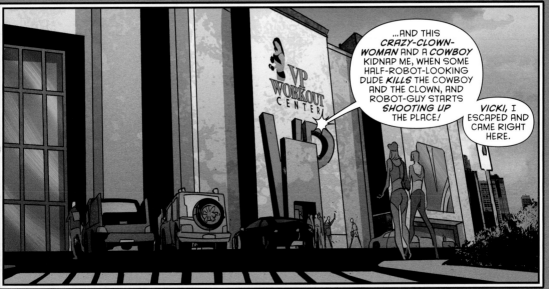

...AND THIS *CRAZY-CLOWN-WOMAN* AND A *COWBOY* KIDNAP ME, WHEN SOME HALF-ROBOT-LOOKING DUDE *KILLS* THE COWBOY AND THE CLOWN, AND ROBOT-GUY STARTS *SHOOTING UP* THE PLACE!

VICKI, I ESCAPED AND CAME RIGHT HERE.

ARE YOU SURE YOU AREN'T ON A BENDER RIGHT *NOW?* THAT STORY SOUNDS A BIT *OVER THE RAINBOW,* SPARROW.

IN ANY CASE, WHAT DO YOU WANT *ME* TO DO ABOUT IT?

I WAS *HOPING* YOU AND HANNAH COULD LET ME CRASH AT *YOUR* PLACE.

YOU OWE ME TEN LARGE ALREADY. WHY SHOULD I GIVE A CRAP WHAT HAPPENS TO YOU?

TO PROTECT YOUR *INVESTMENT?*

I COULD JUST *WASTE* YOU AND CALL IT A LOSS.

I BROUGHT A LOT OF *BUSINESS* YOUR WAY, *REMEMBER?*

WHAT YOU BROUGHT BY *BEING HERE* IS *TROUBLE.* LET ME GUESS, YOU'RE *SO STUPID* YOU PARKED YOUR CAR RIGHT OUT FRONT?

I CAN *MOVE* IT!

LET'S TALK TO HANNAH FIRST. GET *HER* OPINION.

I'M LEANING TOWARDS OFFING YOU *MYSELF,* JUST SO YOU KNOW.

HEY, HANNAH-BANANA, I NEED YOU A SECOND.

VICK, *PLEASE.* I HAVE A CLIENT.

WAIT IN THE OFFICE, SWEETIE. WE CAN ALL TALK THERE.

SORRY, BABY. MY BAD.

SO IT DOESN'T HAVE ANY *MISSILE LAUNCHERS* OR ANYTHING? NO *BAT-SHARK REPELLENT?*

IT'S JUST A *PROP CAR.* NOTHING IN THIS TOWN IS REAL.

JUST AS I THOUGHT. THAT'S HER CAR OUTSIDE HER DEALERS' PLACE.

I'M *NOT* GOING *IN* THERE, HARLEY.

FINE. YOU WAIT FOR ME. DRIVE AWAY, AN' I'LL HUNT YA DOWN AND DECAPACITATE YA, CAPEESH?

YEAH...I *GET* IT. JUST BE CAREFUL... YOU'RE ON *THEIR* TURF.

IT'S *THEM* THAT OUGHTA BE WORRIED. YOU JUST KEEP THAT CAR *RUNNIN'.*

I NEED TA SPEAK TA THE OWNERS?

WHO WANTS TO KNOW?

ME. *ME,* WHO JUST *ASKED* YOU. JUST A SECOND AGO. RIGHT HERE. IN FRONT A' YA.

IS IT THE *AIR* OUT HERE OR THE *CONSTANT SUNLIGHT* CAUSING THE BRAIN DAMAGE?

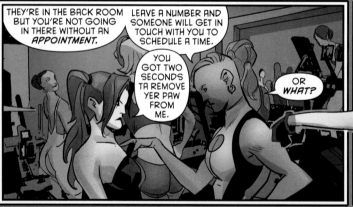

THEY'RE IN THE BACK ROOM BUT YOU'RE NOT GOING IN THERE WITHOUT AN *APPOINTMENT.*

LEAVE A NUMBER AND SOMEONE WILL GET IN TOUCH WITH YOU TO SCHEDULE A TIME.

YOU GOT TWO SECONDS TA REMOVE YER PAW FROM ME.

OR *WHAT?*

OR *THIS.*

FROM THE *LOOKS* A' YER *CLIENTELE* HERE, I'M SURE ONE OF 'EM CAN RECOMMEND A PLASTIC SURGEON TA FIX THAT *BUSTED SCHNOZZ.*

VP RKOUT

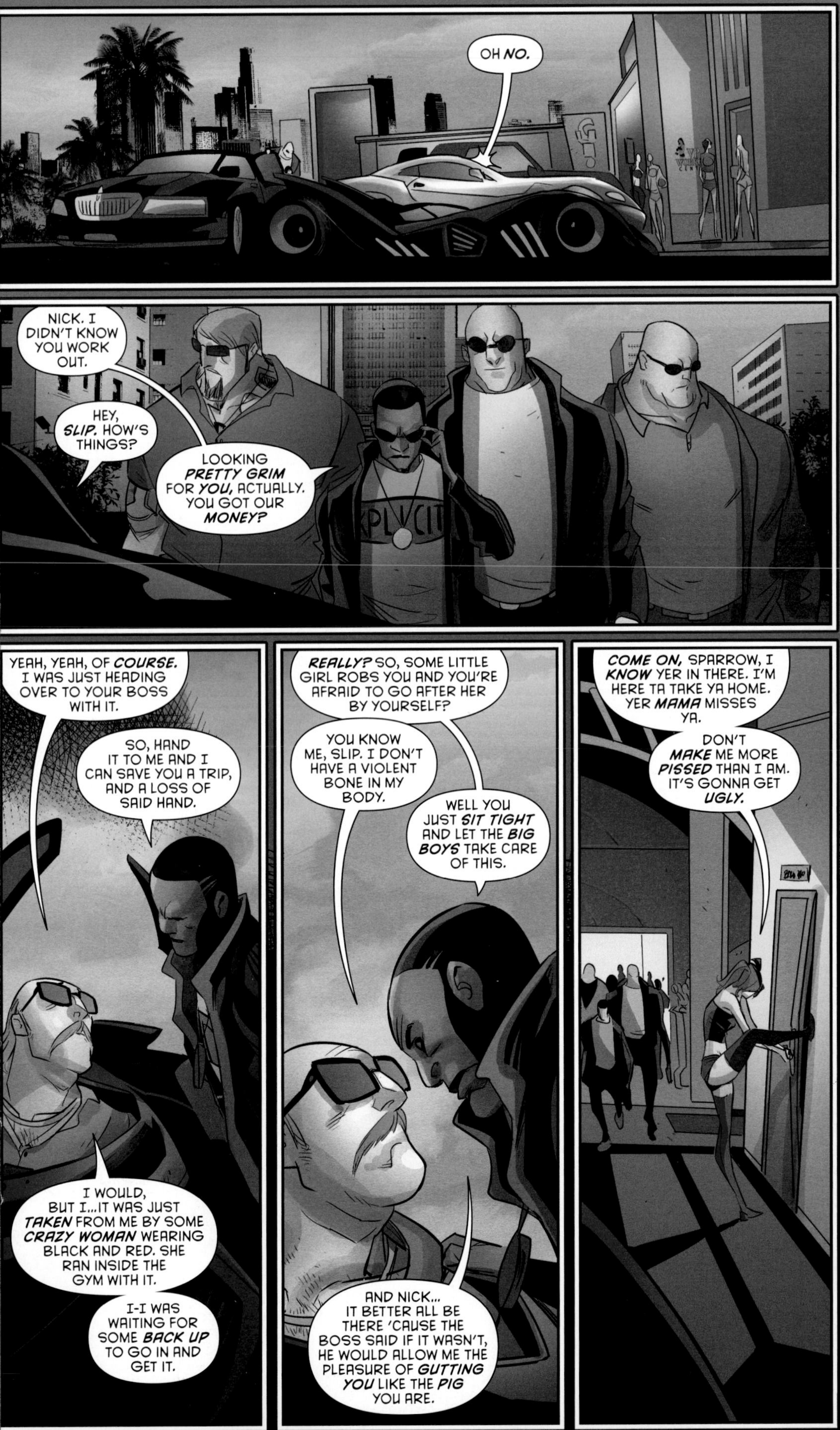
OH NO.
NICK. I DIDN'T KNOW YOU WORK OUT.
HEY, SLIP. HOW'S THINGS?
LOOKING PRETTY GRIM FOR YOU, ACTUALLY. YOU GOT OUR MONEY?
XPLICIT
YEAH, YEAH, OF COURSE. I WAS JUST HEADING OVER TO YOUR BOSS WITH IT.
SO, HAND IT TO ME AND I CAN SAVE YOU A TRIP, AND A LOSS OF SAID HAND.
I WOULD, BUT I...IT WAS JUST TAKEN FROM ME BY SOME CRAZY WOMAN WEARING BLACK AND RED. SHE RAN INSIDE THE GYM WITH IT.
I-I WAS WAITING FOR SOME BACK UP TO GO IN AND GET IT.
REALLY? SO, SOME LITTLE GIRL ROBS YOU AND YOU'RE AFRAID TO GO AFTER HER BY YOURSELF?
YOU KNOW ME, SLIP. I DON'T HAVE A VIOLENT BONE IN MY BODY.
WELL YOU JUST SIT TIGHT AND LET THE BIG BOYS TAKE CARE OF THIS.
AND NICK... IT BETTER ALL BE THERE 'CAUSE THE BOSS SAID IF IT WASN'T, HE WOULD ALLOW ME THE PLEASURE OF GUTTING YOU LIKE THE PIG YOU ARE.
COME ON, SPARROW, I KNOW YER IN THERE. I'M HERE TA TAKE YA HOME. YER MAMA MISSES YA.
DON'T MAKE ME MORE PISSED THAN I AM. IT'S GONNA GET UGLY.

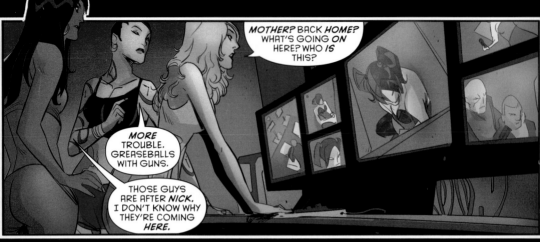

MOTHER? BACK *HOME?* WHAT'S GOING *ON* HERE? WHO *IS* THIS?

MORE TROUBLE. GREASEBALLS WITH GUNS.

THOSE GUYS ARE AFTER *NICK.* I DON'T KNOW WHY THEY'RE COMING *HERE.*

WELL, I'M *NOT* GOING TO HAVE THIS PLACE TURN INTO A WAR ZONE.

VICK, UNLOCK THE BACK DOOR.

PLEASE COME *IN.*

WHO'RE *YOU?*

MY NAME IS *HANNAH,* AND I'M PART-OWNER. YOU DECKED ONE OF MY STAFF LOOKING FOR ME. *REMEMBER?*

HEY! WHERE DO YOU THINK YOU'RE *GOING?*

YOU TALKIN' TA *ME?*

EVERYONE, WON'T YOU STEP INTO MY OFFICE?

GENTLEMEN, *PLEASE* PUT THE GUNS AWAY.

LISTEN TO ME *CLOSELY.*

WHATEVER BUSINESS ALL OF YOU HAVE WITH EACH OTHER IS NOT *MINE* OR *VICKI'S* PROBLEM.

I WOULD APPRECIATE IF YOU CAN RESPECT OUR SPACE AND TAKE IT OUTSIDE TO THE ALLEYWAY IN BACK AND WORK IT OUT AMONGST *YOURSELVES.*

DO THIS FOR ME, AND EACH OF YOU CAN HAVE A *FREE MEMBERSHIP* AT THE GYM FOR SIX MONTHS, PLUS PARKING.

DO WE ALL *UNDERSTAND* EACH OTHER?

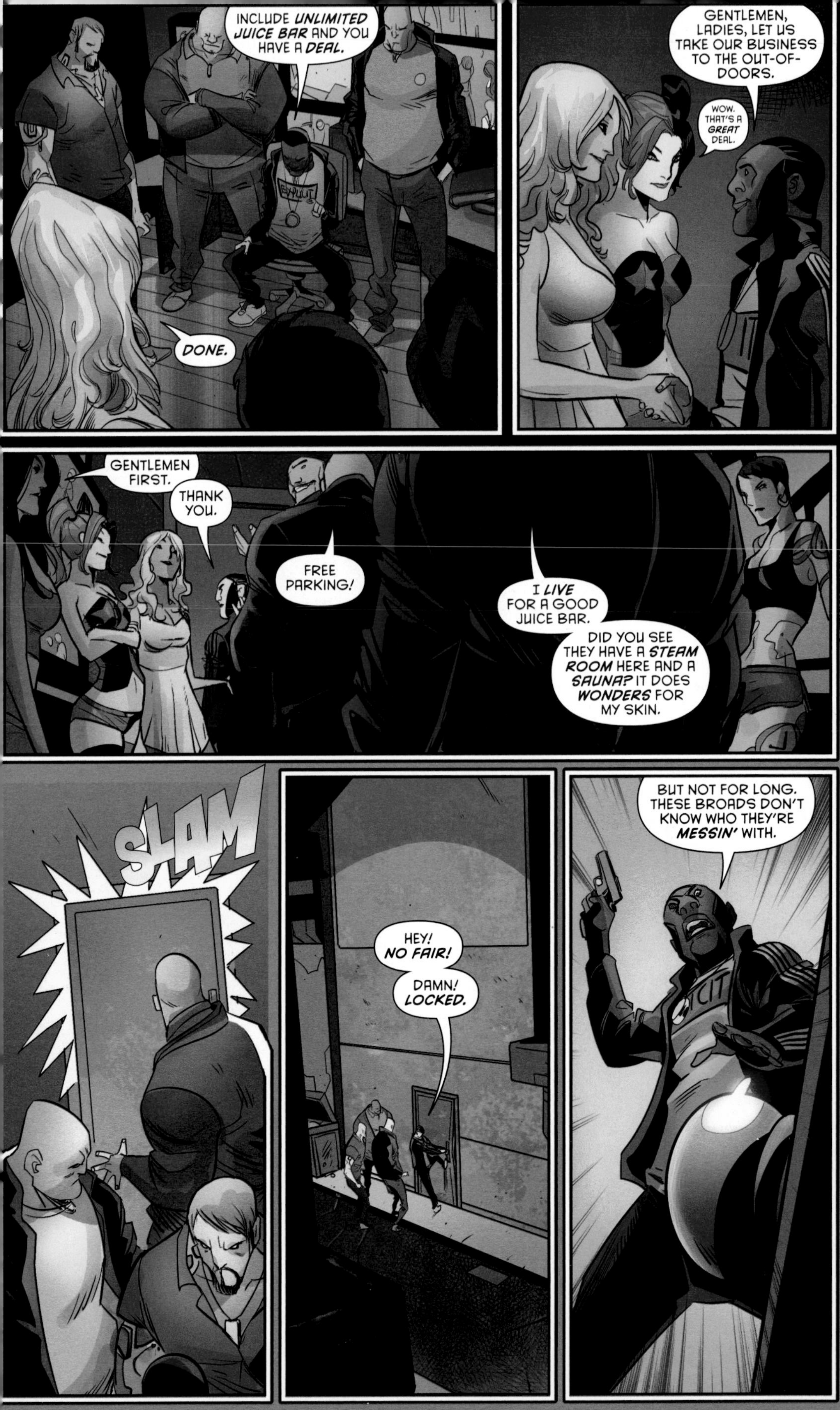
INCLUDE UNLIMITED JUICE BAR AND YOU HAVE A DEAL.
DONE.
GENTLEMEN, LADIES, LET US TAKE OUR BUSINESS TO THE OUT-OF-DOORS.
WOW. THAT'S A GREAT DEAL.
GENTLEMEN FIRST.
THANK YOU.
FREE PARKING!
I LIVE FOR A GOOD JUICE BAR.
DID YOU SEE THEY HAVE A STEAM ROOM HERE AND A SAUNA? IT DOES WONDERS FOR MY SKIN.
SLAM
HEY! NO FAIR!
DAMN! LOCKED.
BUT NOT FOR LONG. THESE BROADS DON'T KNOW WHO THEY'RE MESSIN' WITH.

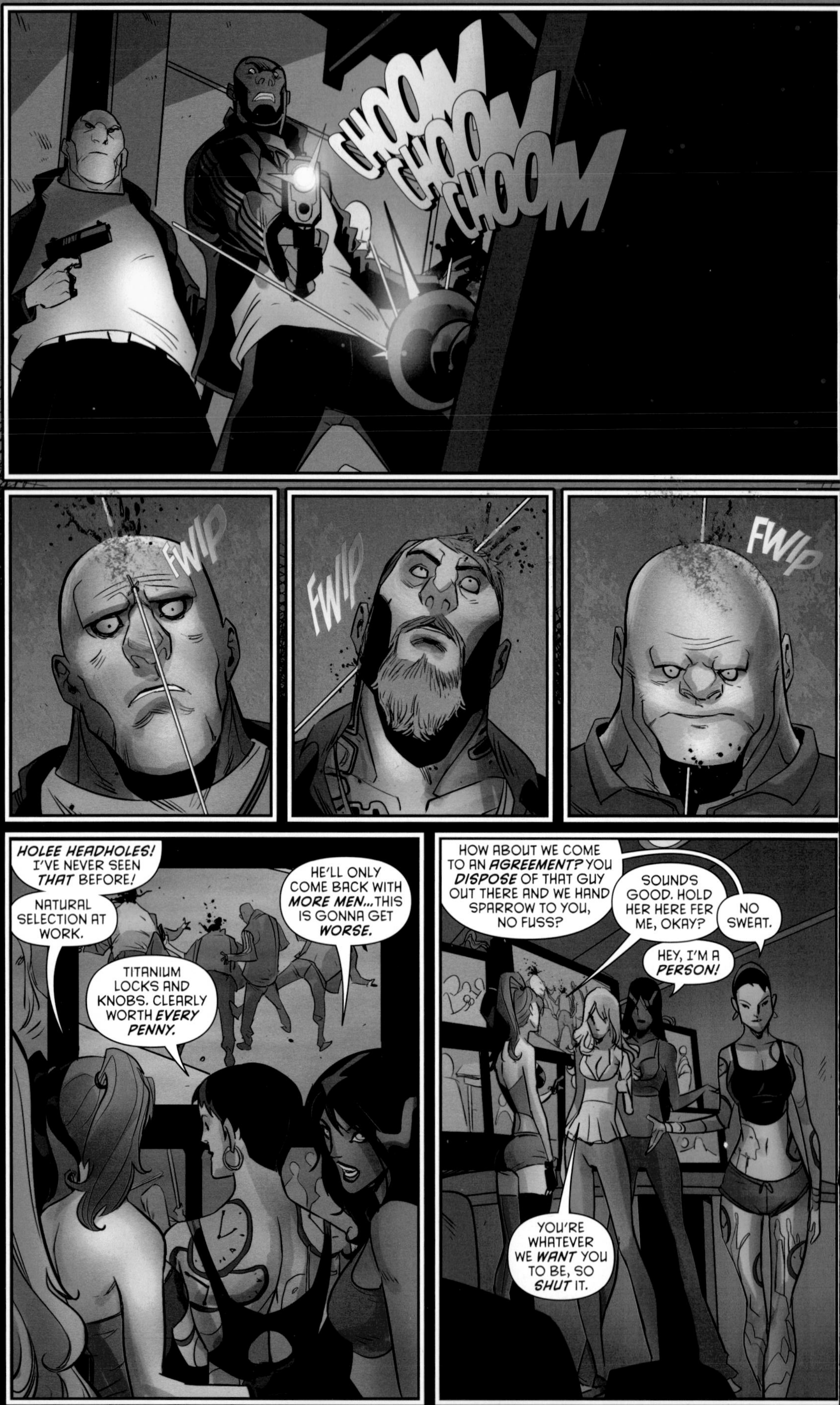
CHOOM
CHOOM
CHOOM
FWIP
FWIP
FWIP
HOLEE HEADHOLES! I'VE NEVER SEEN THAT BEFORE!
NATURAL SELECTION AT WORK.
HE'LL ONLY COME BACK WITH MORE MEN... THIS IS GONNA GET WORSE.
TITANIUM LOCKS AND KNOBS. CLEARLY WORTH EVERY PENNY.
HOW ABOUT WE COME TO AN AGREEMENT? YOU DISPOSE OF THAT GUY OUT THERE AND WE HAND SPARROW TO YOU, NO FUSS?
SOUNDS GOOD. HOLD HER HERE FER ME, OKAY?
NO SWEAT.
HEY, I'M A PERSON!
YOU'RE WHATEVER WE WANT YOU TO BE, SO SHUT IT.

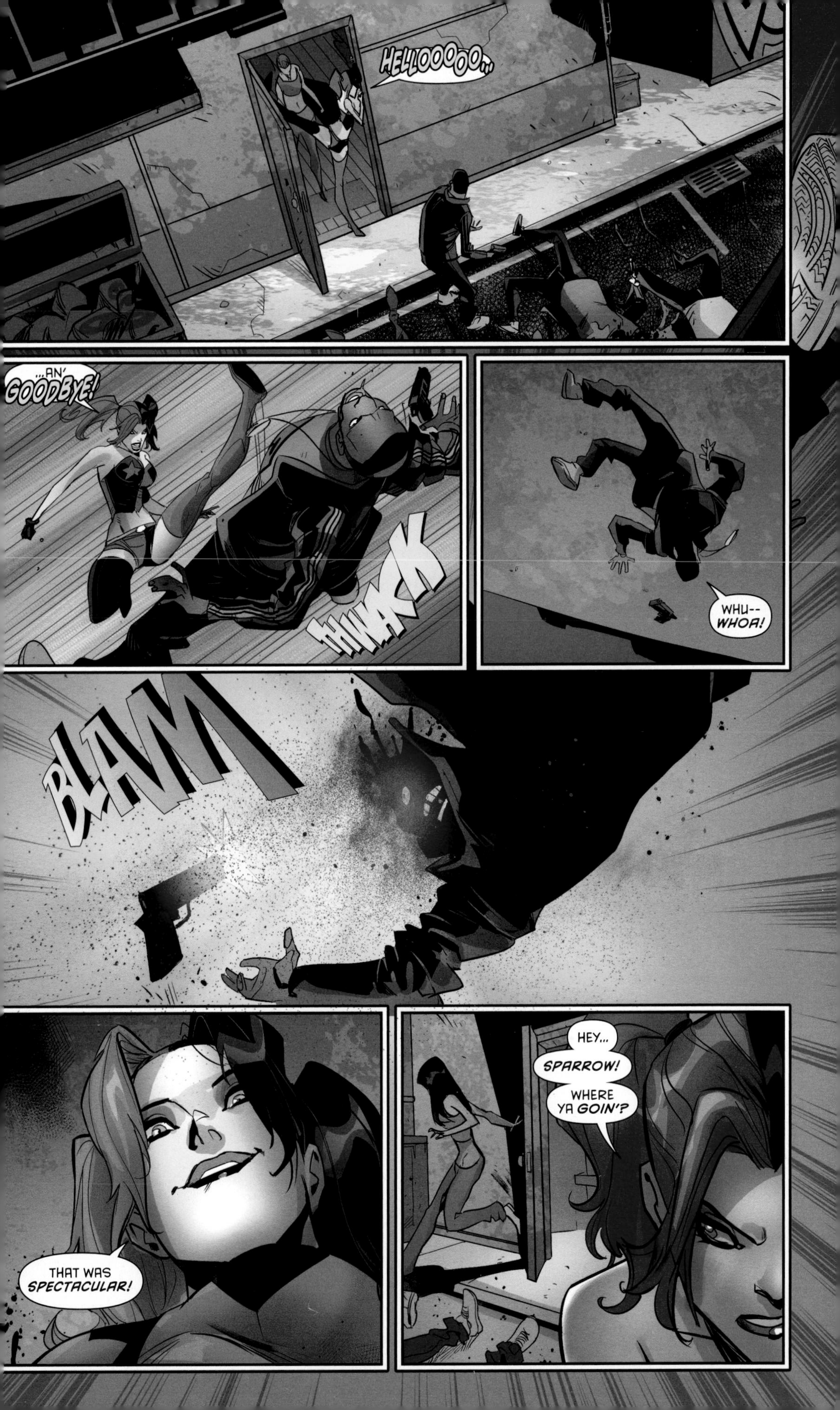
HELLOOOOO...
...AN' GOODBYE!
THWACK
WHU-- WHOA!
BLAM
THAT WAS SPECTACULAR!
HEY... SPARROW!
WHERE YA GOIN'?

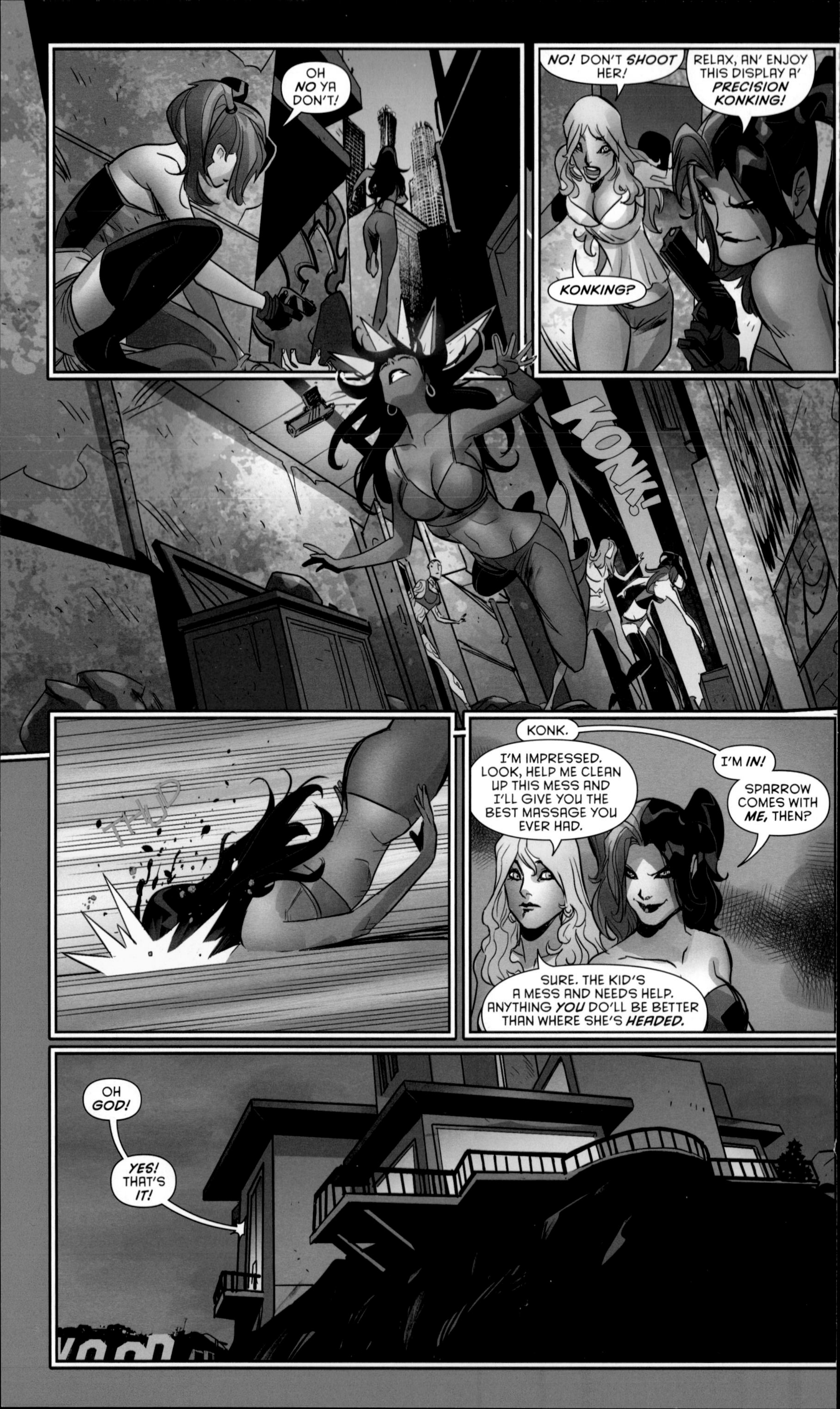
OH NO YA DON'T!
NO! DON'T SHOOT HER!
RELAX, AN' ENJOY THIS DISPLAY A' PRECISION KONKING!
KONKING?
KONK!
THUD
KONK.
I'M IN!
SPARROW COMES WITH ME, THEN?
I'M IMPRESSED. LOOK, HELP ME CLEAN UP THIS MESS AND I'LL GIVE YOU THE BEST MASSAGE YOU EVER HAD.
SURE. THE KID'S A MESS AND NEEDS HELP. ANYTHING YOU DO'LL BE BETTER THAN WHERE SHE'S HEADED.
OH GOD!
YES! THAT'S IT!

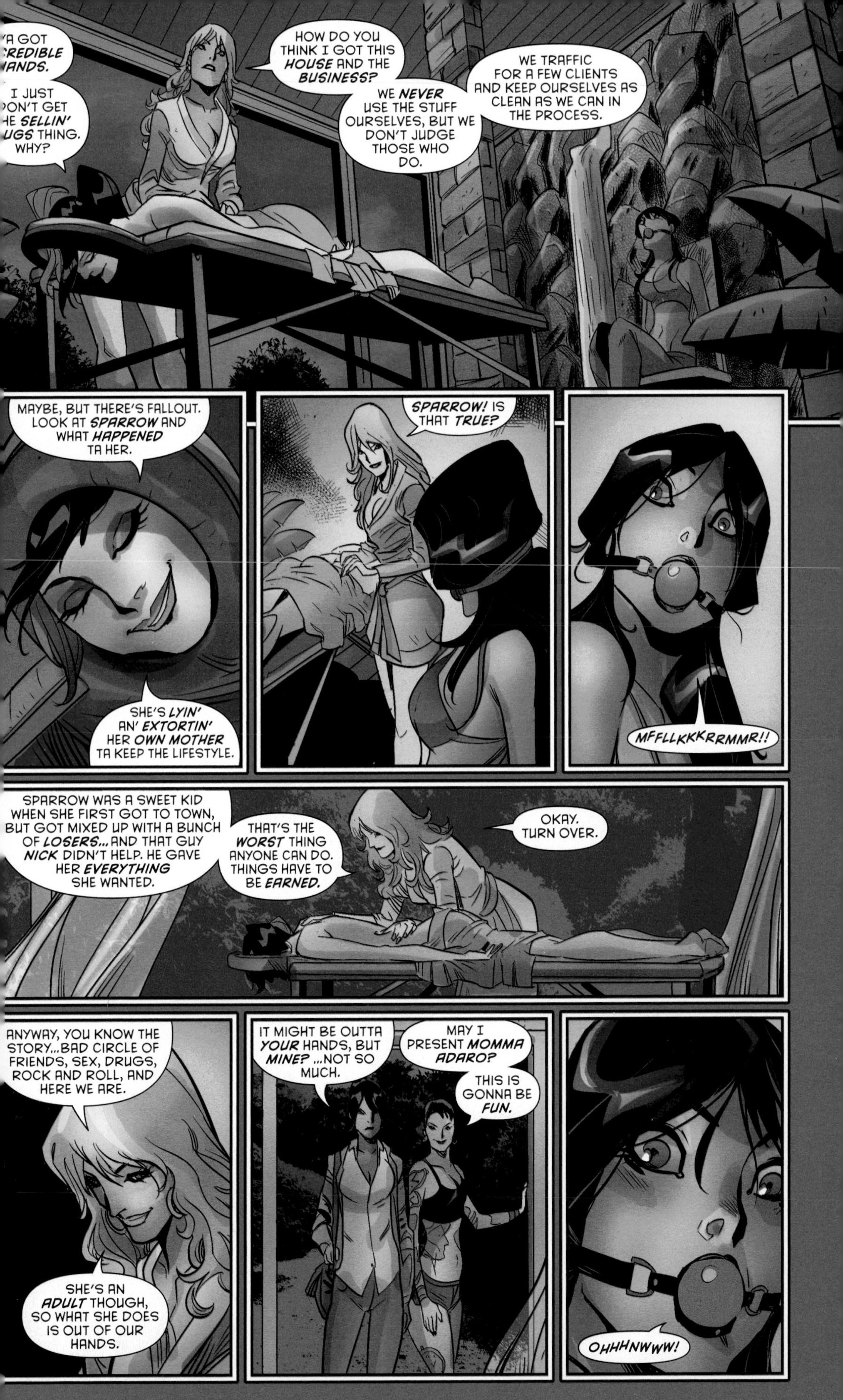

'A GOT
CREDIBLE
HANDS.
I JUST
DON'T GET
HE SELLIN'
UGS THING.
WHY?
HOW DO YOU THINK I GOT THIS HOUSE AND THE BUSINESS?
WE NEVER USE THE STUFF OURSELVES, BUT WE DON'T JUDGE THOSE WHO DO.
WE TRAFFIC FOR A FEW CLIENTS AND KEEP OURSELVES AS CLEAN AS WE CAN IN THE PROCESS.
MAYBE, BUT THERE'S FALLOUT. LOOK AT SPARROW AND WHAT HAPPENED TA HER.
SHE'S LYIN' AN' EXTORTIN' HER OWN MOTHER TA KEEP THE LIFESTYLE.
SPARROW! IS THAT TRUE?
MFFLLKKKRRMMR!!
SPARROW WAS A SWEET KID WHEN SHE FIRST GOT TO TOWN, BUT GOT MIXED UP WITH A BUNCH OF LOSERS... AND THAT GUY NICK DIDN'T HELP. HE GAVE HER EVERYTHING SHE WANTED.
THAT'S THE WORST THING ANYONE CAN DO. THINGS HAVE TO BE EARNED.
OKAY. TURN OVER.
ANYWAY, YOU KNOW THE STORY... BAD CIRCLE OF FRIENDS, SEX, DRUGS, ROCK AND ROLL, AND HERE WE ARE.
SHE'S AN ADULT THOUGH, SO WHAT SHE DOES IS OUT OF OUR HANDS.
IT MIGHT BE OUTTA YOUR HANDS, BUT MINE? ...NOT SO MUCH.
MAY I PRESENT MOMMA ADARO?
THIS IS GONNA BE FUN.
OHHHNWWW!

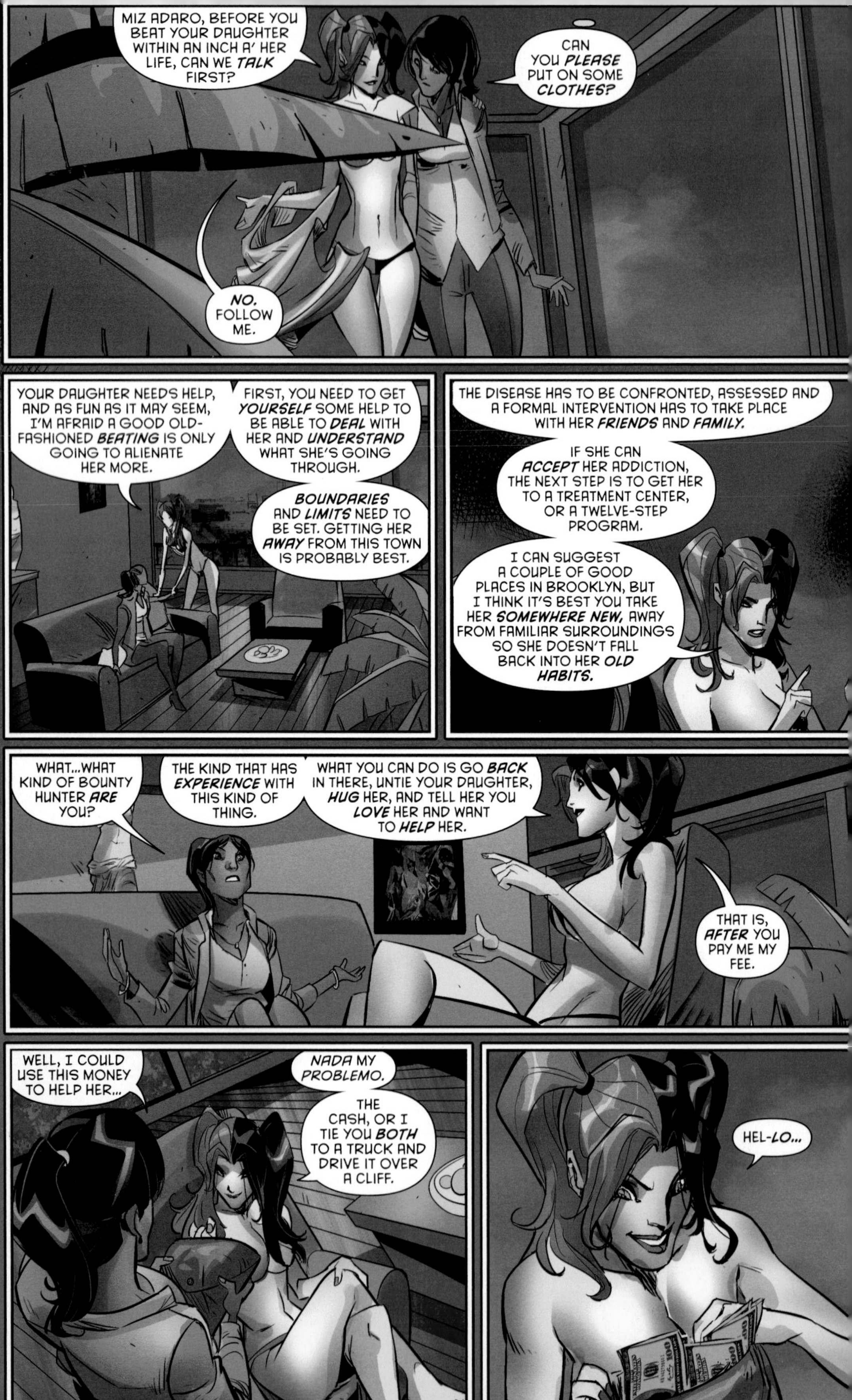
MIZ ADARO, BEFORE YOU BEAT YOUR DAUGHTER WITHIN AN INCH A' HER LIFE, CAN WE TALK FIRST?
CAN YOU PLEASE PUT ON SOME CLOTHES?
NO. FOLLOW ME.
YOUR DAUGHTER NEEDS HELP, AND AS FUN AS IT MAY SEEM, I'M AFRAID A GOOD OLD-FASHIONED BEATING IS ONLY GOING TO ALIENATE HER MORE.
FIRST, YOU NEED TO GET YOURSELF SOME HELP TO BE ABLE TO DEAL WITH HER AND UNDERSTAND WHAT SHE'S GOING THROUGH.
BOUNDARIES AND LIMITS NEED TO BE SET. GETTING HER AWAY FROM THIS TOWN IS PROBABLY BEST.
THE DISEASE HAS TO BE CONFRONTED, ASSESSED AND A FORMAL INTERVENTION HAS TO TAKE PLACE WITH HER FRIENDS AND FAMILY.
IF SHE CAN ACCEPT HER ADDICTION, THE NEXT STEP IS TO GET HER TO A TREATMENT CENTER, OR A TWELVE-STEP PROGRAM.
I CAN SUGGEST A COUPLE OF GOOD PLACES IN BROOKLYN, BUT I THINK IT'S BEST YOU TAKE HER SOMEWHERE NEW, AWAY FROM FAMILIAR SURROUNDINGS SO SHE DOESN'T FALL BACK INTO HER OLD HABITS.
WHAT...WHAT KIND OF BOUNTY HUNTER ARE YOU?
THE KIND THAT HAS EXPERIENCE WITH THIS KIND OF THING.
WHAT YOU CAN DO IS GO BACK IN THERE, UNTIE YOUR DAUGHTER, HUG HER, AND TELL HER YOU LOVE HER AND WANT TO HELP HER.
THAT IS, AFTER YOU PAY ME MY FEE.
WELL, I COULD USE THIS MONEY TO HELP HER...
NADA MY PROBLEMO.
THE CASH, OR I TIE YOU BOTH TO A TRUCK AND DRIVE IT OVER A CLIFF.
HEL-LO...

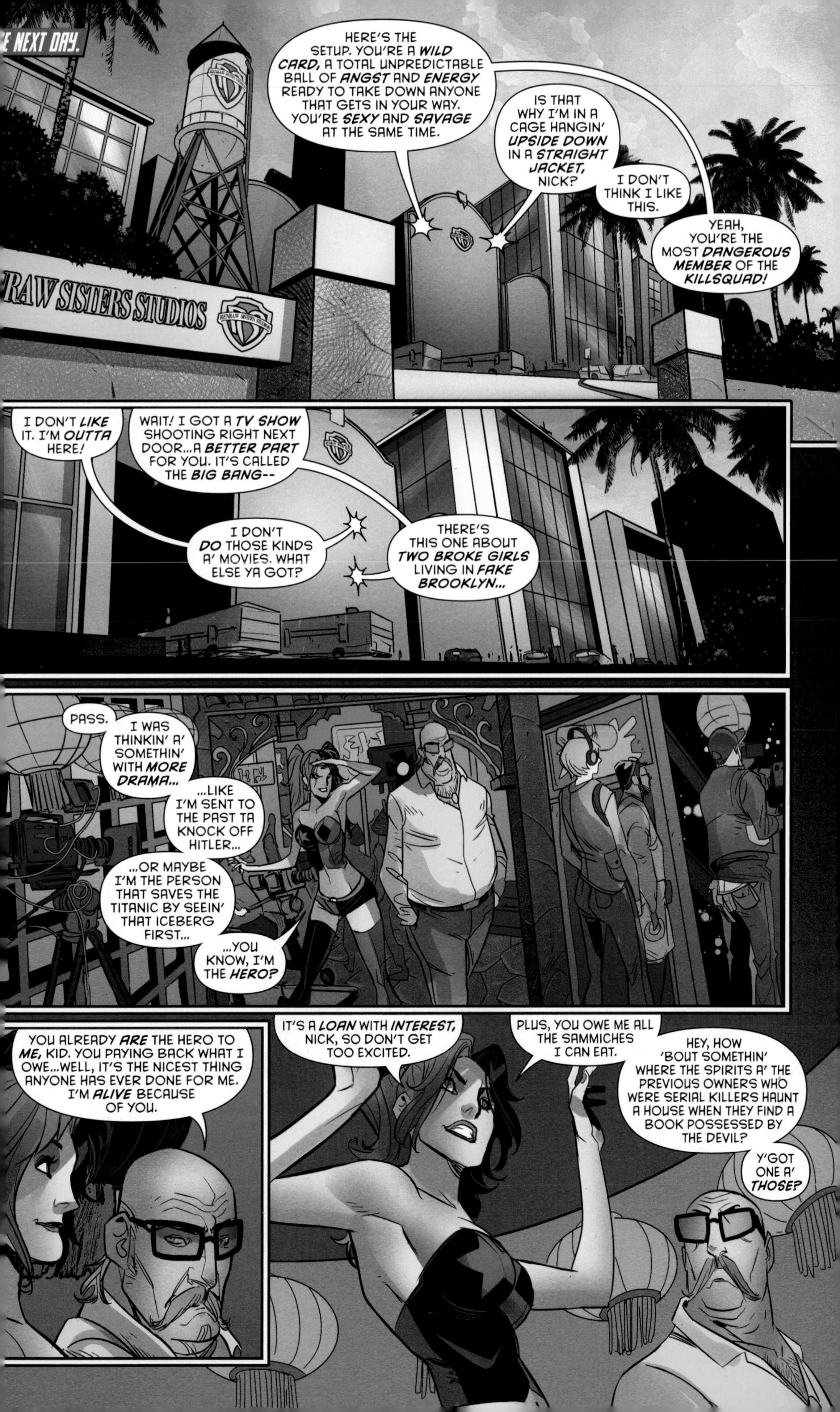

E NEXT DAY.
RAW SISTERS STUDIOS
HERE'S THE SETUP. YOU'RE A WILD CARD, A TOTAL UNPREDICTABLE BALL OF ANGST AND ENERGY READY TO TAKE DOWN ANYONE THAT GETS IN YOUR WAY. YOU'RE SEXY AND SAVAGE AT THE SAME TIME.
IS THAT WHY I'M IN A CAGE HANGIN' UPSIDE DOWN IN A STRAIGHT JACKET, NICK?
I DON'T THINK I LIKE THIS.
YEAH, YOU'RE THE MOST DANGEROUS MEMBER OF THE KILLSQUAD!
I DON'T LIKE IT. I'M OUTTA HERE!
WAIT! I GOT A TV SHOW SHOOTING RIGHT NEXT DOOR...A BETTER PART FOR YOU. IT'S CALLED THE BIG BANG--
I DON'T DO THOSE KINDS A' MOVIES. WHAT ELSE YA GOT?
THERE'S THIS ONE ABOUT TWO BROKE GIRLS LIVING IN FAKE BROOKLYN...
PASS.
I WAS THINKIN' A' SOMETHIN' WITH MORE DRAMA...
...LIKE I'M SENT TO THE PAST TA KNOCK OFF HITLER...
...OR MAYBE I'M THE PERSON THAT SAVES THE TITANIC BY SEEIN' THAT ICEBERG FIRST...
...YOU KNOW, I'M THE HERO?
YOU ALREADY ARE THE HERO TO ME, KID. YOU PAYING BACK WHAT I OWE...WELL, IT'S THE NICEST THING ANYONE HAS EVER DONE FOR ME. I'M ALIVE BECAUSE OF YOU.
IT'S A LOAN WITH INTEREST, NICK, SO DON'T GET TOO EXCITED.
PLUS, YOU OWE ME ALL THE SAMMICHES I CAN EAT.
HEY, HOW 'BOUT SOMETHIN' WHERE THE SPIRITS A' THE PREVIOUS OWNERS WHO WERE SERIAL KILLERS HAUNT A HOUSE WHEN THEY FIND A BOOK POSSESSED BY THE DEVIL?
Y'GOT ONE A' THOSE?

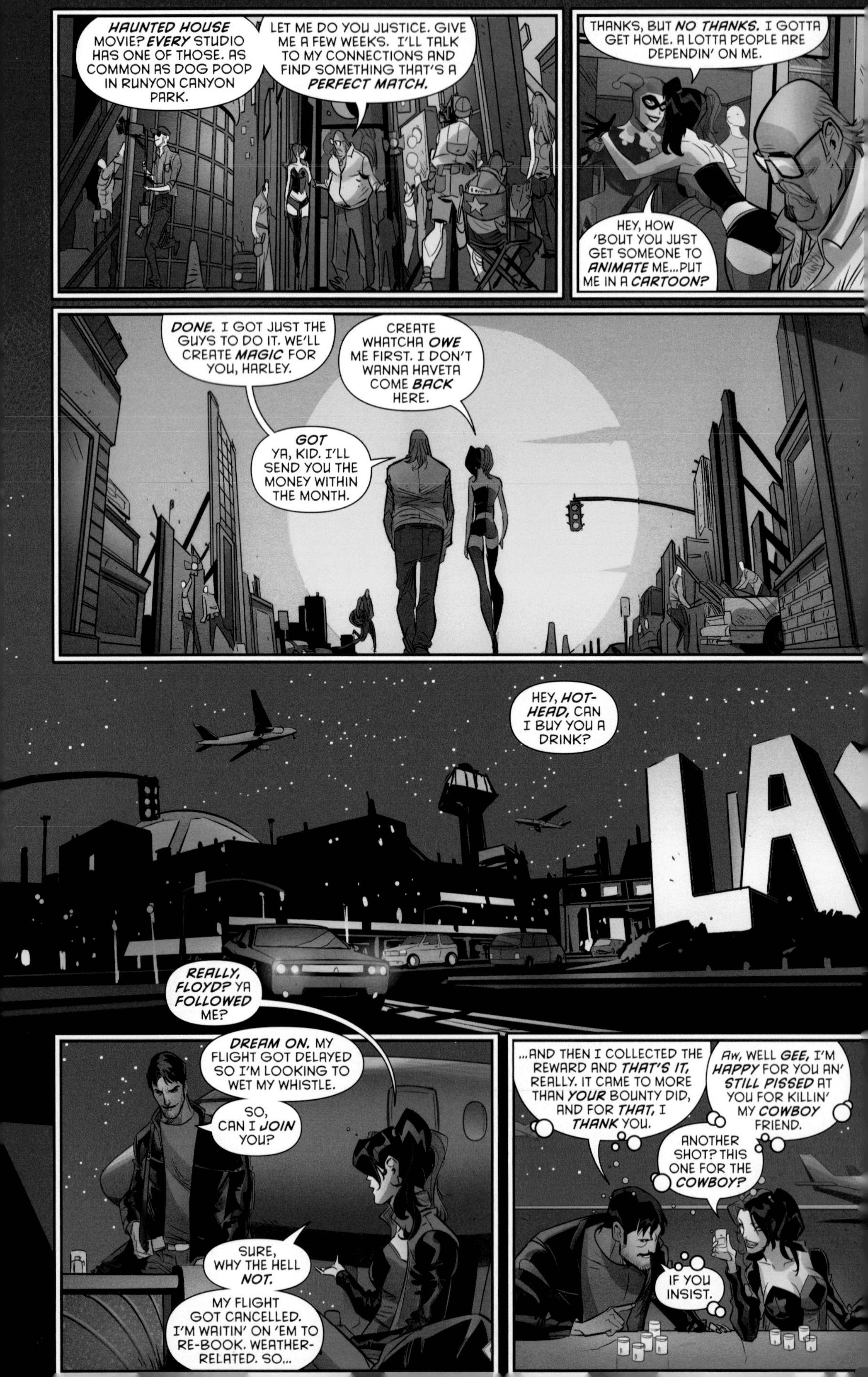
HAUNTED HOUSE MOVIE? EVERY STUDIO HAS ONE OF THOSE. AS COMMON AS DOG POOP IN RUNYON CANYON PARK.
LET ME DO YOU JUSTICE. GIVE ME A FEW WEEKS. I'LL TALK TO MY CONNECTIONS AND FIND SOMETHING THAT'S A PERFECT MATCH.
THANKS, BUT NO THANKS. I GOTTA GET HOME. A LOTTA PEOPLE ARE DEPENDIN' ON ME.
HEY, HOW 'BOUT YOU JUST GET SOMEONE TO ANIMATE ME...PUT ME IN A CARTOON?
DONE. I GOT JUST THE GUYS TO DO IT. WE'LL CREATE MAGIC FOR YOU, HARLEY.
CREATE WHATCHA OWE ME FIRST. I DON'T WANNA HAVETA COME BACK HERE.
GOT YA, KID. I'LL SEND YOU THE MONEY WITHIN THE MONTH.
HEY, HOT-HEAD, CAN I BUY YOU A DRINK?
REALLY, FLOYD? YA FOLLOWED ME?
DREAM ON. MY FLIGHT GOT DELAYED SO I'M LOOKING TO WET MY WHISTLE.
SO, CAN I JOIN YOU?
SURE, WHY THE HELL NOT.
MY FLIGHT GOT CANCELLED. I'M WAITIN' ON 'EM TO RE-BOOK. WEATHER-RELATED. SO...
...AND THEN I COLLECTED THE REWARD AND THAT'S IT, REALLY. IT CAME TO MORE THAN YOUR BOUNTY DID, AND FOR THAT, I THANK YOU.
AW, WELL GEE, I'M HAPPY FOR YOU AN' STILL PISSED AT YOU FOR KILLIN' MY COWBOY FRIEND.
ANOTHER SHOT? THIS ONE FOR THE COWBOY?
IF YOU INSIST.

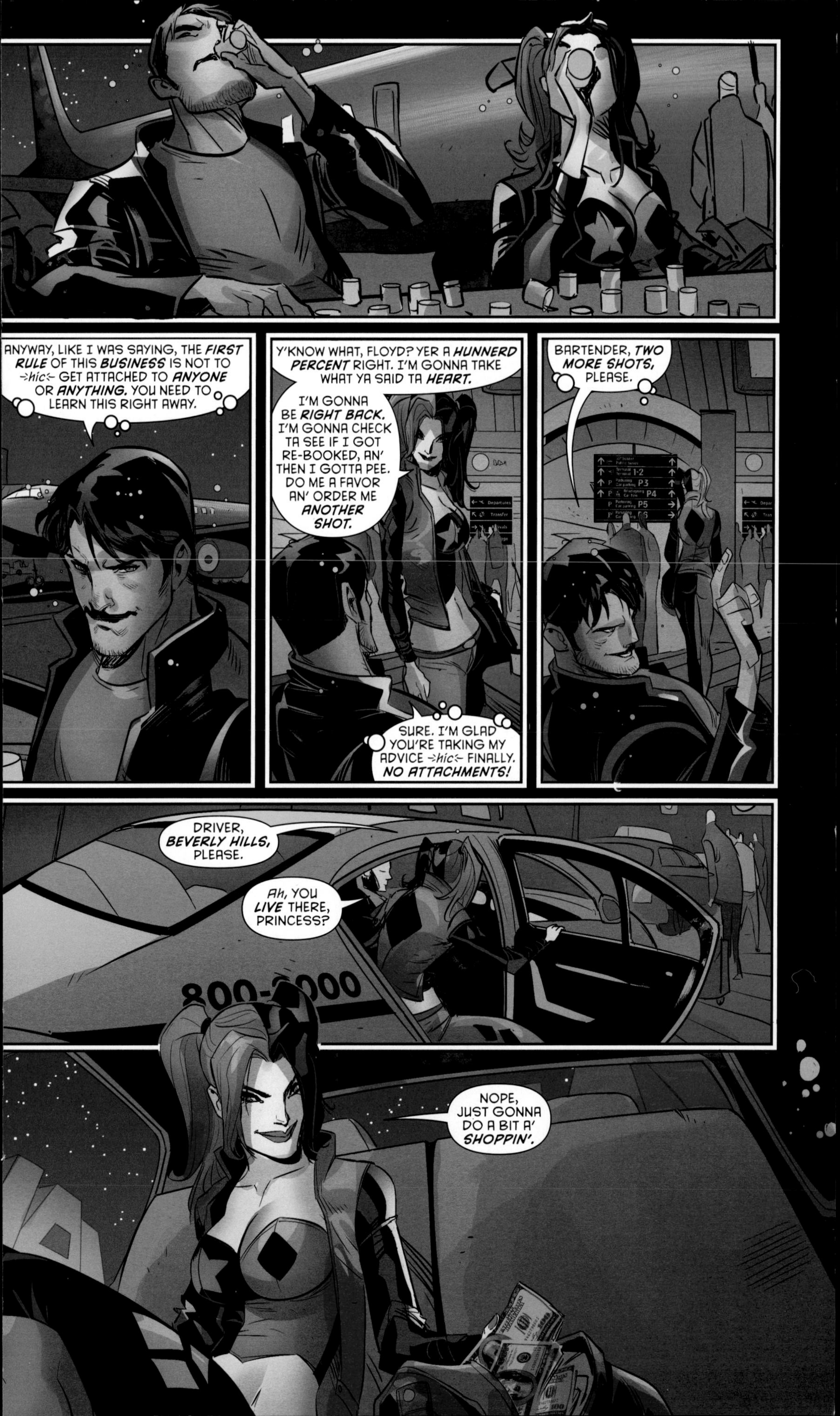
ANYWAY, LIKE I WAS SAYING, THE FIRST RULE OF THIS BUSINESS IS NOT TO ->hic<- GET ATTACHED TO ANYONE OR ANYTHING. YOU NEED TO LEARN THIS RIGHT AWAY.
Y'KNOW WHAT, FLOYD? YER A HUNNERD PERCENT RIGHT. I'M GONNA TAKE WHAT YA SAID TA HEART.
I'M GONNA BE RIGHT BACK. I'M GONNA CHECK TA SEE IF I GOT RE-BOOKED, AN' THEN I GOTTA PEE. DO ME A FAVOR AN' ORDER ME ANOTHER SHOT.
SURE. I'M GLAD YOU'RE TAKING MY ADVICE ->hic<- FINALLY. NO ATTACHMENTS!
BARTENDER, TWO MORE SHOTS, PLEASE.
Departures
Transfer
DRIVER, BEVERLY HILLS, PLEASE.
Ah, YOU LIVE THERE, PRINCESS?
NOPE, JUST GONNA DO A BIT A' SHOPPIN'.

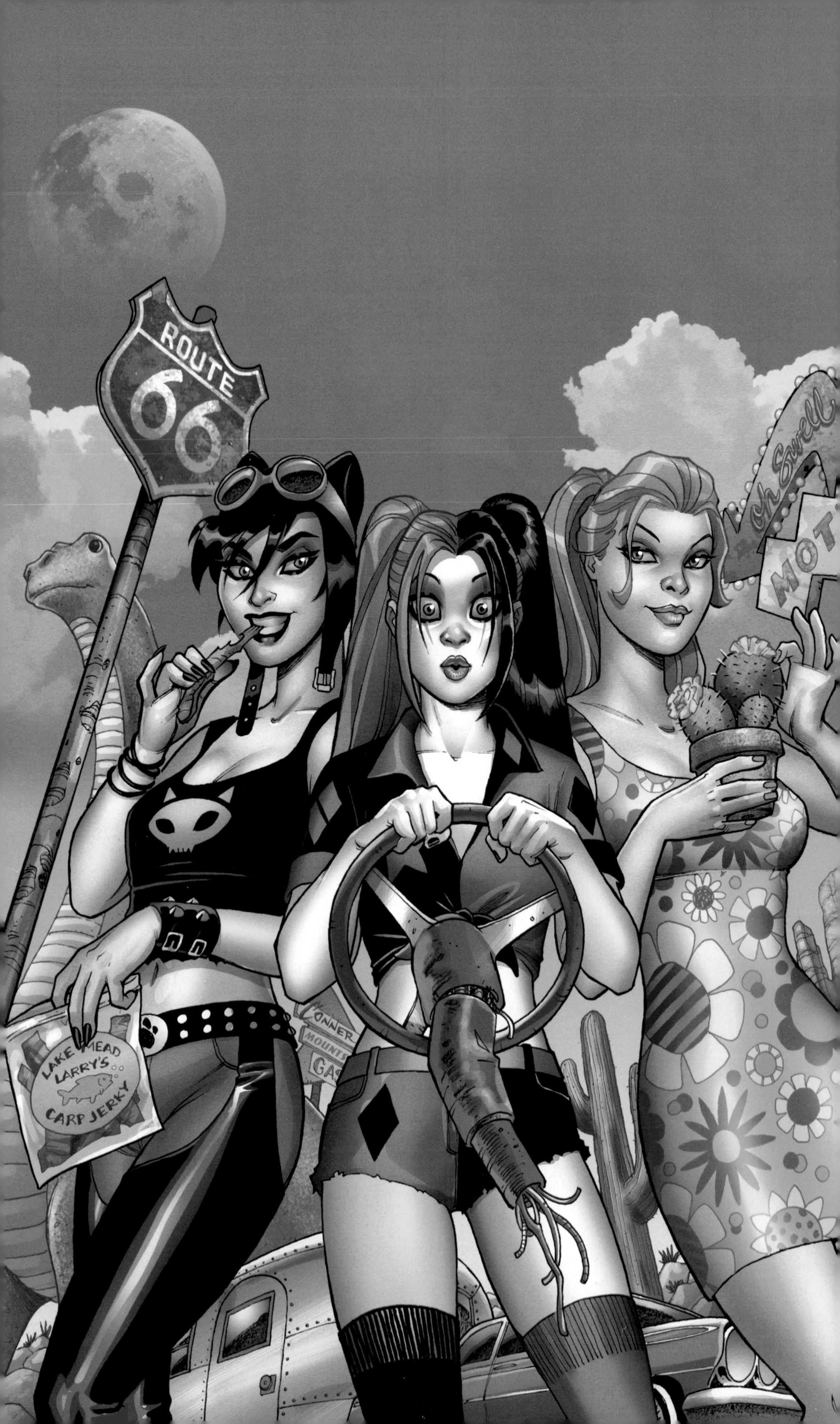
ROUTE
66
LAKE MEAD
LARRY'S
CARP JERKY
MOT

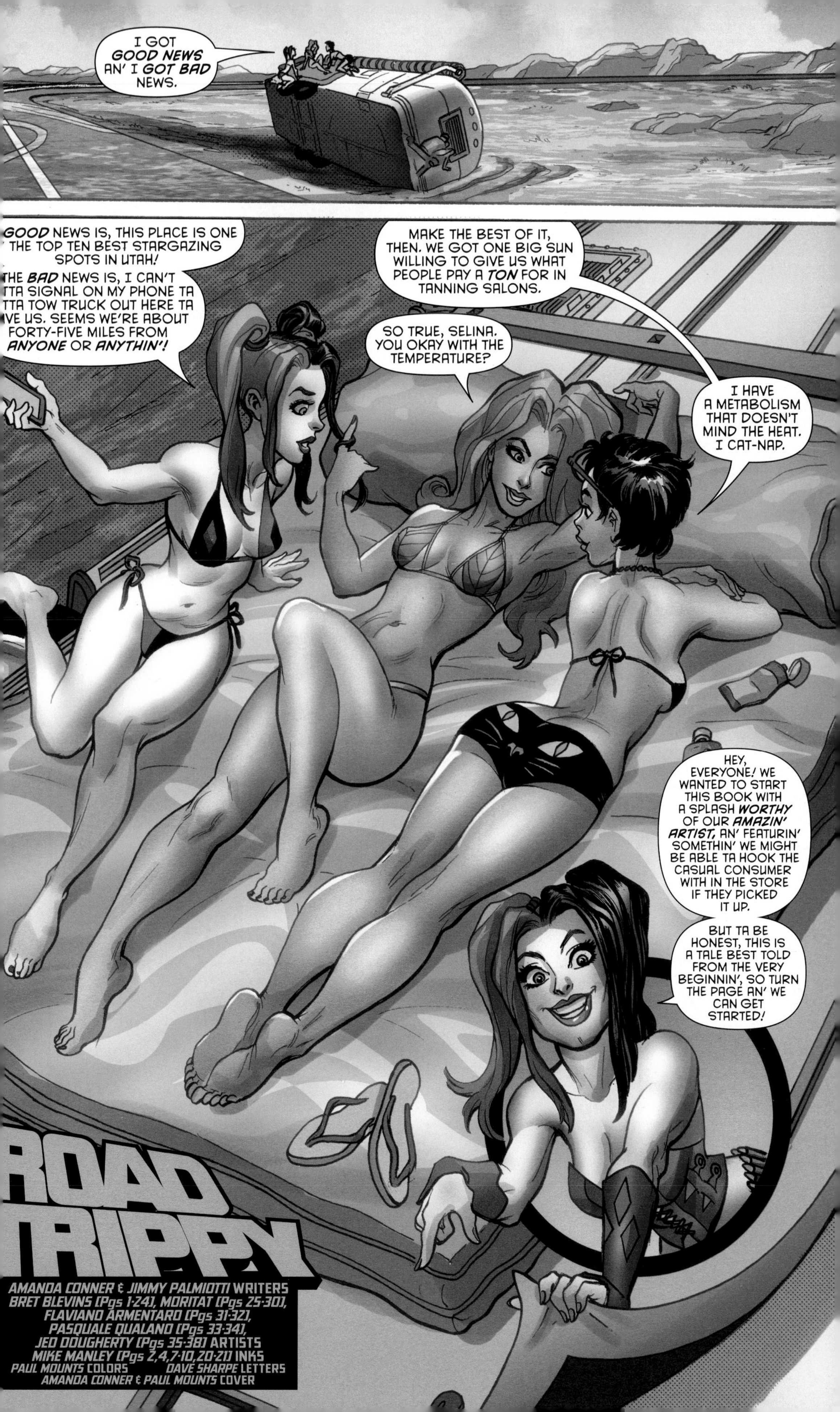

I GOT GOOD NEWS AN' I GOT BAD NEWS.
GOOD NEWS IS, THIS PLACE IS ONE THE TOP TEN BEST STARGAZING SPOTS IN UTAH!
THE BAD NEWS IS, I CAN'T TTA SIGNAL ON MY PHONE TA TTA TOW TRUCK OUT HERE TA VE US. SEEMS WE'RE ABOUT FORTY-FIVE MILES FROM ANYONE OR ANYTHIN'!
MAKE THE BEST OF IT, THEN. WE GOT ONE BIG SUN WILLING TO GIVE US WHAT PEOPLE PAY A TON FOR IN TANNING SALONS.
SO TRUE, SELINA. YOU OKAY WITH THE TEMPERATURE?
I HAVE A METABOLISM THAT DOESN'T MIND THE HEAT. I CAT-NAP.
HEY, EVERYONE! WE WANTED TO START THIS BOOK WITH A SPLASH WORTHY OF OUR AMAZIN' ARTIST, AN' FEATURIN' SOMETHIN' WE MIGHT BE ABLE TA HOOK THE CASUAL CONSUMER WITH IN THE STORE IF THEY PICKED IT UP.
BUT TA BE HONEST, THIS IS A TALE BEST TOLD FROM THE VERY BEGINNIN', SO TURN THE PAGE AN' WE CAN GET STARTED!
ROAD TRIPPY
AMANDA CONNER & JIMMY PALMIOTTI WRITERS
BRET BLEVINS [Pgs 1-24], MORITAT [Pgs 25-30], FLAVIANO ARMENTARO [Pgs 31-32], PASQUALE QUALANO [Pgs 33-34], JED DOUGHERTY [Pgs 35-38] ARTISTS
MIKE MANLEY [Pgs 2,4,7-10,20-21] INKS
PAUL MOUNTS COLORS DAVE SHARPE LETTERS
AMANDA CONNER & PAUL MOUNTS COVER

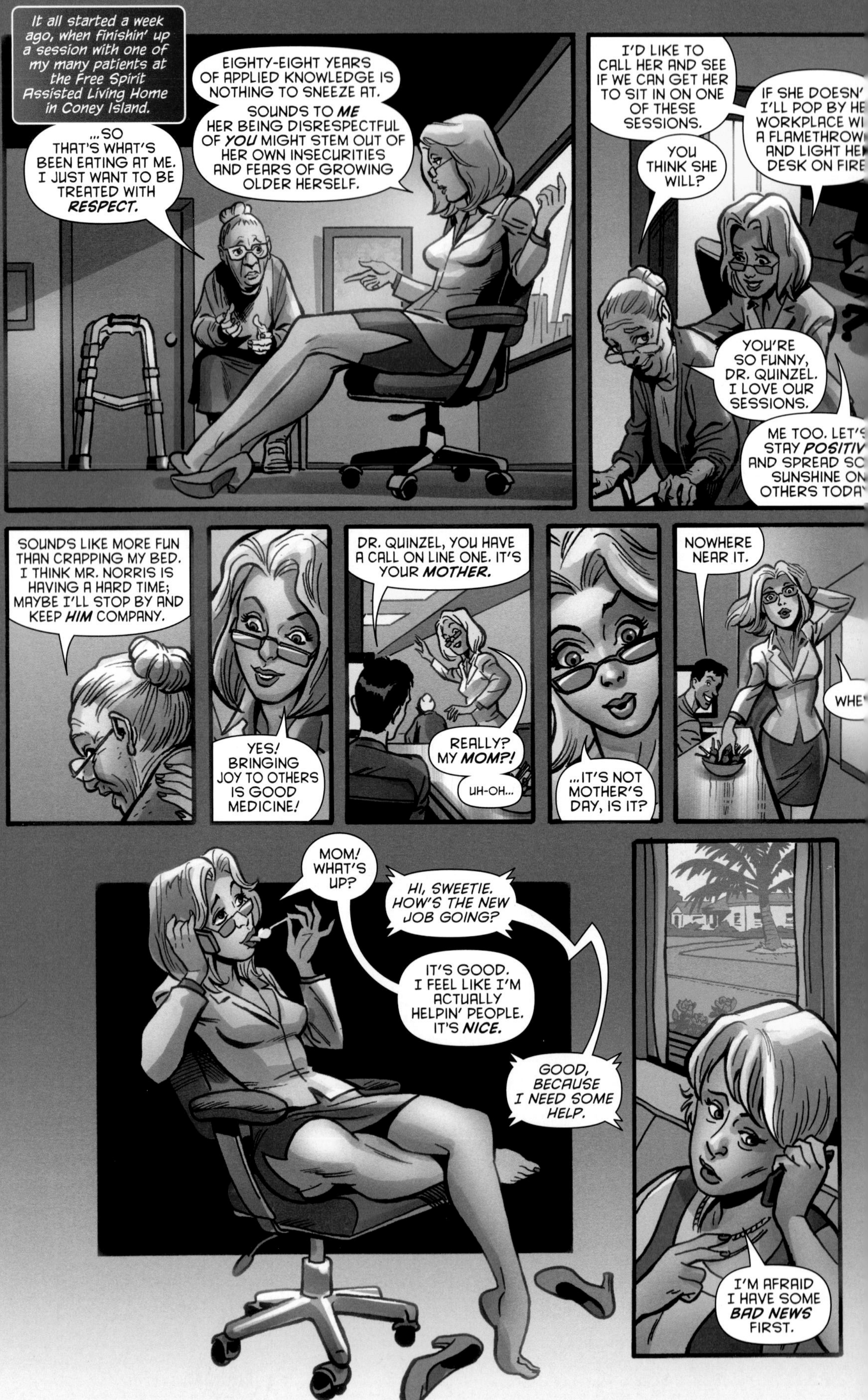
It all started a week ago, when finishin' up a session with one of my many patients at the Free Spirit Assisted Living Home in Coney Island.
...SO THAT'S WHAT'S BEEN EATING AT ME. I JUST WANT TO BE TREATED WITH RESPECT.
EIGHTY-EIGHT YEARS OF APPLIED KNOWLEDGE IS NOTHING TO SNEEZE AT.
SOUNDS TO ME HER BEING DISRESPECTFUL OF YOU MIGHT STEM OUT OF HER OWN INSECURITIES AND FEARS OF GROWING OLDER HERSELF.
I'D LIKE TO CALL HER AND SEE IF WE CAN GET HER TO SIT IN ON ONE OF THESE SESSIONS.
YOU THINK SHE WILL?
YOU'RE SO FUNNY, DR. QUINZEL. I LOVE OUR SESSIONS.
SOUNDS LIKE MORE FUN THAN CRAPPING MY BED. I THINK MR. NORRIS IS HAVING A HARD TIME; MAYBE I'LL STOP BY AND KEEP HIM COMPANY.
YES! BRINGING JOY TO OTHERS IS GOOD MEDICINE!
DR. QUINZEL, YOU HAVE A CALL ON LINE ONE. IT'S YOUR MOTHER.
REALLY? MY MOM?!
UH-OH...
...IT'S NOT MOTHER'S DAY, IS IT?
NOWHERE NEAR IT.
MOM! WHAT'S UP?
HI, SWEETIE. HOW'S THE NEW JOB GOING?
IT'S GOOD. I FEEL LIKE I'M ACTUALLY HELPIN' PEOPLE. IT'S NICE.
GOOD, BECAUSE I NEED SOME HELP.
I'M AFRAID I HAVE SOME BAD NEWS FIRST.

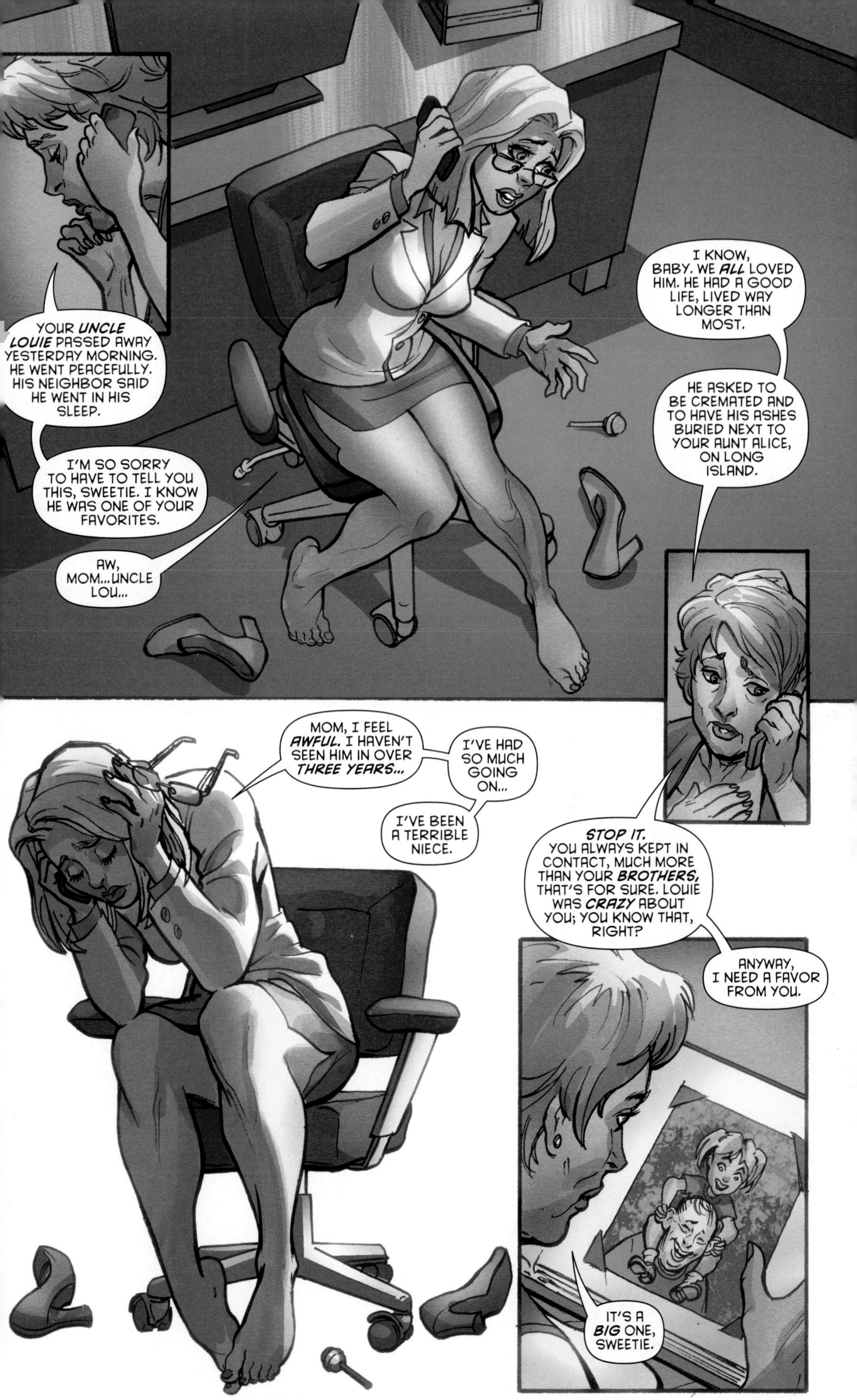
YOUR UNCLE LOUIE PASSED AWAY YESTERDAY MORNING. HE WENT PEACEFULLY. HIS NEIGHBOR SAID HE WENT IN HIS SLEEP.
I'M SO SORRY TO HAVE TO TELL YOU THIS, SWEETIE. I KNOW HE WAS ONE OF YOUR FAVORITES.
AW, MOM...UNCLE LOU...
I KNOW, BABY. WE ALL LOVED HIM. HE HAD A GOOD LIFE, LIVED WAY LONGER THAN MOST.
HE ASKED TO BE CREMATED AND TO HAVE HIS ASHES BURIED NEXT TO YOUR AUNT ALICE, ON LONG ISLAND.
MOM, I FEEL AWFUL. I HAVEN'T SEEN HIM IN OVER THREE YEARS...
I'VE HAD SO MUCH GOING ON...
I'VE BEEN A TERRIBLE NIECE.
STOP IT. YOU ALWAYS KEPT IN CONTACT, MUCH MORE THAN YOUR BROTHERS, THAT'S FOR SURE. LOUIE WAS CRAZY ABOUT YOU; YOU KNOW THAT, RIGHT?
ANYWAY, I NEED A FAVOR FROM YOU.
IT'S A BIG ONE, SWEETIE.

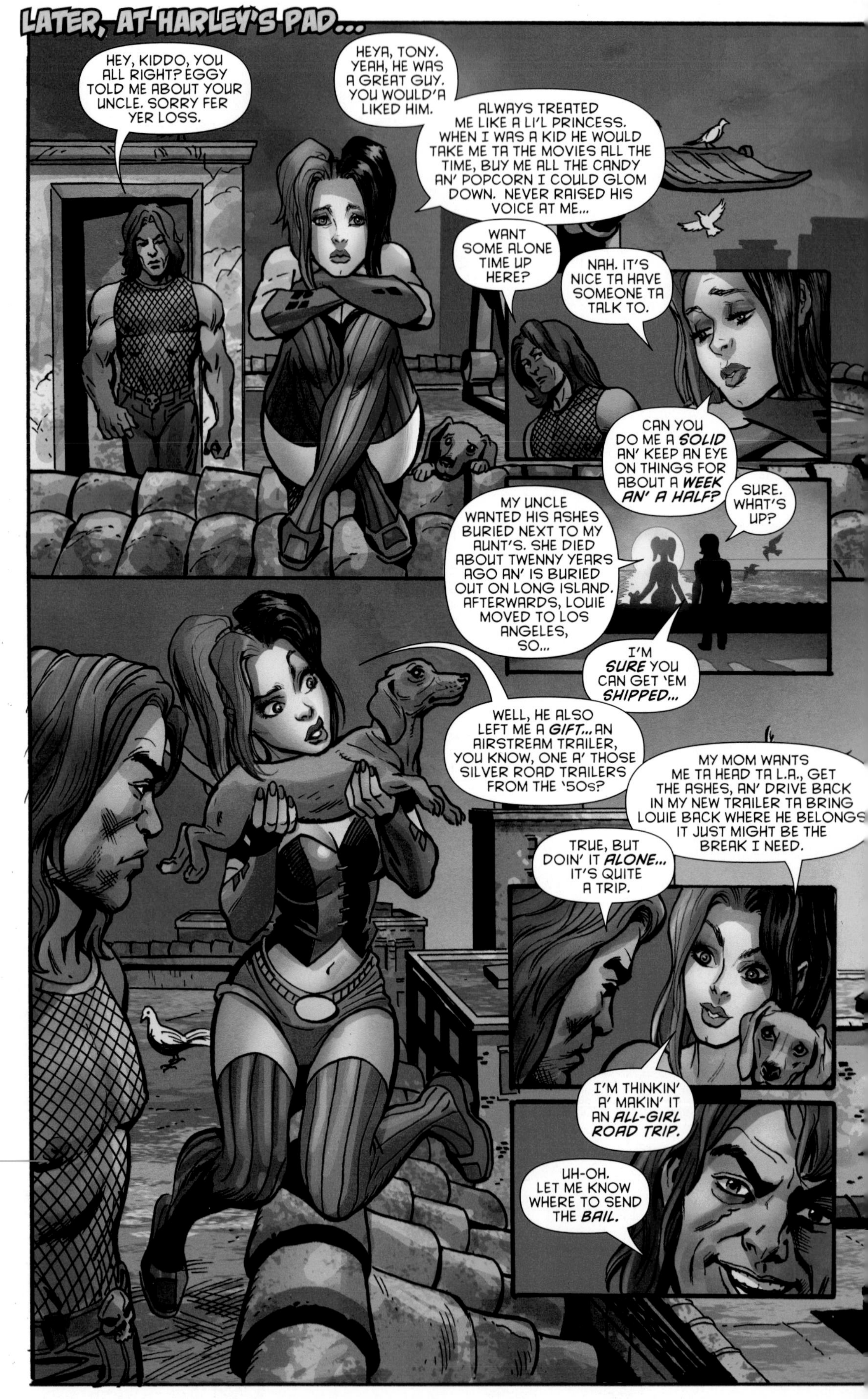
LATER, AT HARLEY'S PAD...
HEY, KIDDO, YOU ALL RIGHT? EGGY TOLD ME ABOUT YOUR UNCLE. SORRY FER YER LOSS.
HEYA, TONY. YEAH, HE WAS A GREAT GUY. YOU WOULD'A LIKED HIM.
ALWAYS TREATED ME LIKE A LI'L PRINCESS. WHEN I WAS A KID HE WOULD TAKE ME TA THE MOVIES ALL THE TIME, BUY ME ALL THE CANDY AN' POPCORN I COULD GLOM DOWN. NEVER RAISED HIS VOICE AT ME...
WANT SOME ALONE TIME UP HERE?
NAH. IT'S NICE TA HAVE SOMEONE TA TALK TO.
CAN YOU DO ME A SOLID AN' KEEP AN EYE ON THINGS FOR ABOUT A WEEK AN' A HALF?
SURE. WHAT'S UP?
MY UNCLE WANTED HIS ASHES BURIED NEXT TO MY AUNT'S. SHE DIED ABOUT TWENNY YEARS AGO AN' IS BURIED OUT ON LONG ISLAND. AFTERWARDS, LOUIE MOVED TO LOS ANGELES, SO...
I'M SURE YOU CAN GET 'EM SHIPPED...
WELL, HE ALSO LEFT ME A GIFT... AN AIRSTREAM TRAILER, YOU KNOW, ONE A' THOSE SILVER ROAD TRAILERS FROM THE '50s?
MY MOM WANTS ME TA HEAD TA L.A., GET THE ASHES, AN' DRIVE BACK IN MY NEW TRAILER TA BRING LOUIE BACK WHERE HE BELONGS. IT JUST MIGHT BE THE BREAK I NEED.
TRUE, BUT DOIN' IT ALONE... IT'S QUITE A TRIP.
I'M THINKIN' A' MAKIN' IT AN ALL-GIRL ROAD TRIP.
UH-OH. LET ME KNOW WHERE TO SEND THE BAIL.

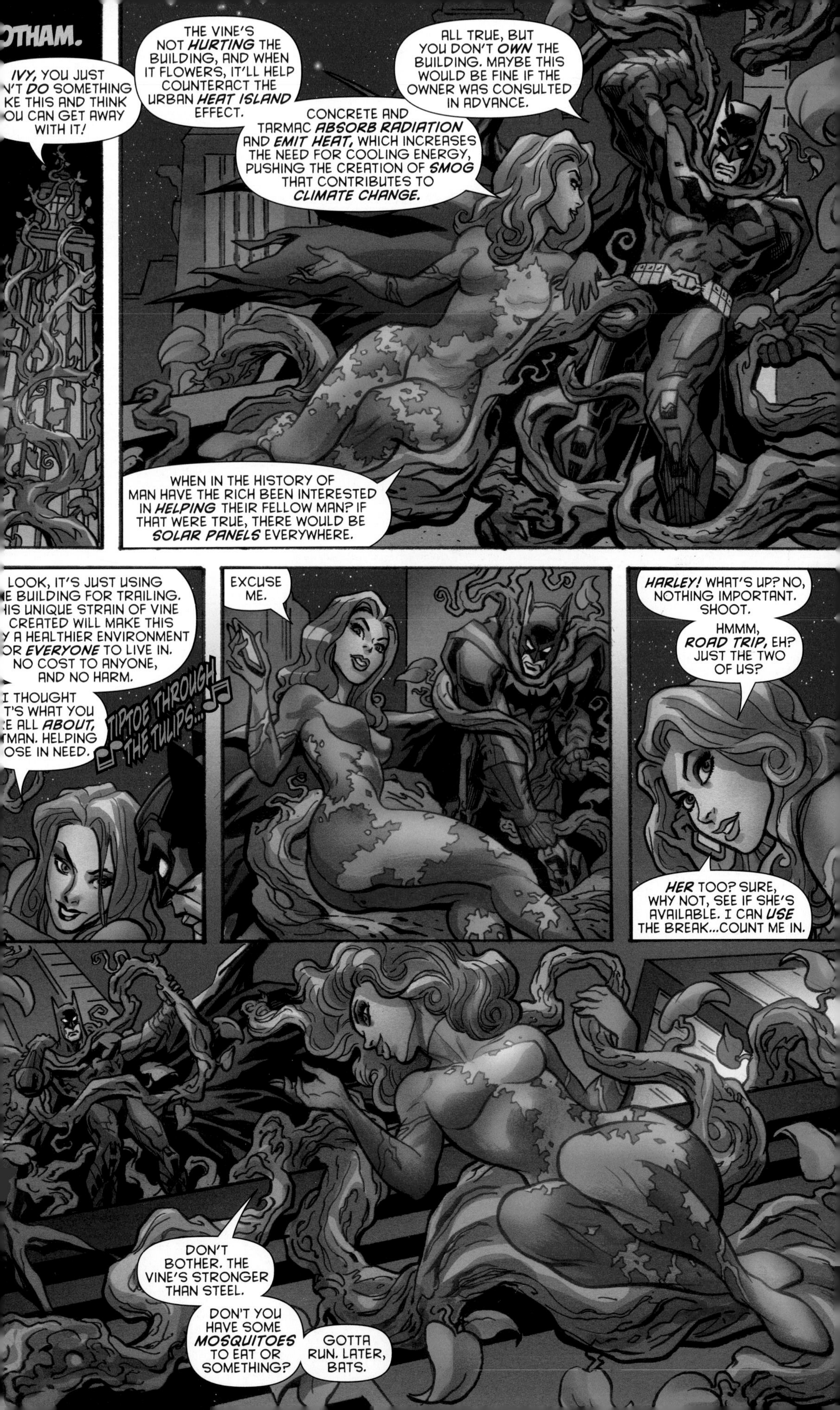

OTHAM.
IVY, YOU JUST N'T DO SOMETHING KE THIS AND THINK OU CAN GET AWAY WITH IT!
THE VINE'S NOT HURTING THE BUILDING, AND WHEN IT FLOWERS, IT'LL HELP COUNTERACT THE URBAN HEAT ISLAND EFFECT.
CONCRETE AND TARMAC ABSORB RADIATION AND EMIT HEAT, WHICH INCREASES THE NEED FOR COOLING ENERGY, PUSHING THE CREATION OF SMOG THAT CONTRIBUTES TO CLIMATE CHANGE.
ALL TRUE, BUT YOU DON'T OWN THE BUILDING. MAYBE THIS WOULD BE FINE IF THE OWNER WAS CONSULTED IN ADVANCE.
WHEN IN THE HISTORY OF MAN HAVE THE RICH BEEN INTERESTED IN HELPING THEIR FELLOW MAN? IF THAT WERE TRUE, THERE WOULD BE SOLAR PANELS EVERYWHERE.
LOOK, IT'S JUST USING E BUILDING FOR TRAILING. HIS UNIQUE STRAIN OF VINE CREATED WILL MAKE THIS Y A HEALTHIER ENVIRONMENT OR EVERYONE TO LIVE IN. NO COST TO ANYONE, AND NO HARM.
I THOUGHT T'S WHAT YOU E ALL ABOUT, TMAN. HELPING OSE IN NEED.
TIPTOE THROUGH THE TULIPS...
EXCUSE ME.
HARLEY! WHAT'S UP? NO, NOTHING IMPORTANT. SHOOT.
HMMM, ROAD TRIP, EH? JUST THE TWO OF US?
HER TOO? SURE, WHY NOT, SEE IF SHE'S AVAILABLE. I CAN USE THE BREAK...COUNT ME IN.
DON'T BOTHER. THE VINE'S STRONGER THAN STEEL.
DON'T YOU HAVE SOME MOSQUITOES TO EAT OR SOMETHING?
GOTTA RUN. LATER, BATS.

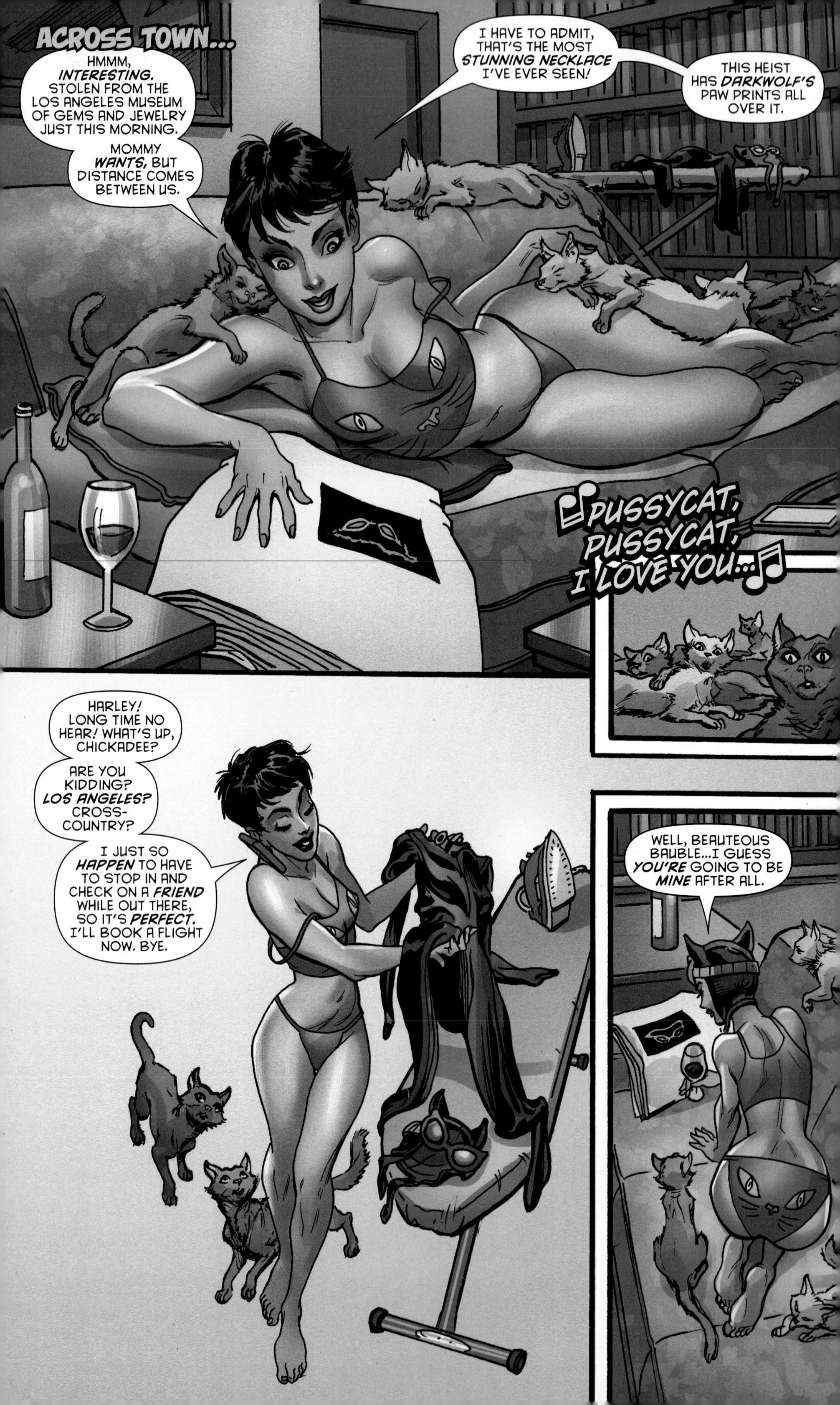

ACROSS TOWN...
HMMM, INTERESTING. STOLEN FROM THE LOS ANGELES MUSEUM OF GEMS AND JEWELRY JUST THIS MORNING.
MOMMY WANTS, BUT DISTANCE COMES BETWEEN US.
I HAVE TO ADMIT, THAT'S THE MOST STUNNING NECKLACE I'VE EVER SEEN!
THIS HEIST HAS DARKWOLF'S PAW PRINTS ALL OVER IT.
PUSSYCAT, PUSSYCAT, I LOVE YOU...
HARLEY! LONG TIME NO HEAR! WHAT'S UP, CHICKADEE?
ARE YOU KIDDING? LOS ANGELES? CROSS-COUNTRY?
I JUST SO HAPPEN TO HAVE TO STOP IN AND CHECK ON A FRIEND WHILE OUT THERE, SO IT'S PERFECT. I'LL BOOK A FLIGHT NOW. BYE.
WELL, BEAUTEOUS BAUBLE...I GUESS YOU'RE GOING TO BE MINE AFTER ALL.

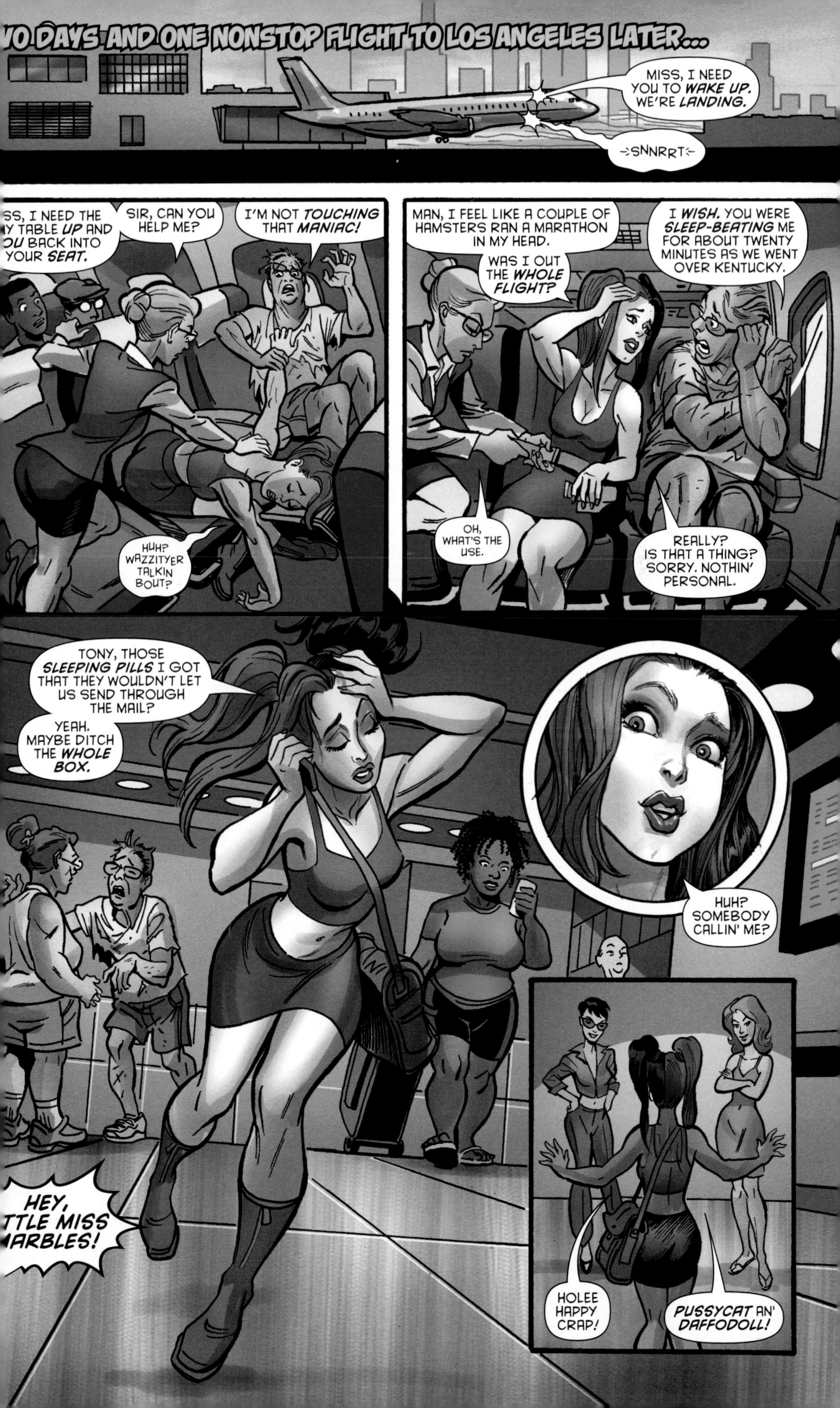

WO DAYS AND ONE NONSTOP FLIGHT TO LOS ANGELES LATER...
MISS, I NEED YOU TO WAKE UP. WE'RE LANDING.
SNNRRT
SS, I NEED THE Y TABLE UP AND OU BACK INTO YOUR SEAT.
SIR, CAN YOU HELP ME?
I'M NOT TOUCHING THAT MANIAC!
HUH? WAZZITYER TALKIN BOUT?
MAN, I FEEL LIKE A COUPLE OF HAMSTERS RAN A MARATHON IN MY HEAD.
WAS I OUT THE WHOLE FLIGHT?
I WISH. YOU WERE SLEEP-BEATING ME FOR ABOUT TWENTY MINUTES AS WE WENT OVER KENTUCKY.
OH, WHAT'S THE USE.
REALLY? IS THAT A THING? SORRY. NOTHIN' PERSONAL.
TONY, THOSE SLEEPING PILLS I GOT THAT THEY WOULDN'T LET US SEND THROUGH THE MAIL?
YEAH. MAYBE DITCH THE WHOLE BOX.
HEY, TTLE MISS ARBLES!
HUH? SOMEBODY CALLIN' ME?
HOLEE HAPPY CRAP!
PUSSYCAT AN' DAFFODOLL!

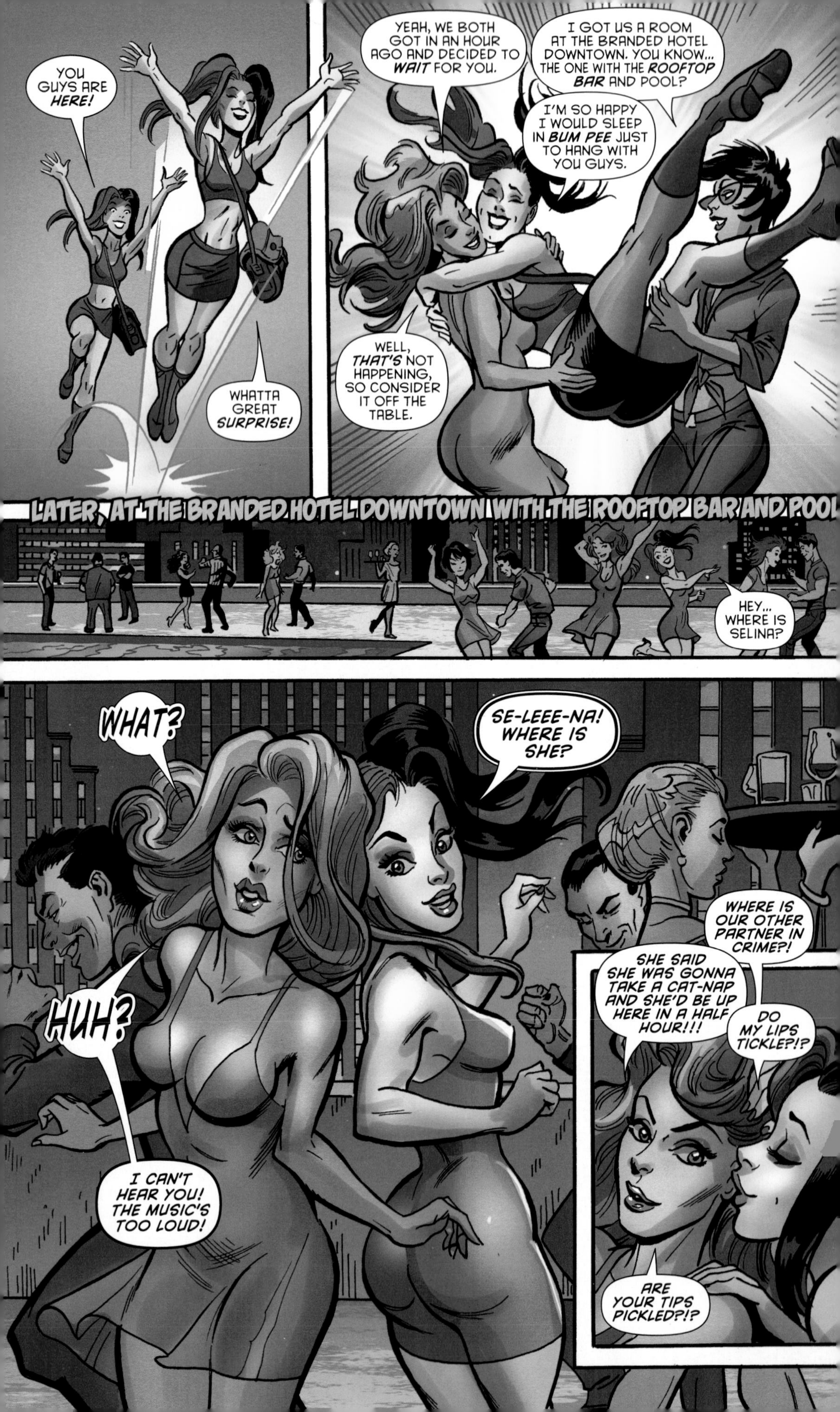
YOU GUYS ARE HERE!
WHATTA GREAT SURPRISE!
YEAH, WE BOTH GOT IN AN HOUR AGO AND DECIDED TO WAIT FOR YOU.
I GOT US A ROOM AT THE BRANDED HOTEL DOWNTOWN. YOU KNOW... THE ONE WITH THE ROOFTOP BAR AND POOL?
I'M SO HAPPY I WOULD SLEEP IN BUM PEE JUST TO HANG WITH YOU GUYS.
WELL, THAT'S NOT HAPPENING, SO CONSIDER IT OFF THE TABLE.
LATER, AT THE BRANDED HOTEL DOWNTOWN WITH THE ROOFTOP BAR AND POOL
HEY... WHERE IS SELINA?
WHAT?
SE-LEEE-NA! WHERE IS SHE?
HUH?
I CAN'T HEAR YOU! THE MUSIC'S TOO LOUD!
WHERE IS OUR OTHER PARTNER IN CRIME?!
SHE SAID SHE WAS GONNA TAKE A CAT-NAP AND SHE'D BE UP HERE IN A HALF HOUR!!!
DO MY LIPS TICKLE?!?
ARE YOUR TIPS PICKLED?!?

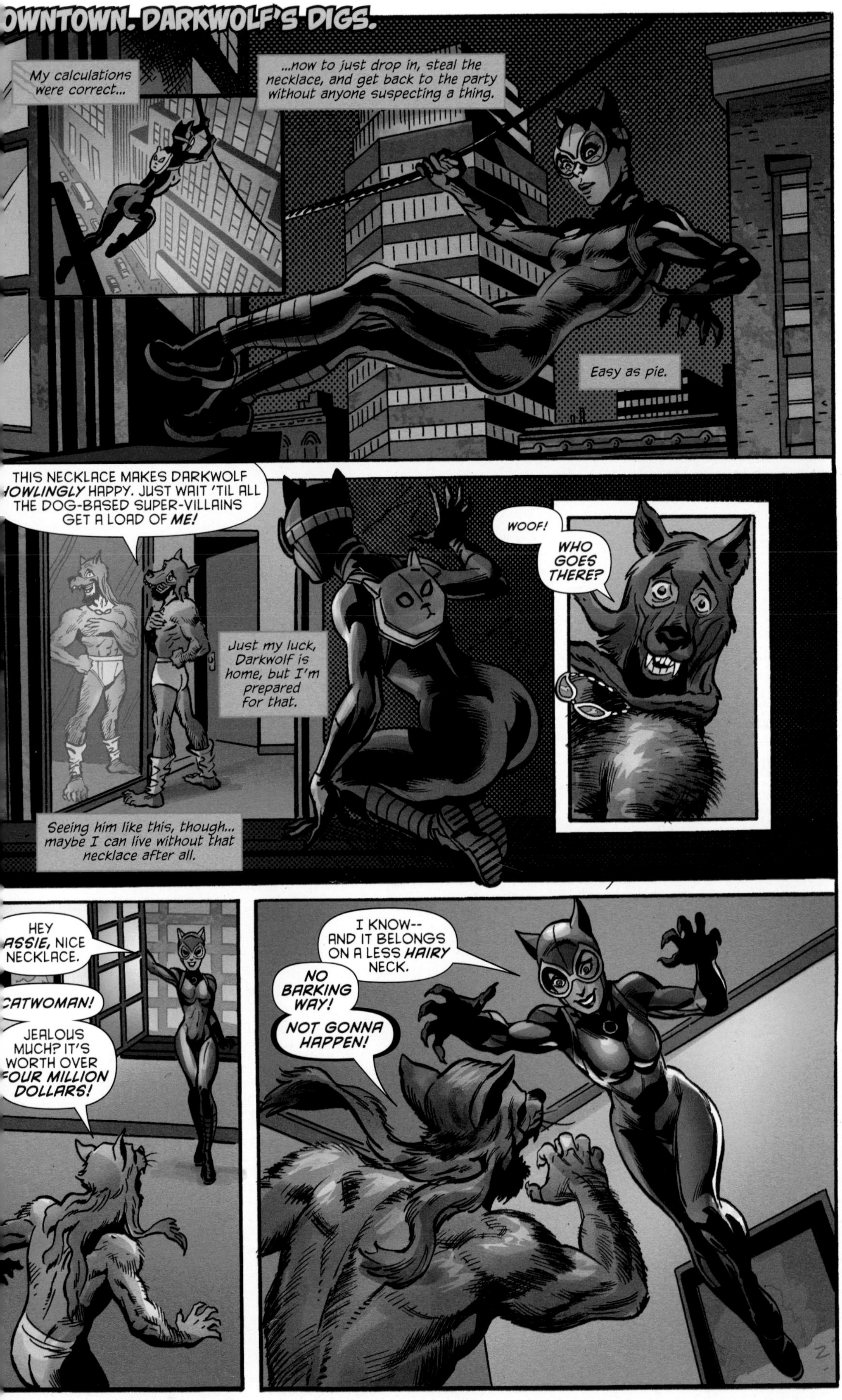

OWNTOWN. DARKWOLF'S DIGS.
My calculations were correct...
...now to just drop in, steal the necklace, and get back to the party without anyone suspecting a thing.
Easy as pie.
THIS NECKLACE MAKES DARKWOLF HOWLINGLY HAPPY. JUST WAIT 'TIL ALL THE DOG-BASED SUPER-VILLAINS GET A LOAD OF ME!
Just my luck, Darkwolf is home, but I'm prepared for that.
Seeing him like this, though... maybe I can live without that necklace after all.
WOOF!
WHO GOES THERE?
HEY ASSIE, NICE NECKLACE.
CATWOMAN!
JEALOUS MUCH? IT'S WORTH OVER FOUR MILLION DOLLARS!
I KNOW-- AND IT BELONGS ON A LESS HAIRY NECK.
NO BARKING WAY!
NOT GONNA HAPPEN!

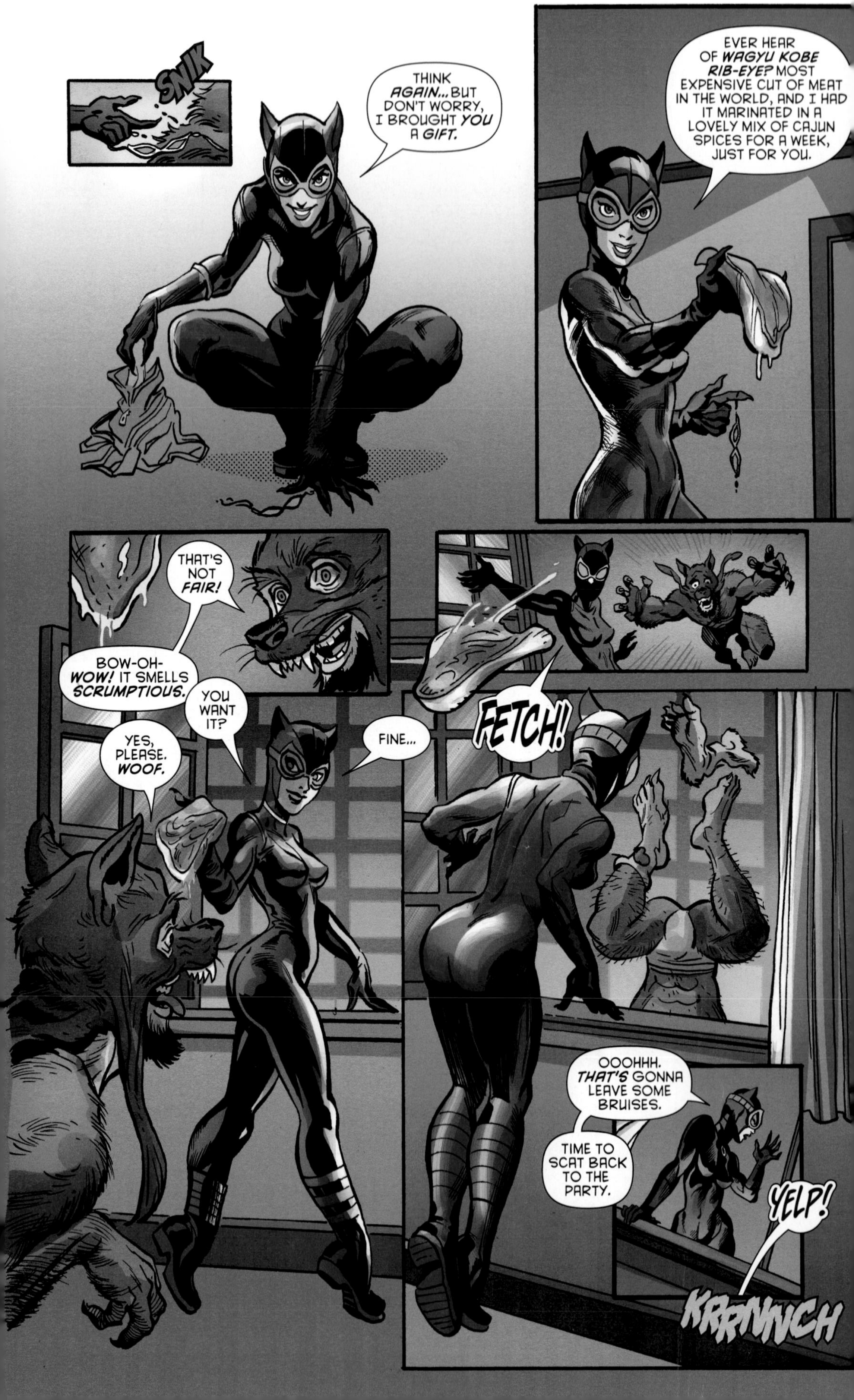
SNIK
THINK AGAIN... BUT DON'T WORRY, I BROUGHT YOU A GIFT.
EVER HEAR OF WAGYU KOBE RIB-EYE? MOST EXPENSIVE CUT OF MEAT IN THE WORLD, AND I HAD IT MARINATED IN A LOVELY MIX OF CAJUN SPICES FOR A WEEK, JUST FOR YOU.
THAT'S NOT FAIR!
BOW-OH-WOW! IT SMELLS SCRUMPTIOUS.
YOU WANT IT?
YES, PLEASE. WOOF.
FINE...
FETCH!
OOOHHH. THAT'S GONNA LEAVE SOME BRUISES.
TIME TO SCAT BACK TO THE PARTY.
YELP!
KRRNNCH

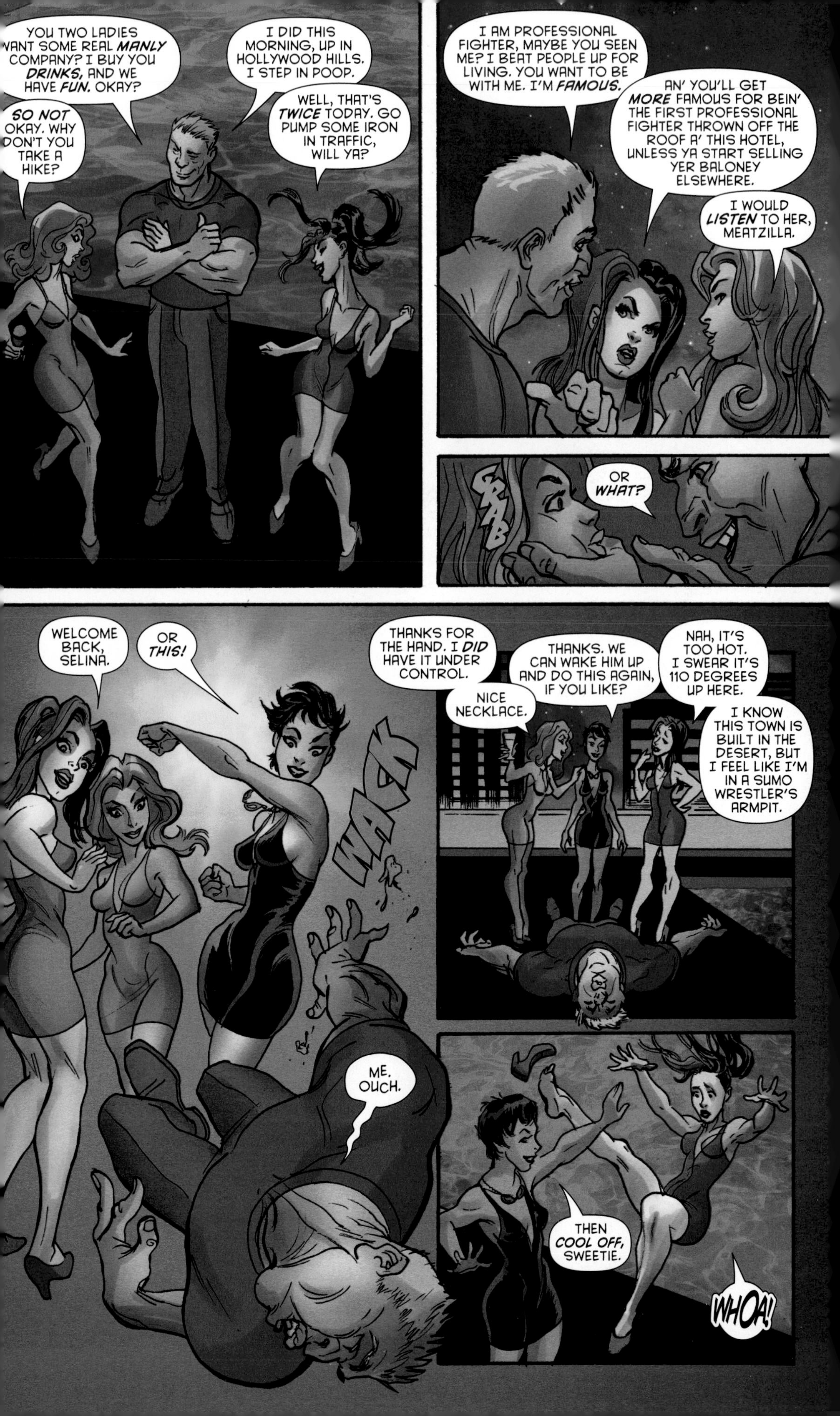
YOU TWO LADIES WANT SOME REAL MANLY COMPANY? I BUY YOU DRINKS, AND WE HAVE FUN. OKAY?
SO NOT OKAY. WHY DON'T YOU TAKE A HIKE?
I DID THIS MORNING, UP IN HOLLYWOOD HILLS. I STEP IN POOP.
WELL, THAT'S TWICE TODAY. GO PUMP SOME IRON IN TRAFFIC, WILL YA?
I AM PROFESSIONAL FIGHTER, MAYBE YOU SEEN ME? I BEAT PEOPLE UP FOR LIVING. YOU WANT TO BE WITH ME. I'M FAMOUS.
AN' YOU'LL GET MORE FAMOUS FOR BEIN' THE FIRST PROFESSIONAL FIGHTER THROWN OFF THE ROOF A' THIS HOTEL, UNLESS YA START SELLING YER BALONEY ELSEWHERE.
I WOULD LISTEN TO HER, MEATZILLA.
GRAB
OR WHAT?
WELCOME BACK, SELINA.
OR THIS!
WACK
ME. OUCH.
THANKS FOR THE HAND. I DID HAVE IT UNDER CONTROL.
NICE NECKLACE.
THANKS. WE CAN WAKE HIM UP AND DO THIS AGAIN, IF YOU LIKE?
NAH, IT'S TOO HOT. I SWEAR IT'S 110 DEGREES UP HERE.
I KNOW THIS TOWN IS BUILT IN THE DESERT, BUT I FEEL LIKE I'M IN A SUMO WRESTLER'S ARMPIT.
THEN COOL OFF, SWEETIE.
WHOA!

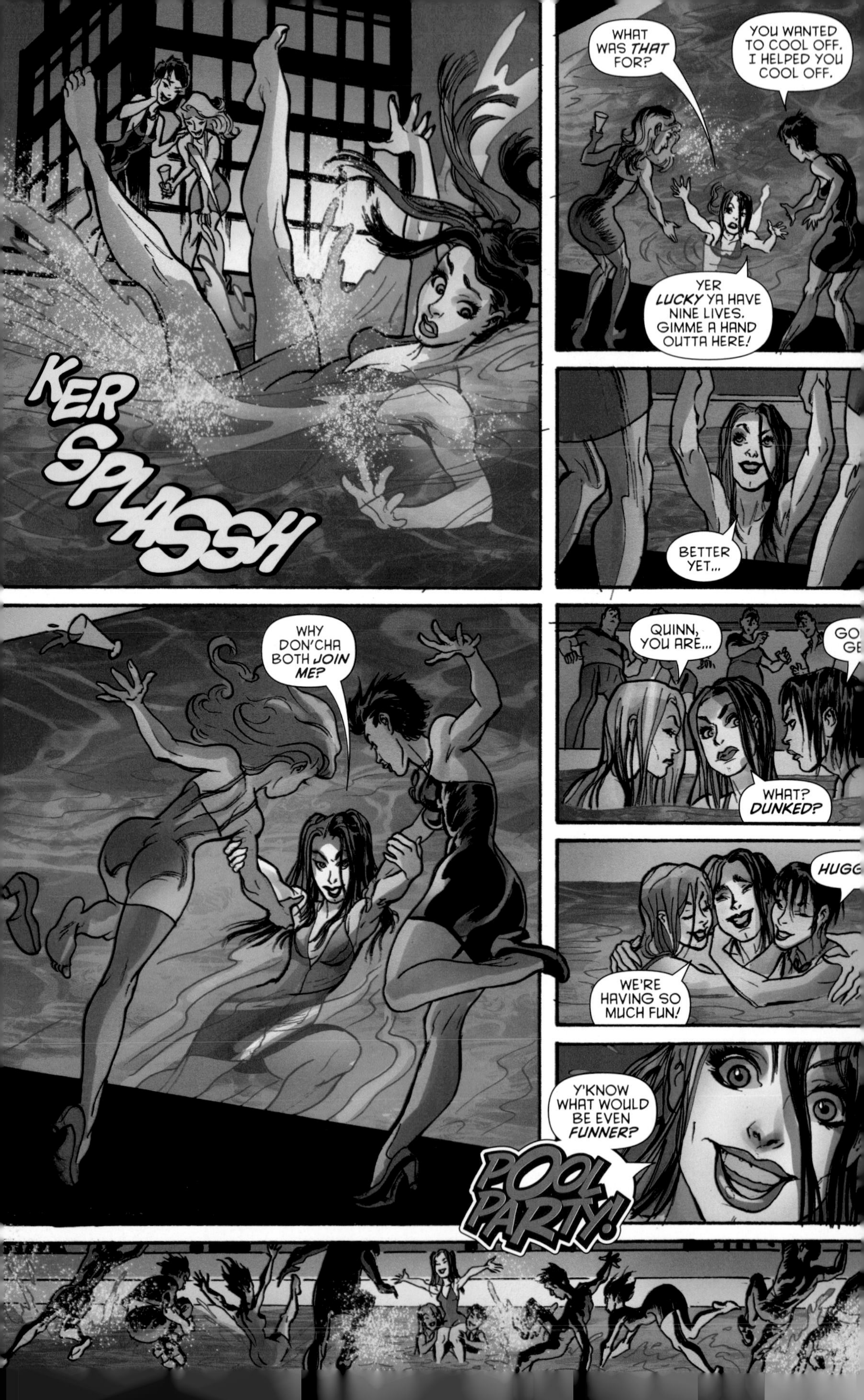
KER SPLASSH
WHAT WAS THAT FOR?
YOU WANTED TO COOL OFF. I HELPED YOU COOL OFF.
YER LUCKY YA HAVE NINE LIVES. GIMME A HAND OUTTA HERE!
BETTER YET...
WHY DON'CHA BOTH JOIN ME?
QUINN, YOU ARE...
WHAT? DUNKED?
WE'RE HAVING SO MUCH FUN!
Y'KNOW WHAT WOULD BE EVEN FUNNER?
POOL PARTY!

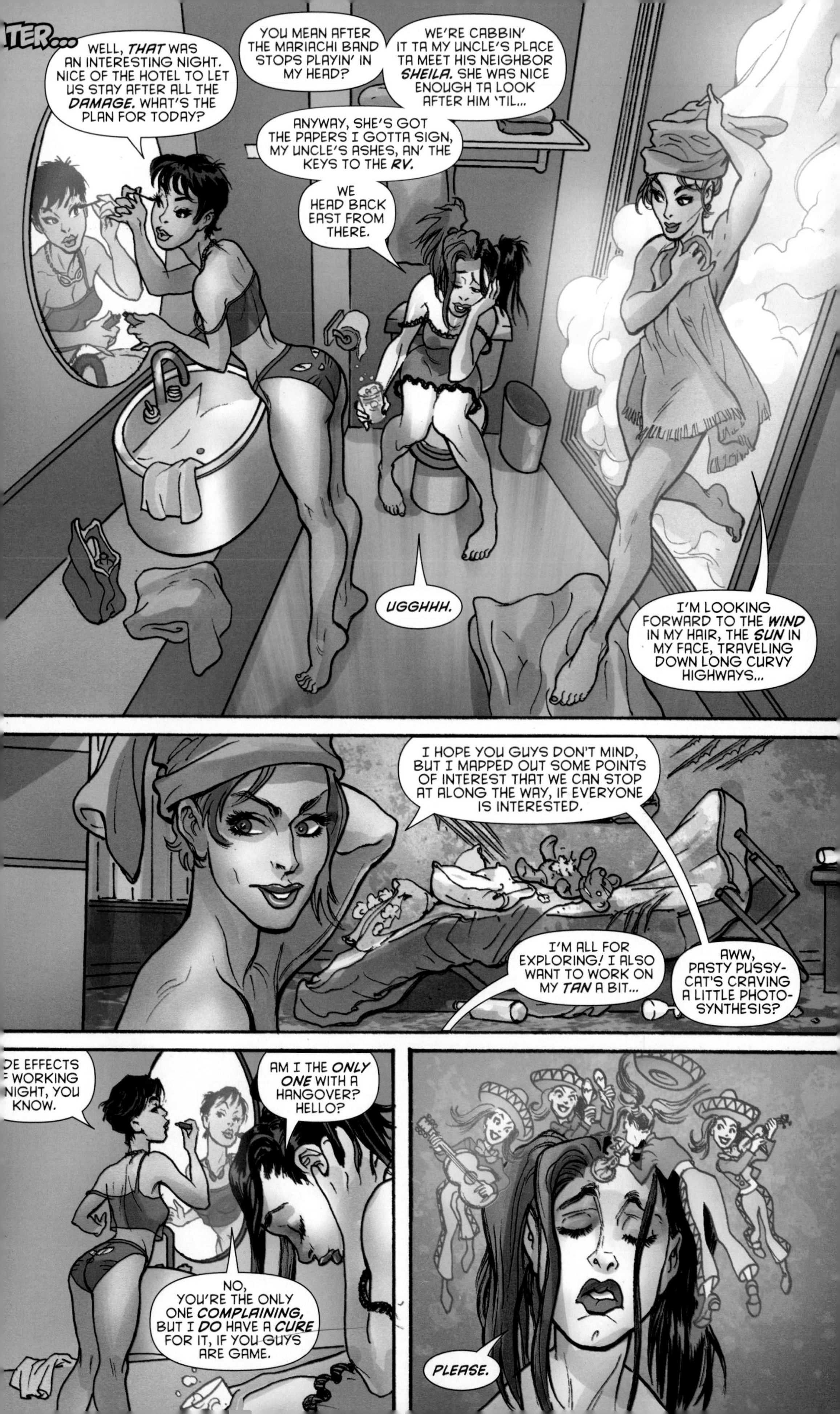
TER...
WELL, THAT WAS AN INTERESTING NIGHT. NICE OF THE HOTEL TO LET US STAY AFTER ALL THE DAMAGE. WHAT'S THE PLAN FOR TODAY?
YOU MEAN AFTER THE MARIACHI BAND STOPS PLAYIN' IN MY HEAD?
WE'RE CABBIN' IT TA MY UNCLE'S PLACE TA MEET HIS NEIGHBOR SHEILA. SHE WAS NICE ENOUGH TA LOOK AFTER HIM 'TIL...
ANYWAY, SHE'S GOT THE PAPERS I GOTTA SIGN, MY UNCLE'S ASHES, AN' THE KEYS TO THE RV.
WE HEAD BACK EAST FROM THERE.
UGGHHH.
I'M LOOKING FORWARD TO THE WIND IN MY HAIR, THE SUN IN MY FACE, TRAVELING DOWN LONG CURVY HIGHWAYS...
I HOPE YOU GUYS DON'T MIND, BUT I MAPPED OUT SOME POINTS OF INTEREST THAT WE CAN STOP AT ALONG THE WAY, IF EVERYONE IS INTERESTED.
I'M ALL FOR EXPLORING! I ALSO WANT TO WORK ON MY TAN A BIT...
AWW, PASTY PUSSY-CAT'S CRAVING A LITTLE PHOTO-SYNTHESIS?
DE EFFECTS F WORKING NIGHT, YOU KNOW.
AM I THE ONLY ONE WITH A HANGOVER? HELLO?
NO, YOU'RE THE ONLY ONE COMPLAINING, BUT I DO HAVE A CURE FOR IT, IF YOU GUYS ARE GAME.
PLEASE.

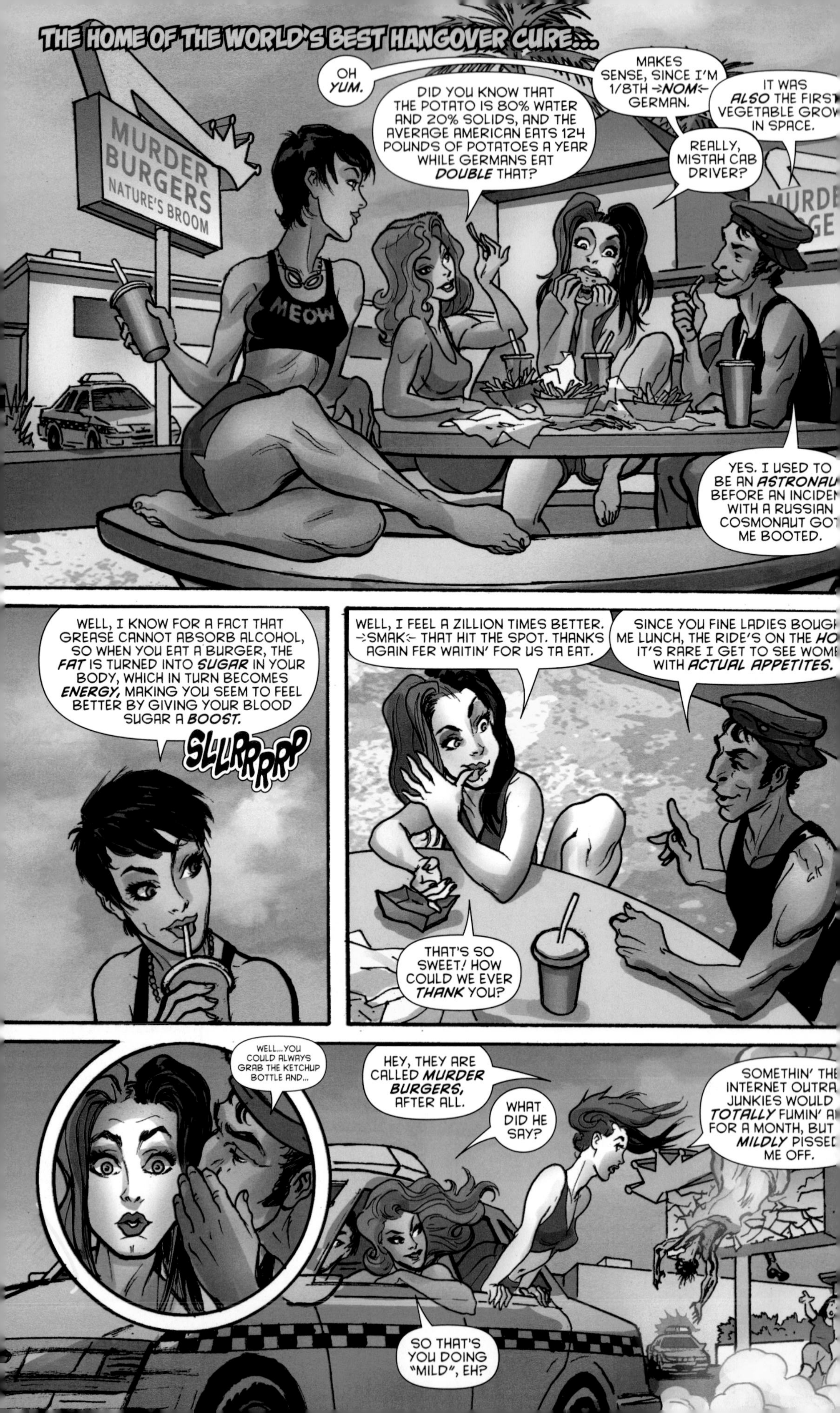
THE HOME OF THE WORLD'S BEST HANGOVER CURE...
MURDER BURGERS NATURE'S BROOM
OH YUM.
DID YOU KNOW THAT THE POTATO IS 80% WATER AND 20% SOLIDS, AND THE AVERAGE AMERICAN EATS 124 POUNDS OF POTATOES A YEAR WHILE GERMANS EAT DOUBLE THAT?
MAKES SENSE, SINCE I'M 1/8TH →NOM← GERMAN.
REALLY, MISTAH CAB DRIVER?
IT WAS ALSO THE FIRST VEGETABLE GROW IN SPACE.
MEOW
YES. I USED TO BE AN ASTRONAU BEFORE AN INCIDEN WITH A RUSSIAN COSMONAUT GOT ME BOOTED.
WELL, I KNOW FOR A FACT THAT GREASE CANNOT ABSORB ALCOHOL, SO WHEN YOU EAT A BURGER, THE FAT IS TURNED INTO SUGAR IN YOUR BODY, WHICH IN TURN BECOMES ENERGY, MAKING YOU SEEM TO FEEL BETTER BY GIVING YOUR BLOOD SUGAR A BOOST.
SLLLRRRRP
WELL, I FEEL A ZILLION TIMES BETTER. →SMAK← THAT HIT THE SPOT. THANKS AGAIN FER WAITIN' FOR US TA EAT.
SINCE YOU FINE LADIES BOUGH ME LUNCH, THE RIDE'S ON THE HO IT'S RARE I GET TO SEE WOME WITH ACTUAL APPETITES.
THAT'S SO SWEET! HOW COULD WE EVER THANK YOU?
WELL...YOU COULD ALWAYS GRAB THE KETCHUP BOTTLE AND...
HEY, THEY ARE CALLED MURDER BURGERS, AFTER ALL.
WHAT DID HE SAY?
SOMETHIN' THE INTERNET OUTRA JUNKIES WOULD TOTALLY FUMIN' A FOR A MONTH, BUT MILDLY PISSED ME OFF.
SO THAT'S YOU DOING "MILD", EH?

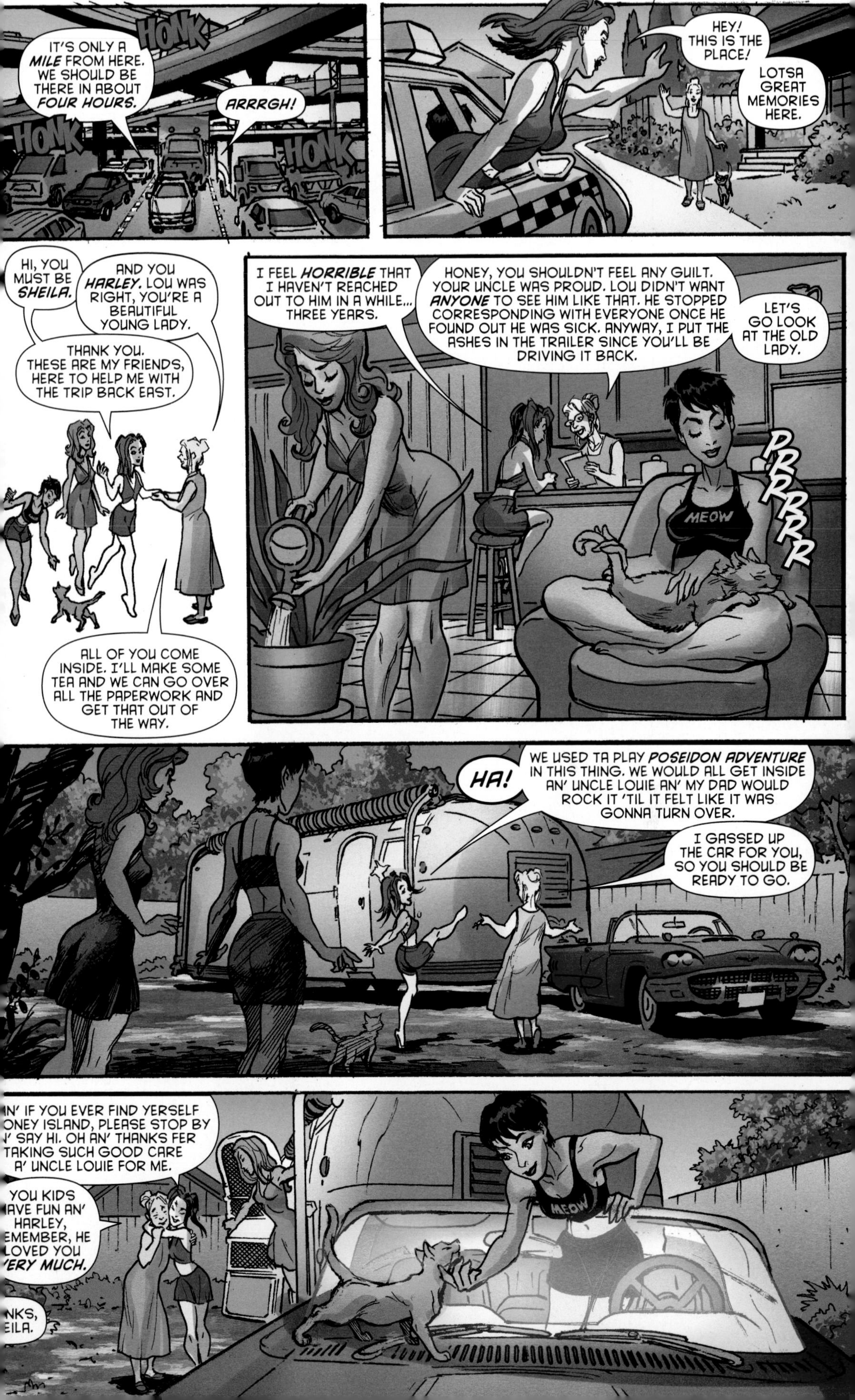
HONK
IT'S ONLY A MILE FROM HERE. WE SHOULD BE THERE IN ABOUT FOUR HOURS.
HONK
ARRRGH!
HONK
HEY! THIS IS THE PLACE!
LOTSA GREAT MEMORIES HERE.
HI, YOU MUST BE SHEILA.
AND YOU HARLEY. LOU WAS RIGHT, YOU'RE A BEAUTIFUL YOUNG LADY.
THANK YOU. THESE ARE MY FRIENDS, HERE TO HELP ME WITH THE TRIP BACK EAST.
ALL OF YOU COME INSIDE. I'LL MAKE SOME TEA AND WE CAN GO OVER ALL THE PAPERWORK AND GET THAT OUT OF THE WAY.
I FEEL HORRIBLE THAT I HAVEN'T REACHED OUT TO HIM IN A WHILE... THREE YEARS.
HONEY, YOU SHOULDN'T FEEL ANY GUILT. YOUR UNCLE WAS PROUD. LOU DIDN'T WANT ANYONE TO SEE HIM LIKE THAT. HE STOPPED CORRESPONDING WITH EVERYONE ONCE HE FOUND OUT HE WAS SICK. ANYWAY, I PUT THE ASHES IN THE TRAILER SINCE YOU'LL BE DRIVING IT BACK.
LET'S GO LOOK AT THE OLD LADY.
PRRRRR
MEOW
HA!
WE USED TA PLAY POSEIDON ADVENTURE IN THIS THING. WE WOULD ALL GET INSIDE AN' UNCLE LOUIE AN' MY DAD WOULD ROCK IT 'TIL IT FELT LIKE IT WAS GONNA TURN OVER.
I GASSED UP THE CAR FOR YOU, SO YOU SHOULD BE READY TO GO.
N' IF YOU EVER FIND YERSELF ONEY ISLAND, PLEASE STOP BY ' SAY HI. OH AN' THANKS FER TAKING SUCH GOOD CARE A' UNCLE LOUIE FOR ME.
YOU KIDS AVE FUN AN' HARLEY, EMEMBER, HE LOVED YOU ERY MUCH.
NKS, EILA.
MEOW

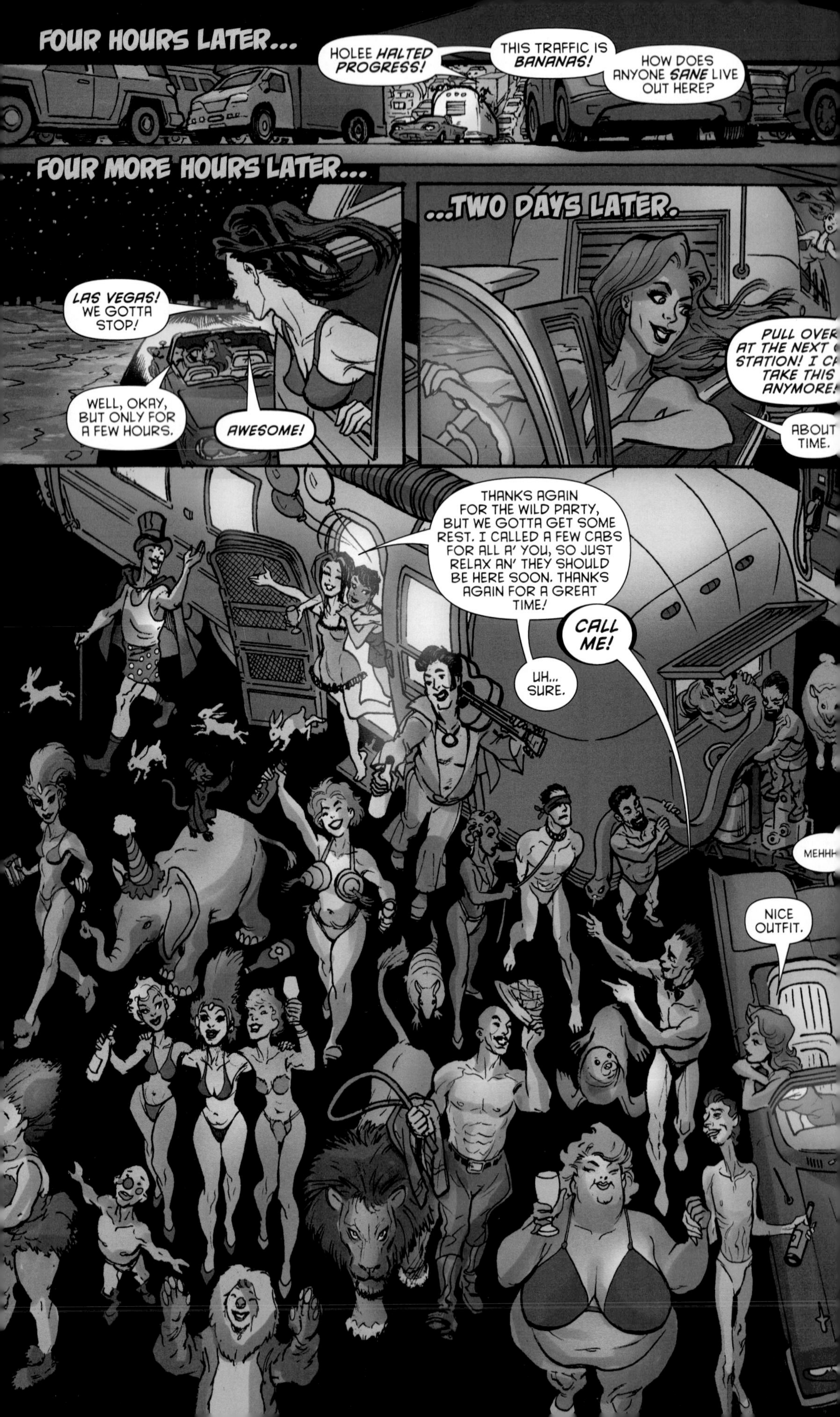
FOUR HOURS LATER...
HOLEE HALTED PROGRESS!
THIS TRAFFIC IS BANANAS!
HOW DOES ANYONE SANE LIVE OUT HERE?
FOUR MORE HOURS LATER...
LAS VEGAS! WE GOTTA STOP!
WELL, OKAY, BUT ONLY FOR A FEW HOURS.
AWESOME!
...TWO DAYS LATER.
ABOUT TIME.
THANKS AGAIN FOR THE WILD PARTY, BUT WE GOTTA GET SOME REST. I CALLED A FEW CABS FOR ALL A' YOU, SO JUST RELAX AN' THEY SHOULD BE HERE SOON. THANKS AGAIN FOR A GREAT TIME!
UH... SURE.
CALL ME!
NICE OUTFIT.

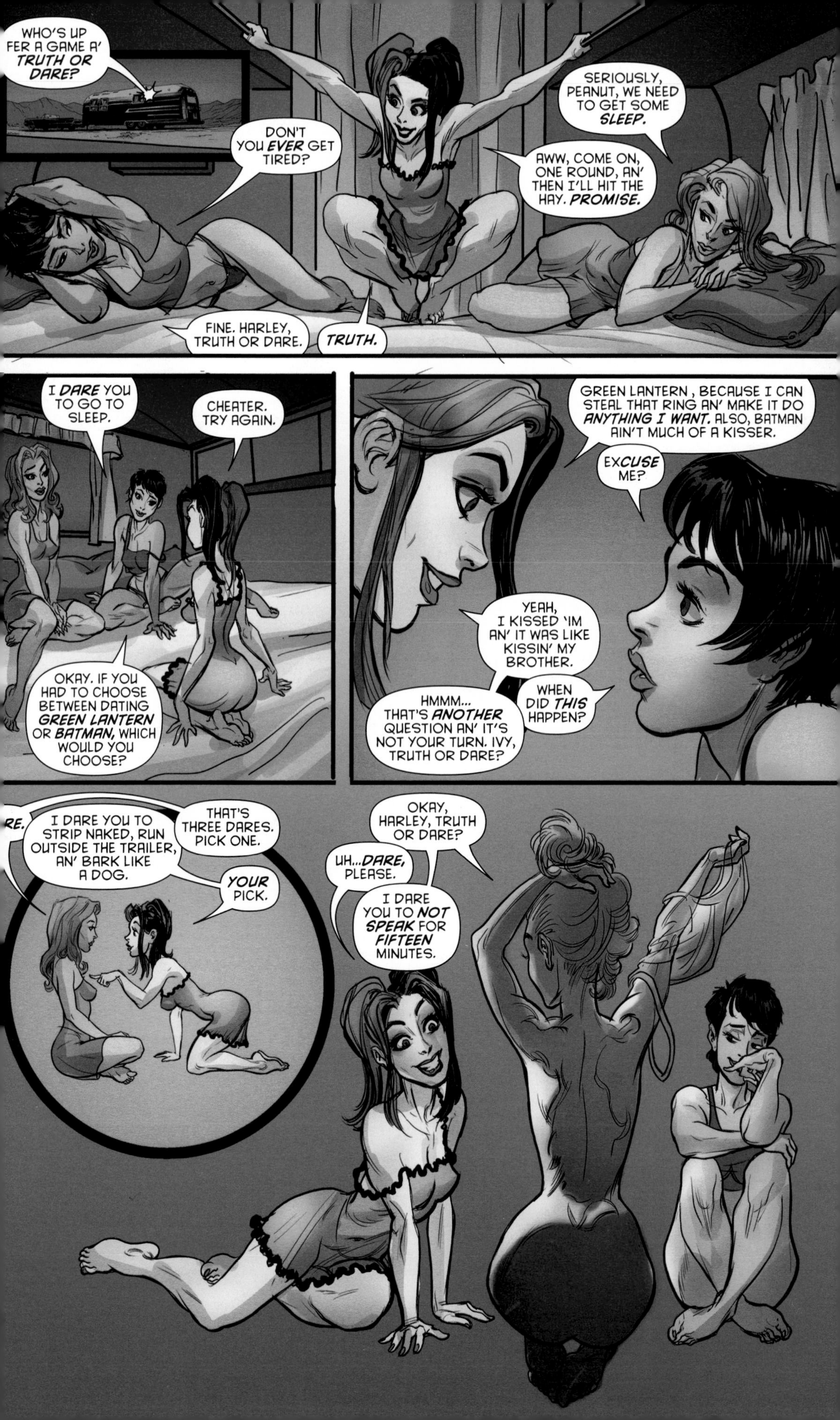
WHO'S UP FER A GAME A' TRUTH OR DARE?
DON'T YOU EVER GET TIRED?
SERIOUSLY, PEANUT, WE NEED TO GET SOME SLEEP.
AWW, COME ON, ONE ROUND, AN' THEN I'LL HIT THE HAY. PROMISE.
FINE. HARLEY, TRUTH OR DARE.
TRUTH.
I DARE YOU TO GO TO SLEEP.
CHEATER. TRY AGAIN.
OKAY. IF YOU HAD TO CHOOSE BETWEEN DATING GREEN LANTERN OR BATMAN, WHICH WOULD YOU CHOOSE?
GREEN LANTERN , BECAUSE I CAN STEAL THAT RING AN' MAKE IT DO ANYTHING I WANT. ALSO, BATMAN AIN'T MUCH OF A KISSER.
EXCUSE ME?
YEAH, I KISSED 'IM AN' IT WAS LIKE KISSIN' MY BROTHER.
WHEN DID THIS HAPPEN?
HMMM... THAT'S ANOTHER QUESTION AN' IT'S NOT YOUR TURN. IVY, TRUTH OR DARE?
RE.
I DARE YOU TO STRIP NAKED, RUN OUTSIDE THE TRAILER, AN' BARK LIKE A DOG.
THAT'S THREE DARES. PICK ONE.
YOUR PICK.
OKAY, HARLEY, TRUTH OR DARE?
UH...DARE, PLEASE.
I DARE YOU TO NOT SPEAK FOR FIFTEEN MINUTES.

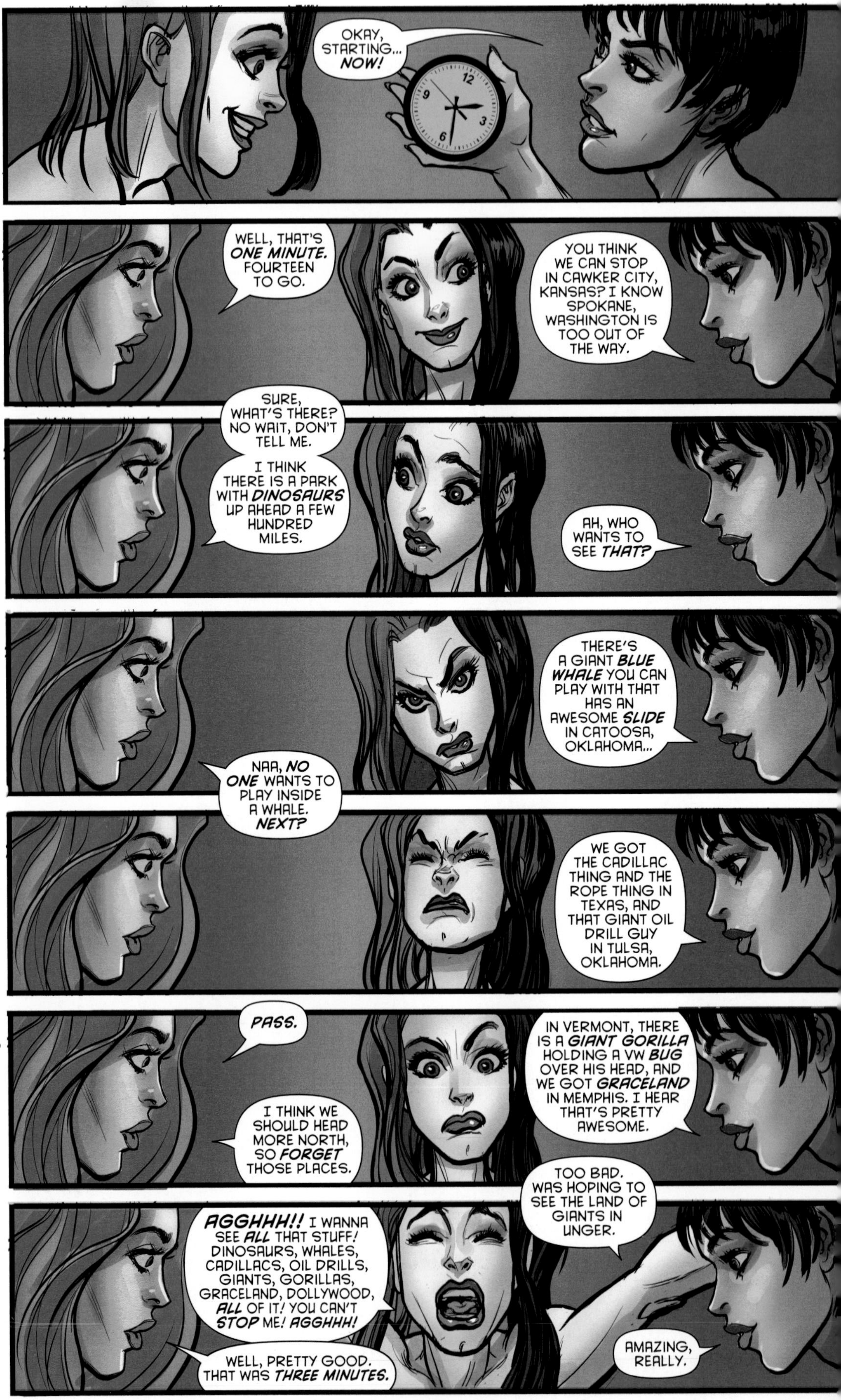
OKAY, STARTING... NOW!
12
9
3
6
WELL, THAT'S ONE MINUTE. FOURTEEN TO GO.
YOU THINK WE CAN STOP IN CAWKER CITY, KANSAS? I KNOW SPOKANE, WASHINGTON IS TOO OUT OF THE WAY.
SURE, WHAT'S THERE? NO WAIT, DON'T TELL ME.
I THINK THERE IS A PARK WITH DINOSAURS UP AHEAD A FEW HUNDRED MILES.
AH, WHO WANTS TO SEE THAT?
THERE'S A GIANT BLUE WHALE YOU CAN PLAY WITH THAT HAS AN AWESOME SLIDE IN CATOOSA, OKLAHOMA...
NAA, NO ONE WANTS TO PLAY INSIDE A WHALE. NEXT?
WE GOT THE CADILLAC THING AND THE ROPE THING IN TEXAS, AND THAT GIANT OIL DRILL GUY IN TULSA, OKLAHOMA.
PASS.
IN VERMONT, THERE IS A GIANT GORILLA HOLDING A VW BUG OVER HIS HEAD, AND WE GOT GRACELAND IN MEMPHIS. I HEAR THAT'S PRETTY AWESOME.
I THINK WE SHOULD HEAD MORE NORTH, SO FORGET THOSE PLACES.
TOO BAD. WAS HOPING TO SEE THE LAND OF GIANTS IN UNGER.
AGGHHH!! I WANNA SEE ALL THAT STUFF! DINOSAURS, WHALES, CADILLACS, OIL DRILLS, GIANTS, GORILLAS, GRACELAND, DOLLYWOOD, ALL OF IT! YOU CAN'T STOP ME! AGGHHH!
WELL, PRETTY GOOD. THAT WAS THREE MINUTES.
AMAZING, REALLY.

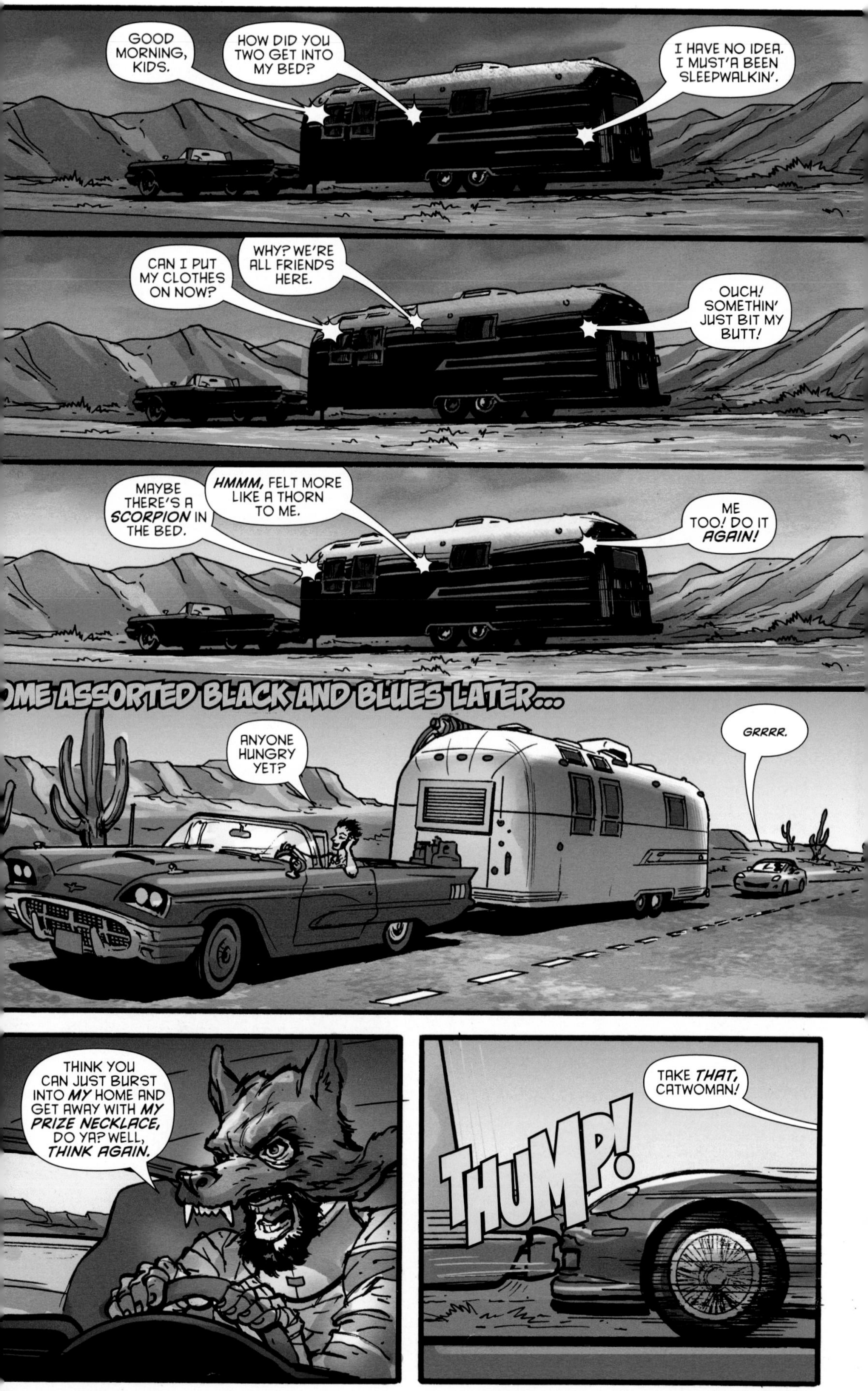
GOOD MORNING, KIDS.
HOW DID YOU TWO GET INTO MY BED?
I HAVE NO IDEA. I MUST'A BEEN SLEEPWALKIN'.
CAN I PUT MY CLOTHES ON NOW?
WHY? WE'RE ALL FRIENDS HERE.
OUCH! SOMETHIN' JUST BIT MY BUTT!
MAYBE THERE'S A SCORPION IN THE BED.
HMMM, FELT MORE LIKE A THORN TO ME.
ME TOO! DO IT AGAIN!
OME ASSORTED BLACK AND BLUES LATER...
ANYONE HUNGRY YET?
GRRRR.
THINK YOU CAN JUST BURST INTO MY HOME AND GET AWAY WITH MY PRIZE NECKLACE, DO YA? WELL, THINK AGAIN.
TAKE THAT, CATWOMAN!
THUMP!

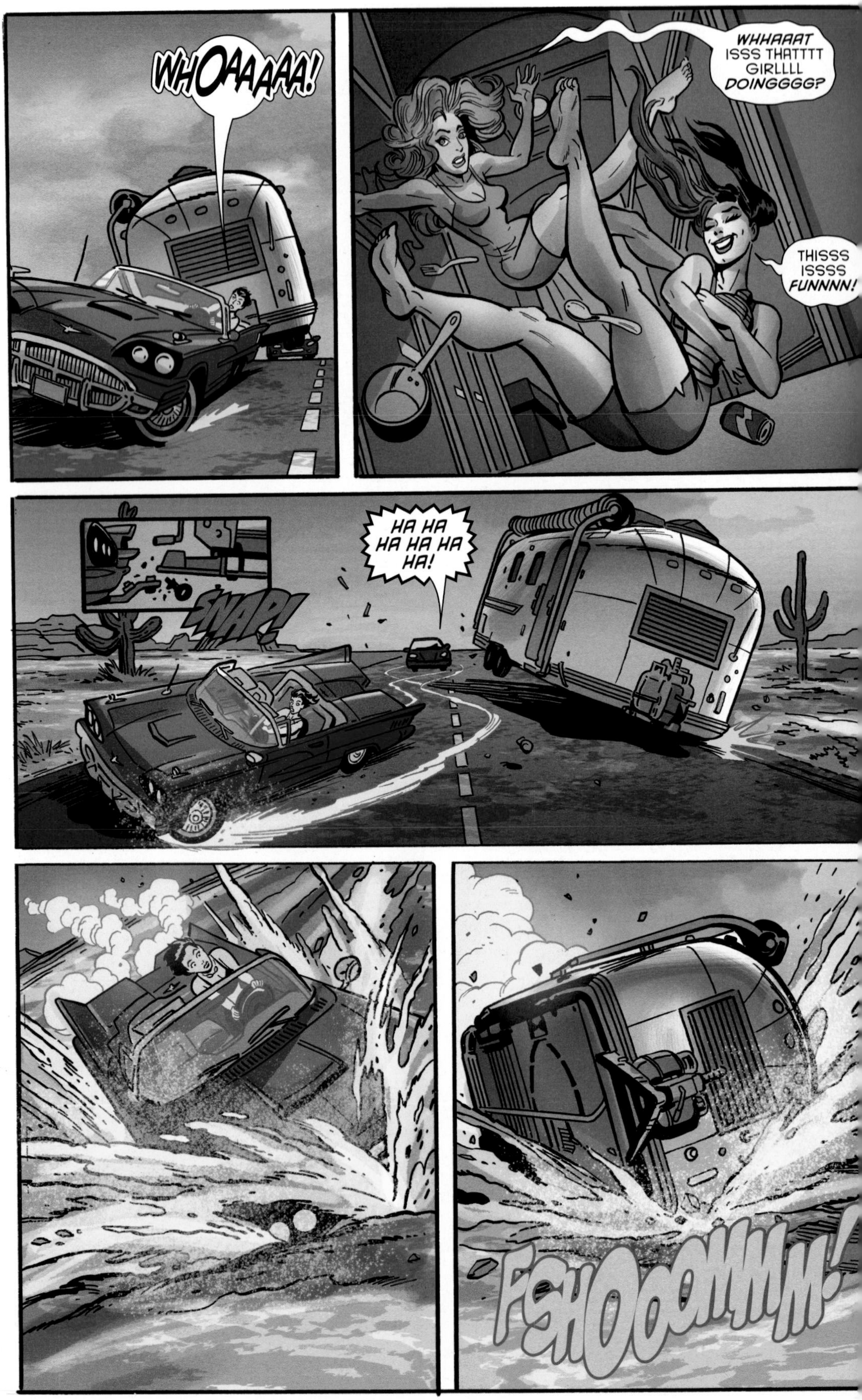
WHOAAAAA!
WHHAAAT ISSS THATTTT GIRLLLL DOINGGGG?
THISSS ISSSS FUNNNN!
SNAP!
HA HA HA HA HA HA!
FSHOOOMMMM!

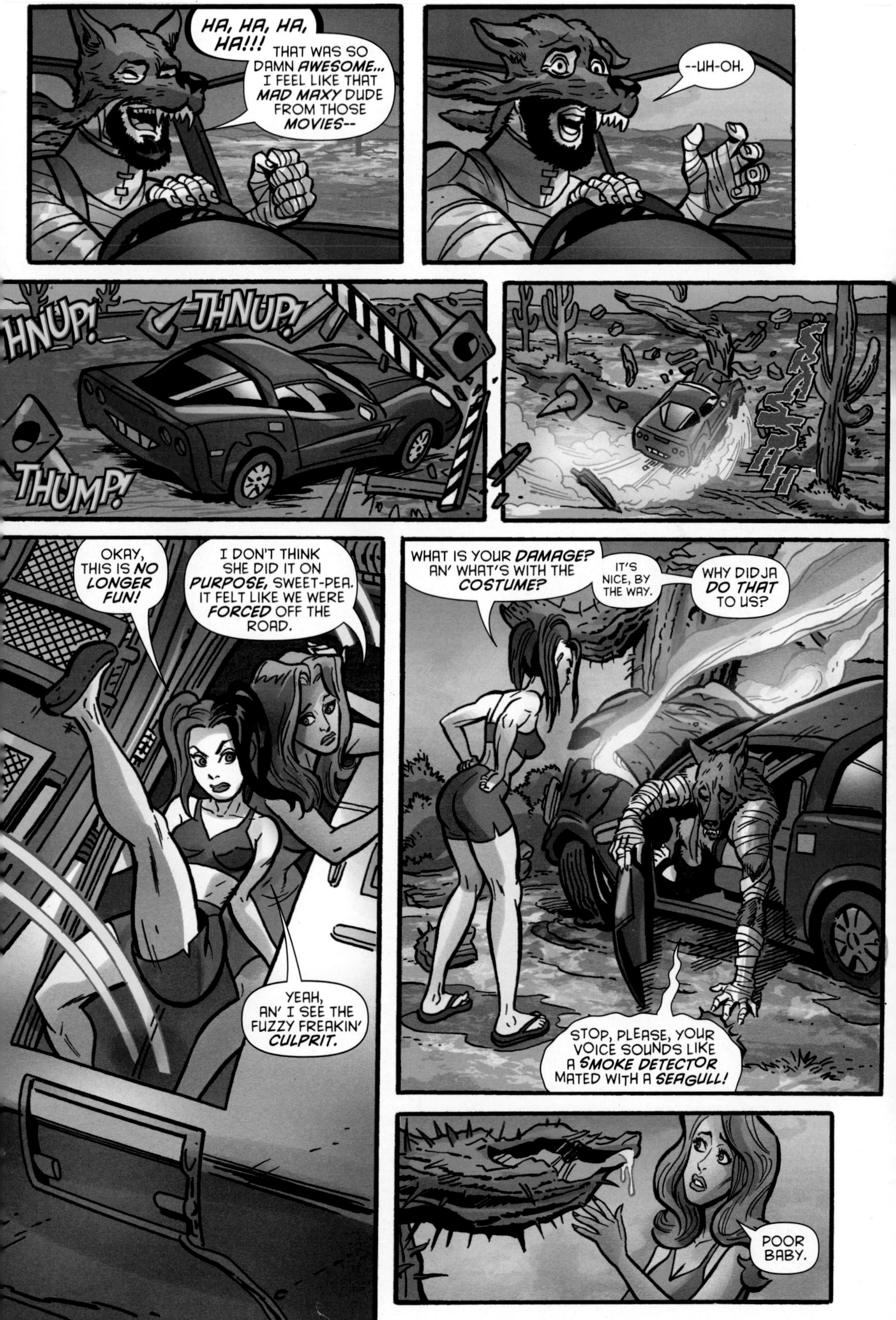

HA, HA, HA, HA!!!
THAT WAS SO DAMN AWESOME... I FEEL LIKE THAT MAD MAXY DUDE FROM THOSE MOVIES--
--UH-OH.
THNUP!
THNUP!
THUMP!
KRASSHH
OKAY, THIS IS NO LONGER FUN!
I DON'T THINK SHE DID IT ON PURPOSE, SWEET-PEA. IT FELT LIKE WE WERE FORCED OFF THE ROAD.
YEAH, AN' I SEE THE FUZZY FREAKIN' CULPRIT.
WHAT IS YOUR DAMAGE? AN' WHAT'S WITH THE COSTUME?
IT'S NICE, BY THE WAY.
WHY DIDJA DO THAT TO US?
STOP, PLEASE, YOUR VOICE SOUNDS LIKE A SMOKE DETECTOR MATED WITH A SEAGULL!
POOR BABY.

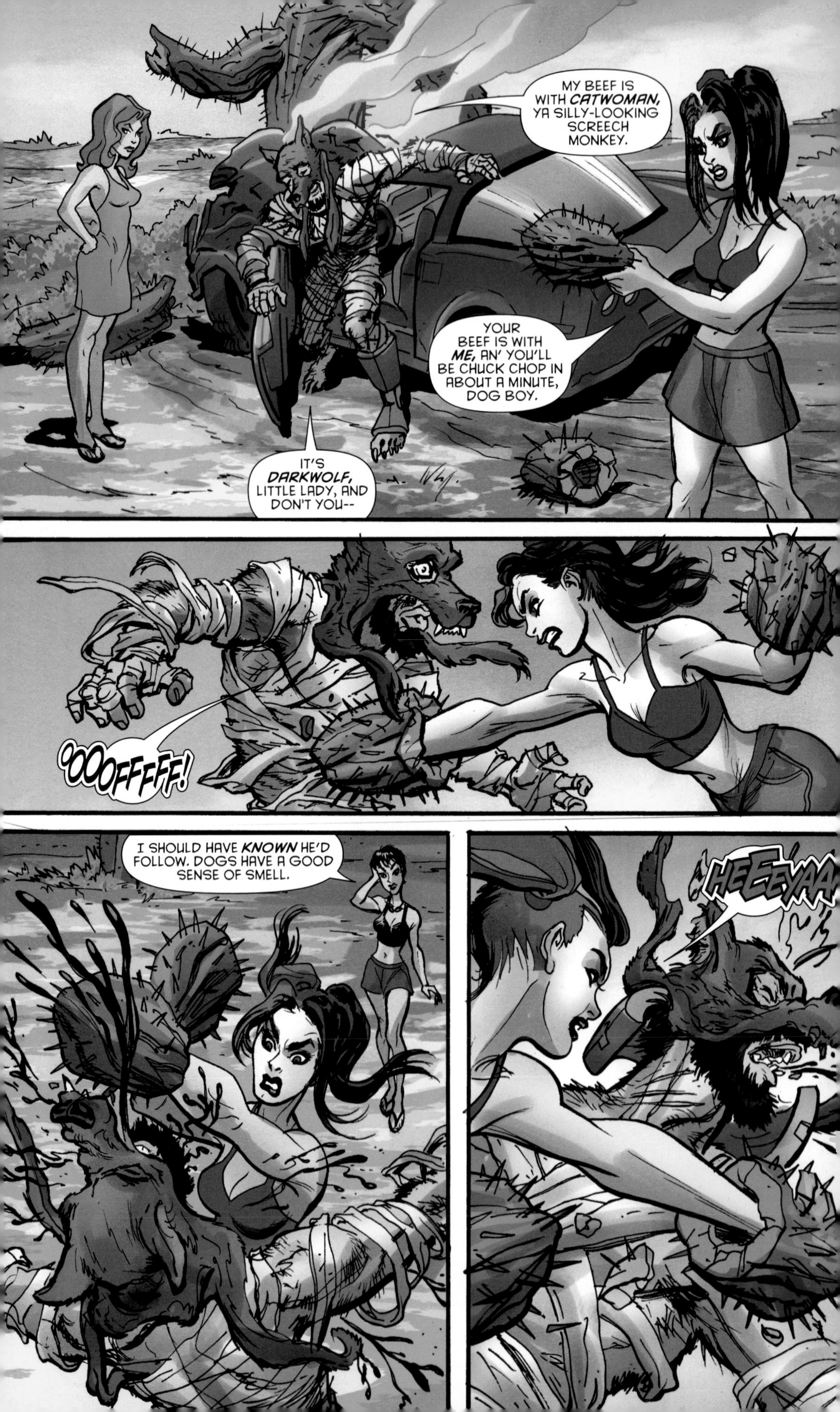
MY BEEF IS WITH CATWOMAN, YA SILLY-LOOKING SCREECH MONKEY.
IT'S DARKWOLF, LITTLE LADY, AND DON'T YOU--
YOUR BEEF IS WITH ME, AN' YOU'LL BE CHUCK CHOP IN ABOUT A MINUTE, DOG BOY.
OOOOFFFFF!
I SHOULD HAVE KNOWN HE'D FOLLOW. DOGS HAVE A GOOD SENSE OF SMELL.
HEEEYAA

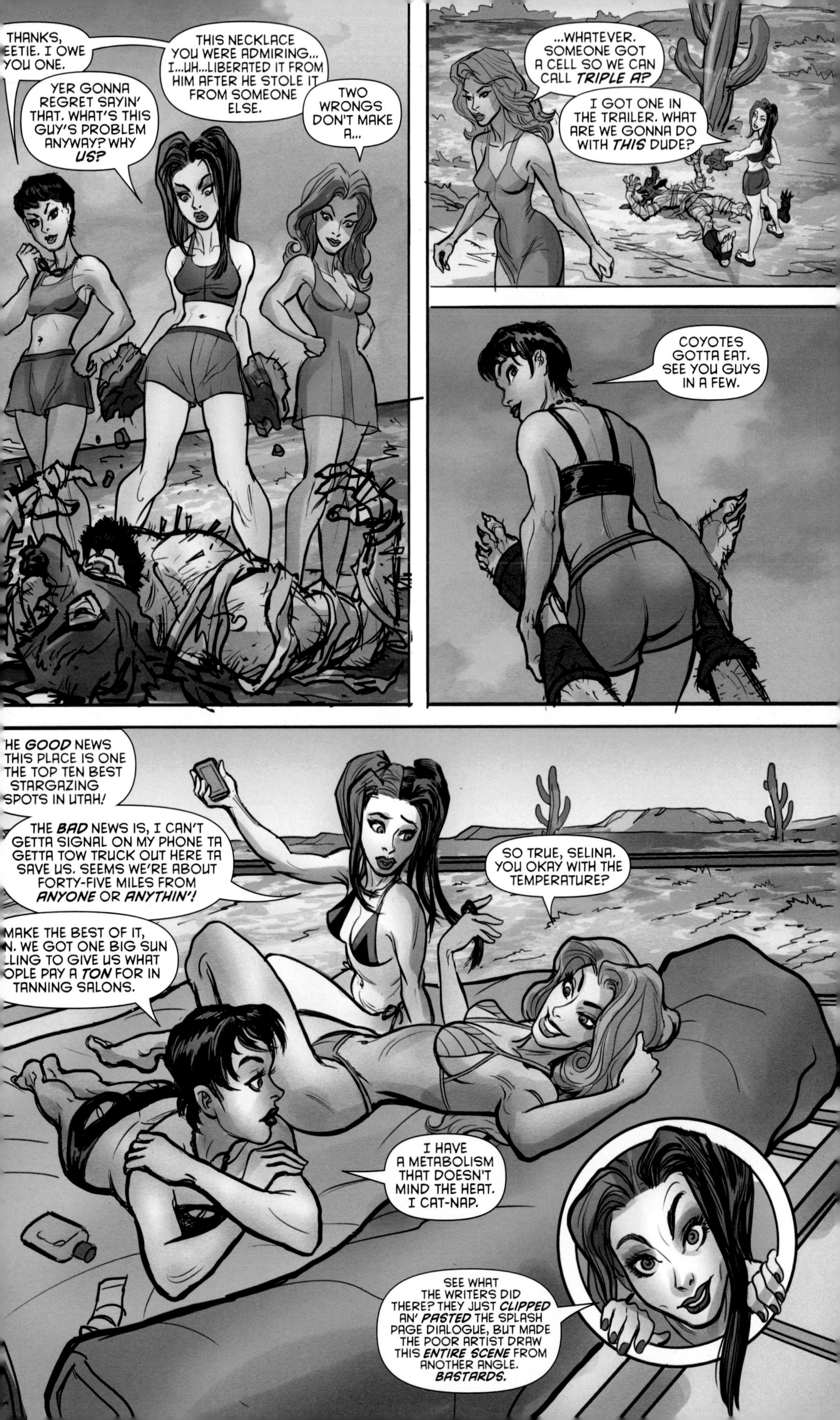

THANKS, EETIE. I OWE YOU ONE.
THIS NECKLACE YOU WERE ADMIRING... I...UH...LIBERATED IT FROM HIM AFTER HE STOLE IT FROM SOMEONE ELSE.
YER GONNA REGRET SAYIN' THAT. WHAT'S THIS GUY'S PROBLEM ANYWAY? WHY US?
TWO WRONGS DON'T MAKE A...
...WHATEVER. SOMEONE GOT A CELL SO WE CAN CALL TRIPLE A?
I GOT ONE IN THE TRAILER. WHAT ARE WE GONNA DO WITH THIS DUDE?
COYOTES GOTTA EAT. SEE YOU GUYS IN A FEW.
HE GOOD NEWS THIS PLACE IS ONE THE TOP TEN BEST STARGAZING SPOTS IN UTAH!
THE BAD NEWS IS, I CAN'T GETTA SIGNAL ON MY PHONE TA GETTA TOW TRUCK OUT HERE TA SAVE US. SEEMS WE'RE ABOUT FORTY-FIVE MILES FROM ANYONE OR ANYTHIN'!
SO TRUE, SELINA. YOU OKAY WITH THE TEMPERATURE?
MAKE THE BEST OF IT, N. WE GOT ONE BIG SUN LING TO GIVE US WHAT OPLE PAY A TON FOR IN TANNING SALONS.
I HAVE A METABOLISM THAT DOESN'T MIND THE HEAT. I CAT-NAP.
SEE WHAT THE WRITERS DID THERE? THEY JUST CLIPPED AN' PASTED THE SPLASH PAGE DIALOGUE, BUT MADE THE POOR ARTIST DRAW THIS ENTIRE SCENE FROM ANOTHER ANGLE. BASTARDS.

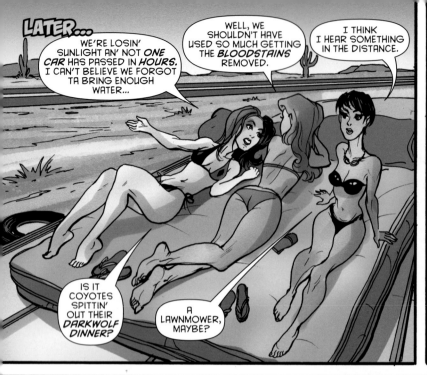

LATER...

WE'RE LOSIN' SUNLIGHT AN' NOT *ONE CAR* HAS PASSED IN *HOURS.* I CAN'T BELIEVE WE FORGOT TA BRING ENOUGH WATER...

WELL, WE SHOULDN'T HAVE USED SO MUCH GETTING THE *BLOODSTAINS* REMOVED.

I THINK I HEAR SOMETHING IN THE DISTANCE.

IS IT COYOTES SPITTIN' OUT THEIR *DARKWOLF* DINNER?

A LAWNMOWER, MAYBE?

HEY! PULL OVER!

DAMSEL DISTRE

HEYA HOT STUFF, WE NEED HELP. WE CRASHED WHEN SOME DUDE RAN US OFF THE ROAD, AN' WE'VE BEEN STRANDED HERE FOR HOURS WITH NO WATER.

GET OFF THE RESERVATION.

I KNOW, HARD TA BELIEVE, AIN'T IT?

NO, I MEAN GET OFF THE *RESERVATION* AND YOU CAN FIND SOME HELP. ABOUT 35 MILES FROM HERE THERE'S A *GARAGE.* HOP IN THE BACK AND DON'T *MESS* WITH ANYTHING.

THERE SHOULD BE SOME BOTTL WATER IN BACK. J *DON'T* DRINK T STUFF IN THE *MAR BOTTLES* IS AL I ASK.

LOOK AT ALL THESE BOTTLES. YOU THINK WE CAN WE HAVE SOME?

YEAH. HE SAID SOMETHIN' ABOUT DRINKIN' ONLY FROM THE MARKED *BOTTLES.*

THE INDIANS MUST MAKE THEIR OWN KIND A' PURIFIED WATER.

HERE, PASS IT AROUND LIKE A *PEACE PIPE.*

I'M NOT SURE IF THAT POLITICALLY CORRECT.

IF YOU HAVE TO ASK, IT PROBABLY ISN'T. NOW GIVE ME A SWIG!

ON SECOND THOUGHT...

HMMM, EVERYTHING'S GETTIN' FUZZZZZ...

SNIFF

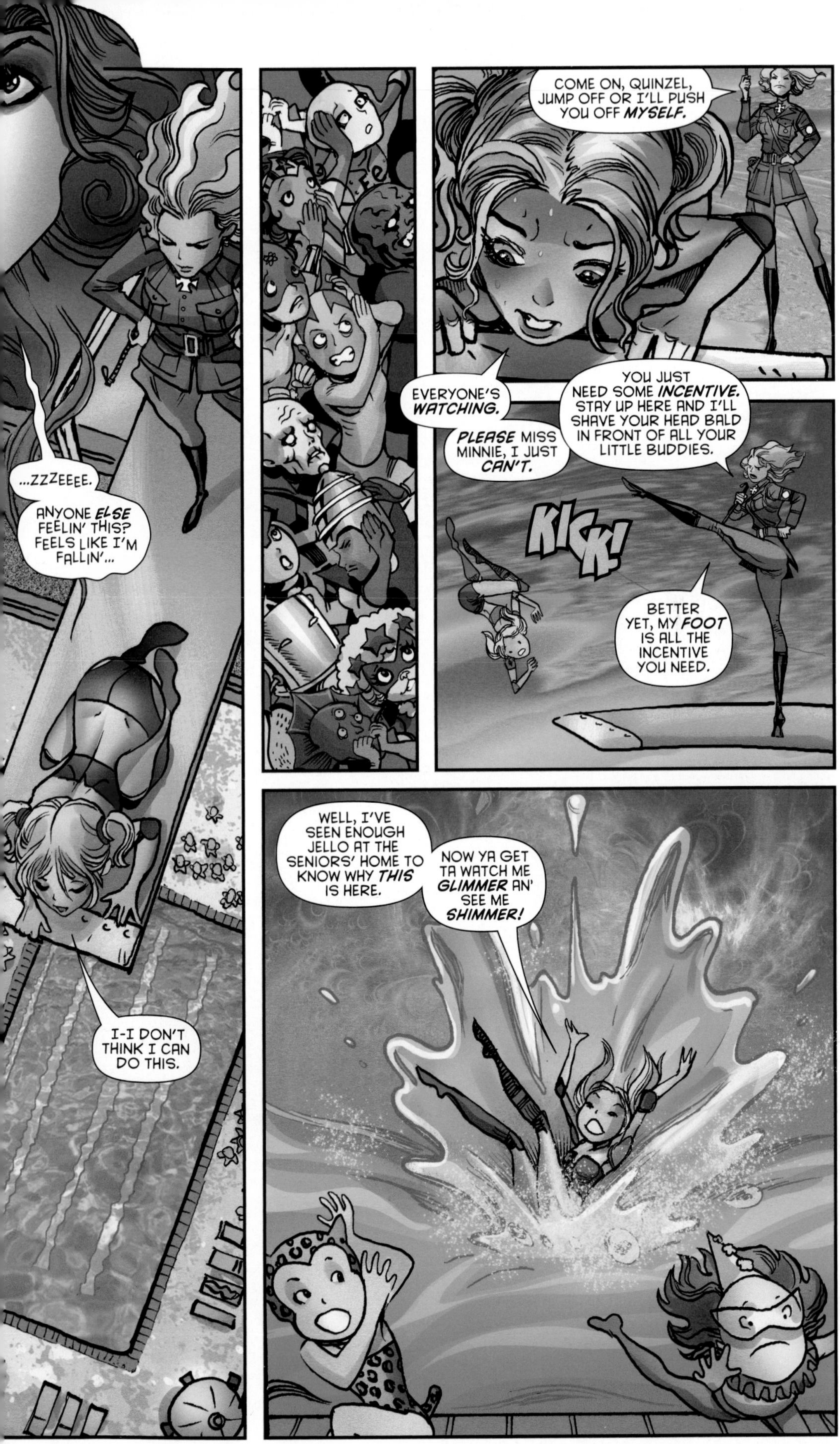
...ZZZEEEE.
ANYONE *ELSE* FEELIN' THIS? FEELS LIKE I'M FALLIN'...
I-I DON'T THINK I CAN DO THIS.
COME ON, QUINZEL, JUMP OFF OR I'LL PUSH YOU OFF *MYSELF.*
EVERYONE'S *WATCHING.*
PLEASE MISS MINNIE, I JUST *CAN'T.*
YOU JUST NEED SOME *INCENTIVE.* STAY UP HERE AND I'LL SHAVE YOUR HEAD BALD IN FRONT OF ALL YOUR LITTLE BUDDIES.
KICK!
BETTER YET, MY *FOOT* IS ALL THE INCENTIVE YOU NEED.
WELL, I'VE SEEN ENOUGH JELLO AT THE SENIORS' HOME TO KNOW WHY *THIS* IS HERE.
NOW YA GET TA WATCH ME *GLIMMER* AN' SEE ME *SHIMMER!*

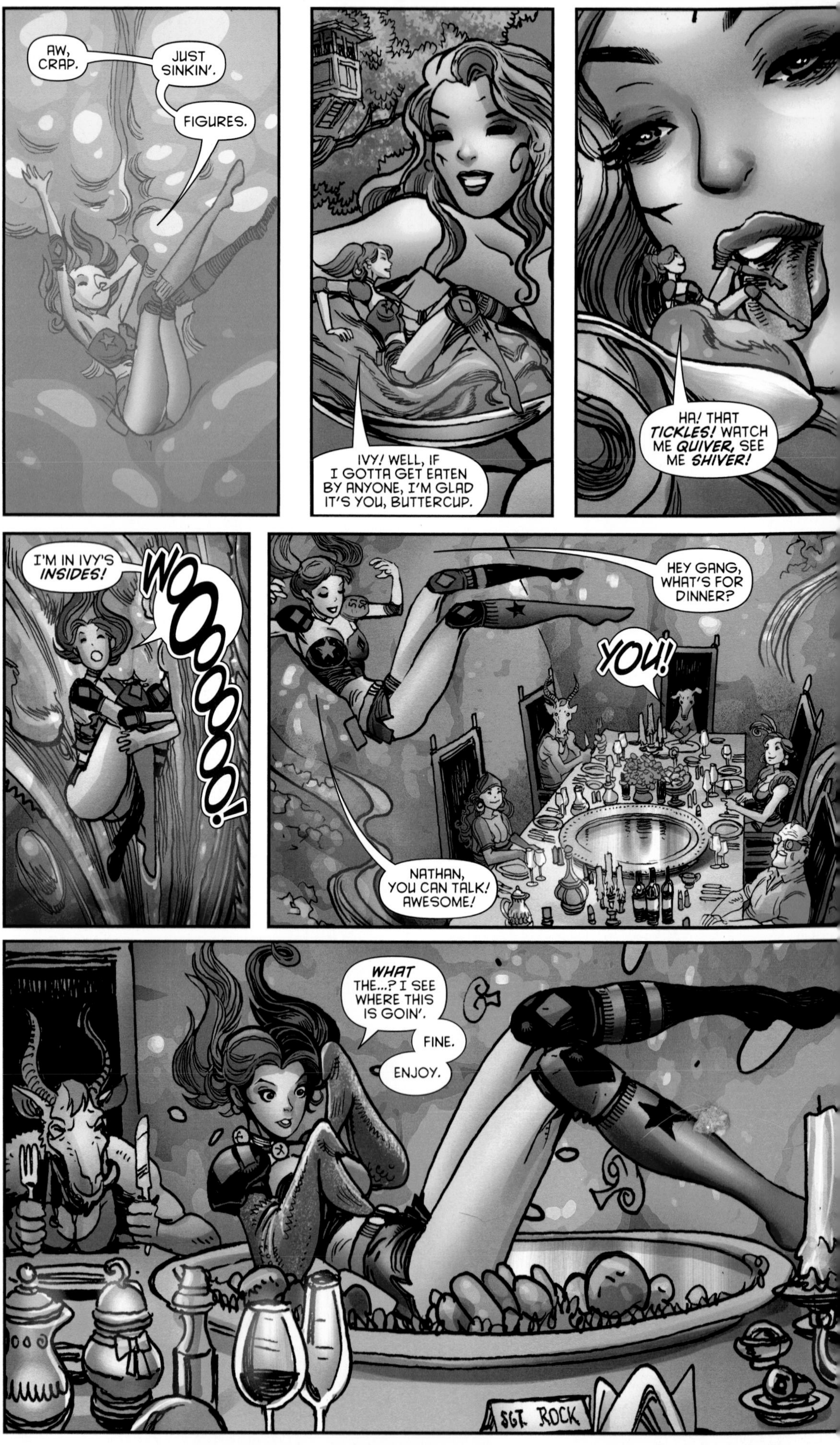
AW, CRAP.
JUST SINKIN'.
FIGURES.
IVY! WELL, IF I GOTTA GET EATEN BY ANYONE, I'M GLAD IT'S YOU, BUTTERCUP.
HA! THAT *TICKLES!* WATCH ME *QUIVER,* SEE ME *SHIVER!*
I'M IN IVY'S *INSIDES!*
WOOOOOOO!
HEY GANG, WHAT'S FOR DINNER?
YOU!
NATHAN, YOU CAN TALK! AWESOME!
WHAT THE...? I SEE WHERE THIS IS GOIN'.
FINE.
ENJOY.
SGT. ROCK

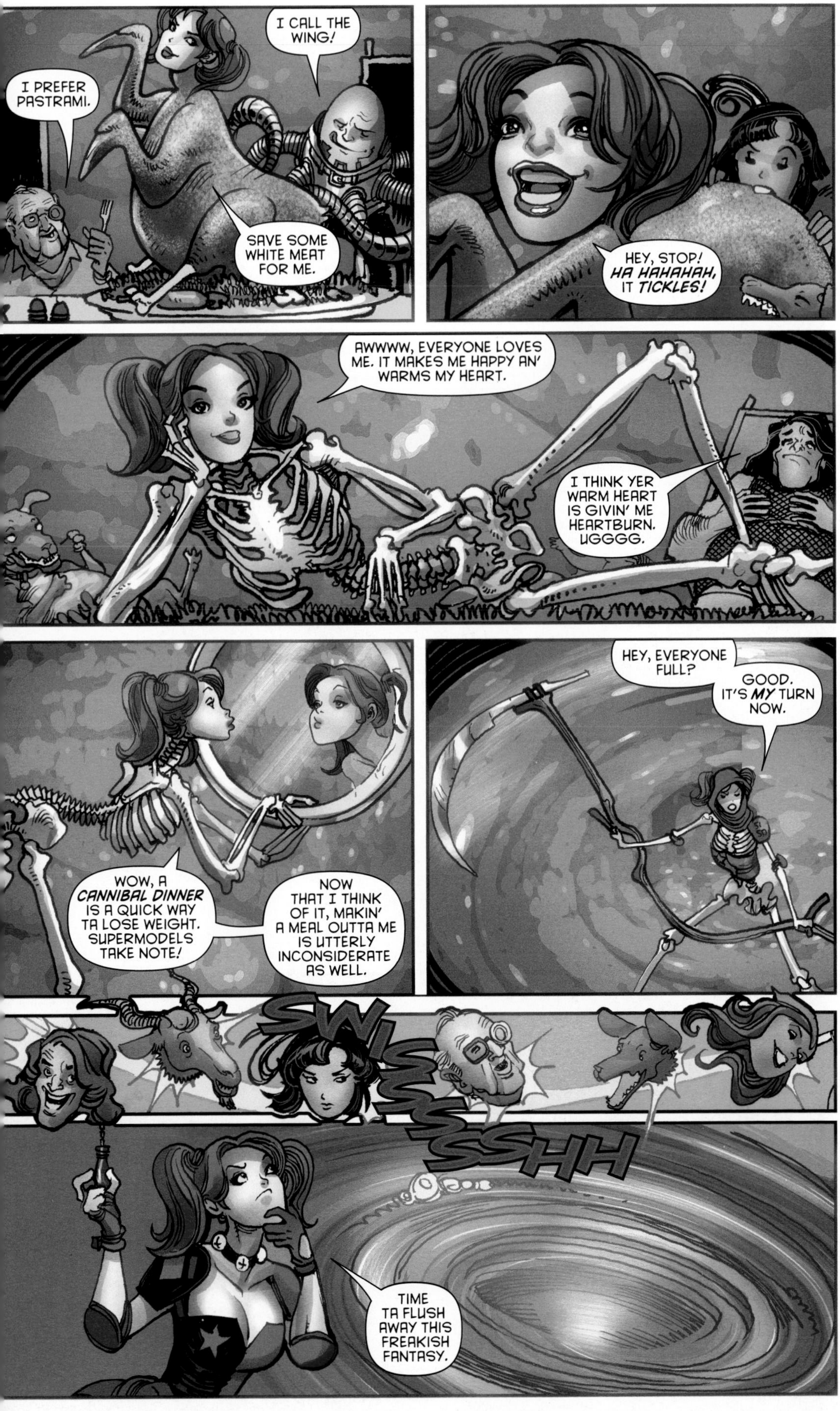

I PREFER PASTRAMI.
I CALL THE WING!
SAVE SOME WHITE MEAT FOR ME.
HEY, STOP! HA HAHAHAH, IT TICKLES!
AWWWW, EVERYONE LOVES ME. IT MAKES ME HAPPY AN' WARMS MY HEART.
I THINK YER WARM HEART IS GIVIN' ME HEARTBURN. UGGGG.
WOW, A CANNIBAL DINNER IS A QUICK WAY TA LOSE WEIGHT. SUPERMODELS TAKE NOTE!
NOW THAT I THINK OF IT, MAKIN' A MEAL OUTTA ME IS UTTERLY INCONSIDERATE AS WELL.
HEY, EVERYONE FULL?
GOOD. IT'S MY TURN NOW.
SWISSSHH
TIME TA FLUSH AWAY THIS FREAKISH FANTASY.

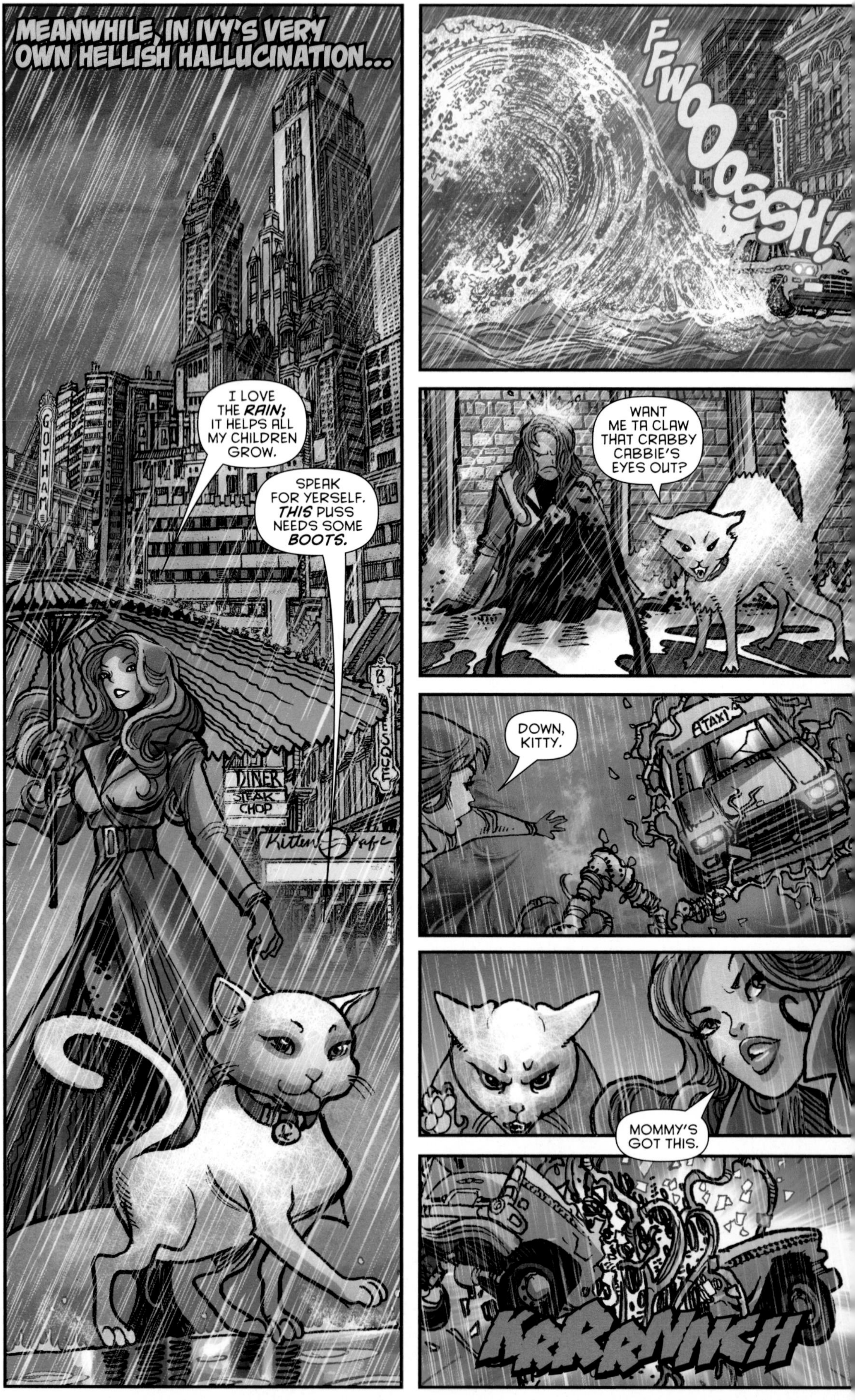
MEANWHILE, IN IVY'S VERY OWN HELLISH HALLUCINATION...
I LOVE THE RAIN; IT HELPS ALL MY CHILDREN GROW.
SPEAK FOR YERSELF. THIS PUSS NEEDS SOME BOOTS.
GOTHAM
DINER
STEAK
CHOP
Kitten Cafe
FFWOOOSSH!
WANT ME TA CLAW THAT CRABBY CABBIE'S EYES OUT?
DOWN, KITTY.
TAXI
MOMMY'S GOT THIS.
KRRRNNCH

FEEL BETTER?

PRRRRRR

AWWW, YOUR PURRING VIBRATION IS A WONDERFUL SENSATION.

WHAT NOW?

PAY ATTENTION, LITTLE ONE. IT'S TIME FOR *GOTHAM CITY* TO GO *GREEN*.

HOLEE VEGE-MOLEE!

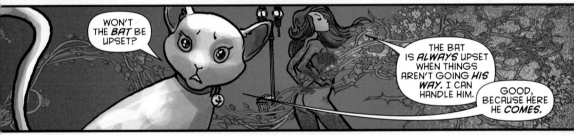

WON'T THE *BAT* BE UPSET?

THE BAT IS *ALWAYS* UPSET WHEN THINGS AREN'T GOING *HIS WAY.* I CAN HANDLE HIM.

GOOD, BECAUSE HERE HE *COMES.*

WHAT HAVE YOU DONE TO MY CITY?

I'VE TAKEN IT BACK TO A TIME BEFORE THE INDUSTRY OF MANKIND POLLUTED EVERYTHING IN ITS PATH.

COOL. I LIKE WHAT I SEE.

YOU *DO? SERIOUSLY?* YOU DON'T MIND ALL THE FOLIAGE?

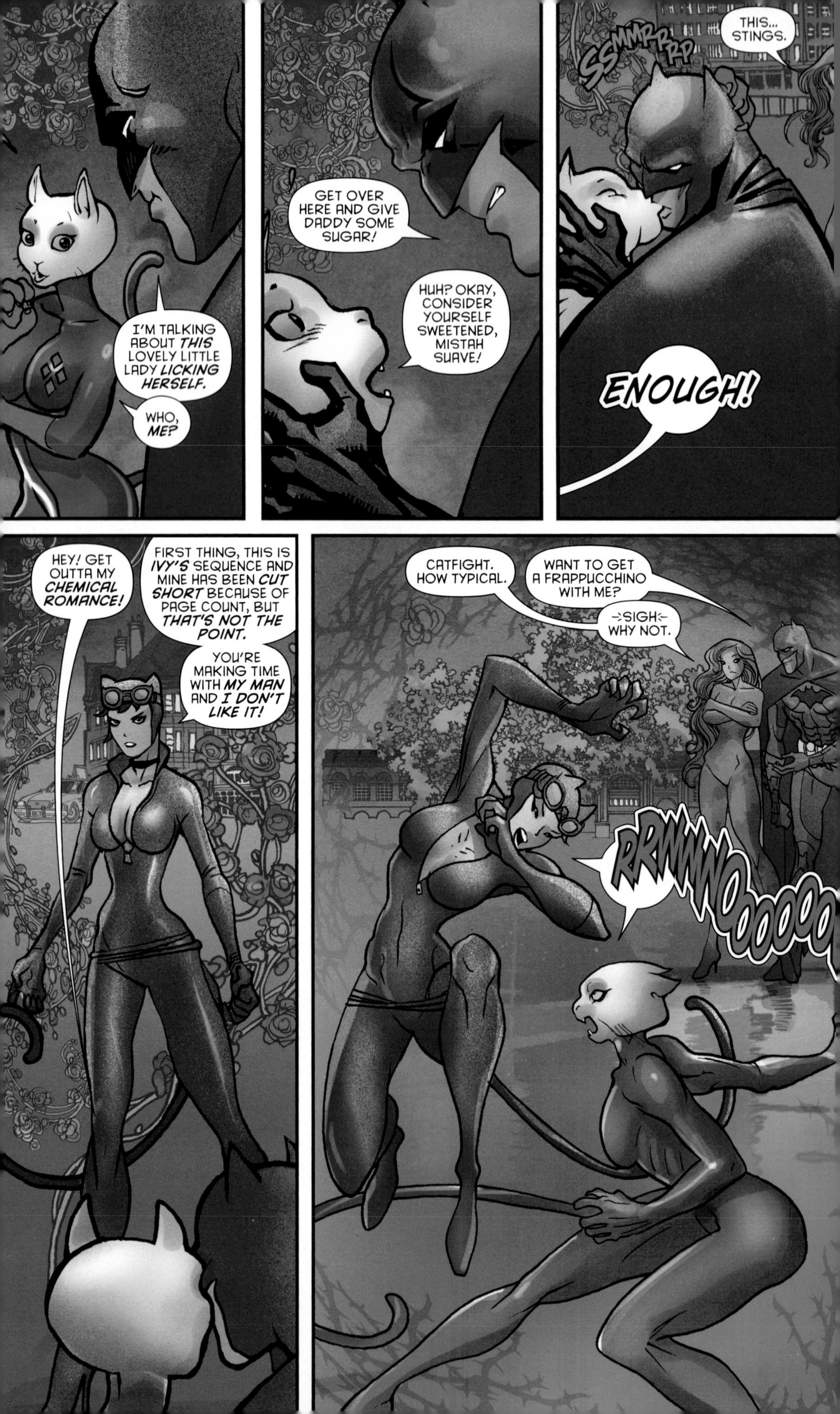
I'M TALKING ABOUT THIS LOVELY LITTLE LADY LICKING HERSELF.
WHO, ME?
GET OVER HERE AND GIVE DADDY SOME SUGAR!
HUH? OKAY, CONSIDER YOURSELF SWEETENED, MISTAH SUAVE!
SSMMRRRRP
THIS... STINGS.
ENOUGH!
HEY! GET OUTTA MY CHEMICAL ROMANCE!
FIRST THING, THIS IS IVY'S SEQUENCE AND MINE HAS BEEN CUT SHORT BECAUSE OF PAGE COUNT, BUT THAT'S NOT THE POINT.
YOU'RE MAKING TIME WITH MY MAN AND I DON'T LIKE IT!
CATFIGHT. HOW TYPICAL.
WANT TO GET A FRAPPUCCHINO WITH ME?
-SIGH- WHY NOT.
RRWWWOOOOOO

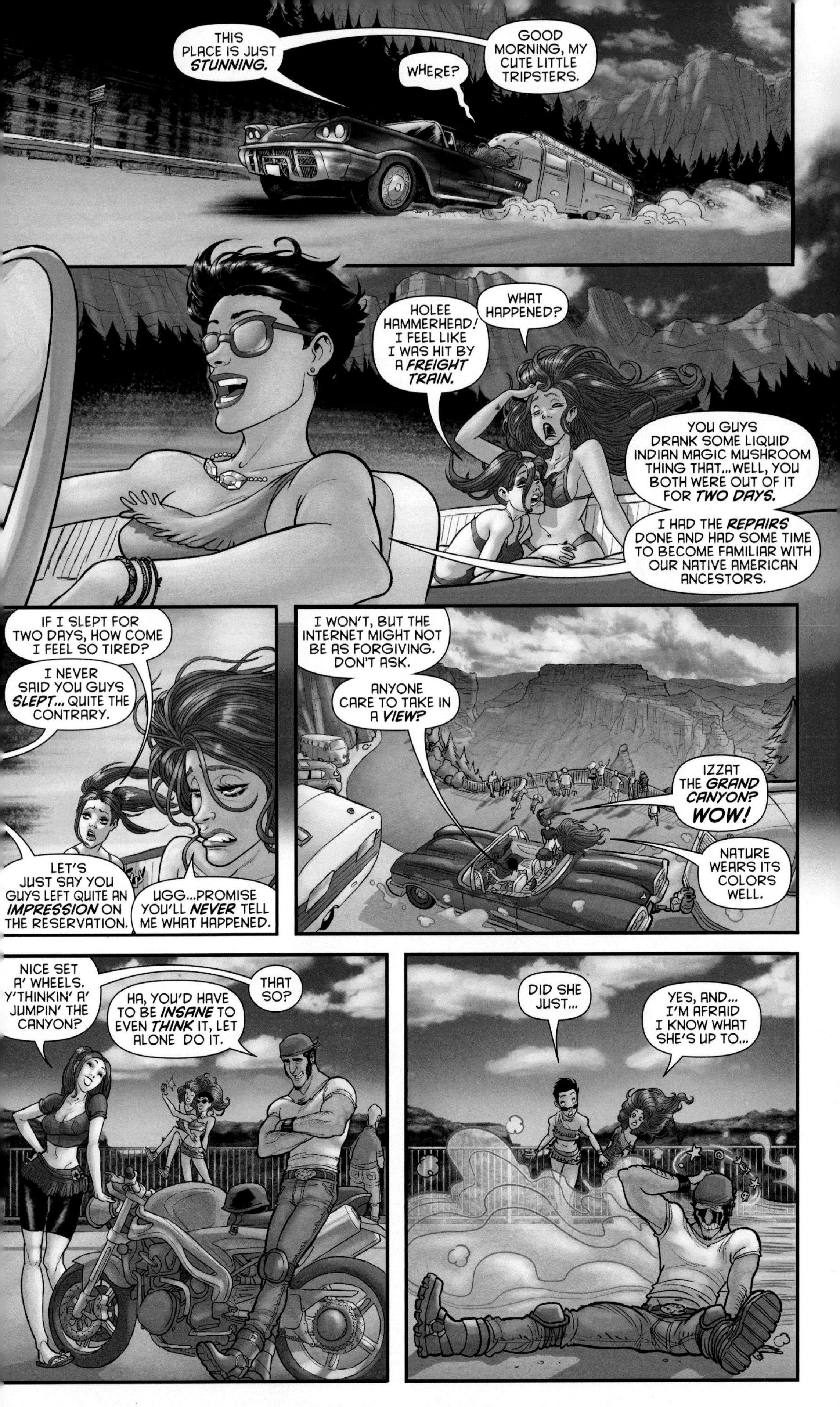

THIS PLACE IS JUST *STUNNING.*
GOOD MORNING, MY CUTE LITTLE TRIPSTERS.
WHERE?
WHAT HAPPENED?
HOLEE HAMMERHEAD! I FEEL LIKE I WAS HIT BY A *FREIGHT TRAIN.*
YOU GUYS DRANK SOME LIQUID INDIAN MAGIC MUSHROOM THING THAT...WELL, YOU BOTH WERE OUT OF IT FOR *TWO DAYS.*
I HAD THE *REPAIRS* DONE AND HAD SOME TIME TO BECOME FAMILIAR WITH OUR NATIVE AMERICAN ANCESTORS.
IF I SLEPT FOR TWO DAYS, HOW COME I FEEL SO TIRED?
I NEVER SAID YOU GUYS *SLEPT...* QUITE THE CONTRARY.
LET'S JUST SAY YOU GUYS LEFT QUITE AN *IMPRESSION* ON THE RESERVATION.
UGG...PROMISE YOU'LL *NEVER* TELL ME WHAT HAPPENED.
I WON'T, BUT THE INTERNET MIGHT NOT BE AS FORGIVING. DON'T ASK.
ANYONE CARE TO TAKE IN A *VIEW?*
IZZAT THE *GRAND CANYON? WOW!*
NATURE WEARS ITS COLORS WELL.
NICE SET A' WHEELS. Y'THINKIN' A' JUMPIN' THE CANYON?
THAT SO?
HA, YOU'D HAVE TO BE *INSANE* TO EVEN *THINK* IT, LET ALONE DO IT.
DID SHE JUST...
YES, AND... I'M AFRAID I KNOW WHAT SHE'S UP TO...

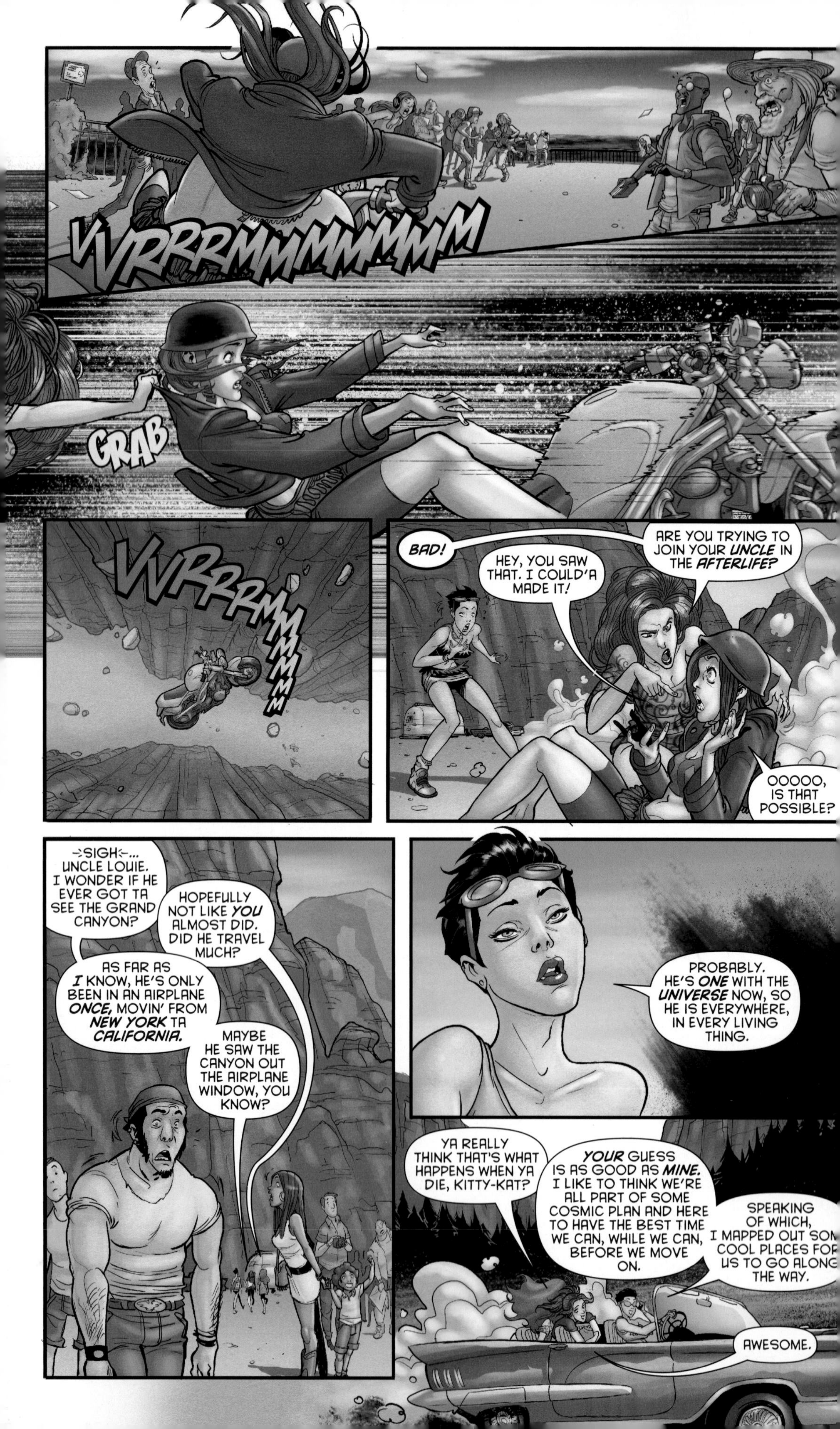
VVRRRMMMMMMMM
GRAB
VVRRRMMMMMMM
BAD!
HEY, YOU SAW THAT. I COULD'A MADE IT!
ARE YOU TRYING TO JOIN YOUR *UNCLE* IN THE *AFTERLIFE?*
OOOOO, IS THAT POSSIBLE?
->SIGH<-... UNCLE LOUIE. I WONDER IF HE EVER GOT TA SEE THE GRAND CANYON?
HOPEFULLY NOT LIKE *YOU* ALMOST DID. DID HE TRAVEL MUCH?
AS FAR AS *I* KNOW, HE'S ONLY BEEN IN AN AIRPLANE *ONCE,* MOVIN' FROM *NEW YORK* TA *CALIFORNIA.*
MAYBE HE SAW THE CANYON OUT THE AIRPLANE WINDOW, YOU KNOW?
PROBABLY. HE'S *ONE* WITH THE *UNIVERSE* NOW, SO HE IS EVERYWHERE, IN EVERY LIVING THING.
YA REALLY THINK THAT'S WHAT HAPPENS WHEN YA DIE, KITTY-KAT?
YOUR GUESS IS AS GOOD AS *MINE.* I LIKE TO THINK WE'RE ALL PART OF SOME COSMIC PLAN AND HERE TO HAVE THE BEST TIME WE CAN, WHILE WE CAN, BEFORE WE MOVE ON.
SPEAKING OF WHICH, I MAPPED OUT SOM COOL PLACES FOR US TO GO ALONG THE WAY.
AWESOME.

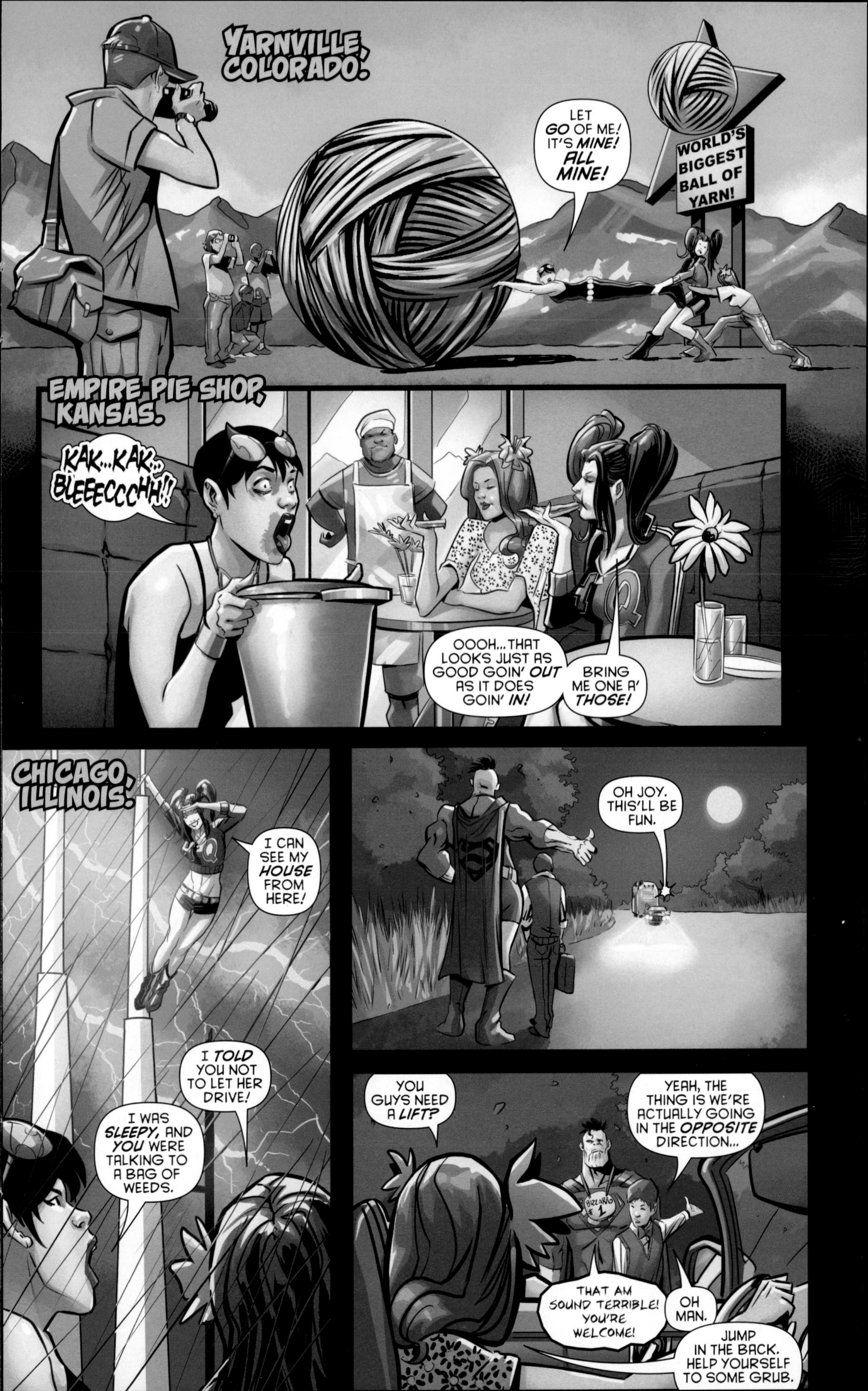

YARNVILLE, COLORADO.
LET GO OF ME! IT'S MINE! ALL MINE!
WORLD'S BIGGEST BALL OF YARN!
EMPIRE PIE SHOP, KANSAS.
KAK...KAK... BLEEECCCHH!!
OOOH... THAT LOOKS JUST AS GOOD GOIN' OUT AS IT DOES GOIN' IN!
BRING ME ONE A' THOSE!
CHICAGO, ILLINOIS.
I CAN SEE MY HOUSE FROM HERE!
I TOLD YOU NOT TO LET HER DRIVE!
I WAS SLEEPY, AND YOU WERE TALKING TO A BAG OF WEEDS.
OH JOY. THIS'LL BE FUN.
YOU GUYS NEED A LIFT?
YEAH, THE THING IS WE'RE ACTUALLY GOING IN THE OPPOSITE DIRECTION...
BIZARRO #1
THAT AM SOUND TERRIBLE! YOU'RE WELCOME!
OH MAN.
JUMP IN THE BACK. HELP YOURSELF TO SOME GRUB.

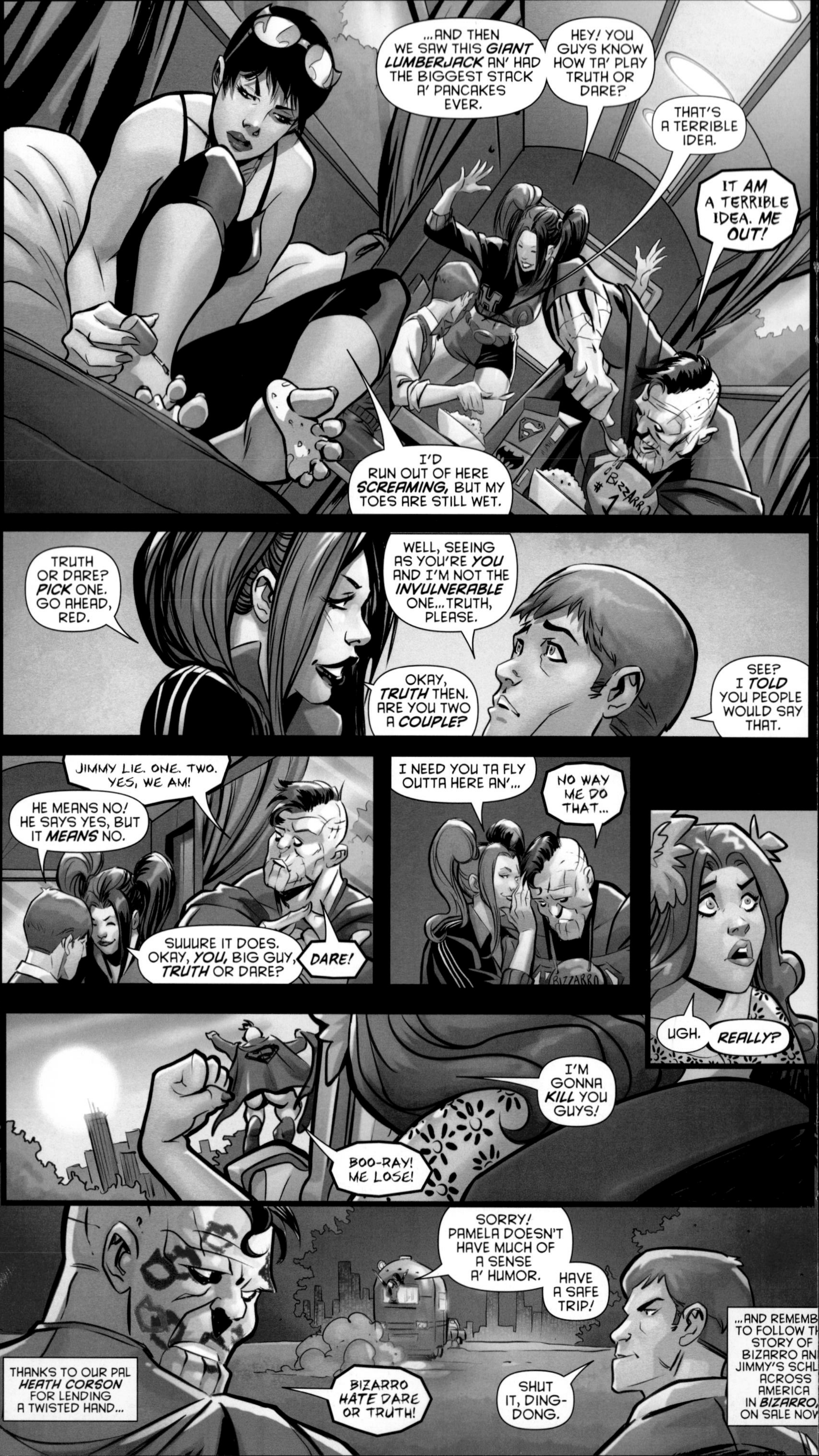
...AND THEN WE SAW THIS GIANT LUMBERJACK AN' HAD THE BIGGEST STACK A' PANCAKES EVER.
HEY! YOU GUYS KNOW HOW TA' PLAY TRUTH OR DARE?
THAT'S A TERRIBLE IDEA.
IT AM A TERRIBLE IDEA. ME OUT!
I'D RUN OUT OF HERE SCREAMING, BUT MY TOES ARE STILL WET.
1 BIZZARRO
TRUTH OR DARE? PICK ONE. GO AHEAD, RED.
WELL, SEEING AS YOU'RE YOU AND I'M NOT THE INVULNERABLE ONE... TRUTH, PLEASE.
OKAY, TRUTH THEN. ARE YOU TWO A COUPLE?
SEE? I TOLD YOU PEOPLE WOULD SAY THAT.
JIMMY LIE. ONE. TWO. YES, WE AM!
HE MEANS NO! HE SAYS YES, BUT IT MEANS NO.
SUUURE IT DOES. OKAY, YOU, BIG GUY, TRUTH OR DARE?
DARE!
I NEED YOU TA FLY OUTTA HERE AN'...
NO WAY ME DO THAT...
UGH.
REALLY?
I'M GONNA KILL YOU GUYS!
BOO-RAY! ME LOSE!
SORRY! PAMELA DOESN'T HAVE MUCH OF A SENSE A' HUMOR.
HAVE A SAFE TRIP!
THANKS TO OUR PAL HEATH CORSON FOR LENDING A TWISTED HAND...
BIZARRO HATE DARE OR TRUTH!
SHUT IT, DING-DONG.
...AND REMEMB TO FOLLOW TH STORY OF BIZARRO AN JIMMY'S SCHL ACROSS AMERICA IN BIZARRO, ON SALE NOV

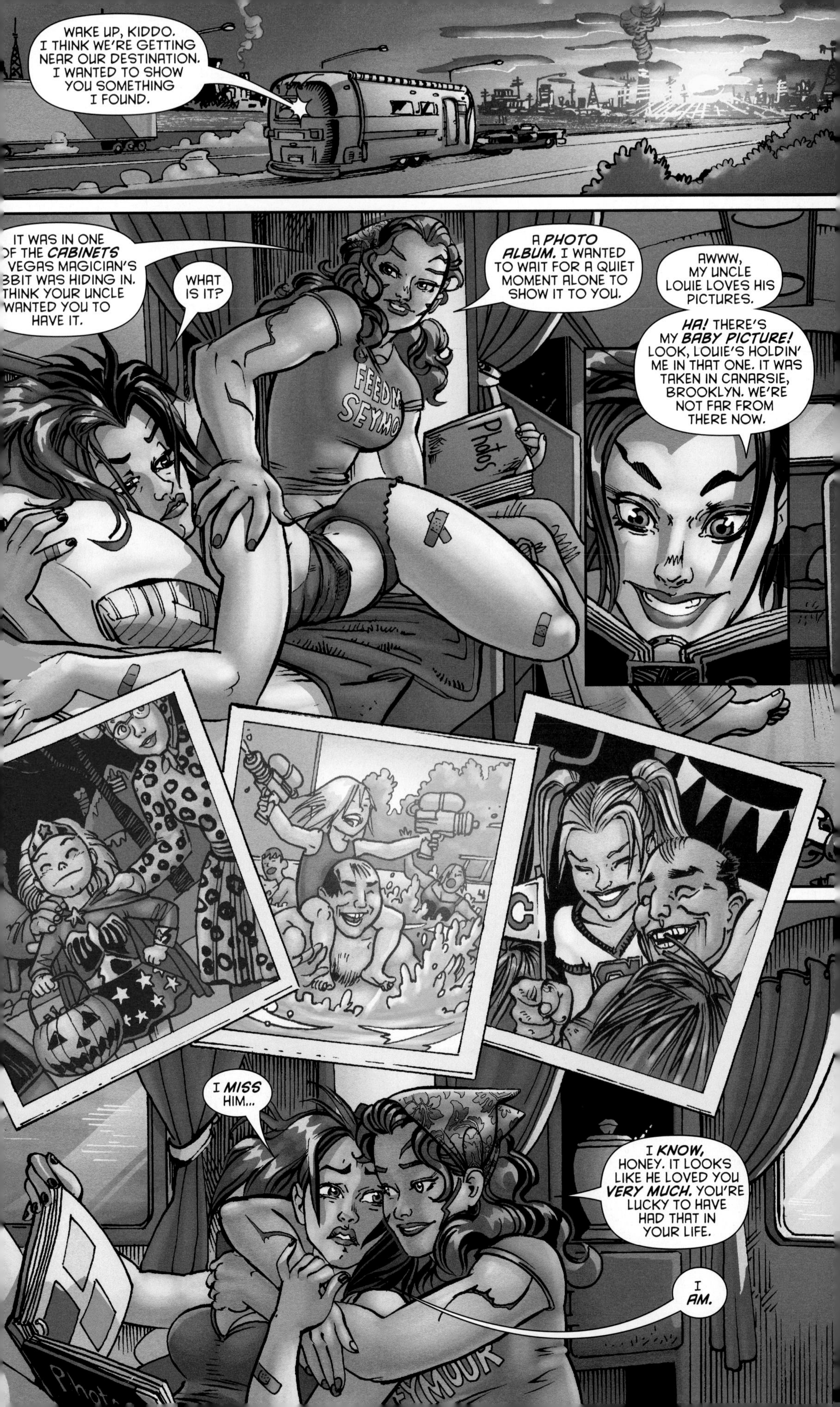

WAKE UP, KIDDO. I THINK WE'RE GETTING NEAR OUR DESTINATION. I WANTED TO SHOW YOU SOMETHING I FOUND.
WHAT IS IT?
IT WAS IN ONE OF THE CABINETS VEGAS MAGICIAN'S BBIT WAS HIDING IN. THINK YOUR UNCLE WANTED YOU TO HAVE IT.
A PHOTO ALBUM. I WANTED TO WAIT FOR A QUIET MOMENT ALONE TO SHOW IT TO YOU.
FEED ME SEYMO
Photos
AWWW, MY UNCLE LOUIE LOVES HIS PICTURES.
HA! THERE'S MY BABY PICTURE! LOOK, LOUIE'S HOLDIN' ME IN THAT ONE. IT WAS TAKEN IN CANARSIE, BROOKLYN. WE'RE NOT FAR FROM THERE NOW.
I MISS HIM...
I KNOW, HONEY. IT LOOKS LIKE HE LOVED YOU VERY MUCH. YOU'RE LUCKY TO HAVE HAD THAT IN YOUR LIFE.
I AM.

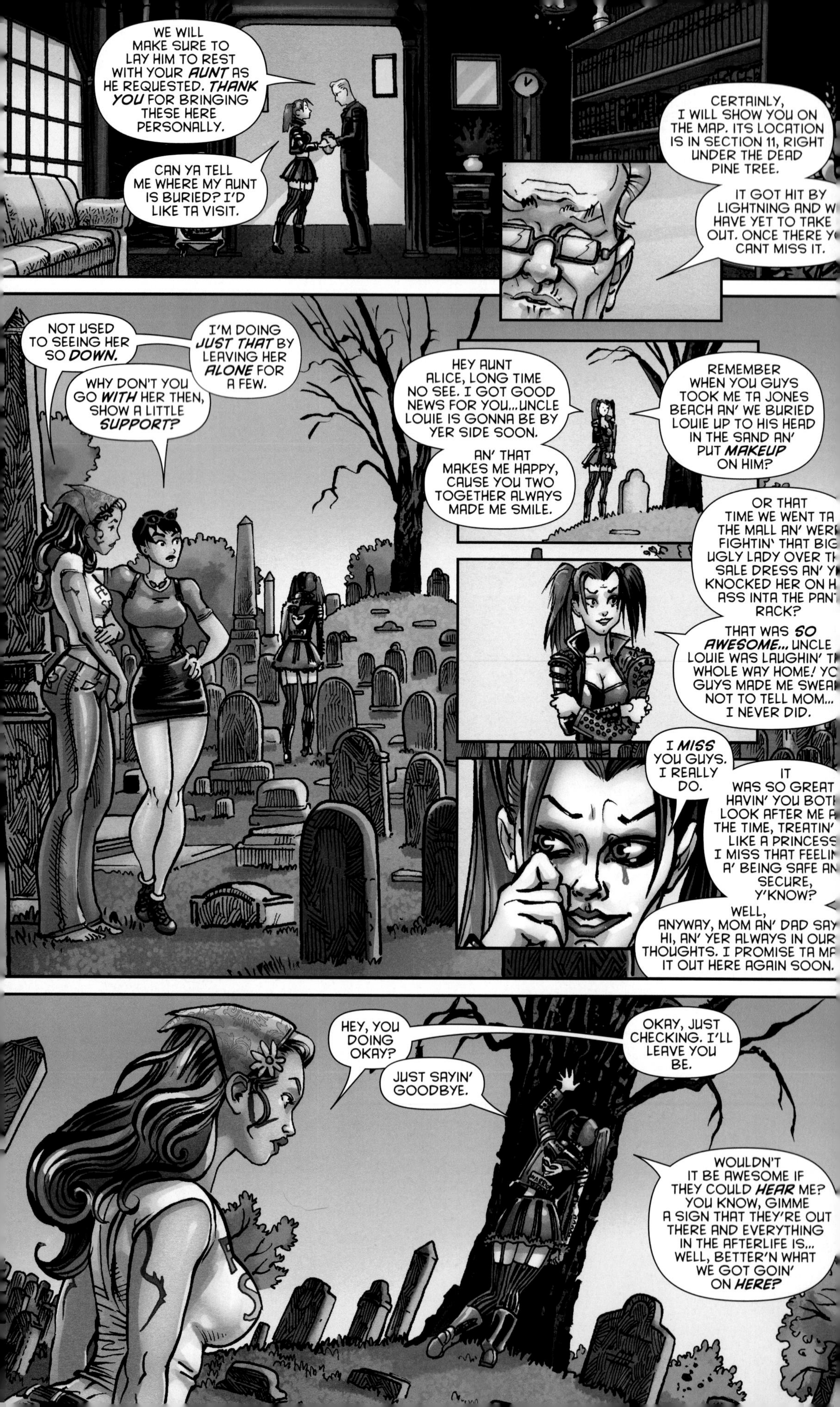
WE WILL MAKE SURE TO LAY HIM TO REST WITH YOUR AUNT AS HE REQUESTED. THANK YOU FOR BRINGING THESE HERE PERSONALLY.
CAN YA TELL ME WHERE MY AUNT IS BURIED? I'D LIKE TA VISIT.
CERTAINLY, I WILL SHOW YOU ON THE MAP. ITS LOCATION IS IN SECTION 11, RIGHT UNDER THE DEAD PINE TREE.
IT GOT HIT BY LIGHTNING AND W HAVE YET TO TAKE OUT. ONCE THERE Y CANT MISS IT.
NOT USED TO SEEING HER SO DOWN.
I'M DOING JUST THAT BY LEAVING HER ALONE FOR A FEW.
WHY DON'T YOU GO WITH HER THEN, SHOW A LITTLE SUPPORT?
HEY AUNT ALICE, LONG TIME NO SEE. I GOT GOOD NEWS FOR YOU...UNCLE LOUIE IS GONNA BE BY YER SIDE SOON.
AN' THAT MAKES ME HAPPY, CAUSE YOU TWO TOGETHER ALWAYS MADE ME SMILE.
REMEMBER WHEN YOU GUYS TOOK ME TA JONES BEACH AN' WE BURIED LOUIE UP TO HIS HEAD IN THE SAND AN' PUT MAKEUP ON HIM?
OR THAT TIME WE WENT TA THE MALL AN' WER FIGHTIN' THAT BIG UGLY LADY OVER T SALE DRESS AN' Y KNOCKED HER ON H ASS INTA THE PAN RACK?
THAT WAS SO AWESOME... UNCLE LOUIE WAS LAUGHIN' T WHOLE WAY HOME! YO GUYS MADE ME SWEA NOT TO TELL MOM... I NEVER DID.
I MISS YOU GUYS. I REALLY DO.
IT WAS SO GREAT HAVIN' YOU BOT LOOK AFTER ME A THE TIME, TREATIN' LIKE A PRINCESS I MISS THAT FEELI A' BEING SAFE AN SECURE, Y'KNOW?
WELL, ANYWAY, MOM AN' DAD SAY HI, AN' YER ALWAYS IN OUR THOUGHTS. I PROMISE TA M IT OUT HERE AGAIN SOON.
HEY, YOU DOING OKAY?
JUST SAYIN' GOODBYE.
OKAY, JUST CHECKING. I'LL LEAVE YOU BE.
WOULDN'T IT BE AWESOME IF THEY COULD HEAR ME? YOU KNOW, GIMME A SIGN THAT THEY'RE OUT THERE AND EVERYTHING IN THE AFTERLIFE IS... WELL, BETTER'N WHAT WE GOT GOIN' ON HERE?

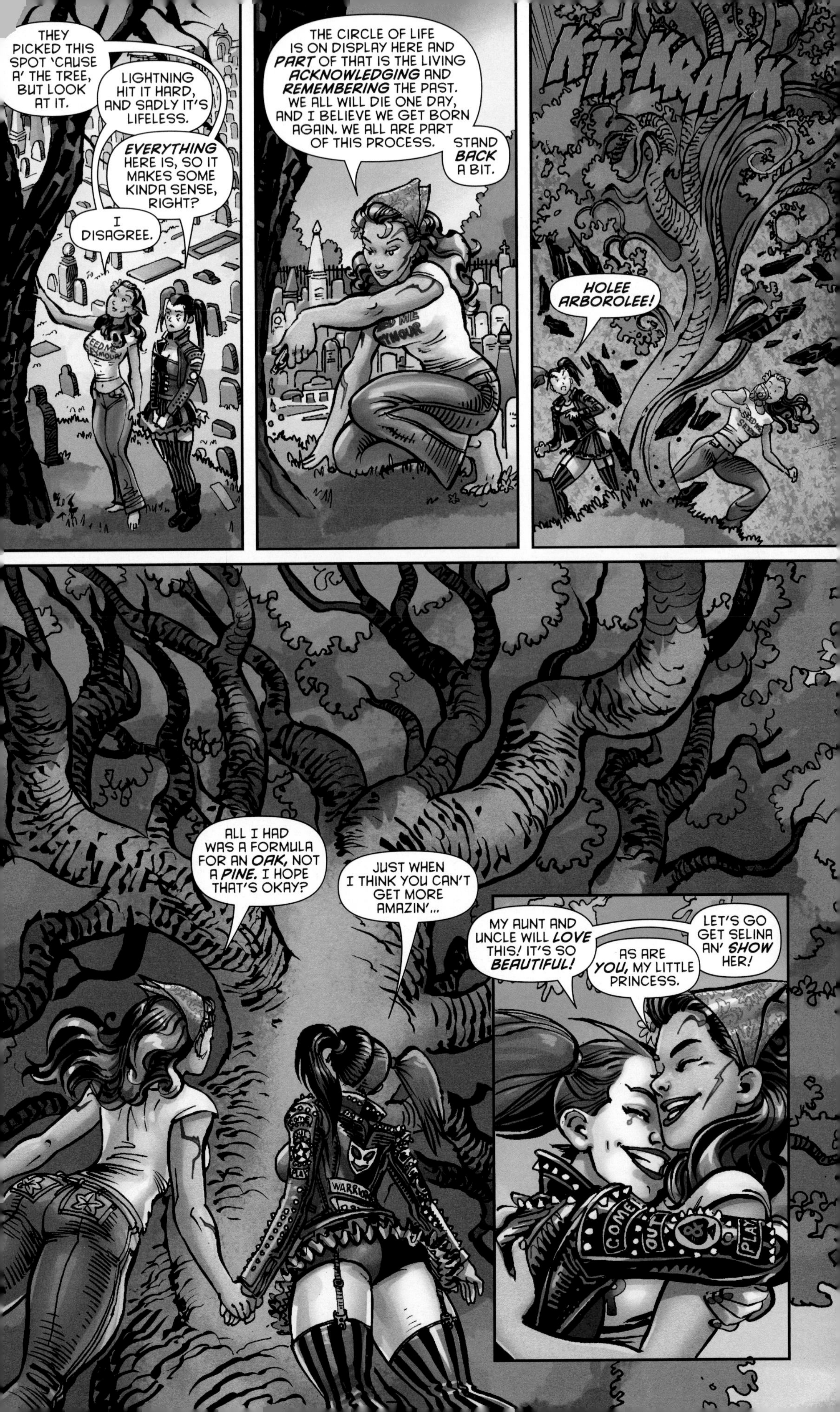
THEY PICKED THIS SPOT 'CAUSE A' THE TREE, BUT LOOK AT IT.
LIGHTNING HIT IT HARD, AND SADLY IT'S LIFELESS.
EVERYTHING HERE IS, SO IT MAKES SOME KINDA SENSE, RIGHT?
I DISAGREE.
THE CIRCLE OF LIFE IS ON DISPLAY HERE AND PART OF THAT IS THE LIVING ACKNOWLEDGING AND REMEMBERING THE PAST. WE ALL WILL DIE ONE DAY, AND I BELIEVE WE GET BORN AGAIN. WE ALL ARE PART OF THIS PROCESS.
STAND BACK A BIT.
K-K-KRAAAK
HOLEE ARBOROLEE!
ALL I HAD WAS A FORMULA FOR AN OAK, NOT A PINE. I HOPE THAT'S OKAY?
JUST WHEN I THINK YOU CAN'T GET MORE AMAZIN'...
MY AUNT AND UNCLE WILL LOVE THIS! IT'S SO BEAUTIFUL!
AS ARE YOU, MY LITTLE PRINCESS.
LET'S GO GET SELINA AN' SHOW HER!

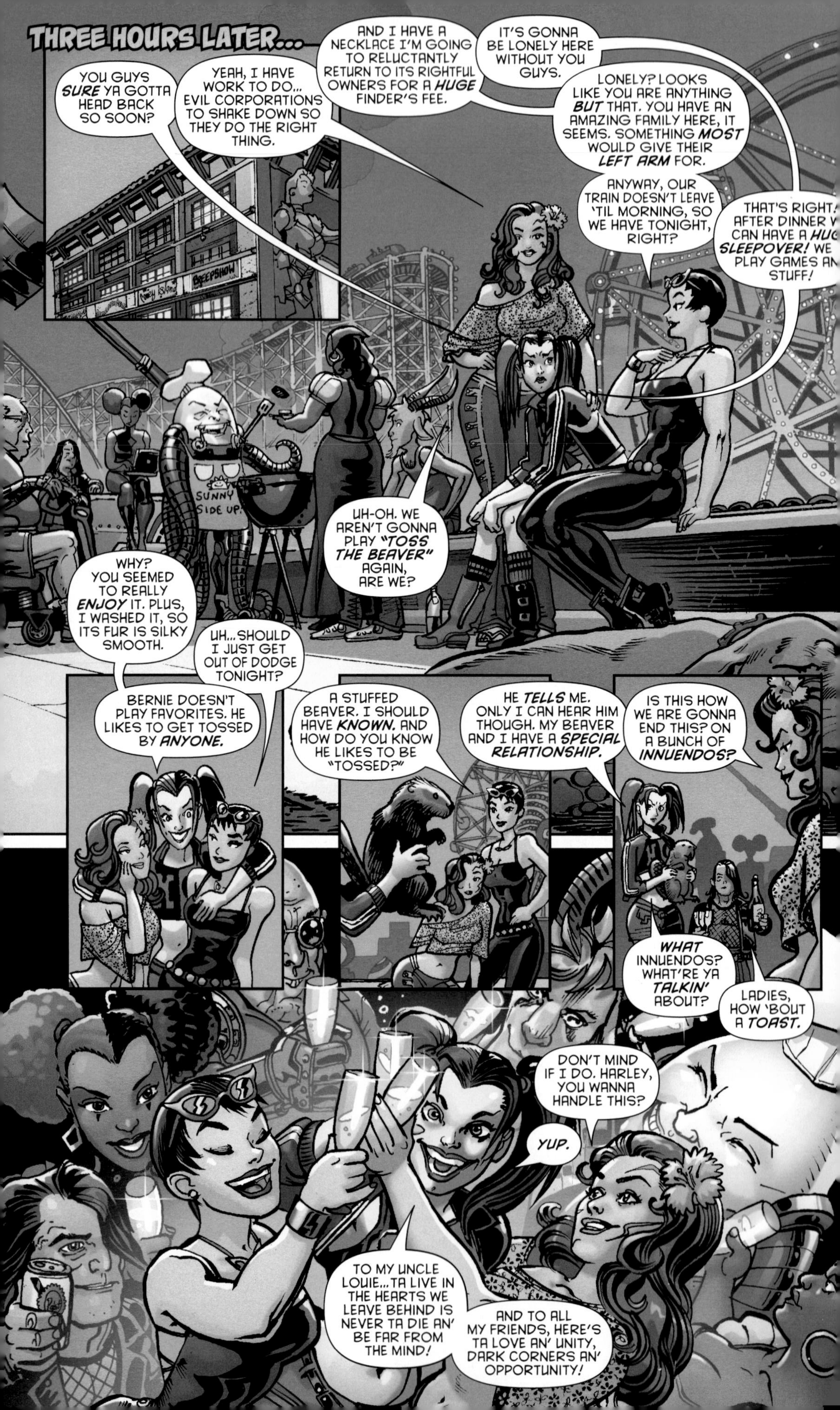
THREE HOURS LATER...
YOU GUYS SURE YA GOTTA HEAD BACK SO SOON?
YEAH, I HAVE WORK TO DO... EVIL CORPORATIONS TO SHAKE DOWN SO THEY DO THE RIGHT THING.
AND I HAVE A NECKLACE I'M GOING TO RELUCTANTLY RETURN TO ITS RIGHTFUL OWNERS FOR A HUGE FINDER'S FEE.
IT'S GONNA BE LONELY HERE WITHOUT YOU GUYS.
LONELY? LOOKS LIKE YOU ARE ANYTHING BUT THAT. YOU HAVE AN AMAZING FAMILY HERE, IT SEEMS. SOMETHING MOST WOULD GIVE THEIR LEFT ARM FOR.
ANYWAY, OUR TRAIN DOESN'T LEAVE 'TIL MORNING, SO WE HAVE TONIGHT, RIGHT?
THAT'S RIGHT! AFTER DINNER W CAN HAVE A HUG SLEEPOVER! WE PLAY GAMES AN STUFF!
SUNNY SIDE UP
UH-OH. WE AREN'T GONNA PLAY "TOSS THE BEAVER" AGAIN, ARE WE?
WHY? YOU SEEMED TO REALLY ENJOY IT. PLUS, I WASHED IT, SO ITS FUR IS SILKY SMOOTH.
UH...SHOULD I JUST GET OUT OF DODGE TONIGHT?
BERNIE DOESN'T PLAY FAVORITES. HE LIKES TO GET TOSSED BY ANYONE.
A STUFFED BEAVER. I SHOULD HAVE KNOWN. AND HOW DO YOU KNOW HE LIKES TO BE "TOSSED?"
HE TELLS ME. ONLY I CAN HEAR HIM THOUGH. MY BEAVER AND I HAVE A SPECIAL RELATIONSHIP.
IS THIS HOW WE ARE GONNA END THIS? ON A BUNCH OF INNUENDOS?
WHAT INNUENDOS? WHAT'RE YA TALKIN' ABOUT?
LADIES, HOW 'BOUT A TOAST.
DON'T MIND IF I DO. HARLEY, YOU WANNA HANDLE THIS?
YUP.
TO MY UNCLE LOUIE...TA LIVE IN THE HEARTS WE LEAVE BEHIND IS NEVER TA DIE AN' BE FAR FROM THE MIND!
AND TO ALL MY FRIENDS, HERE'S TA LOVE AN' UNITY, DARK CORNERS AN' OPPORTUNITY!

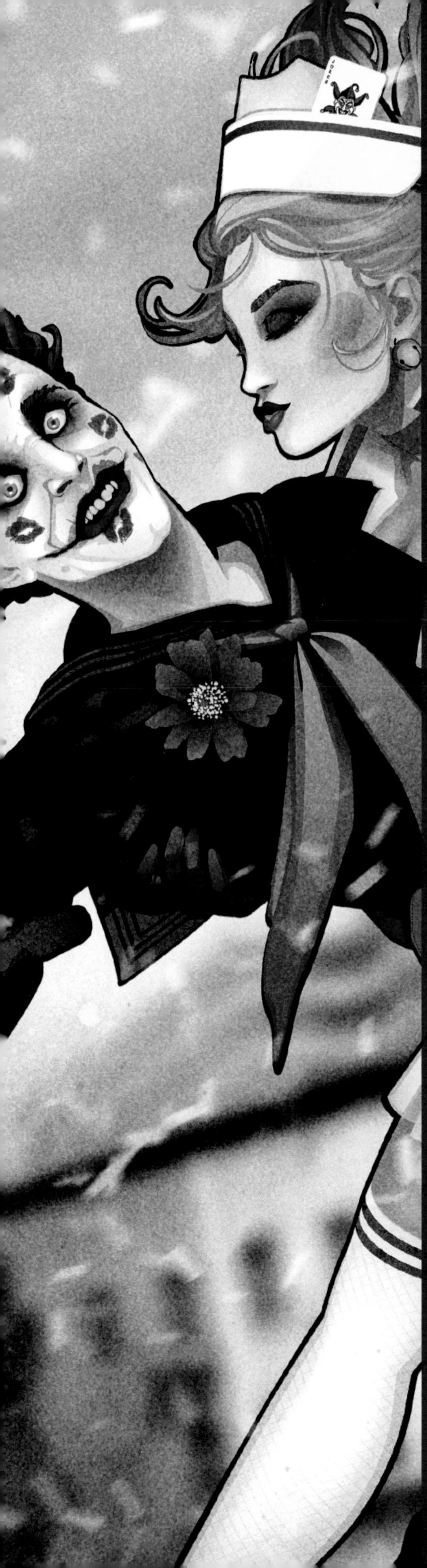

VARIANT COVER GALLERY

HARLEY QUINN #17
JOKER 75TH ANNIVERSARY
VARIANT BY
EDUARDO RISSO

HARLEY QUINN #17
SAN DIEGO COMIC-CON VARIANT BY
AMANDA CONNER & PAUL MOUNTS

HARLEY QUINN #18
TEEN TITANS GO! VARIANT BY
BEN CALDWELL

HARLEY QUINN #19
BOMBSHELLS VARIANT COVER BY
ANT LUCIA

HARLEY QUINN #19
ALAMO CITY COMIC-CON VARIANT BY
CHAD HARDIN

HARLEY QUINN #19
AMAZING HOUSTON COMIC CON
VARIANT BY ANT LUCIA

HARLEY QUINN #20
GREEN LANTERN 75TH ANNIVERSARY
VARIANT BY DAN PANOSIAN

HARLEY QUINN #21
MONSTER VARIANT BY RYAN SOOK

HARLEY QUINN
ROAD TRIP SPECIAL #1
VARIANT BY
BRET BLEVINS & PAUL MOUNTS

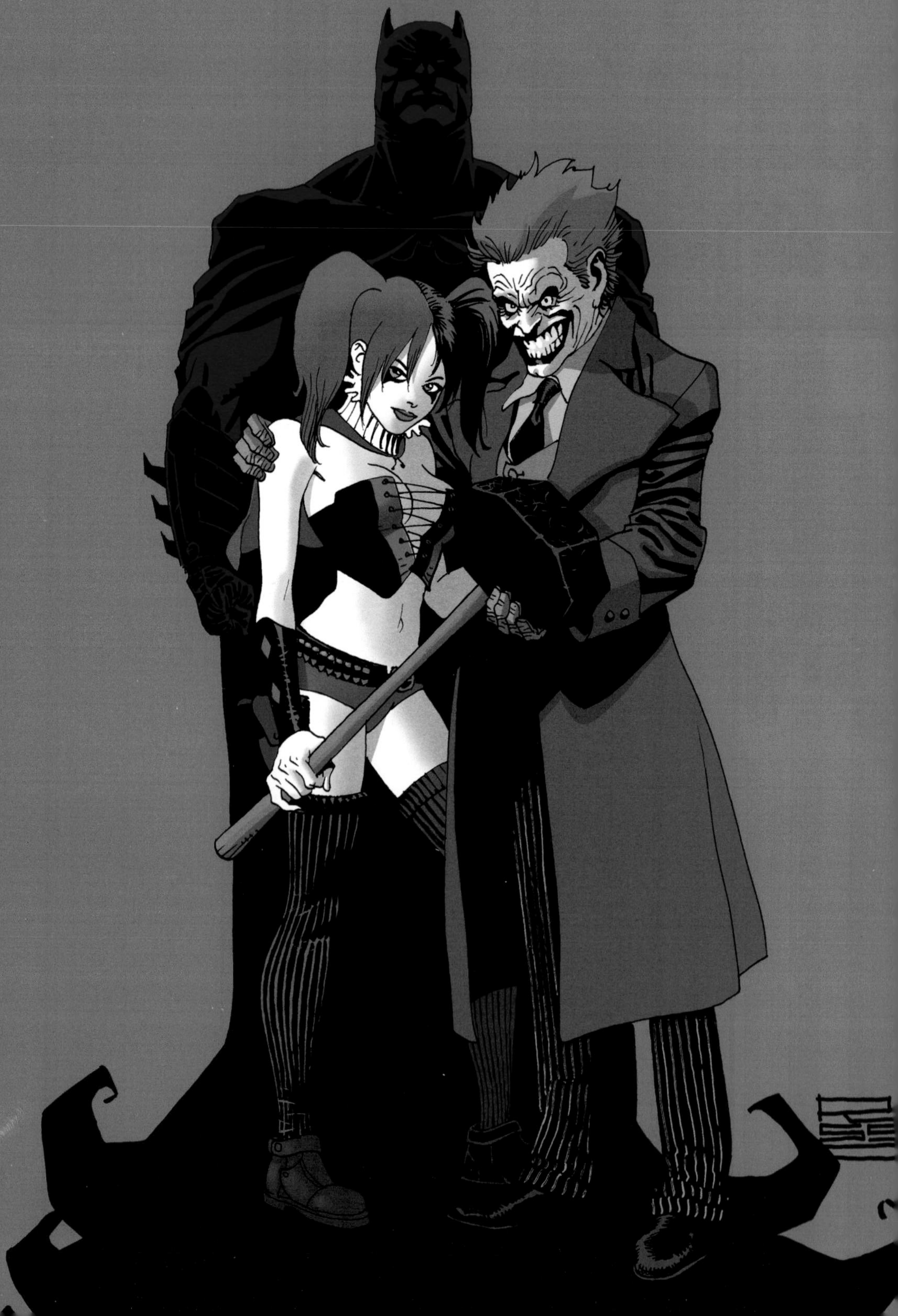

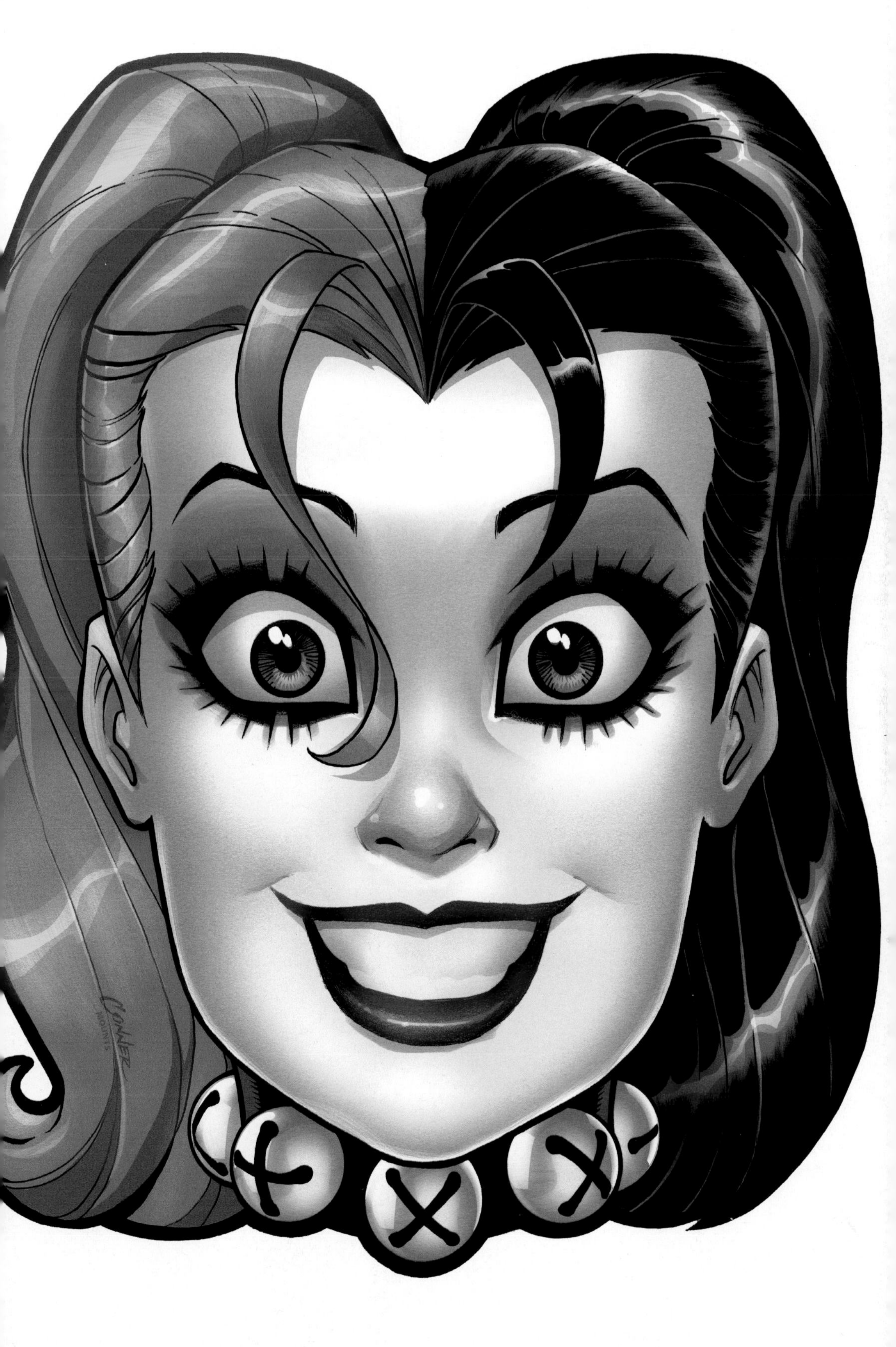

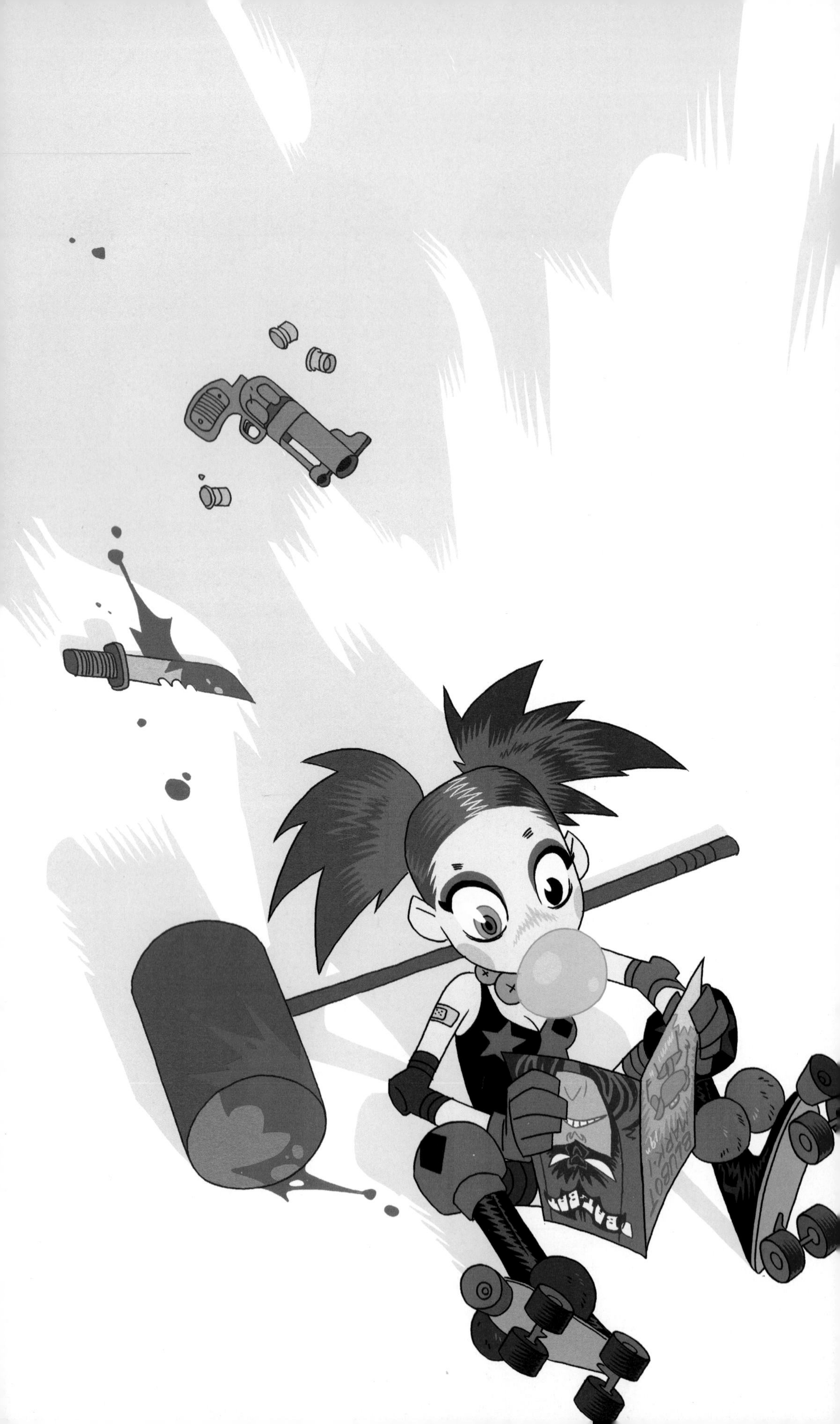
BLUBOT MARK-I
BATBAR

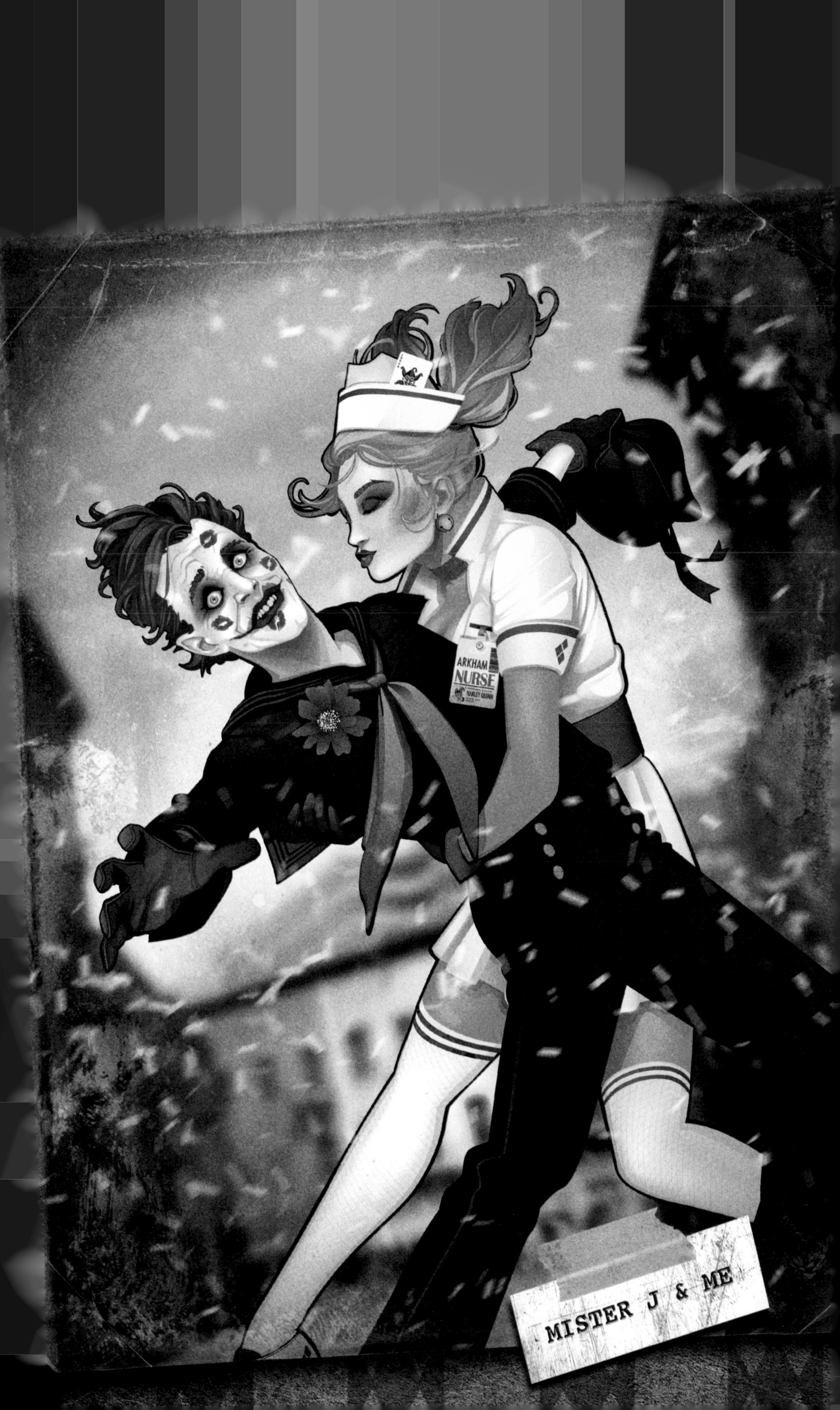
ARKHAM
NURSE
HARLEY QUINN
MISTER J & ME

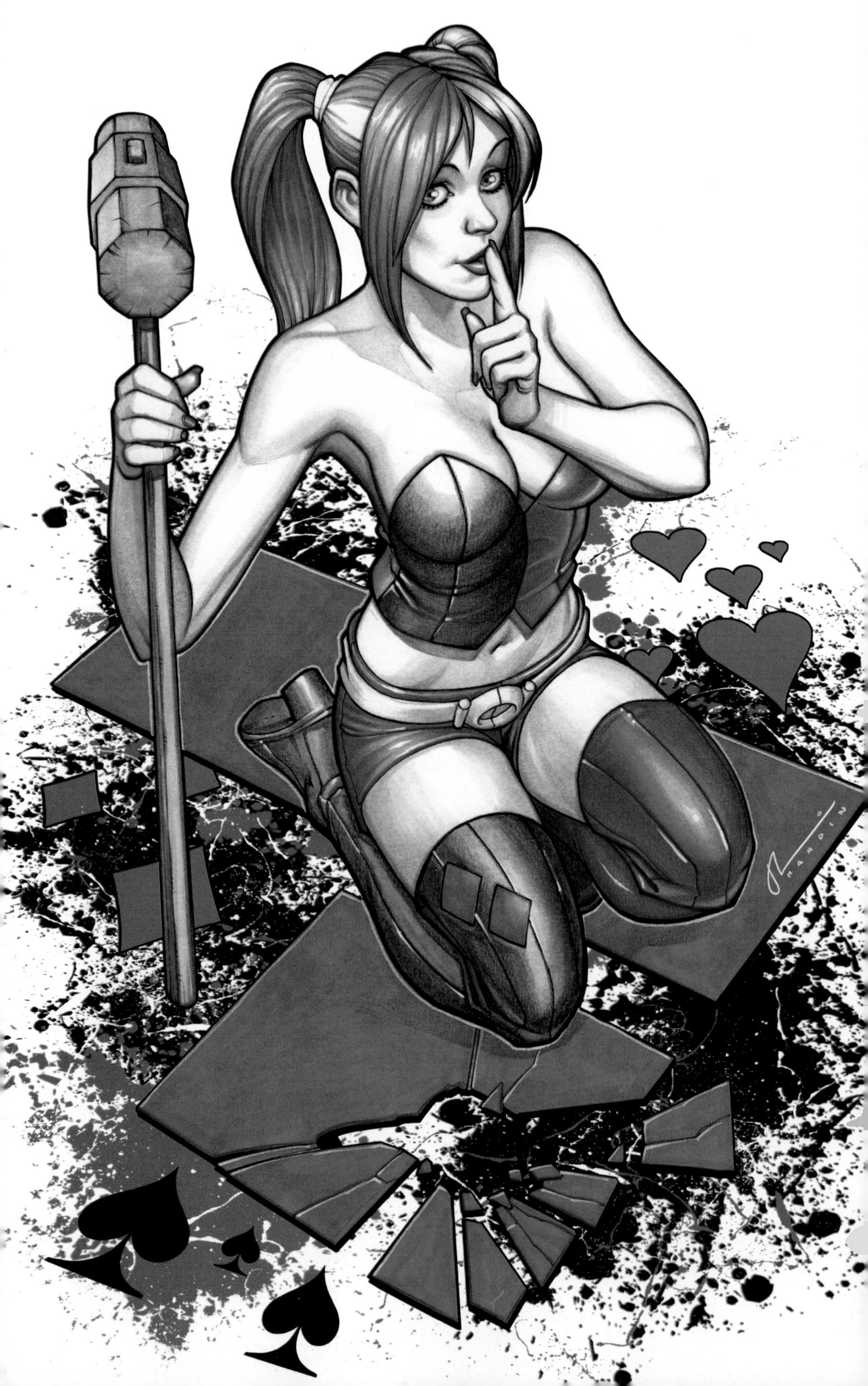
HARDIN

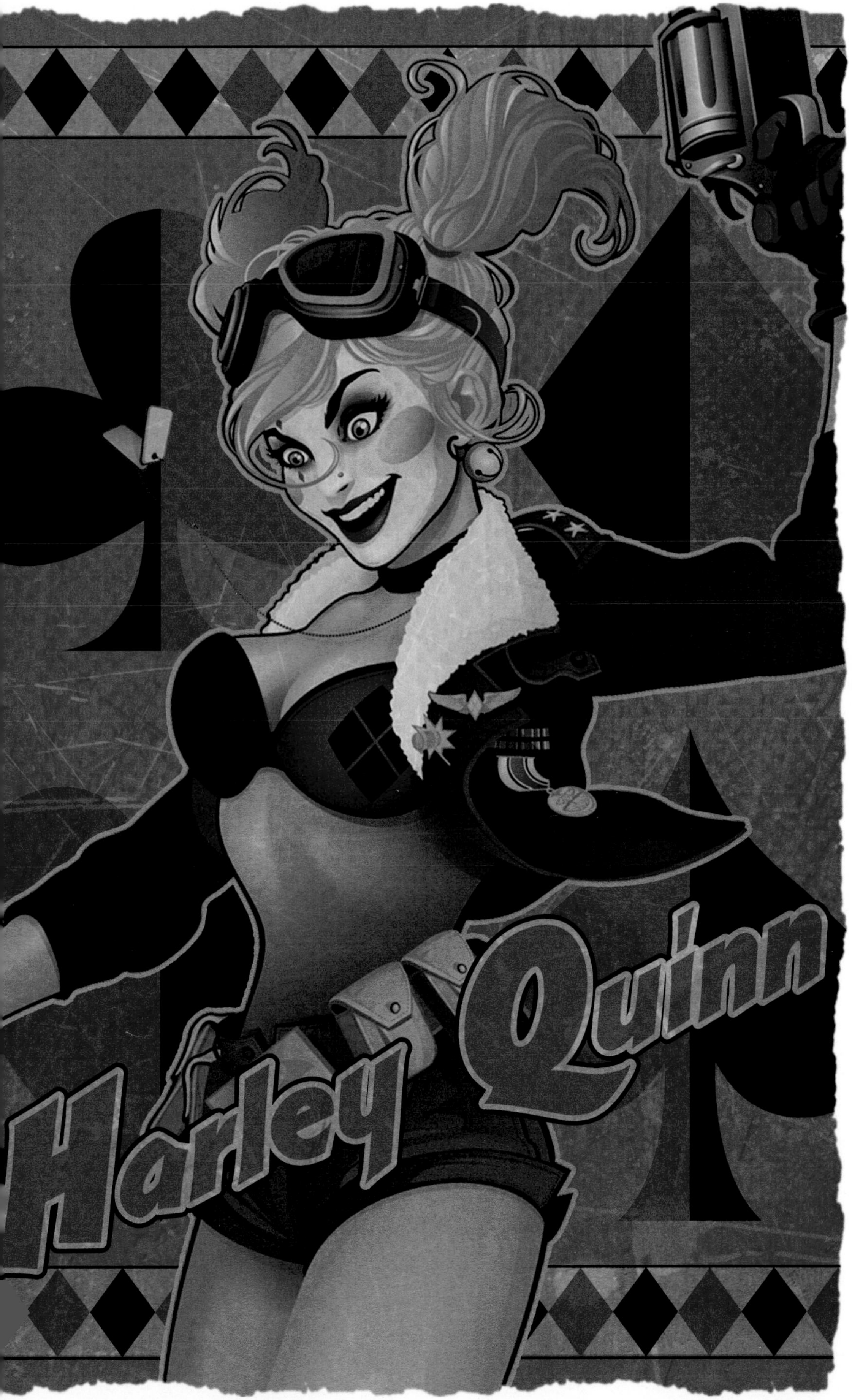
Harley Quinn

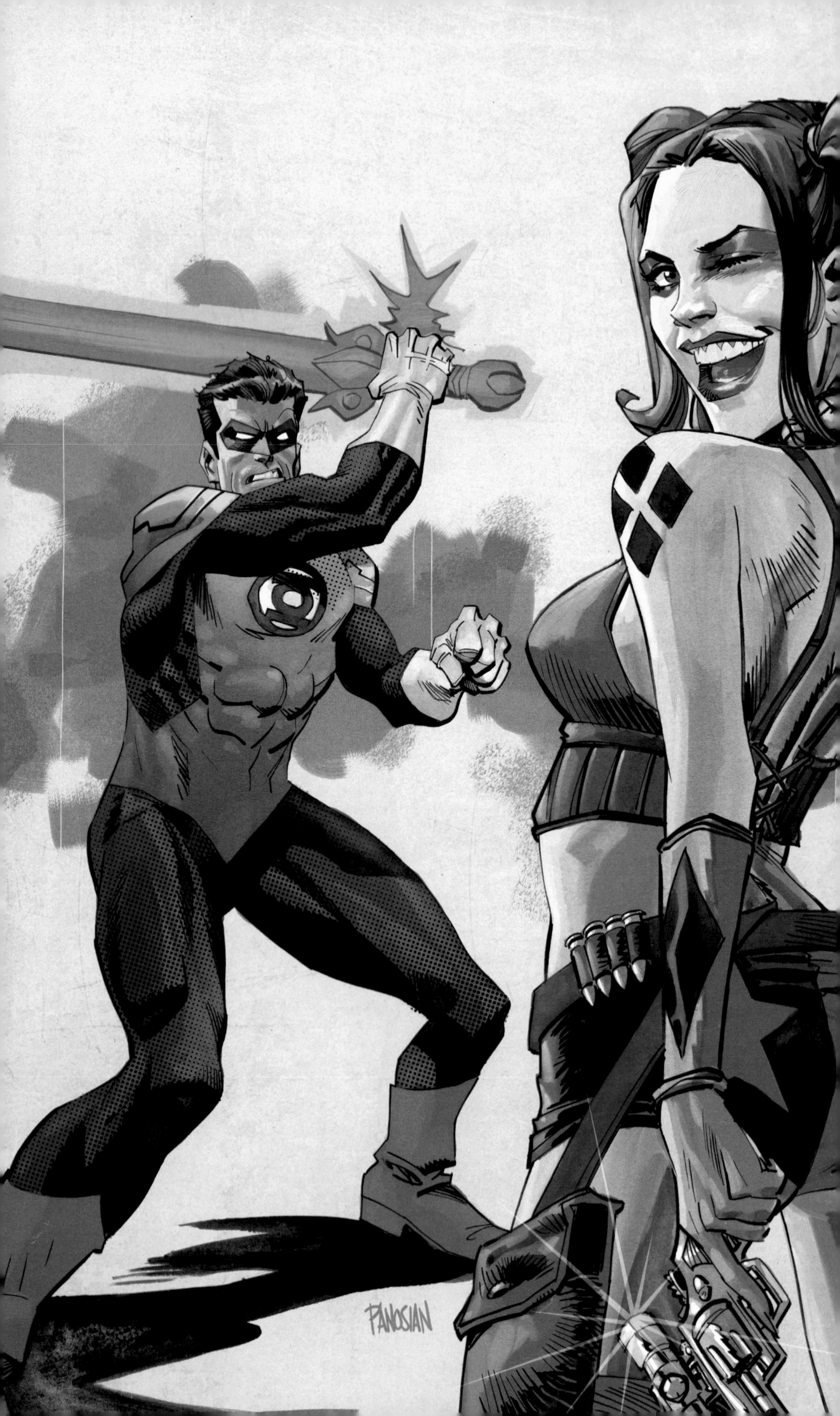
PANOSIAN

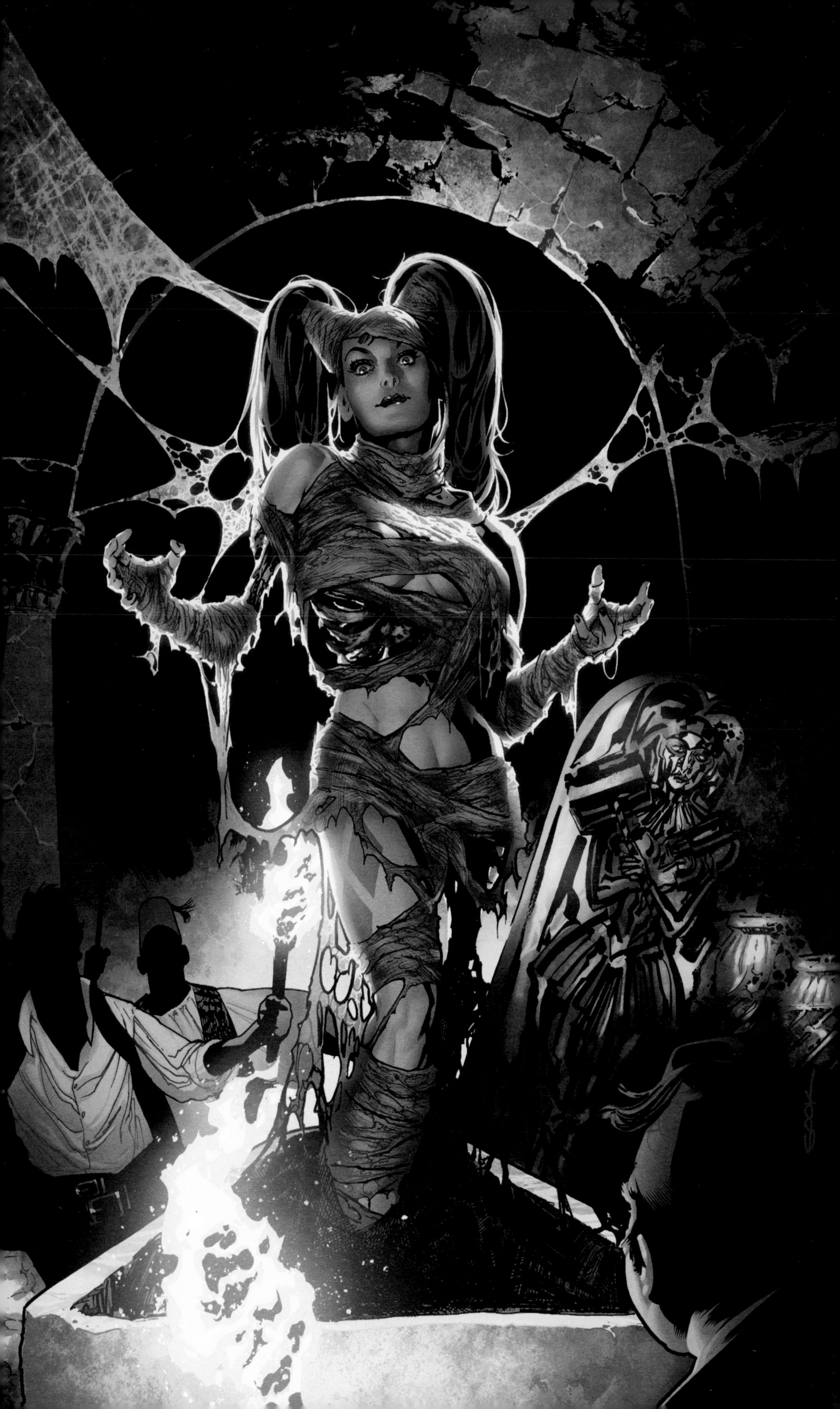

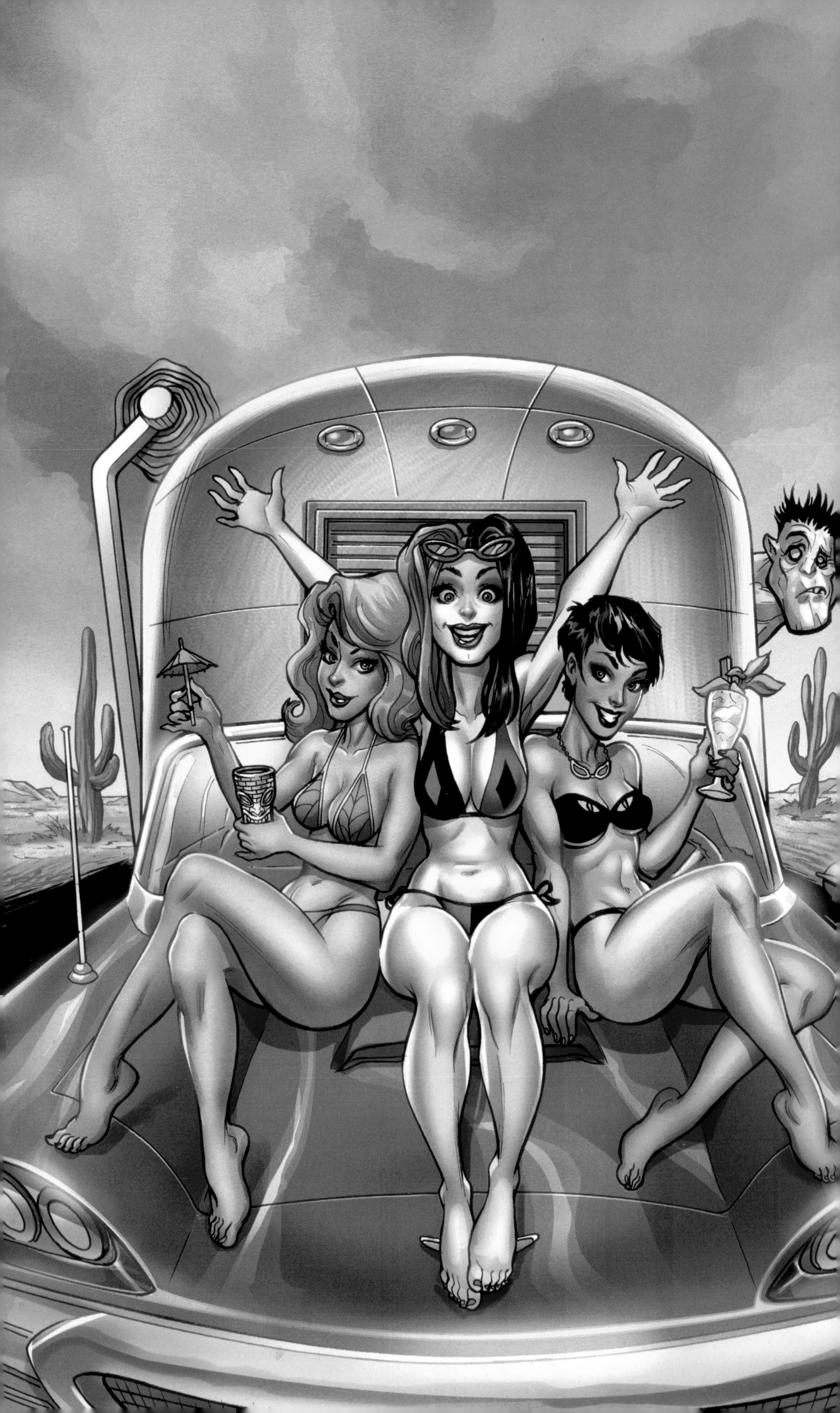

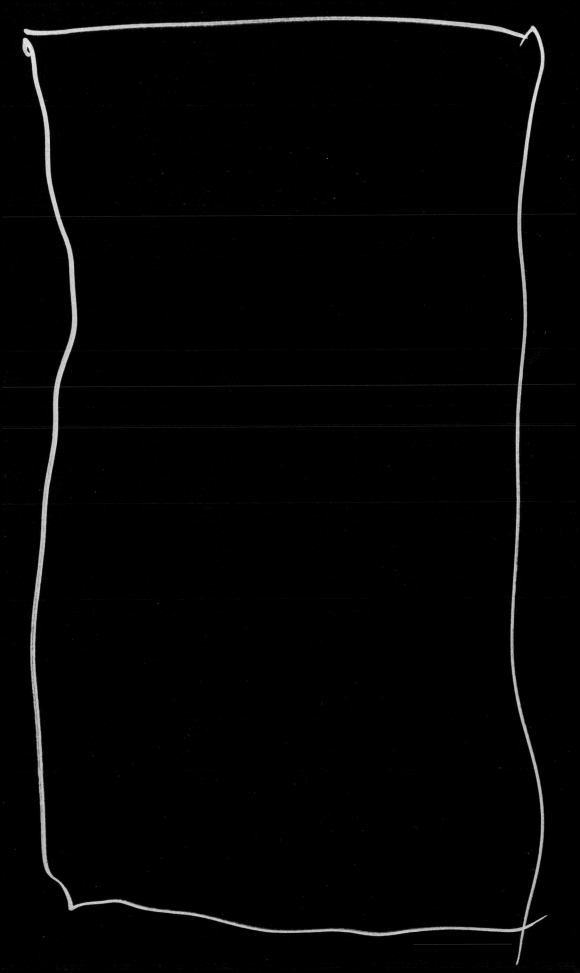

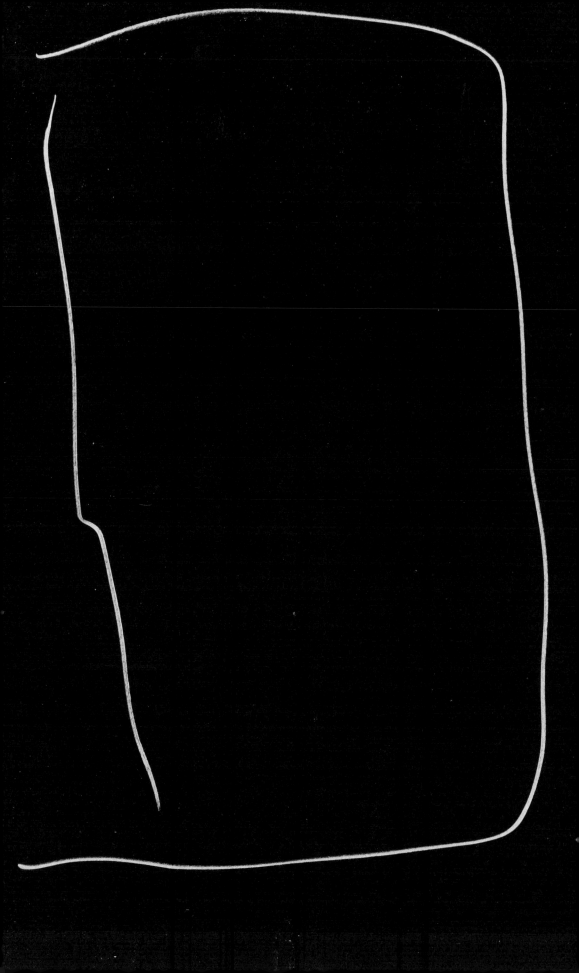